W9-AUE-513

Toronto
City Guide

Marconi Baird

FIREFLY BOOKS

A FIREFLY BOOK

Published by Firefly Books Ltd. 2005

Revised and expanded edition

Publisher Cataloging-in-Publication Data (U.S.)

Baird, Marconi.
   Toronto City Guide / Marconi Baird.
Revised and expanded.
[240] p. : ill., maps ;   cm.
Includes index.
Summary: A guide to tourist attractions,
restaurants, night life and shopping, supple-
mented by detailed maps.
ISBN 1-55407-124-0 (pbk.)
1. Toronto (Ont.) — Guidebooks. 2. Toronto
(Ont.) — Guides. I. Title.
917.13/541044 dc22   F1059.5.T683M878   2005

Library and Archives Canada Cataloguing in Publication

Baird, Marconi
Toronto city guide / Marconi Baird. — Rev. and expanded ed.

Includes index.
ISBN 1-55407-124-0

1. Toronto (Ont.)—Guidebooks. I. Title.

FC3097.18.M88 2005 917.13'541045 C2005-903547-1

Published in the United States by
Firefly Books (U.S.) Inc.
P.O. Box 1338, Ellicott Station
Buffalo, New York 14205

Published in Canada by
Firefly Books Ltd.
66 Leek Crescent
Richmond Hill, Ontario L4B 1H1

Cover design by George Walker
Interior layout by Brian Lehen Graphic Design Ltd.

Printed in Canada

The publisher gratefully acknowledges the financial support for our publishing program by the Canada Council for the Arts, the Ontario Arts Council and the Government of Canada through the Book Publishing Industry Development Program.

Contents

Preface
A new kind of guide book, **5**

Arrival
Airports, **6**
Highways, **8**
Trains & buses, **11**
Customs & Immigration, **11**
Currency, **13**
Southern Ontario airports map, **13**
GO Train regional transit system map, **13**

Toronto
From 1613–2006, **14**
Toronto quotes, **16**
Toronto map, **17**
TTC subway map, **18**
Downtown map, **20**
Underground walkways map, **21**
Suburbs & neighbourhoods map, **22**
Inner-city neighbourhoods, 23
  Toronto Islands, **24**
  Exhibition, **26**
  Queen's Quay West, **28**
  Harbourfront Park, **30**
  Harbourfront Centre, **32**
  Queen's Quay East, **34**
  Port Area, **36**
  Queen Street West, **38**
  Fashion District, **40**
  Financial District, **42**
  St Lawrence, **44**
  Town of York, **46**
  Portugal Village, **48**
  Chinatown, **50**

Discovery District, **52**
Dundas Square, **54**
Regent Park, **56**
Little Italy, **58**
University of Toronto, **60**
Queen's Park, **62**
Church-Wellesley Village, **64**
Old Cabbagetown, **66**
Koreatown, **68**
The Annex, **70**
Yorkville, **72**
Bloor East, **74**
Davenport, **76**
Casa Loma, **78**
Summerhill, **80**
Rosedale, **82**
North & South Rosedale, **84**
Yonge & St Clair, **86**
Davisville, **88**
Yonge & Eglinton, **90**
North York Centre, **92**

Neighbourhood street index, **94**
Origins of street names, **98**

Accommodation

By neighbourhood, **99**
Bed & breakfast, **103**

Places

Buildings, **104**
Historical sites & churches, **113**
Markets, **123**

Museums, galleries & public art, **126**
Parks, beaches, squares & zoos, **136**

Entertainment

Annual events, **148**
Ballet & dance, **160**
Cinema, **161**
Bars & clubs, **163**
Family entertainment centres, **164**

Opera & classical music, **166**
Sport, **169**
Stage companies, **172**
Theatres, concert halls & stadiums, **175**

Restaurants

General information, **182**
Listings by cuisine, **183**
Restaurant reviews, **187**

Local information

Alcohol & bars, **213**
Clothing, **213**
Crime, **214**
Cycling, **214**
Directions, **214**
Distress centres, **215**
Driving, **215**
Drug stores, **216**
Electrical current, **216**
Gay community, **216**
Holidays, **217**
Hospitals, **217**
Media, **217**
Medical & dental, **218**

Metric system, **219**
Multiculturalism, **219**
People with disabilities, **219**
Politeness, **220**
Postal services, **220**
Prostitution, **221**
Security, **221**
Smoking, **221**
Taxes, **222**
Telephones, **222**
Walking, **222**
Washrooms/toilets, **223**
Weather, **223**
Toronto trivia, **225**

Index

General index, **232**

Preface

This is a new kind of guide book for a new generation of travellers.

It is based on my experiences as a journalist travelling more than a million kilometres to hundreds of cities in 17 countries. And after walking every neighbourhood street and alley in Toronto. Not once, but four times.

The idea of writing a guide book came to me during my first visit to Rome about 35 years ago. After arriving at a small hotel early one evening, I had this irrational craving for some French food. French food in Rome? Go figure. Anyway, I went downstairs to ask where I could find a nice little Parisian bistro. I spoke no Italian. The guy at the desk didn't speak English or French. First problem.

So I decided to roam around the neighbourhood, sniffing the air for any fleeting aroma of coq au vin. After about an hour I would have settled for frites. Finally, I bumped into some locals who spoke English and they directed me to a place 'just down there past the gardens of the Villa Borghese and turn right – or maybe left – anyway, down near the fountain. You can't miss it.' Sure. Ever tried finding your way around Rome's back streets in the dark? Problem two.

As I have no sense of direction whatsoever, and often come close to getting lost in my own house, I gave in and got a taxi back to the hotel. I went straight into the bar and ate peanuts.

I didn't know there was an incredible outdoor exhibition of Italian sports cars scattered throughout the gardens of the Villa Borghese. And I didn't know one of the best French restaurants outside France was two blocks from my hotel.

That's when I decided someone should write a guide book for naïve and somewhat clueless wanderers like myself: a book for people like me who are holed-up in a big city hotel with not the faintest idea of what's outside. I wanted them to write a book that would take me by the hand and lead me around with a quiet understanding of my directional disabilities and abysmal lack of local knowledge.

Because of the Internet, times have changed for travellers since my first visit to Rome. So, this time around, I still want them to take me by the hand, but I also want their book to seduce me on to the Internet and let me wander though its constantly opening doors in the hope of finding those Italian sports cars.

Marconi Baird
Toronto

Arrival

The following arrival information is designed to get you into town with the minimum of fuss and bother.
No matter how you get here – by plane, train, bus, or car – there's a warm welcome waiting for you!

Airports, **6**
Highways, **8**
Trains & buses, **11**

Customs & Immigration, **11**
Currency, **13**
GO Train regional transit, **13**

Half the city's 16,500,000 annual visitors come by car, 40% by plane and 10% by either train or bus. Over 40% arrive from other parts of Canada, a third from the United States and the remainder from overseas. Chances are better than 70% that you'll return to the city after your first visit. This is due mainly to a variety of things to do, diverse cultures, inexpensive shopping, interesting attractions, safe streets and open-mindedness.

Arrival **Airports**

Three airports serve the city. The massively re-developed Lester B Pearson International Airport is the one you will most likely use for your arrival and departure. Commuter airlines and private pilots use the City Centre Airport, located downtown on the Toronto Islands. Private aircraft have exclusive use of the Toronto Buttonville Municipal Airport.

LESTER B PEARSON INTERNATIONAL AIRPORT (YYZ)

It's named after Canada's 19th prime minister, who won the 1957 Nobel Peace Prize. Mostly referred to simply as 'Pearson', the airport is located about 25 km (17 miles) northwest of downtown. It's the busiest airport in the country, and has just completed a massive $4.5 billion re-development program that added new road systems, runways and a spectacular new major terminal building. The facility serves 60 domestic and international airlines and has direct service to 140 destinations in 45 countries. Surrounding Pearson is the 'Strip', a combination of hotels, restaurants and conference and exhibition facilities. It's also renowned for its lively nightlife, especially for those people staying at a nearby hotel. Together with the airport, the Strip generates about $10-billion in annual revenues and employs around 100,000 people. It's one of the most important economic districts in the region.

Pearson terminal buildings

The airport has three terminals – Terminals 1, 2 and 3 – so make sure you know which one your airline uses by checking your ticket, or phoning ahead. And don't forget to tell any one who is picking you up. Highway signs into the area clearly show what road to take to your terminal's arrival or departure level. All terminals are busy from before 5:00 AM until after midnight. A free shuttle bus connects the buildings. The terminals have duty-free shopping, rental car offices, banks, restaurants, bookstores, bars, indoor parking and personal services. A 496-room Sheraton hotel is linked directly to Terminal 3. For additional information, including maps of the airport terminals, visit the airport Web site at **gtaa.com**

Pearson porter services

If you're arriving from outside the country, you could have a long walk before getting outside the terminal. A private company handles porter services, which means the cost is not necessarily cheap. There is a flat rate of $10.50 for a porter carrying up to three bags and $3.00 for each additional bag. Charges are based on standard tourist-sized luggage. You have to pay a cashier before you proceed to your destination with the porter.

Pearson transportation

Apart from the airport's new internal **rail shuttle**, there are free, wheelchair accessible **inter-terminal shuttle** LINK buses available curbside on the departures level of Terminals 2 and 3 and on the arrivals level of Terminal 1 to take you to a different terminal. There are **taxi and limousine** stands outside the arrivals level at each terminal building and a sidewalk dispatcher will organize your ride. Even though a limo costs a little more than the average $43 taxi ride downtown, it's usually the better and more comfortable buy. The trip to downtown averages about 40 minutes but can take a lot longer in heavy traffic or bad weather. About 20 **regional bus services** operate to and from the airport. You can link to their Web sites for schedules at **gtaa.com** The Pacific Western Airport Express provides **downtown bus service**. It operates every 20 minutes during peak periods and every 30 minutes during off-peak hours and offers pick-up and delivery at many downtown hotels. Their Web site is **torontoairportexpress.com** The cheapest way to get to and from the airport is by **public transit**. Bus connections to and from the subway are frequent and cost the regular cash transit fare of around $2.50. For more information, including schedules and general transit information, call 416-393-4636, or visit the TTC Web site at **ttc.ca** If you are **driving from the airport** and headed for downtown, take Highway 427 south to the QEW, then east to downtown. As you leave the airport you'll find the highways are all very well-marked. The QEW becomes the Gardiner Expressway and there are exits to all major north-south streets in the downtown area. If you are going to places in the middle of the city, take highway 401 east to the north-south exit you want. It's a good idea to stay in the collector lanes if you are not familiar with the 401, otherwise you could miss your exit. See the *Toronto* map, page 17.

Pearson parking

The terminals have combined parking for over 16,000 vehicles. In addition to the multi-level garages, there are also areas for metered and long-term parking. Terminal 1 has 8,976 public parking spaces, including special designations for disabled persons. A short-term parking area is cost-effective if you aren't there for more than four hours. Terminal 2 has 3,376 parking spaces and Terminal 3 has 3,446. This might sound like a lot of spaces, but chances are you will have to hunt around to find a spot.

TORONTO CITY CENTRE AIRPORT (YTZ)

Better known locally as 'The Island Airport,' it's on Centre Island in Toronto's Inner Harbour right next to downtown. It's used, on average, by about 400 passengers a day who travel on short-haul regional airlines. It's also a popular airport for private pilots. A 122 m (133 yds) ferry ride to the foot of Bathurst Street gets you from the island. A free shuttle bus operates between the airport and the downtown Royal York Hotel. For more information, phone 416-203-6942. Web site: **torontoport.com**

TORONTO BUTTONVILLE MUNICIPAL AIRPORT (YKZ)

This ranks as the tenth busiest airport in Canada, handling about 190,000 takeoffs and landings a year. It's used mainly by private and corporate aircraft. Access to downtown is south on highway 404 and the DVP. For more information, phone 905-477-8100. Web site: **markham.ca**

Arrival Highways

Ontario has an excellent highway system giving easy access to Toronto. Together with Massachusetts, the province has the safest highways on the continent. The map above shows major routes in southern Ontario serving the Toronto area. The QEW and all 400-series highways are multi-lane and well-marked. During winter months and bad weather conditions, use extra caution while you are on the road. A good idea is to check out road conditions by logging on to **theweathernetwork.com** before starting your trip. Buckle-up (it's the law), always obey highway signs and drive safely.

Queen Elizabeth Way *(The QEW)* and the **Gardiner Expressway** *(The Gardiner).*

The QEW runs from the Ontario-New York border at Fort Erie, Ontario, to Toronto. Be careful during the winter as the highway passes through a 'micro-climate' for a 15 km (10 mile) stretch on the Canadian side of the border. This phenomenon, brought about by the close proximity of Lake Erie to Lake Ontario, often causes sudden blinding snow squalls or dense fog. As the QEW approaches downtown Toronto it becomes the Gardiner Expressway. The Gardiner cuts through the downtown core dividing business and commercial areas from the waterfront. You have exits to all the major north-south downtown streets, the lakefront entertainment complexes, Rogers Centre and the CN Tower. The Gardiner can become very congested during rush hour in both directions. Speed limits: QEW is 100 km/h (62 mph) and the Gardiner is 90 km/h (56 mph).

Highway 400

This is the major highway that connects Toronto with northern Ontario and western Canada. As it approaches Toronto it expands to eight, then 12 lanes. Use extra caution during winter because this highway is renowned for its whiteouts just north of Toronto. It's also known as a 'boring' highway, so keep your wits about you and watch out for drivers who are speeding. Speed limit: 100 km/h (62 mph).

Highway 401 *(The 401)*

This is a major four-lane provincial highway running from the Ontario-Québec border to Windsor on the Ontario-Michigan border. As it goes through Toronto it expands to 16 lanes and becomes the second busiest highway in North America. There are eight express lanes with four collector lanes on either side. If you are unfamiliar with the 401 keep in the collector lanes to avoid missing your exit. Despite its size it can come to a standstill in bad weather, because of an accident, or during rush hour. If possible avoid using it from 6:30 AM – 10:00 AM and from 3:00 PM – 7:00 PM weekdays, as well as evenings on the first and last days of a holiday weekend when traffic is especially heavy. Speed limit: 100 km/h (62 mph).

Highway 403

If you're heading east along the QEW coming into Toronto and want to get to Pearson International Airport, or the middle of Toronto, take highway 403 north from the QEW. The 403/QEW interchange is just before you get to Mississauga. The 403 connects with the 401 and the 407 ETR. This way you'll avoid having to go through downtown's congested traffic. Speed limit: 100 km/h (62 mph).

Highway 404 and the **Don Valley Parkway** *(The Parkway,* or *The DVP)*

Highway 404 runs south from the Town of Newmarket to the 401 in the middle of Toronto. As it continues southwest to downtown it becomes the six-lane Don Valley Parkway. It's a wise idea to avoid the DVP during the morning rush hour into town (6:30 AM – 10:00 AM) and the afternoon rush hour going out of town (3:00 PM – 7:00 PM). During these times it's known locally as 'The Don Valley Parking Lot'. It's not at all unusual to experience congestion just south of the 401 any time due to volume. A new interchange design here doesn't seem to have helped the problem. From the DVP you have access to many of Toronto's main east-west streets including interchanges at Lawrence Avenue, Eglinton Avenue, Don Mills Road, Bloor Street, Richmond Street and Lakeshore Boulevard. Speed limits: the 404 is 100 km/h (62 mph) and the DVP is 90 km/h (56 mph).

Highway 407 - ETR

Highway 407 ETR (Express Toll Route) is 108 km (67 miles) long and was the world's first open-access, electronically controlled toll highway without toll booths. Drivers who are in a hurry and want to use a northern east-west bypass of the city are the main users. It operates by photographing and recording up to 14,000 license plates each hour as drivers enter and exit. You get a bill through the mail. That bill might come as a shock because the 407 is one of the most expensive toll highways in North America and calculates its tolls according to the time of day and distance travelled. It runs from Highway 7 in the east to the QEW just west of Highway 1. If you have out-of-province license plates, don't think you can get away without paying the toll. The 407 folk are well connected with vehicle databases throughout North America and, sooner or later, you will be discovered. The speed limit is 100 km/h (62 mph). Web site: **407etr.com**

Highway 427 *(The 427)*

The 427 is the north-south expressway linking Pearson International Airport with the QEW. It can get very busy in the morning going south into town and again in the afternoon, starting around 3:00 PM, going north. If you are using the 427 to get to or from Pearson during these periods make sure you leave yourself plenty of time. The Gardiner/QEW combination, leading from downtown to the 427, is always busy.

HIGHWAY SIGNS

In keeping with Canada's metric system, distances and speeds are given in kilometres (km) and metres (m) only. There's no posted conversion into miles and yards. Each major provincial highway shows its number inside a crown logo. This tradition goes back many years to when a provincial highway was known as 'The King's Highway'. All highway signs are clearly marked and the information is posted well in advance. Some signs provide basic information in French. Always keep alert for signs indicating that your lane is about to end. This is especially important when you are using the 401. There are special overhead electronic signs on most of the major highways that give you current traffic conditions ahead. You can also find out about any problems by phoning 416-599-9090, 24hr. Web information: **highwayconditions.com/on**

DRIVING TIMES TO/FROM TORONTO

The following are approximate driving times from downtown to downtown, based on daytime summer driving conditions and an average wait at Canada Customs where applicable. For real-time waits at the Canada-USA border, check out: **cbsa-asfc.gc.ca**

Albany, NY: 6 $^1/_2$ hours
Boston, MA: 9 $^1/_2$ hours
Buffalo, NY: 1 $^3/_4$ hours
Detroit, MI: 4 hours
Montréal, PQ: 6 hours

New York City, NY: 9 $^1/_2$ hours
Niagara Falls, ON: 1 $^1/_2$ hours
Ottawa, ON: 5 hours
Pittsburgh, PA: 5 $^1/_2$ hours
Stratford, ON: 1 $^1/_2$ hours

Arrival Trains & buses

TRAIN

If you are coming to Toronto by train from the United States you will clear Canada Customs and Immigration at the border. The train will pull into Union Station, in the centre of downtown's financial district. Union is the city's major rail terminal serving inter-city trains, the regional GO Transit system and the subway (map 10). Union Station is linked directly to the PATH underground walkway system (page 21). Outside Union's main entrance on Front Street you'll find a major taxi stand. Opposite, outside the Royal York Hotel on the northeast corner of Front and York streets, you can board the Airport Express bus for Pearson Airport, or catch the shuttle bus to the Toronto City Centre Airport. The station has bars, restaurants, coffee shops, ATMs, newsstands and personal services. It's linked to the Toronto Convention Centre next to the CN Tower along an elevated Skywalk. For more information, phone 416-366-8411 for Via Rail arrivals and departures; 416-869-3200 for GO Transit; or 416-393-4636 for the TTC. For Web site information: **city.toronto.on.ca/union_station.com** or **gotransit.com** or **ttc.ca**

BUS

If you are travelling from the United States by bus you will clear Canada Customs and Immigration at the border. Upon arrival in Toronto you will disembark at the Toronto Coach Terminal in the centre of downtown with easy access to the PATH underground system, subway and hotels. (Map 15 for the coach terminal and the map on page 21 for PATH). The terminal, which is open from 5:30 AM till midnight daily, is served by several inter-city, regional and local bus lines and handles about 2,500 people a day. Inside, there's a coffee shop, storage lockers, bar, restaurant and newsstand. Just outside the door there are lots of shops, restaurants and ATMs. You're also right on the doorstep of Chinatown, major downtown hospitals, city hall, the Eaton Centre and Dundas Square. For more information, phone 416-393-7911.

Arrival Customs & Immigration

CUSTOMS

You are allowed to bring into the country all the personal effects needed for your visit. If you are bringing medication with you, make sure it is clearly la-

11

belled as such. It's a good idea to get your doctor or pharmacist to list your prescriptions on their letterhead, especially if the drugs have narcotic content. If you are at least 19 years old you can bring with you, duty-free, 200 cigarettes and 50 cigars; 1.1 litres (40 oz) of wine *or* liquor *or* 24 x 355 ml (24 x 12 oz) cans of beer *or* ale. Coolers with an alcohol content of 0.5% or less are not considered to be alcoholic beverages for customs purposes. If you bring more than these amounts of tobacco or alcohol you will have to pay high taxes to both Canada Customs and the government of Ontario. You can also bring, duty-free, unlimited gifts valued at less than $CA 60.00 each, providing they are not tobacco or alcohol products. Pets, plants and food carry some restrictions, so find out ahead of time what you're allowed to bring. Either phone, or visit the Web site noted below. It is a very serious criminal offence, carrying heavy penalties, to bring illegal drugs or undeclared firearms into Canada. If you are bringing firearms into the country for sport or hunting, for use in competitions, or for in-transit movement through Canada, you must declare them to customs at the border. Weapons that are totally prohibited from entering the country include 'mufflers' and 'silencers' for guns, 'switchblade' knives, fully automatic firearms, sawed-off rifles and shotguns. It is a criminal offence for foreigners to carry their hand guns in Canada. If you have any questions, give Canada Customs a call at 905-676-8022, Monday to Friday, 8:30 AM – 4:30 PM. You'll find them very helpful, particularly by keeping Americans up to date on the latest customs benefits under the North American Free Trade Agreement (NAFTA). Web site: **cbsa-asfc.gc.ca**

Customs tax rebate for visitors

Visitors to Canada are entitled to a rebate of the 7% federal GST tax on their accommodation and goods purchased. You must submit original receipts, showing at least a total of $14 paid in tax. Photocopies will not be accepted. Each receipt must show tax of at least $3.50. Get these receipts stamped by Canada Customs when you leave Canada and get an application form to fill out so you can get your tax refunded. You can also get a refund of your 8% Ontario PST tax providing it has been paid on goods amounting to at least $625. For more information, phone Global Refund Canada at 905-791-5007, or visit their Web site: **ca.globalrefund.ca**

IMMIGRATION

You'll meet Canadian immigration officials when you land at the airport or when you cross over the border in your vehicle. You'll be on Canadian territory and under Canadian law. If you're an American you can be asked for proof of citizenship, so carry a passport or your birth certificate. Naturalized Americans should carry their naturalization papers. Americans should also check with their local authorities before leaving home in case they might need a passport to re-enter the United States after a Canadian visit. All other nationals must have a valid passport and, in some cases, a visa. Check with your travel agent to see if the visa requirement applies to you. It is a serious offence to enter Canada to work unless you have the required documentation. Web site: **cic.gc.ca**

CURRENCY

If you are coming here from the UK, Europe, or the United States, the pound is worth about $2.50 Canadian; the euro close to $1.50; and the American dollar is usually around $1.25. American currency is accepted by businesses around town, but you might not get a good exchange rate. No other foreign currency is accepted. Therefore, bring Canadian money with you in $20 bills (notes). Charge everything you can to your credit card while you're here and never carry around more cash than you can easily afford to lose.

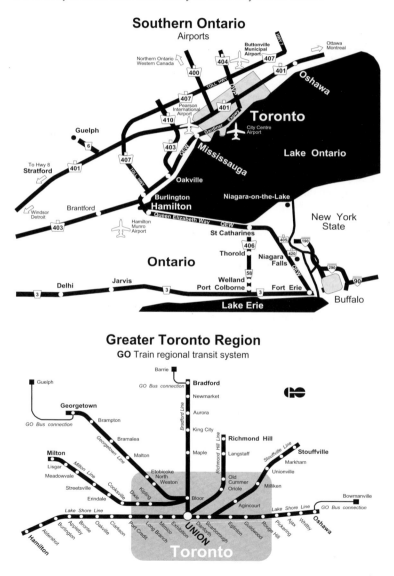

Southern Ontario
Airports

Greater Toronto Region
GO Train regional transit system

Toronto

Once upon a time, Iroquois was the only language spoken here. Then it was French. Then English. Now it's any one of around 160 languages and dialects. The world has come to live in Toronto's wonderfully diverse neighbourhoods.

Toronto **From 1613 – 2006**

 For centuries, this part of Canada was Iroquois territory. Aboriginal peoples came through here to take advantage of trails leading north to Lake Simcoe and for canoe routes that provided a short cut between lakes Ontario and Huron.

In 1615 the French explorer Étienne Brûlé was the first European to see Lake Iroquois (now Lake Ontario) and it soon became well known to French fur traders. A small settlement took root in 1720 and the modest Fort Toronto was erected in 1748. It wasn't long before British soldiers captured the place and Loyalists from the American Revolution ventured north to this and other sites further downstream along the St Lawrence River. In 1791 the area became known as Upper Canada, because it was up stream from the French settlements in Québec, known as Lower Canada.

Today, the Greater Toronto Area extends along that historic curve in Lake Ontario from St Catharines to Oshawa. Often referred to as the 'Golden Horseshoe', its population of over 5,500,000 people makes it one of the continent's largest urban areas. It's home to a third of Ontario's residents and represents about 17% of Canada's population.

The region, which has one of the world's most envied economies, is the national centre for performing arts, communications, high technology, finance and banking, business, medical research, manufacturing, transportation and media enterprises.

The focal point is Toronto, Canada's largest city.

During the 1950s it was known as 'Toronto the Good', or 'Toronto the Sanctimonious'. This was not surprising considering the then *Lord's Day Act* almost completely shut down any commercial activity on a Sunday. Not only that, but men were forbidden to wear shorts during the hot summer months "lest it offend the moral values of the community." As far as anyone can remember there was only one half-decent restaurant open downtown on the Sabbath. And it wasn't allowed to serve alcohol. Not surprisingly, people rushed in droves over the border to Buffalo, NY, for food, some shopping, a drink and excitement.

Toronto, back in those days, was a very conservative and thoroughly boring place. A member of Oxford University's debating team even went so far as to say: "Toronto is so boring the Indians don't want it back." A snobbish debating point, or a hard truth to be faced?

Either way, things have really changed.

On January 1, 1998, Toronto amalgamated with five surrounding munici-palities – most being cities in their own right – to bring the collective popu-lation under a common and better organized form of government. It became the fourth most populous city in North America after New York, Los Angeles and Chicago and was dubbed the 'Megacity' by local media intent on going to great lengths to bask in the newly found statistic.

However, it's the diversity of neighbourhoods that makes Toronto unique, not its size. Unlike other places that insist on a cultural melting pot, we take the opposite view and vigourously promote the preservation and individu-alism of our diverse cultural communities. Every year that pride is celebrat-ed in scores of parades, festivals and community events.

Regrettably, it wasn't always like this. After the First World War, for exam-ple, Toronto was rife with anti-Semitism and racism. It even took firm steps to ban Chinese immigration.

That low point in our history is now contrasted with the fact that during the first 12 months of this century, Toronto was the continent's strongest mag-net for immigrants. Just over 108,000 foreigners made Toronto their home that year, whereas only 85,867 settled in New York, and 47,404 headed west to Los Angeles. Perhaps this was because the newcomers could continue being themselves here without fear of becoming homogenized into a less interesting whole.

Consequently, Toronto has become an intriguing boutique city. The niche we have carved out for ourselves focuses on this amazing mélange of cul-tures. Here's a city rooted in North America, yet offering an international style and cosmopolitan experiences. It's where you can take a summer stroll in the evening along safe downtown streets that evoke European, Asian and African environments. It's where civility and politeness are noticed, and it's where you'll hear more resident languages spoken around open-air markets and sidewalk cafés than anywhere else. In fact, more than half of us came here from another country. Toronto is no longer the predominantly Anglo-Saxon place it used to be. By 2017, over 50% of the population will be non-European.

Because of this cultural diversity and our open acceptance for one anoth-er, the city we have created has become a vibrant and interesting place. It shows how people of every race, social group and creed from around the world can come together in harmony to share rich traditions, differing cus-toms and fascinating ways of life. It is truly a city of nations.

Toronto has come a long way since 1788 when the Mississauga Indians traded the place to the English for a bit of money and 149 barrels of provi-sions.

Today, they might even want it back.

Toronto **Quotes**

Over the years, ordinary and famous people have come and gone and left their impressions of the city. Here's some of what they had to say.

"I found here good food and wine." *Fr Picuet, at Fort Rouillé, 1751.*

"Toronto makes a Sunday in a Scotch village seem like a hashish dream." *Aleister Crowley, British writer, 1913.*

"It couldn't be any worse. You can't imagine it. I'm not going to describe it." *Ernest Hemingway, American journalist and author, 1923.*

"We all hate Toronto. It's the only thing Canadians have in common." *Lister Sinclair, Canadian author and broadcaster, 1948.*

"It's like New York run by the Swiss." *Peter Ustinov, British actor and raconteur, 1976.*

"It's the cleanest city. And it works." *Buckminster Fuller, American urban guru, 1978.*

"I've never been to a city I've fallen in love with more than Toronto." *Billy Graham, American evangelist, 1978.*

"Toronto is still a jewel. It's a great place to live and work. But if you want something extra, you still have to go to Paris." *David Crombie, Toronto mayor, 1979.*

"It's a worldly place that doesn't take itself too seriously." *Linda Farron, English immigrant, 1999.*

"Toronto is like New York with all the crap scraped off." *Ed Feldman, American television personality, 2000.*

"Toronto is really cool. I find that in Toronto I live this ideal lifestyle. It's wonderful. I don't want to leave." *Jason Priestley, Hollywood actor, 2001.*

"Canada's premier city for business and finance is still considered a model." *New York Times, 2002.*

"It's the greatest city on earth!" *Mel Lastman, Toronto mayor, 2003.*

"I love Toronto. It's cosmopolitan, there's all sorts of different kinds of people everywhere you go in Toronto, there's all sorts of great music, great restaurants, great night spots that don't respond to a lot of American play lists and have play lists that I really dig. It's a real melting pot in every sense of the word." *Prince, American entertainer and Toronto resident, 2004.*

"Toronto is the engine that drives Canada. If it wasn't for us, the whole country would fall apart – period. I don't know why people in other provinces are so down on us. Guess it's jealousy. Yeah, that's it. They're jealous." *Toronto resident interviewed on the street, 2005.*

Toronto

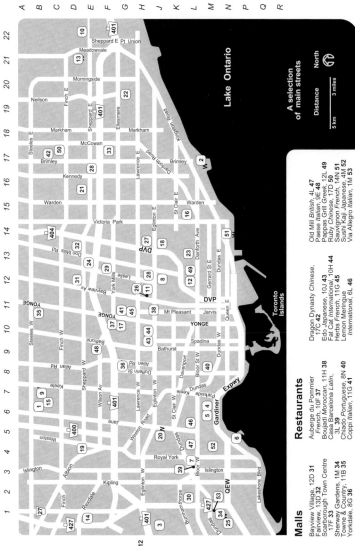

Lake Ontario

A selection
of main streets

Distance   North

5 km   3 miles

Toronto
Islands

---

*For Uptown, Midtown and
Downtown, see Maps 1 - 35*

Places

Black Creek Pioneer Village,
6B **1**
Bluffer's Park, 17M **2**
Centennial Park, 1J **3**
Colborne Lodge, 6M **4**
High Park, 6M **5**
Humber Bay Park, 5P **6**
Montgomery's Inn Museum,
3L **7**
Ontario Science Centre, 12J **8**
Rexall Centre, 7B **9**
Rouge Park, 22E **10**
Sunnybrook Park, 12H **11**
Todmorden Mills Museum, 12L **12**
Toronto Zoo, 21D **13**
Woodbine Racetrack, 1E **14**
York University, 6C **15**

Golf courses

Dentonia Park, 15L **16**
Don Valley, 10G **17**
Flemingdon Park, 14J **18**
Humber Valley, 4D **19**
Scarlett Woods, 5J **20**
Tam O'Shanter, 16E **21**

Hospitals

Centenary, 20G **22**
East General, 13K **23**
North York, 13E **24**
Queensway, 1N **25**
Sunnybrook, 12H **26**

Accommodation

Crowne Plaza Don Valley,
14H **27**
Delta Toronto East, 17E **28**
Prince Hotel, 13F **29**
Valhalla Inn, 2L **30**

Malls

Bayview Village, 12D **31**
Fairview, 13D **32**
Scarborough Town Centre
17F **33**
Sherway Gardens, 1M **34**
Towne & Country, 11B **35**
Yorkdale, 8G **36**

Restaurants

Auberge du Pommier
French, 10F **37**
Boujadi *Moroccan,* 11H **38**
Casa Barcelona *Latin,*
3L **39**
Chiado *Portuguese,* 8N **40**
Coppi *Italian,* 11G **41**

Dragon Dynasty *Chinese,*
17C **42**
Edo *Japanese,* 10J **43**
Fat Cat International, 10H **44**
Herbs *French,* 11G **45**
Lemon Meringue
International, 6L **46**

Old Mill *British,* 4L **47**
Paese *Italian,* 9E **48**
Pappas Grill *Greek,* 12L **49**
Ruby *Chinese,* 17D **50**
Sauvignon *French,* 14N **51**
Sushi Kaji *Japanese,* 14N **52**
Via Allegro *Italian,* 1M **53**

17

TTC subway

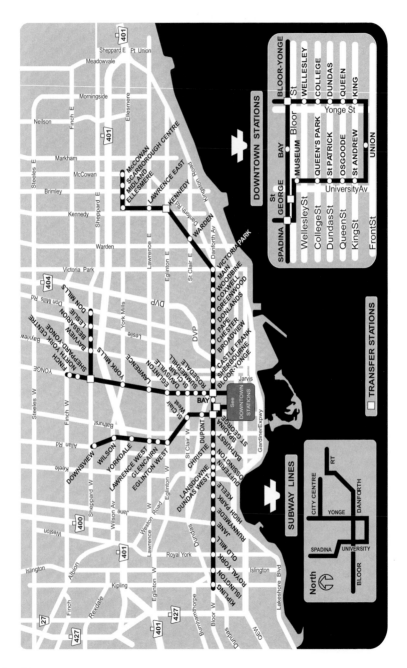

Public transit **TTC subway**

 Toronto's public rapid transit system is called **The TTC** (Toronto Transit Commission). It is one of the safest and most reliable systems on the continent.

The TTC is the quick way to get around town. (The folks who operate it like to remind you that "It's the better way.") The **subway system** is linked directly with buses and streetcars. You can transfer between vehicles as many times as necessary to get to your destination. The **cash fare is $2.50**, regardless of distance travelled, provided you make a one-way trip with no stopovers. If you need to connect with another vehicle, get a **free transfer** when you first board the system and show it to the operator of each subsequent vehicle. If you will be using the TTC a lot, it's cheaper to buy 5 tokens for $10, or 10 for $20 from any subway ticket booth.

On weekdays and Saturdays, **subway trains** run every few minutes from about 6:00 AM – 1:30 AM. On Sundays, they run from about 9:00 AM – 1:30 AM. Most **buses and streetcars** start about 5:00 AM and run to about 1:30 AM weekdays, with reduced service on weekends. You'll find localized transit area maps at main intersections where TTC routes intersect.

There's a late-night service called the **Blue Night Network**. Buses and streetcars run on most major routes (transit stops are marked with a reflective blue band) every morning from about 1:30 AM to 5:00 AM. Service is provided every 30 minutes or better.

Later on, this book will show you how to get to most of the popular places around town using the TTC.

Wheel-Trans is a special service for people with disabilities who cannot ride on conventional TTC vehicles. It provides door-to-door accessible transit service seven days a week, weekdays from 6:00 AM – 1:00 AM and weekends and holidays from 7:00 AM – 1:00 AM within the city limits. You have to book a pick-up time by phoning 416-393-4222. Regular TTC fares apply.

The TTC is also the cheapest way to get to and from **Pearson airport**. Take the 192 bus from Kipling subway station to the airport, or the 58A bus from Lawrence West subway. You can get to and from Pearson for the regular $2.50 cash fare.

A good idea is to get a free *Ride Guide* from any TTC subway collector booth. It's full of maps, fares and general information. Check out their Web site as well at **ttc.ca**

For more answers, call 416-393-3636. They operate their call service in 160 languages, 24 hours a day, seven days a week. If you want to write them a note, their address is: Toronto Transit Commission, 1900 Yonge Street, Toronto, Ontario M4S 1Z2. If you lose anything on a TTC vehicle, contact their **Lost and Found** office at the Bay subway station by calling 416-393-4100. Chances are you'll get it back. Torontonians are generally pretty honest people.

Downtown

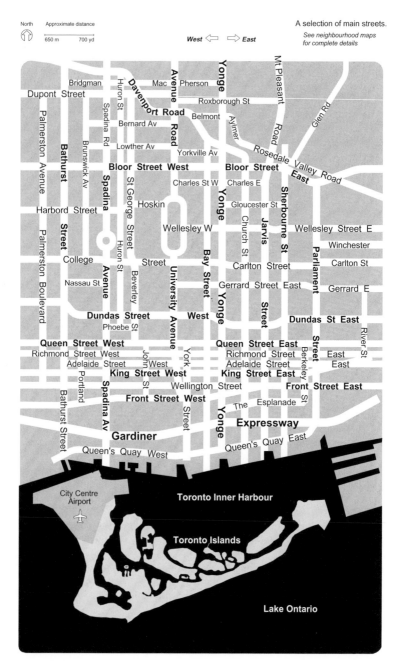

North
Approximate distance
650 m   700 yd

West ⇐   ⇒ East

A selection of main streets.

*See neighbourhood maps
for complete details*

Bridgman
Dupont Street
Mac Pherson
Roxborough St
Huron St
Davenport Road
Belmont
Avenue
Yonge
Mt Pleasant
Glen Rd
Bernard Av
Aylmer
Spadina Rd
Lowther Av
Yorkville Av
Road
Palmerston Avenue
Bathurst
Brunswick Av
Bloor Street West
Bloor Street
Rosedale Valley Road
East
Spadina
Charles St W
Charles E
Harbord Street
Hoskin
St George Street
Yonge
Gloucester St
Sherbourne St
Street
Palmerston Boulevard
Wellesley W
Wellesley Street E
Huron St
Jarvis
Winchester
College
Avenue
Street
Church St
Carlton Street
Parliament
Carlton St
Nassau St
Beverley
University Avenue
Bay Street
Gerrard Street East
Gerrard E
Dundas Street
West
Yonge
Dundas St East
Phoebe St
Queen Street West
Queen Street East
River St
Richmond Street West
Richmond Street
East
Adelaide Street
John West
King Street West
York
King Street East
Berkeley Street
East
Adelaide Street
Portland
Spadina Av
Wellington Street
Front Street East
Front Street West
St
Front Street West
Bathurst Street
Street
The Esplanade
St
Yonge
Expressway
Gardiner
Queen's Quay East
Queen's Quay West
Street

City Centre
Airport
Toronto Inner Harbour

Toronto Islands

Lake Ontario

Underground walkways

North Subway

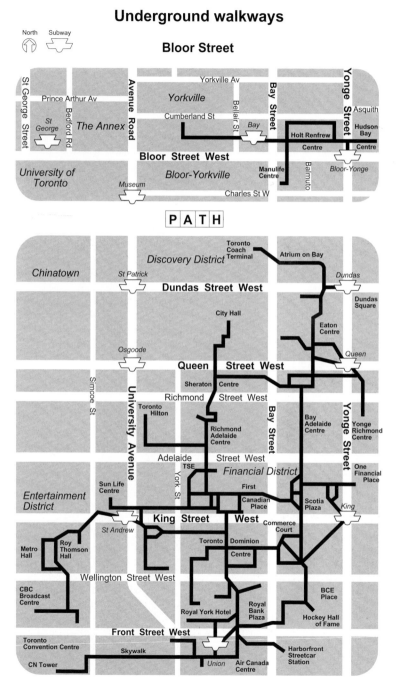

Bloor Street

St George Street

Prince Arthur Av

Avenue Road

Bedford Rd

St George

The Annex

Yorkville Av

Yorkville

Cumberland St

Bellair St

Bay Street

Yonge Street

Asquith

Bay

Holt Renfrew
Centre

Hudson
Bay
Centre

Bloor Street West

University of Toronto

Bloor-Yorkville

Manulife
Centre

Balmuto

Bloor-Yonge

Museum

Charles St W

P A T H

Chinatown

Discovery District

Toronto Coach Terminal

Atrium on Bay

St Patrick

Dundas Street West

Dundas

Dundas
Square

City Hall

Eaton
Centre

Osgoode

Queen Street West

Queen

Simcoe St

Sheraton Centre

Richmond Street West

Bay Street

Bay
Adelaide
Centre

Yonge Street

Toronto
Hilton

Yonge
Richmond
Centre

University Avenue

Richmond
Adelaide
Centre

Adelaide Street West

York St

TSE

Financial District

One
Financial
Place

Sun Life
Centre

First

Canadian
Place

Scotia
Plaza

Entertainment
District

King Street West

King

St Andrew

Commerce
Court

Metro
Hall

Roy
Thomson
Hall

Toronto Dominion

Centre

Wellington Street West

CBC
Broadcast
Centre

BCE
Place

Royal York Hotel

Royal
Bank
Plaza

Hockey Hall
of Fame

Front Street West

Toronto
Convention Centre

Skywalk

Harborfront
Streetcar
Station

CN Tower

Union

Air Canada
Centre

Suburbs & neighbourhoods

For Uptown, Midtown and Downtown neighbourhoods, see maps 1 – 35

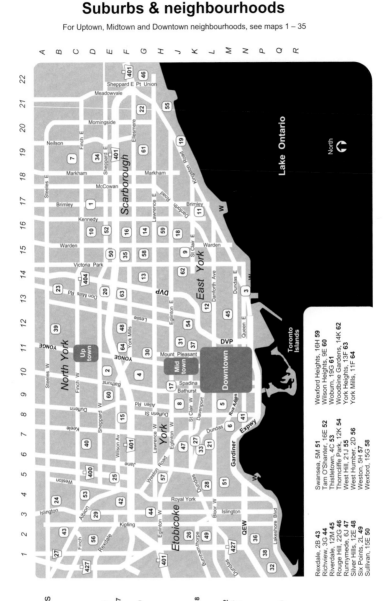

Suburban neighbourhoods Index

Agincourt, 17D **1**
Amour Heights, 10E **2**
Beaches, The, 13N **3**
Bedford, 10G **4**
Bloorcourt Village, 8M **5**
Brockton, 7M **6**
Browne's Corners, 19C **7**
Cedarvale, 8J **8**
Clairlea, 15K **9**
Clark's Corners, 16D **10**
Cliffside, 17L **11**
Danforth, The, 12L **12**
Don Mills, 14G **13**
Dorset Park, 16G **14**
Downsview, 8F **15**
Ellesmere, 16F **16**
Forest Hill, 9J **17**
Golden Mile, The, 15J **18**
Guildwood, 19J **19**
Henry Farm, 13E **20**
High Park, 7L **21**
Highland Creek, 21G **22**
Hillcrest Village, 13B **23**
Humber Summit, 4B **24**
Humberlea, 5E **25**
Islington, 2J **26**
Junction, The, 7K **27**
Kingsway, The, 5J **28**
Kipling Heights, 3D **29**
Lawrence Park, 11G **30**
Leaside, 11J **31**
Long Branch, 1Q **32**
Malta Village, 6K **33**
Malvern, 19D **34**
Maryvale, 15F **35**
Mimico, 2P **36**
Moore Park, 11K **37**
New Toronto, 1P **38**
Newtonbrook, 12B **39**
Northwood, 7D **40**
Parkdale, 8N **41**
Pine Point, 3F **42**

Rexdale, 2B **43**
Richview, 3G **44**
Riverdale, 12M **45**
Rouge Hill, 22G **46**
Runnymede, 6J **47**
Silver Hills, 12E **48**
Six Points, 2J **49**
Sullivan, 15E **50**

Swansea, 5M **51**
Tam O'Shanter, 16E **52**
Thistletown, 4C **53**
Thorncliffe Park, 12K **54**
West Hill, 21J **55**
West Humber, 2D **56**
Weston, 5H **57**
Wexford, 15G **58**

Wexford Heights, 16H **59**
Wilson Heights, 9E **60**
Woburn, 19G **61**
Woodbine Gardens, 14K **62**
York Heights, 13F **63**
York Mills, 11F **64**

North Lake Ontario

Scarborough

North York

Etobicoke

York

East York

Uptown

Midtown

Downtown

Toronto Islands

Inner-city neighbourhoods

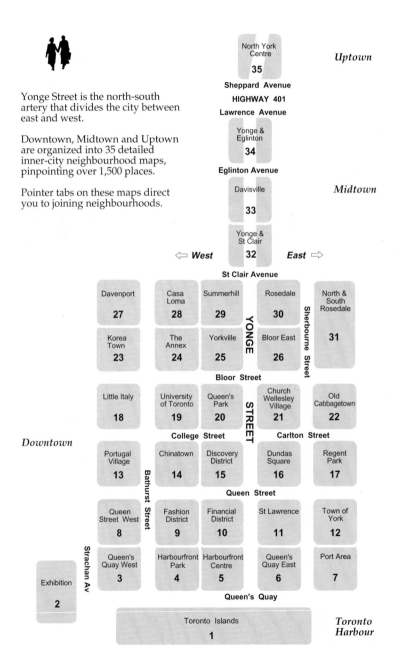

Yonge Street is the north-south artery that divides the city between east and west.

Downtown, Midtown and Uptown are organized into 35 detailed inner-city neighbourhood maps, pinpointing over 1,500 places.

Pointer tabs on these maps direct you to joining neighbourhoods.

Uptown

North York Centre
35

Sheppard Avenue

HIGHWAY 401

Lawrence Avenue

Yonge & Eglinton
34

Eglinton Avenue

Midtown

Davisville
33

Yonge & St Clair
32

⇦ *West*   *East* ⇨

St Clair Avenue

Davenport **27**	Casa Loma **28**	Summerhill **29**	Rosedale **30**	North & South Rosedale **31**
Korea Town **23**	The Annex **24**	Yorkville **25**	Bloor East **26**	

YONGE

Sherbourne Street

Bloor Street

Downtown

Little Italy **18**	University of Toronto **19**	Queen's Park **20**	Church Wellesley Village **21**	Old Cabbagetown **22**

College Street   Carlton Street

STREET

Portugal Village **13**	Chinatown **14**	Discovery District **15**	Dundas Square **16**	Regent Park **17**

Bathurst Street

Queen Street

Queen Street West **8**	Fashion District **9**	Financial District **10**	St Lawrence **11**	Town of York **12**

Strachan Street

Queen's Quay West **3**	Harbourfront Park **4**	Harbourfront Centre **5**	Queen's Quay East **6**	Port Area **7**

Strachan Av

Exhibition
2

Queen's Quay

Toronto Islands
1

Toronto Harbour

MAP

1

Toronto Islands

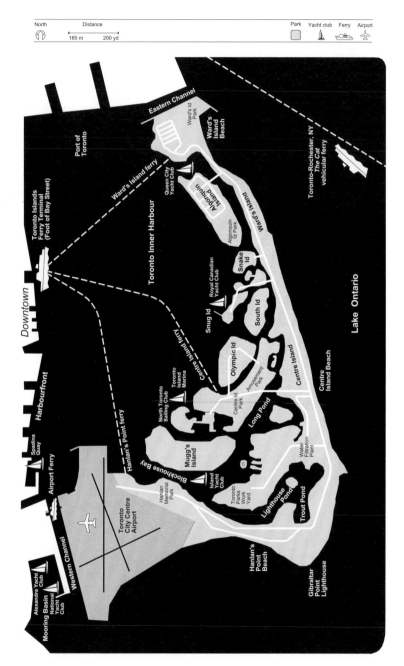

North | Distance | Park | Yacht club | Ferry | Airport
185 m | 200 yd

Eastern Channel

Ward's Id Park

Ward's Island Beach

Port of Toronto

Ward's Island ferry

Queen City Yacht Club

Algonquin Island

Algonquin Id Park

Ward's Island

Toronto-Rochester, NY The Cat vehicular ferry

Toronto Islands Ferry Terminal (Foot of Bay Street)

Toronto Inner Harbour

Royal Canadian Yacht Club

Snake Id

Downtown

Snug Id

South Id

Lake Ontario

Centre Island ferry

Olympic Id

Centre Island

Harbourfront

Amusement Park

Centre Id Park

Centre Island Beach

North Toronto Sailing Club

Toronto Island Marina

Long Pond

Spadina Quay

Mugg's Island

Water Filtration Plant

Airport Ferry

Hanlan's Point ferry

Blockhouse Bay

Island Yacht Club

Hanlan Memorial Park

Toronto Parks Work Yard

Lighthouse Pond

Trout Pond

Toronto City Centre Airport

Western Channel

Hanlan's Point Beach

Gibraltar Point Lighthouse

Alexandra Yacht Club

National Yacht Club

Mooring Basin

Toronto Islands **Profile**

For thousands of years, this is where people have come to relax. And that's the naked truth.

Before the arrival of the first Europeans here in the early part of the 17th century, the delta of what is now the Don River spilled out around two islands into what we know today as Lake Ontario. The delta, where Ashbridges Bay is now, was part of a large marsh that extended almost as far east as the Scarborough Bluffs. Off-shore there was a sand bank, formed from the Don's silt, that became an archipelago just west of the Don's delta. The isolation and tranquility of this finger of land with its small islands and sandy beaches became a kind of Caribbean vacation spot for Aboriginals throughout the region. They came here to harvest medicinal plants, relax in sweat lodges and generally rejuvenate their bodies and spirits. The Iroquois called the place 'Taronto', which meant 'a meeting place near trees in the water.'

Early French explorers named the islands Presq'ile, or 'nearly an island'. Elizabeth Simcoe, wife of the first British lieutenant-governor, referred to them as "my favourite sands." In 1858 a violent storm tore at the sandbank and separated the archipelago at a point where the Eastern Channel now stands. By then, Toronto's early settlers had already begun to fill the marshes around the mouth of the Don and join many of the scattered islands with construction debris and soil from the expanding city. The idea was twofold: to give the city more room, and to secure a more solid coast for the harbour.

Today's archipelago is one of the largest public parks in the city, except for a couple of small and stalwart communities that have claimed parts of Ward's Island and Algonquin Island as their own. Over the years, the residents have been hassled unsuccessfully by civic fathers to renounce their communities so the city can extend the islands' popular public facilities.

Centre Island, with its Centreville Amusement Park, is where a lot of us like to get away from the city with our kids and have a good time. It's also the place to be for the post-parade Caribana party. Mugg's Island is usually a domain for birds, and Snug Island is taken over by some of us who can afford to be members of the RCYC (Royal Canadian Yacht Club). Olympic Island, with its snack bars and nice sandy beach, is for folk without cell phones and international portfolios.

But it's Hanlan's Point Beach that attracts a really note-worthy crowd. On July 17, 1894 the city passed a by-law permitting nude swimming and sunbathing there "at all times."

Toronto Islands **Experience:** Go sailing around the Inner Harbour • take pictures of a great skyline view • have a summer picnic • be nice to a member of the RCYC • get an overall sun tan

MAP

2

Exhibition

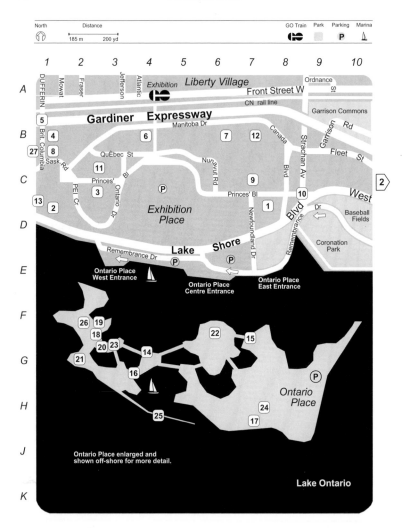

Exhibition Place

Automotive Building, 7D **1**
Bandshell, 1D **2**
Better Living Centre, 2D **3**
Centennial Square, 1B **4**
Dufferin Gate, 1B **5**
Food Products Building, 4B **6**
Horse Palace, 6B **7**
Horticultural Building, 1C **8**
National Trade Centre, 7C **9**
Princes' Gate, 8D **10**

Queen Elizabeth Building, 2C **11**
Ricoh Coliseum, 7B **12**
Scadding Cabin, 1D **13**

Ontario Place

Atlantis, 4H **14**
Bumper Boats, 7H **15**
Cinesphere IMAX, 3J **16**
Hydrofuge, 7K **17**
Go Zone Stage, 2H **18**

H2O Generation Station, 2H **19**
Japanese Temple Bell, 3H **20**
Megamaze, 2H **21**
Molson Ampitheatre, 5H **22**
OP Driving School, 3H **23**
Rush River Raft Ride, 7K **24**
Sunken Ships, 4K **25**
Wilderness Adventure Ride, 2G **26**

Restaurants

Medieval Times *Ancient*, 1C **27**

Exhibition **Profile**

There's been human activity around here since 8,000 BC. The first European settlers were French and they built Fort Taronto on this site. Some will argue it was the birthplace of the modern city.

 A year later, Fort Rouillé replaced Fort Taronto and in 1759 the French garrison burned it to the ground as they fled from British forces. During the next 30 years minor trading took place on this site before the British bought it from the Mississauga Indians and built a permanent settlement, the Town of York, a few kilometres to the east.

As the centuries changed, this area went from a place of conflict to one for leisure, entertainment and discovery.

The transition started in 1878 when 20 ha of land were leased to start a permanent fairground. Twenty-three wooden buildings and a spectacular Crystal Palace would house the Toronto Industrial Exhibition. Twenty-five years later the fairgrounds were the first to be lit by electricity and the following year saw the introduction of an electric railway. In 1912 the fair expanded to cover 141 ha and was re-named the Canadian National Exhibition. 'The Ex', or 'CNE', had entrenched itself into our psyche.

It became one of the world's finest permanent amusement and exhibition sites, featuring celebrity concerts, entertainment spectaculars, vast agricultural and industrial shows and the first television broadcast in the country. Every summer we flocked to the grounds like so many pilgrims. Being first through the Princes' Gate on opening day was to guarantee your photo on the front page of that evening's newspaper.

The CNE magic began to wane in the late Sixties when Montréal staged the hugely successful Expo '67. It seemed the CNE, by comparison, was not all that inspiring anymore. The second blow came four years later when three man-made islands joined the CNE's shoreline to form Ontario Place. The old CNE grandstand shows were challenged by Ontario Place's 16,000 seat Molson Amphitheatre, one of the country's then largest and most popular outdoor stages. The islands spawned parks, *avant-garde* architecture and lots of fun places for kids. They became home for the first permanent IMAX theatre and the venerable Ex never really recovered.

Some suggest Ontario Place was built to show Montréalers that Toronto could up the ante when it came to creating a spectacular public playground. Others muse, tongue in cheek, that Expo '67 was Montréal trying to get back at us for the defeat at Fort Rouillé.

Exhibition **Experience:** Enjoy some fun at the CNE • attend a concert at the Molson Amphitheatre • walk through the parks inside Ontario Place • have an unusual dinner at Medieval Times • visit Scadding Cabin – Toronto's oldest building.

MAP

3

Queen's Quay West

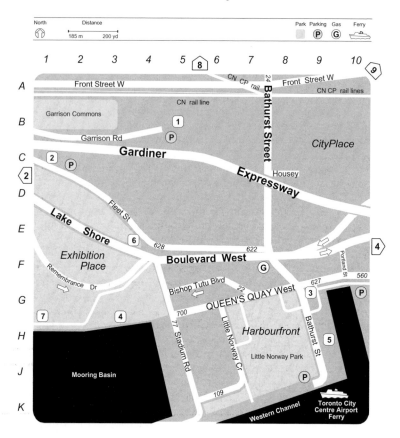

Places

Fort York (1793), 5B **1**
Fort York Armoury, 1C **2**
Harbourfront Community Centre, 8G **3**
HMCS York
  (Department of National Defence), 3G **4**
Metronome (Under development), 9H **5**
Queen's Wharf Lighthouse (1861), 3E **6**
Victory Garden, 1G **7**

Development

Over the next 10 years, the area east of
Bathurst Street will undergo a massive
redevelopment costing $1,500,000,000

Construction is well under way at *CityPlace*, a
557,000 sq m, 6,000-unit housing complex
that's the biggest of its kind in Toronto.

An area of 17.8 ha will see the construction
of 20 highrise condominium towers, lowrise
residential properties and commercial space.

Further to the south, next to the Toronto
City Centre Airport ferry terminal, the old
Canada Malting Silo is about to be
transformed into the *Metronome*, which is
being billed as "the world's first music city."

The complex is designed to be the national
showcase for the Canadian music industry.
When completed, it will occupy about
3,700 square metres (40,000 square feet) of
interior space.

Queen's Quay West **Profile**

In 1812, America declared war on Upper Canada. Twelve months later Fort York surrendered. The following year British forces retaliated in a most ungentlemanly fashion.

 Fort York was built in 1793 to provide protection for the fledgling Town of York against the United States. But, on April 27, 1813 superior numbers of Americans stormed ashore just west of here and defeated a comparatively small band of British, Canadian, Mississaugan and Ojibway forces. Before retreating, the British blew-up Fort York's gunpowder magazine which led to the death of America's commander, Brigadier General Zebulon Pike. It was a nasty six-hour battle with defenders outnumbered nearly four to one by the invaders. When the bloody affair was all over, British forces had lost 157 men and the Americans 320.

Americans occupied the Town of York for six days and went on a rampage of looting homes and pillaging supplies. They even burned down Upper Canada's parliament buildings and government house. It was a week the British wouldn't easily forget.

Toronto took over restoration of Fort York in 1924 and it later became a national historical site, housing Canada's largest collection of original War of 1812 buildings. These days, it lies in the shadow of yet another of the neighbourhood's high rise condominium towers.

During World War II, this part of the city became directly involved in war once again. This time it opened its doors to Norwegian air force pilots who trained at the nearby island airport. Their barracks occupied what is now Little Norway Park. On the northeast corner there's an ancient stone brought from Norway to commemorate the wartime alliance. A bit further west, on the shore of Mooring Basin, is the quiet dignity of Victory Garden. The understated circle of memory was dedicated to peace on the 50th anniversary of the end of World War II.

There's a piece of naval history wedged between Lake Shore Boulevard West and Fleet Street near the entrance to Stadium Road. It's the operating portion of a lighthouse that began guiding ships into Toronto harbour from 1861.

This was the same year that this neighbourhood was on war footing once again, fearing another American invasion. It never materialized. Perhaps the Americans remembered what happened the last time that they attacked here: within a year the British had retaliated for the American attack on Fort York by raiding Washington, DC. While they were there they burned down the Capitol and White House.

> *Queen's Quay West* **Experience:** Learn some history at Fort York • roam around Little Norway Park's alcoves • take Canada's shortest ferry ride • pause at the Victory Garden for a reflective moment • enjoy the view around the Mooring Basin • see Garrison Commons.

MAP
4

Harbourfront Park

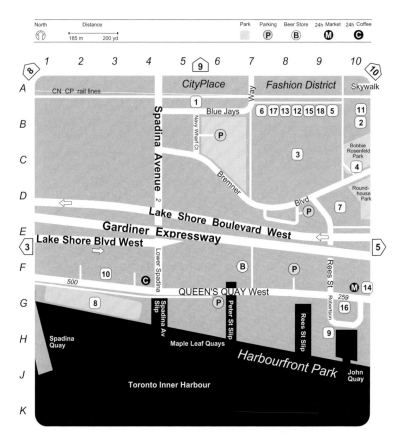

Places

Chinese Railroad Memorial, 5A **1**
CN Tower, 10B **2**
Rogers Centre, 8C **3**
Salmon Run, 10C **4**
The Audience, Part 1, 9B **5**
The Audience, Part 2, 7B **6**
The Roundhouse, 10D **7**
Toronto Music Garden, 2G **8**
Toronto Police Marine Unit, 9H **9**
Walter Carson Centre,
   National Ballet of Canada, 3F **10**

Restaurants

360 Restaurant (CN Tower)
   International, 10B **11**
Hard Rock Café *American,* 8B **12**
Sightlines *American,* 8B **13**

Spice Thai *Thai,* 10F **14**
Windows on Sightline *International,* 8B **15**

Accommodation

Radisson Plaza Admiral Hotel, 10G **16**
Renaissance Downtown Hotel, 8B **17**

Shops

Blue Jays' Bullpen *Blue Jays stuff,*
   9B **18**

Harbourfront Park **Profile**

Here's where you'll find lots of those postcard places. But there's more to address in this part of town.

 Looking east along Queen's Quay from Lower Spadina Avenue there's a continuous line of high-rise condominium towers. Look straight up and the CN Tower dominates the sky. These are modern counterparts of ancient forests that once inspired Aboriginal people and then became a source of lumber for European settlers.

Few neighbourhoods in the city have been so thoroughly stamped with Toronto's modern icons than Harbourfront Park. The CN Tower has become the city's signature, while the Rogers Centre is an integral part of North America's baseball photo album. But, if you look closer at less obvious things, the place can evoke other kinds of powerful emotions.

On Blue Jays Way at Navy Wharf there's the moving Chinese Workers monument. It is a stark memorial to the 4,000 people from Kwangtung, China who died between 1880 and 1885 while building the trans-continental Canadian Pacific railway through Alberta and British Columbia. Eldon Garnet conceived the monument and Francis Le Bouthillier sculpted the two working figures. The 13,000 Chinese labourers who survived didn't have enough money to return home and disappeared into Canadian anonymity.

An inscription reads: "Rich is the hand that holds the stone of memory."

On the other side of Rogers Centre is another aspect of the realities of western Canada. It's Susan Schelle's sculpture, Salmon Run. The strangely realistic sight of two-dimensional salmon swimming and jumping through waterfalls on their way to spawn has a serene strength that rivals the surrounding concrete. It draws us to it and provides a relaxing spot to sit for awhile.

Another place for quiet contemplation is the beautiful Toronto Music Garden that evokes botanical themes for classical music. Joining it at the eastern end is the Spadina Quay Wetland. This small, natural refuge for animals and plants shows you what the shore looked like before the advent of Europeans. Look back to the west and see the old Canada Malting silos. One day it might become the Metronome, "an international symbol of a vital Canadian music community."

In the midst of concrete icons, this neighbourhood is also a place for art and nature in their many forms.

Harbourfront Park **Experience:** Do what lots of tourists do and take that express ride up the CN Tower to see if you can spot Niagara Falls • attend a game at Rogers Centre • walk along Bremner boulevard • stop and look at the street art • sit down in the Toronto Music Garden • check out Roundhouse Park • buy some Blue Jays stuff.

MAP
5
Harbourfront Centre

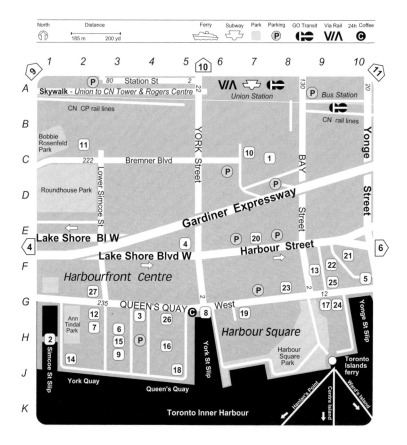

Places

Air Canada Centre, 7C **1**
Amsterdam Bridge, 1H **2**
Artists' Gardens, 3G **3**
Auto Pound, 5E **4**
Between the Eyes, 10F **5**
Canada Quay, 3H **6**
   Information Web site
International Marketplace, 2H **7**
Pier 6 (1907), 6G **8**
Power Plant, 3J **9**
Search Light, Star Light, Spot Light,
   7C **10**
Toronto Convention Centre, 2B **11**
   South entrance
York Quay Centre, 2G **12**
Westin Harbour Castle Convention Centre,
   9F **13**

Entertainment

CIBC Stage, 2J **14**

Harbourfront Centre Theatre, 3H **15**
Premier Dance Theatre, 4H **16**

Accommodation

Westin Harbour Castle Hotel, 9G **17**

Restaurants

Boathouse *International*, 5J **18**
Cocoberry Café *International*, 7G **19**
Harbour Sixty *Steakhouse*, 7E **20**
Harbour Sports Grill, 10F **21**
Oyshi *Japanese*, 9F **22**
Piazza Manna *Italian*, 8G **23**
Toulà (Harbour Castle Hotel) *Italian*,
   9G **24**

Shops

Eskimo Art *Canadian art*, 9G **25**
Queen's Quay Terminal *Mall*, 4G **26**
Vineyards *Wine shop*, 2G **27**

Harbourfront Centre **Profile**

Not that long ago, this was a pretty run down place. Today, following an urban renewal program, it's where people come to play.

 In 1974 the city began a significant 4 ha redevelopment of the waterfront between York and Simcoe slips. A quarter century later that modest beginning had escalated into a more ambitious project that spread west to Exhibition Place. This lakeside stretch of playground south of the Gardiner Expressway is known simply as Harbourfront, while the original 4 ha at the bottom of York Street is called Harbourfront Centre.

This is about the busiest area on the waterfront. About 4,000 events take place in this neighbourhood every year. They range from music and dance performances on several stages, to art exhibitions, ethnic festivals, literary readings and international marketplace activity. And there's Canada Quay, a wired building open seven days a week, where you can use the latest technology to surf the Canadian government's databases. The state-of-the-art LED monitors are alone worth a visit.

Following completion of the CN Tower and Rogers Centre (originally called the SkyDome), the barren lands to the east underwent a transformation that has changed them dramatically. The stub of Bremner Boulevard – that had previously not ventured much past the Rogers Centre – was pushed eastward to join with York Street. Book-ending this section of the boulevard is the Air Canada Centre and the southern entrance to the Toronto Convention Centre.

Ground broke for the Air Canada Centre in February, 1997 on the site of the old Canada Post Delivery Building. It was designed to accommodate basketball (Toronto Raptors), ice hockey (Toronto Maple Leafs), concerts, trade shows and circuses. Seating capacity ranges from 19,000 for hockey to 22,000 for concerts. The old post office building's historic eastern façade was blended into the new stadium's architecture. On the west side of the arena is John McEwen's rusted 11-ton sculpture *Search Light, Star Light, Spot Light*.

When the Toronto Convention Centre on Front Street West was expanded towards the lake, its southern entrance spilled out on to Bremner Boulevard. There, on the edge of Bobbie Rosenfeld Park, sit two huge birds on the dauntingly black *Woodpecker Column*.

The total economic benefit for the first decade of the 21st century generated by the Air Canada Centre, Harbourfront Centre and Convention Centre should come to over $4,000,000,000. That's a lot of play money.

Harbourfront Centre **Experience:** Spend time watching the boats • enjoy a live show • attend something at the Air Canada Centre • take a ferry to the islands • see what's inside the Power Plant and Canada Quay • go shopping in the Queen's Quay Terminal mall.

MAP
6

Queen's Quay East

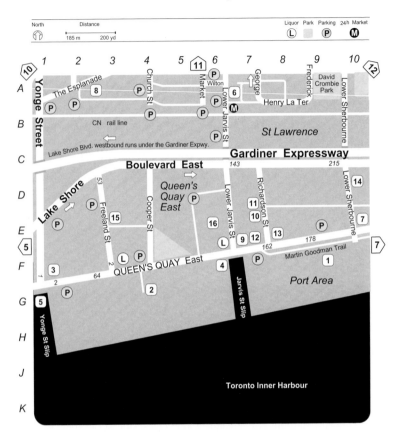

Places

Cinespace studios, 9F **1**
Redpath Sugar Museum, 4G **2**
Toronto Star Newspaper, 1F **3**
Whale mural, 6F **4**

Restaurants

Captain John's *Seafood*, 1G **5**
Casa di Giorgio *Italian*, 7A **6**
Town & Country *Buffet*, 10E **7**

Accommodation

Novotel Toronto Centre Hotel, 2A **8**

Entertainment

Charlies *Club*, 7F **9**
Guvernment *Club*, 7E **10**
Koolhaus *Club*, 7D **11**
Orange Room *Club*, 7F **12**

Shops

Dock Shoppe *Ship Chandlers*, 7E **13**
Eurolite *Lighting fixtures*, 10D **14**
LCBO Specialty Wine Store,
    Private vintage ordering, 3E **15**
Queen's Quay Market, 6E **16**
    Caban *Home décor*
    Holy Smokes *Cigars*
    Loblaws *Supermarket*
    Moneysworth & Best *Shoe repair*

Queen's Quay East **Profile**

Yonge Street is the longest street in the world. It starts here and goes all the way to Rainy River on the border of Ontario and Michigan.

 Yonge Street – pronounced 'young' – is one of the oldest thoroughfares in the city.

It started as an Aboriginal trail that headed north from what was Lake Iroquois (Lake Ontario) to Lake Simcoe. Using this pathway as a rough guide, early settlers mapped out Yonge Street to serve as the north-south spine for the Town of York. The first few muddy kilometres were completed on February 16, 1796, and named after Sir George Yonge who was the British Secretary of War and an authority on Roman roads.

At the beginning of the 20th century, docks at the bottom of Yonge Street were a place of bustling commercial enterprise. Steamers berthed here for their passenger and freight runs from Toronto to Buffalo, NY, Niagara Falls and Grimsby. The area now occupied by the *Toronto Star* building and Westin Harbour Castle hotel was crowded with horse-drawn wagons and merchants. The only marine memories left are the tour boats and a permanently moored ferry housing Captain John's Restaurant.

The area roughly south of The Esplanade is built entirely on landfill. In fact, The Esplanade gets its name because it was once literally an esplanade along the lake's shore and a popular spot for early residents during the summer. By 1900, Yonge Street had reached about as far south into the lake as it has today.

The significant redevelopment of the lakeshore west of Yonge Street, with its forest of condominium towers, hasn't spilled over into Queen's Quay East. However, the large and popular Queen's Quay Market at the bottom of Lower Jarvis Street, and four popular clubs a block further east, have started to jazz the place up. The former has attracted trendy folk from the condominium neighbourhoods along Queen's Quay West, while the clubs act as a magnet for the young crowd from all over the city.

The Redpath Sugar Refinery holds the distinction of being one of the few – if not the only – commercial building in the city opened by Queen Elizabeth II. Tucked away at the back is a small, informal museum devoted to all you would ever want to know about sugar and its manufacture. Just go to reception in the main building and ask to be shown around.

They say that a journey starts with the first step. So, if you really want to go all the way up Yonge Street, remember that it's 1,896 km long.

Queen's Quay East **Experience:** Get out at the weekend and go to a club • browse around the Queen's Quay Market shops • place your order for an unusual wine at the LCBO Specialty Wine Store • do lunch in an old railway freight car or on-board a ferry.

MAP

7

Port Area

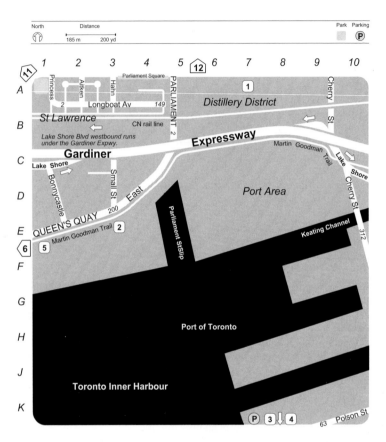

Places

Gooderham & Worts distillery (1837),
7A **1**
Royal Canadian Yacht Club (RCYC)
private ferry, 3E **2**

Restaurants

The Docks *International*, 8K **3**

Entertainment

The Docks *Nightclub & entertainment centre.
Drive in cinema.* 8K **4**
Waterside Golf & Tennis Centre, 1E **5**

Development

Toronto has long been considered a major film
production location. Over the years, Hollywood
producers – bolstered by the low Canadian dollar and
expert Toronto production crews – have invested
hundreds of millions of dollars filming block buster
movies here.

The area just to the east of Cherry Street is about
to undergo extensive redevelopment into an
independent film studio complex containing one of
the world's largest sound stages.

The winning bid to build and operate the complex
went to the Canadian company Toronto Film Studios.
The cost of the state-of-the-art facility, covering a
12 ha site, will be approximately $100,000,000. The
complex is due to open for production in the spring
of 2007.

Port Area **Profile**

The area was once the centre of the city's bustling 19th century industrial complex. In this 21st century, the industries are entertainment and media. But the past lives on through handsome rejuvenation.

 The shoreline from the mouth of the Don River east to Scarborough Bluffs was one long marsh when European settlers arrived. John Graves Simcoe, who established the Town of York in 1793, had a vision for the place: convert land around the Don River delta into a public park. Accordingly, early layouts for the settlement included a significant allotment for parks east of Parliament Street.

Within 40 years commercial interests had redefined the future of the delta and that future didn't include Simcoe's visionary parkland. To satisfy an appetite for industrial expansion and workers' housing – especially by the liquor giant Gooderham and Worts – the neighbourhood was redesigned to accommodate business rather than pleasure. By the end of the 1800s the place was a thriving industrial complex.

Gooderham and Worts was the largest 19th century distillery in the country. It started in 1832 as a gristmill to convert surplus grain into whiskey. Exploiting the technology of the day, the company grew steadily, paralleling Toronto's rise as a manufacturing centre. The stone distillery that remains today was built between 1859 and 1861 and the rest of the complex was completed before the turn of the century. The distillery is no longer in business. What remains is a national historic site and Toronto's best example of Victorian industrial design.

Within this complex the city has created a strikingly handsome commercial space with art galleries, boutiques, stores, a live theatre stage and restaurants that easily challenge similar groupings in the city's upscale neighbourhoods. There's even a microbrewery for old time's sake.

In an otherwise desolate part of the city, with its flat and anonymous landscape, there has emerged one of Toronto's largest and most successful entertainment complexes. The Docks is a bar, restaurant, activity centre, nightclub, midway, swimming pool, putting course, drive-in cinema, and virtual reality kind of place. It attracts thousands of our twentysomethings to Polson Street – and to one of the best views of the downtown skyline.

Go further down Cherry Street towards the lake and you can look across to an evolving bird sanctuary on Tommy Thompson Park that's open to us on weekends. Perhaps it's the closest the city will get to accomplishing the 200-year-old vision of John Graves Simcoe.

Port Area **Experience**: Follow the crowd to The Docks • jog along the Martin Goodman trail • find someone important to take you to the RCYC • visit the historic Distillery District and tell your friends all about it.

MAP

8

Queen Street West

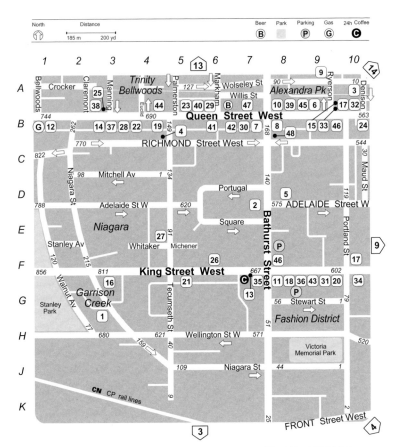

Places

Buddhist Temple, 3G **1**
St Mary's Church (1885)
   Roman Catholic, 7D **2**
St Stanislaus Kostka (1879)
   Roman Catholic, 10A **3**
Ukrainian Baptist Church, 5B **4**

Entertainment

Factory Theatre, 8D **5**
   John Mulvey House (1869)
Funhaus *Club*, 9A **6**
Healey's *Club*, 7B **7**
Reverb *Club*, 8B **8**
Théâtre Passe Muraille, 9A **9**

Restaurants

Azul *International*, 8A **10**
Banknote Grill *Pub*, 8F **11**
Cities *Continental*, 1B **12**

Coco Rice *Thai*, 7F **13**
Dufflet *Pastries*, 3B **14**
Epicure *Café*, 9B **15**
Foggy Dew *Pub*, 3F **16**
Friendly Thai *Thai*, 10A **17**
Giovanna *Italian*, 8F **18**
Habitat *Continental*, 4B **19**
Innocenti *Italian*, 9F **20**
Jalapeño *Mexican*, 5F **21**
Irie *Café*, 4B **22**
La Hacienda *Spanish*, 5A **23**
Left Bank *American*, 10B **24**
Little Tibet *Tibetan*, 2A **25**
Loft *International*, 6F **26**
Nonna's *Italian*, 5E **27**
Paddy Murphy's *Pub*, 4B **28**
Portobello *Café*, 6A **29**
Queenshead *Pub*, 7B **30**
Susur *International*, 9F **31**
Taro *International*, 10A **32**
Tequilla Bookworm
   International, 10A **33**
Toshi Sushi *Japanese*, 10F **34**

Wheat Sheaf (1849) *Pub*,
   7F **35**

Accommodation

Travelodge Motel, 8F **36**

Shops

Bullet *Home Décor*, 3B **37**
Doc's Leather *Cycle gear*, 2A **38**
EQ3 *Furniture*, 8A **39**
Intheory *Furniture*, 5A **40**
Jalan *Antiques*, 6B **41**
Morba *Lighting*, 6B **42**
Navaro *Art gallery*, 8F **43**
Pavilion *Home décor*, 4B **44**
Red Indian *Art déco*, 8A **45**
Six In One *Fine arts*, 9B **46**
Urban Barn *Furniture*, 7A **47**
Xexe *Gallery*, 8B **48**

Queen Street West **Profile**

At the end of the 1800s the Polish community settled here. Since then, they've moved on and the neighbourhood has become a place where funky folk can relax and do their thing.

 The Poles moved here from the notorious slums of The Ward, about a kilometre to the east, attracted by employment opportunities in the light manufacturing industries. The Roman Catholic faith was the cornerstone of their lives and places like St Stanislaus Kostka on Denison Avenue became the focal point to help families through some rough times. It is the oldest of the Polish churches in this area and keeps traditions alive with Polish language classes for kids and Old Country dance lessons for adults. However, the community has largely moved on again to what's known as 'Little Poland' along Roncesvalles Avenue.

The vacuum was filled with a wider cultural mix of people and for the last 40 years there's been a feeling of the Sixties here. Nowhere else in town will you see such a concentration of funky shops, nerdish people reading obscure literature in coffee shops, off-beat clothes hanging in windows and strange neon-coloured street art. It's all part of a modern-day hippiedom that this working class neighbourhood preserves for its residents. The young crowd comes here for an earthy urban experience, the clubs and a plethora of reasonably priced restaurants devoted to almost any cuisine your mood dictates. It's a place to take it easy and browse around on the weekend. 'Queen West' is a distinctive kind of place. And it's quite content believing that it's not really part of the predictable and stressed-out city.

This part of town also has stories to tell as far back as the days when a British garrison was in charge. Even the streets tell a story: Niagara was named after the original capital of Upper Canada; Tecumseth was the great chief of the Shawnee; Wellington after Lord Wellington. Garrison Creek that flowed through Stanley Park provided fresh water to the British forces at Fort York. It now flows anonymously through an underground Victorian brick sewer. The park is named to commemorate Stanley Barracks that once stood on the present Exhibition Place.

The men who died as a result of the American attack on Fort York in 1813 are remembered in Victoria Memorial Park. This is where you'll see some of the old headstones that were collected and placed here for a final acknowledgement of their acts of courage.

Queen Street West **Experience:** Read the inscriptions and map on the sidewalk at the northwest corner of Walnut and Wellington streets • take in a show at the 135-year-old Factory Theatre • have a drink at the 155-year-old Wheat Sheaf Pub, just to say you've been there • torture yourself trying to choose where to eat • visit a bit of history among the headstones in Victoria Memorial Park.

MAP

9

Fashion District

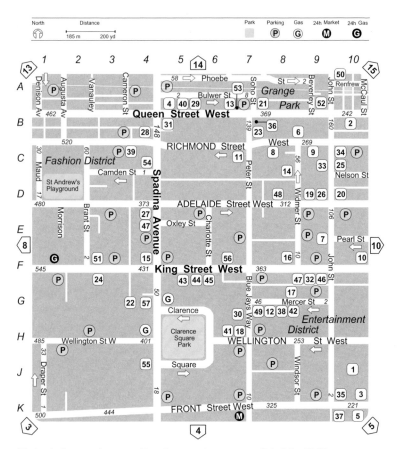

Entertainment

CBC Broadcast Centre, 10J **1**
CITY-*Muchmusic-Bravo!*, 10B **2**
Glenn Gould Studio, 10K **3**
Horseshoe Tavern, 5B **4**
John Bassett Theatre, 10K **5**
Joker *Club*, 8B **6**
Lucid *Club*, 9E **7**
Oxygen *Club*, 8C **8**
Paramount Cinemas, 9C **9**
Princess of Wales Thtr, 10F **10**
Privilege, 7C **11**
Second City *Comedy*, 8G **12**
Ultra *Supper Club*, 6A **13**

Accommodation

Canadiana *Backpack*, 8C **14**
Global Village *Backpack*, 4F **15**
Holiday Inn Hotel, 8F **16**
Le Germain Hotel, 8G **17**
Soho Hotel, 7H **18**

Restaurants

Alice Fazooli's *Italian*, 9D **19**
Avalon, *Continental*, 10D **20**
Black Bull (1833) *Tavern*, 7B **21**
Brassai *International*, 3G **22**
Fez Batik *Eclectic*, 7B **23**
Fionn MacCool's *Pub*, 3F **24**
Frisco's *International*, 10C **25**
Hooters *American*, 9D **26**
Imagine *Vegetarian*, 4E **27**
Le Gourmand *Café* 4B **28**
Le Select *French*, 5A **29**
Leoni's *Italian*, 7G **30**
Lettieri *Café*, 4B **31**
Milano *Italian*, 9F **32**
Milestones *International*, 9D **33**
Montana *American*, 10C **34**
Palavrion *Continental*, 10K **35**
Peter Pan *International*, 7B **36**
Planet Hollywood *American*,
   10K **37**

Rain *Asian*, 8G **38**
Rasoee *Indian*, 4C **39**
Rivoli *International*, 5A **40**
Sen5es *Continental*, 6H **41**
Schmooze *Continental*, 8G **42**
Solo *International*, 5G **43**
Spoon *International*, 5F **44**
Thai Princess *Thai*, 6F **45**
Urban *International*, 9F **46**
Verona *Continental*, 8F **47**
Waterfall *International*, 8D **48**
Wayne Gretzky *Canadian*, 7G **49**
Young Thailand *Thai*, 10A **50**

Shops

Acton *Leather furniture*,2F **51**
Caban *Home accents*, 9B **52**
Flea Market (Seasonal), 6B **53**
Homeproud *Bed-bath*, 4C **54**
MacGregor *Sox*, 4J **55**
Mountain Equipment, 6F **56**
Sistemlux *Lighting*, 4G **57**

Fashion District **Profile**

Funky and anti-establishment clothing shops influence the Queen West strip. But, if it's something more au courant and up-market you're looking for, you'll have to check out the clubs.

 York Hospital, built in 1829 to replace an existing military hospital, stood at the corner of King and John streets. It was so over-burdened by the cholera epidemic of 1847 that makeshift wooden sheds had to be constructed to the north to take care of patients. It was not a warm welcome for Toronto's fledgling Jewish community who came to this neighbourhood in the early 1830s. Nevertheless, 60,000 people banded together to build synagogues and open a variety of small businesses, including tailoring and furrier enterprises. It wasn't the greatest place to set-up shop, because it bordered a district known as 'The Ward'. Few would disagree that The Ward was the worst slum in Canada, if not North America. Nevertheless, large red brick industrial buildings began housing a flourishing needle trade that eventually included some of the city's most sought after furriers.

For all practical purposes, the Jewish community has moved away from Spadina Avenue to more affluent neighbourhoods. They've been replaced with a mainly Asian population. Even though the people and traditions have visibly changed, you'll still find Jewish-owned businesses carrying on the needle trade of their forebears. The short Queen Street West strip between Vanauley and Denison, for example, has the city's largest concentration of fabric and needlework shops. However, the big old buildings east of Spadina Avenue that once housed hundreds of tailors and seamstresses have largely made way for another fashion: the club scene.

The neighbourhood from Queen Street West down to Front Street is where the affluent young crowd – and those who wish they were – head for a night on the town. It's a blossoming mélange of clubs, bars, restaurants and little *avant garde* shops that spill into the traditional Entertainment District.

This is also the most concentrated mass media neighbourhood in Canada. The national English-language networks of the Canadian Broadcasting Corporation are centred here. So is the street-savvy CITY-TV organization that runs a half-dozen cable networks, including the hip MuchMusic and the prestigious Bravo! The national *Globe and Mail* newspaper is down on Front Street West.

In the midst of it all is Draper Street, one of the city's least known enclaves. Its impeccable heritage cottages are so close to this playground of the Now Generation, yet so far away in time.

Fashion District **Experience:** Eat, play and get up late next morning • rant at CITY-TV's 'Speakers' Corner' • walk down Draper Street for something completely different • buy some utterly outlandish clothes on Queen Street West.

MAP
10   Financial District

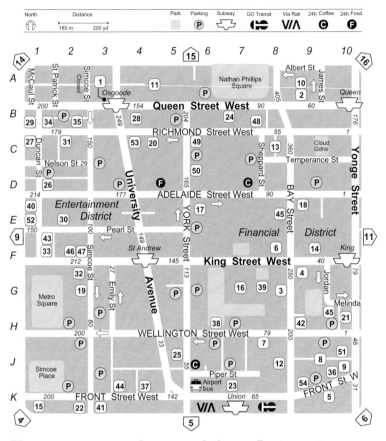

Places

Campbell House (1822), 3A **1**
Cenotaph, 9B **2**
Design Exchange, 8G **3**
Commerce Court, 9F **4**
Dominion Public Building, 9K **5**
First Canadian Place, 8F **6**
Gallery of Inuit Art, 7H **7**
Heritage Square (BCE Pl), 9J **8**
Hockey Hall of Fame, 10J **9**
Old City Hall (1899), 9A **10**
Osgoode Hall (1832), 4A **11**
Royal Bank Plaza, 8J **12**
Sapphire Tower (uc), 8C **13**
Scotia Plaza, 9F **14**
Toronto Convention Cntr, 1K **15**
Toronto Dominion Cntr, 7G **16**
Toronto Stock Exchange, 6D **17**
Trump Tower (uc),9D **18**
Walk of Fame, 2G **19**

Accommodation

Hilton Hotel, 4C **20**
Hotel Victoria, 10G **21**
Intercontinental Hotel, 2K **22**
Royal York Hotel, 6K **23**
Sheraton Centre Hotel, 7B **24**
Strathcona Hotel, 5J **25**

Entertainment

Crocodile Rock *Club*, 1D **26**
Fluid *Club*, 1C **27**
Four Seasons Centre, 4B **28**
Joe Inc *Club*, 1B **29**
Mink *Club*, 2E 31 **30**
Money *Club*, 2B **31**
Roy Thomson Hall, 2F **32**
Royal Alex Theatre, 1F **33**
Sugar *Club*, 1B **34**
Yuk Yuk's *Comedy*, 2B **35**

Restaurants

Acqua *Italian*, 10J **36**
Armadillo *Texan*, 4K **37**
Bymark *International*, 6H **38**
Canoe *Canadian*, 8G **39**
Duncan Street *Grill*, 1E **40**
East Side Marios *Italian*, 3K **41**
Far Niente *Continental*, 9H **42**
Filet of Sole *Seafood*, 1E **43**
Joe Badali's *Italian*, 3J **44**
Jump *International*, 9G **45**
Kama *Indian*, 2F **46**
King's Garden *Chinese*, 2F **47**
Le Bifthéque, *Steakhouse*, 7B **48**
Little Anthony's *Italian*, 6C **49**
Mövenpick *Continental*, 6C **50**
Mövenpick *Marché*, 10J **51**
RD's *Ribs*, 1E **52**
Ruth's Chris *Steakhouse*, 4C **53**
Takesushi *Japanese*, 8J **54**

Financial District **Profile**

Four of Canada's 'Big Five' banks have built their monuments to wealth on the corners of King and Bay streets. If all their towers were placed end to end they would top 323 storeys. They call it 'Mint Corner.'

There are more banks, accountants, money traders and lawyers in this area than anywhere in the country. One of the buildings they occupy is made of matched Italian white marble. Another is clad with $950,000 worth of real gold, calculated on the 2005 price for bullion. (Mint Corner is an acronym for the Bank of **M**ontreal, Canadian **I**mperial Bank of Commerce, Bank of **N**ova Scotia and the **T**oronto Dominion Bank.) The Toronto Stock Exchange is the fourth largest in North America in terms of market capitalization. During an average trading day about $2,000,000,000 changes hands. The five major banks here each make more than a billion dollars in profit annually. Some of the legal firms in this area have more than 190 lawyers on staff. After a while, statistics in this part of town rise above the comprehension of mere mortals.

The mind boggled around here as far back as 70 years ago. The old 34-storey Bank of Commerce building was the tallest in the British Empire when it opened in 1931. The Royal York hotel, which opened in 1929, was the largest hotel in the Empire commanding the downtown skyline in height and width.

Despite the intensity of size, this neighbourhood has been able to make room for quiet little parks and a spawning of street art. Catherine Widgery's cut-out *City People* can be seen scurrying up a staircase outside the south entrance to Royal Bank Plaza; Joe Fafard's *Reclining Cows* rests on lawns in the Toronto Dominion Centre; and Anish Kapoor's *Untitled (Mountain)* are forever catching the eyes of wandering camera buffs in Simcoe Place. Francesco Pirelli's *The Monument to Multiculturalism*, which was a gift to the city from the Italian community, stands outside Union Station. The park in First Canadian Place, fronting King Street West, has a full-length waterfall cascading down its northern wall. These are all favourite summer spots for office workers brown-bagging their lunches.

In 1869, at the northwest corner of Queen and Yonge streets, Timothy Eaton opened his first shop in Toronto. Just across the street, Robert Simpson set-up competition in the department store business. For generations both Simpson's and Eaton's were household names in Canadian merchandising. Today they're both gone. Simpson's was taken over by the Hudson's Bay Company and Eaton's became part of Sears in the fall of 1999. Business can be rough in this part of town.

Financial District **Experience:** Gawk at skyscrapers • eat at trendy places • go to a club or show • put your feet up in one of the small parks • don't forget to walk through the impressive Heritage Square gallery in BCE Place • get lost somewhere in the PATH walkway.

MAP
11
St Lawrence

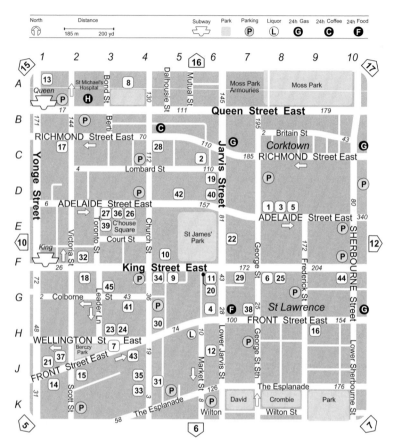

Places

Bank of Upper Canada (1827), 8D **1**
Central Fire Hall (1886), 6C **2**
De La Salle Institute (1871), 8D **3**
Farmer's Market, 6G **4**
First Post Office (1835) and Museum, 8D **5**
First Public School site (1807), 8F **6**
Flatiron Building (1892), 3H **7**
Metropolitan Church (1870), *United*, 3A **8**
Sculpture Garden, 5F **9**
St James Cathedral (1853) *Anglican*, 5F **10**
St Lawrence Hall (1850), 6F **11**
St Lawrence Market, 6H **12**

Entertainment

Elgin & Winter Garden Theatres, 1A **13**
Hummingbird Centre, 1J **14**
St Lawrence Centre, 2J **15**
  Bluma Appel Theatre
  Jane Mallett Theatre
Theatre for Young People, 9H **16**

Accommodation

Cambridge Suites Hotel, 1C **17**
King Edward Hotel, 2F **18**
Quality Hotel, 6C **19**

Restaurants

Biagio *Italian*, 6F **20**
Biff's *French bistro*, 1J **21**
Bombay Palace *Indian*, 6E **22**
Bouchon *Bistro*, 3H **23**
Bravi *Continental*, 3H **24**

Chocolate *International*, 8F **25**
Courthouse *Grill*, 3D **26**
Fig Leaf *Italian*, 3D **27**
Golden Thai *Thai*, 4C **28**
Hiro Sushi *Japanese*, 7F **29**
Hot House *Italian*, 4H **30**
Jamie Kennedy *Wine Bar*, 4J **31**
Kabuki *Japanese*, 2F **32**
Keg *Steakhouse*, 4K **33**
La Maquette *International*, 4F **34**
Le Papillon *French*, 4J **35**
Nami *Japanese*, 3D **36**
Penelope *Greek*, 1J **37**
Romagna Mia *Italian*, 7G **38**
Rosewater *International*, 3E **39**
Sakura *Japanese*, 6D **40**
Spinello *Italian*, 4G **41**
Starfish *Seafood*, 5D **42**
Sultan's Tent *Moroccan*, 4J **43**
Toba *International*, 10F **44**
Tom Jones *Steakhouse*, 3G **45**

St Lawrence **Profile**

Gallows once stood here under the spire of a church. And one of the local buildings is haunted. Few neighbourhoods give us a sense of Toronto's deadly past more than St Lawrence.

 Nothing reminds us more about the deadly history of this part of town than little Courthouse Square. Almost hidden among buildings and filled with lunchtime office workers, it is where the last public hangings took place. Three men, convicted for their part in the 1837 Rebellion, were put to death here in April 1838. Their crime was to demand that the British crown hear the voices of concerned farmers. Queen Victoria commuted their sentences, but news of this didn't arrive in the colony in time to stay the executions.

The spire across the street from the gallows was that of St James church, which burned to the ground less than a year after the hangings. A replacement building suffered a similar fate in 1849. Today's Georgian-styled cathedral opened in 1853. In the porch wall is the tombstone of John Rideout, killed in 1817 in the last fatal duel held in the Town of York.

A few blocks further east is the 1827 Bank of Upper Canada building, the oldest surviving bank building in town. Founded by some of York's powerful élite, it became one of the most powerful and influential financial institutions on the continent. It collapsed in 1886. Next door is the De La Salle Institute, representing the first Jesuit foothold in what was then a staunchly Church of England colony. The next building to the east is the York post office, built a year before York changed its name to Toronto. It then became known as The First Post Office in Toronto and is now the oldest continuously operating post office in Canada. Its modest museum is worth a visit.

There's a building on the southeast corner of King and St George streets that once served as the Little George Hotel. It was built in 1879 and replaced the Town of York's first public school that opened 200 years ago.

British architect William Thomas, who imprinted a Gothic style onto the city's landscape, designed more than 100 buildings throughout Toronto in only 17 years. One major project that remains is the still elegant 150-year-old St Lawrence Hall, where Ralph Waldo Emerson and D'Arcy McGee once spoke.

As for the ghost, it's believed to be that of Sister Vincenza. She was one of the Sisters of St Joseph who owned and operated St Michael's Hospital. She died in the late 1950s, but is still apparently doing her rounds switching lights on and off. They say she's the only 'person' in the hospital who wears a habit.

St Lawrence **Experience:** Brown bag a lunch in Courthouse Square • be inquisitive and walk through history • applaud good theatre • graze in popular restaurants • do the St Lawrence Market ritual on a Saturday morning and stock up on great produce.

MAP

12

Town of York

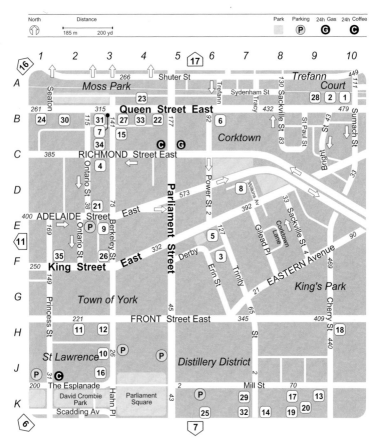

Places

Dominion Hotel (1875), 10A **1**
Dominion Square (1873), 9A **2**
Enoch Turner School (1843), 6F **3**
Greek Orthodox Church, 3C **4**
Little Trinity Church (1842) *Anglican*, 6E **5**
St Paul's Basilica (1889) *Catholic*, 6B **6**
Wesleyan Methodist Church (1871), 3B **7**
Worker's cottages, 7D **8**

Entertainment

Alumnae Theatre, 3E **9**
Canadian Stage, 3H **10**
  Berkeley Street Theatre
  Théâtre Français

Imperial Opera Theatre, 2H **11**
Tanenbaum Opera Centre, 3H **12**
Young Centre for the Performing Arts, 9K **13**
  George Brown Theatre
  Soulpepper Theatre

Restaurants

Balzac's *Coffee shop*, 7K **14**
Berkeley Café *Continental*, 3B **15**
Berkeleys *Café*, 3J **16**
Boiler House *American*, 8K **17**
Canary *American*, 10H **18**
Mill Street Brewery *Canadian* 8K **19**
Pure Spirits *Oysters*, 8K **20**
VOX *American*, 2D **21**

Shops

Allen Gallery *Prints*, 4B **22**
Arabesque *Antique carpets*, 4A **23**
Art Nouveau *Stained Glass*, 2B **24**
Fluid Living *Furniture*, 6K **25**
Klaus *Furniture*, 2F **26**
Kober Wrentree *Home décor*, 3B **27**
Librairie Champlain *French books*, 9A **28**
Lileo *Clothing*, 7K **29**
Ontario Decorative Hardware *Design centre*, 2B **30**
Robert Deveau *Fine art auctioneers*, 3B **31**
Sandra Ainsley *Gallery*, 7K **32**
Studio Gallery *Fine art*, 4B **33**
Turko-Persian *Carpets*, 3C **34**
Ziggurat *Furniture*, 2F **35**

Town of York **Profile**

In 1793 John Graves Simcoe established a garrison on the shore of Lake Ontario. A small settlement built nearby was called York.

At the time Simcoe was lieutenant-governor of Upper Canada, a not-too-inspiring colony in British North America. He was worried about an impending war with America and planned to establish a naval base here so the British could control Lake Ontario. Another part of his strategy was to move the capital of Upper Canada from Niagara to York to make it less vulnerable to American attack. York's town limits were set by what are now Parliament, Peter, Front and Queen streets. In the old days, Front Street East was called Palace Street, Richmond was Hospital Street, Adelaide was Newgate Street, and Queen was Lot Street. Lot Street was named that way for a purpose. In order to lure men of distinction to York, Simcoe offered them extensive lots of land fronting Lot Street and going as far north as present-day Bloor Street. Lot was then renamed Queen to add a little more tone.

The first parliament buildings, consisting of two single storey structures, were erected in 1798 near the corner of Berkeley Street and The Esplanade. They were also used as a courthouse and for religious meetings. When the Americans finally attacked York in late-April 1813, they set fire to them. Seven years later the structures were repaired, only to burn again in 1824 after a chimney fire. A third attempt was made in 1832 to establish a place for parliament at Front and Simcoe streets.

Not much of the old Town of York remains here. Three notable exceptions are Little Trinity Church, Dominion Square and the Enoch Turner School.

Little Trinity is the oldest church in town. It was built in 1842 to serve the hundreds of poor immigrants who had come here to work at places like the Gooderham and Worts distillery. People referred to it as "the poor man's church." Next door is Enoch Turner School, built in 1843. It's not only the oldest school building, but it was the first to offer free public education to underprivileged kids of working class parents. Inside, some of the original desks, stoves and blackboards are still there as a reminder of much more stoic times. Dominion Square opened in 1873 in a neighbourhood known as Corktown. It got its name from the folk who came here from Cork, Ireland, to work in the nearby distillery and brewing enterprises.

Regrettably, Toronto's genesis is fast disappearing under civic apathy and uninformed development. The only promising sign of sanity here – albeit too late – is the magnificent restoration of the Distillery District.

Town of York **Experience:** Ramble around what's left of the historic buildings • spend lots of time in the Distillery District and be amazed by the superb interior designs • and, while you're there, have a meal, take in a show and browse through the galleries.

MAP
13

Portugal Village

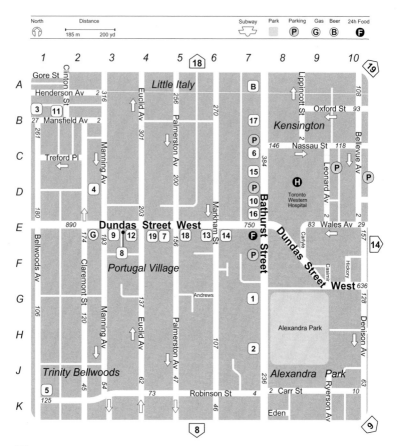

Places

Ching Kwok Temple *Buddhist*, 7G **1**
Church of the Assumption of the Virgin Mary
    Ukrainian Catholic, 7H **2**
St Francis of Assisi Church (1914) *Catholic*,
    1B **3**
St Francis of Assisi School, 2D **4**
St Matthias Church (1873) *Anglican*, 1K **5**
St Vladimir Cathedral *Ukrainian Orthodox*,
    7C **6**

Restaurants

Benfica Aguia *Portuguese*, 5E **7**
Caffe Brasiliano *International*, 3E **8**
Churrasqueira Vila Verde *Portuguese*,
    3E **9**
Kim Bo *Vietnamese*, 7D **10**
Monarch Tavern *Pub*, 2B **11**
Musa *International*, 4E **12**

Portuguese Café *Portuguese*, 6E **13**
Tommy's Backyard *Greek*, 6E **14**

Shops

Balloon King *Party supplies*, 7C **15**
Irene's *Florist*, 7D **16**
Kromer Radio *Audio-Video*, 7B **17**
Liberal *Home accents*, 5E **18**
Portuguese Market, 4E **19**

Portugal Village **Profile**

Portuguese explorers got to know Canada as far back as the 15th century. And in 1705 Pedro Silva was the country's first letter carrier.

When the *Saturnia* docked in Halifax in 1953, it carried 85 Portuguese male passengers. Even though most of them were recruited as farm labourers, they soon made their way west to take advantage of Toronto's booming post-war construction industry. Since then, the Portuguese community has grown from this modest number to about 160,000, making it the fourth-largest cultural group in the city. Most have come from the Azores, but there's also a good representation from Madeira, Macao and the Cape Verde Islands.

They put down roots in the working-class neighbourhood around Dundas and Bathurst streets. This area goes back to the early 1800s when much of it was owned by Samuel Smith. It was named Gore Vale after Lieutenant Governor Francis Gore. There's a Gore Street in the neighbourhood and, interestingly, it runs into Clinton Street.

Except for a few small front gardens displaying a dwindling number of statues of Our Lady of Fatima, there's little about the homes here to make you think they're distinctively Portuguese. However, the commercial corridor along Dundas Street West is regaining a more obvious Portuguese character. The Ukrainian Orthodox Cathedral of St Vladimir stands just north of the Bathurst Street intersection. The impressive Ching Kwok Buddhist Temple faces Alexandria Park to the south. Little Italy presses down from College Street. East, across Bathurst Street, is the cultural mélange of Kensington.

The absence of noticeable Portuguese icons here may be due, in part, to the new generation of Canadian-born Portuguese who have moved into other parts of the city away from the comfortable traditions of their parents. You'll find the Portuguese restaurants these days further to the west, mostly along College and Dundas streets. And the city's two oldest Portuguese bakeries are still in business across on Augusta Avenue in Kensington, where they've been joined by a multi-national array of busy markets.

The real flavour of Portugal Village, however, comes not so much from food as it does from the Day of Portugal parade. The closest Saturday to June 10th brings thousands of people in traditional Portuguese dress out into the streets for Canada's largest Portuguese street festival.

It's something that would have made Pedro Silva proud.

Portugal Village **Experience:** Spend time exploring a mix of the world's religious faiths • take advantage of that once a year opportunity to celebrate the Day of Portugal • say "hi" to people sitting on their front porches • salivate over some great Portuguese food.

MAP
14

Chinatown

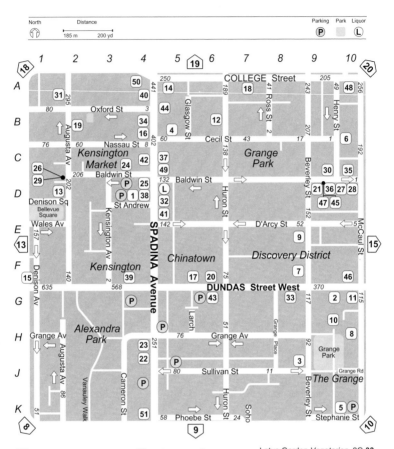

North   Distance
185 m   200 yd

Parking   Park   Liquor
(P)   (L)

Places

Anshei Minsk Synagogue
(1930), 3D **1**
Art Gallery of Ontario (AGO),
9G **2**
Chinese Baptist Church (1886),
8J **3**
Cecil Community Centre
(Church of Christ, 1890), 5B **4**
Church of St George the Martyr
(1844), 10K **5**
Holy Trinity Russian Orthodox
Church, 10C **6**
Italian Consulate (1872), 8F **7**
Ontario College of Art & Design
(OCAD), 10H **8**
Ontario Gallery of Chinese Arts,
8E **9**
The Grange (1817), 9G **10**
Two Forms, 10G **11**
Workers' cottages, 6B **12**

Restaurants

Amadeu's *Portuguese*, 1D **13**
Asean *Asian*, 5A **14**
Ban Vanipha *Lao-Thai*, 1F **15**
Bangkok *Thai*, 4B **16**
Champion House *Chinese*, 5F **17**
Ein-stein *Pub*, 7A **18**
El Trompo *Mexican*, 2B **19**
Forestview *Chinese*, 6F **20**
Fujiyama *Japanese*, 9D **21**
Furama *Desserts*, 4J **22**
Gold Stone *Chinese*, 4H **23**
Graffiti's *American*, 3C **24**
Happy Seven *Chinese*, 4D **25**
HungAry Thai *Eclectic*, 2C **26**
Jodhpore *Indian*, 9D **27**
John's *Italian*, 10D **28**
King's *Vegetarian*, 2D **29**
La Bodega *French*, 9C **30**
La Palette *French*, 2A **31**
Lee Garden *Chinese*, 5D **32**

Lotus Garden *Vegetarian*, 8G **33**
Lucky Dragon *Szechuan*, 4B **34**
Margarita's *Mexican*, 10C **35**
Mata Hari *Malaysian,* 9D **36**
New Sky *Szechuan*, 4C **37**
Pho Hu'ng *Vietnamese*, 4D **38**
Rainbow *Vietnamese*, 3F **39**
Red Book *American*, 4A **40**
Rol San *Seafood*, 4E **41**
Saigon *Vietnamese*, 4C **42**
Sen Ming *Seafood*, 6G **43**
Shanghai Lily *Chinese*, 4B **44**
Tuscany *Café*, 9D **45**
Village Idiot *Pub*, 10F **46**
Wah Sing *Seafood*, 9D **47**
Woodlands *Vegetarian Thali*
10A **48**
Xam Yu *Seafood*, 5C **49**

Shops

Computer stores, 4A **50**
Fur stores, 4K **51**

Chinatown **Profile**

Sam Ching's Chinese laundry was first listed in the telephone book in 1878. This is where you'll find his roots.

 It's believed that Toronto's 272,000 Chinese residents have now formed the largest Chinese community in North America. Their roots go back to the 1870s when 17,000 of them came from China to work as labourers on the western sections of the Canadian Pacific Railway. When the railway was completed many remained in Canada and some came east to start a new life in Toronto around the intersection of Bay and Dundas streets. Today, most of Chinatown has moved west along Dundas Street towards Spadina Avenue and it's here that you'd be forgiven if you thought you were in Hong Kong.

The 1815 estate of Captain John Denison once occupied over 40 ha of dense forest on the west side of Spadina Avenue. His house, known as the Bellevue Homestead, was built on the present site of Bellevue Square. By 1870 the estate had been divided into a respectable middle-class English neighbourhood with British street names such as Kensington, Oxford, St Andrew and Wales. Around 1900 the British moved north and Jewish people moved in to replace them. Many were new immigrants escaping persecution in Europe; others came here to avoid the persecution they had experienced in other parts of town. Jews were not welcomed into Toronto's business community during that time, so in 1905 they opened street stalls outside their homes and sold produce and merchandise to each other. This is how the century-old Kensington Market, around Augusta Avenue and Baldwin Street, came into being.

The Jewish community has now followed prosperity to North York and neighbourhoods along Bathurst Street, leaving behind only a couple of synagogues as a testament to its past. This part of town is now our most colourful, consisting of Chinese, Vietnamese, Portuguese, Malaysian and Laotian heritages.

In the midst of all this is The Grange. It's about the last tangible reminder of the once huge old estates fronting Queen Street that were given to respectable citizens by Governor Simcoe in the early days of York. This one belonged to D'Arcy Boulton Jr. In 1911 it was bequeathed to the Art Museum of Toronto, which later became the Art Gallery of Ontario.

Although this might be the original Chinatown, there are a few others around town: 'Chinatown East' around Broadview and Gerrard and another in Scarborough's Agincourt neighbourhood. A fourth is the most affluent one of all. It's out of town in Richmond Hill. Like the British and Jews before them, the Chinese are prospering and moving north.

Chinatown **Experience:** Discover Kensington Market • have dinner on Baldwin Street • watch architect Frank Gehry's fascinating new exterior of the AGO take shape.

MAP

15   Discovery District

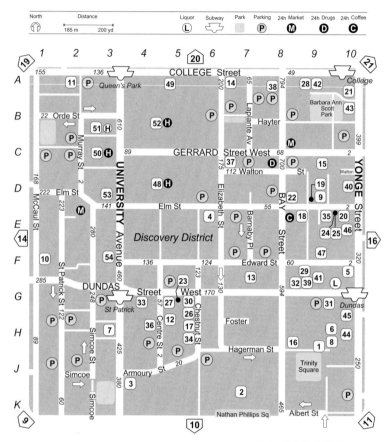

Places

Church of the Holy Trinity
  (1847) *Anglican*, 9H **1**
City Hall, 7K **2**
Court House, 4J **3**
Laughlen Lodge (1848), 6E **4**
Media Tower, 10F **5**
Old Rectory (1861), 9H **6**
Royal Cdn. Military Inst., 3H **7**
Scadding House (1860), 9H **8**
St George's Hall (1891), 9D **9**
St Patrick's *Catholic*, 1F **10**
Stewart Building (1894), 2A **11**
Textile Museum, 4H **12**
Toronto Coach Terminal, 7F **13**
Victoria Hospital (1892) 7A **14**

Accommodation

Chelsea Inn Hotel, 9C **15**
Marriott Eaton C'tr Hotel, 8H **16**
Metropolitan Hotel, 5H **17**

Restaurants

Adega *Portuguese*, 8E **18**
Bangkok Garden *Thai*, 9D **19**
Barberian's *Steakhouse*, 10E **20**
Carlu *Continental*, 10A **21**
Commensal *Vegetarian*, 8D **22**
Cugini *Sandwiches*, 5G **23**
Donatello *Italian*, 9E **24**
Frascatti *Italian*, 9E **25**
Hemispheres *Continental*, 5H **26**
Hong Shin *Chinese*, 4G **27**
Hughie's *American*, 9A **28**
Indian Flavour *Indian*, 9F **29**
Indochine *Pan-Asian*, 5G **30**
J J Muggs *American grill*, 9G **31**
Japango *Japanese*, 9G **32**
Kim Sang *Chinese*, 4G **33**
Lai Wah Heen *Chinese*, 5H **34**
Oro *Italian*, 9E **35**
Pegasus *Continental*, 4H **36**
Saffron Tree *Indian*, 7C **37**
Sangam *Indian*, 8A **38**

Spring Rolls *Thai*, 9G **39**
The One *Thai-Asian*, 10D **40**

Shops

Atrium on Bay *Mall*, 9G **41**
College Park *Mall*, 9A **42**
De Boer's *Furniture*, 10B **43**
Eaton Centre *Mall*, 10H **44**
Sears *Department store*, 10H **45**
Sunrise *Recordings*, 10E **46**
World's Biggest Book Store, 9F **47**

Medical Centres

Hospital for Sick Children, 5D **48**
MaRS Centre, 5A **49**
Mount Sinai Hospital, 3C **50**
Princess Margaret Hospital, 3B **51**
Toronto General Hospital, 4B **52**
Toronto Rehab Centre, 3D **53**
U of T Rehabilitation Centre, 3F **54**

Discovery District **Profile**

During the latter half of the 19th century, this area had the worst slums in North America. Today, it's a leading medical research centre.

 The neighbourhood was known as 'The Ward'. Many homes sat on lots measuring just three metres by six. There was a lack of running water, flush toilets and drains. It was an awful place, and residents were charged 25 cents a week to live here.

A witness of the day wrote: "Worries about sanitation were exacerbated by suspicion of the increasingly non-British character of the area's population. The cultural and lifestyle differences that they attributed to Jews, Italians, and other southeast European immigrants were regarded as additional obstacles to 'improvement'." Another said: "It's a strange and fearful place. It is unwise to enter, even in daylight. No sane person would dream of running such a risk. Perhaps it is the dagger of an Italian desperado of which they dream, perhaps the bearded faces of the Sheenies are sufficient in themselves to inspire terror."

Gladys Marie Smith was born in The Ward in 1893 near the intersection of University Avenue and Elm Street. She's better known as Mary Pickford, the first genuine Hollywood film star and the first of an avalanche of talented Canadians who have since found fame and fortune south of the border. Her Broadway début was in 1907 and her first movie, Her First Biscuits, was released in 1909. All that's left of The Ward is Laughlen Lodge. It was built in 1848 as a charitable institution, known as the 'House of Industry', "to provide lodging, food and fuel to the needy". It's now a home for seniors.

The city gradually chipped away at The Ward's boundaries. The Victoria Hospital for Sick Children, the first pediatric hospital in Canada, was built on College Street in 1892. The Toronto General Hospital was erected next door in 1911. St George's Hall, designed as a place to help British immigrants, was opened in 1891. It's now the Arts and Letters Club that was once frequented by The Group of Seven artists. Along the Queen Street side, the (old) city hall was built, as was Osgoode Hall. Slowly, the ugly realities of The Ward, and all it stood for, were quietly and systematically erased.

These days, the neighbourhood houses city hall, the Eaton Centre and perhaps the largest hospital complex on the continent. In June, 2002 the area north of Dundas Street West, was designated the 'Discovery District' because it has the largest concentration of biotechnology and biomedical research facilities in North America. No one is scared about coming here any more.

Discovery District **Experience:** Check out the Eaton Centre • visit the Textile Museum of Canada • star gaze at Mary Pickford's statue on the northeast corner of University and Elm • splurge on dinner at Lai Wah Heen • see the atrium in Sick Kid's hospital • regain your sanity by exploring Trinity Square.

MAP

16   Dundas Square

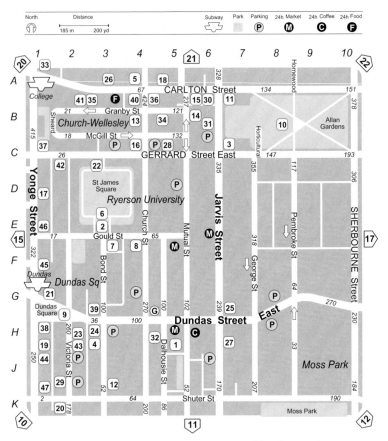

Places

Arena Gardens (1912), 5H **1**
Egerton Ryerson statue, 3E **2**
Jarvis Street Baptist Church
(1832), 7C **3**
Mackenzie House (1859),
3H **4**
Maple Leaf Gardens, 4A **5**
Normal & Model School, (1851),
3E **6**
O'Keefe House (1879), 3F **7**
Oakham House (1848), 4F **8**
Olympic Spirit, 2G **9**
Palm House (1910), 8B **10**
St Andrew's Lutheran Church
(1878), 7B **11**
St Michael's Catholic Cathedral
(1848), 3K **12**

Gay places

Barn-Stables *Bars*, 4B **13**

Club Toronto *Sauna*, 6B **14**
Excess *Sauna*, 5A **15**
Hassle Free Clinic, 4C **16**
Remington's *Strip club*, 1D **17**
Zipperz *Bar*, 5A **18**

Entertainment

Canon Theatre, 1H **19**
Massey Hall, 2K **20**
Metropolis, 1G **21**
Ryerson Theatre, 3C **22**
Top o' Senator *Jazz*, 2H **23**

Accommodation

Bond Place Hotel, 3H **24**
Comfort Suites Hotel, 7G **25**
Day's Hotel, 3A **26**
Grand Hotel, 7H **27**
Neill-Wycik *Backpackers*, 5C **28**
Pantages Hotel, 2K **29**
Primrose Hotel, 6B **30**
Ramada Hotel, 6B **31**

Restaurants

Amalfi *Italian*, 4H **32**
Baroli *Caffé*, 1A **33**
Bulldog *Café*, 5B **34**
Daio *Japanese*, 3A **35**
Eggstacy *Café*, 4A **36**
Ginger 2 *Vietnamese*, 1C **37**
Hard Rock Cafe *American*,
1H **38**
Imperial *Pub*, 3G **39**
Mick E Fynn's *Pub*, 4B **40**
Peach *Vietnamese*, 2A **41**
Rock 'n Roll *American*, 2C **42**
Senator Diner *American*, 2H **43**
Superior *American*, 1J **44**

Shops

HMV *Recordings*, 1F **45**
Sam the Record Man *Recordings*,
1E **46**
Urban Outfitters *Clothing*, 1K **47**

Dundas Square **Profile**

This is where Canada's greatest ice hockey arena thrilled millions of fans. Today the body checks have gone and will be replaced with checkouts. Maple Leaf Gardens is destined to become a supermarket.

 The first of the great arenas in this part of town was the Horticultural Pavilion. It was built in 1879 on the site of Allan Gardens and designed as a concert venue to raise money for the Toronto Horticultural Society. The building held 3,000 people, which was impressive for its day. Gradually the pavilion attracted a host of famous writers who came to Toronto to give readings. They included Mark Twain and Oscar Wilde. "I find that one great trouble all over is that your workmen are not given to noble designs," Wilde, then 27, said. "You cannot be indifferent to this, because art is not something which you can take or leave. It is a necessity to human life."

The Arena Gardens was the largest indoor facility in the country when it was built in 1912 on Mutual Street, just south of Dundas Street East. It was home to the Toronto Arenas, the city's first professional hockey team that would later become the Toronto Maple Leafs. Glenn Miller dropped by the 'Mutual Street Arena' to give a concert in 1942, and so did Frank Sinatra in 1948. The first Boat Show opened here in 1954. But, perhaps the most famous event to take place on these grounds was on June 10, 1925. This was when Methodists, Congregationalists and Presbyterians came from across the country to this site to form the United Church of Canada.

The third arena was Maple Leaf Gardens. For almost 70 years, 'The Gardens' hosted an almost endless parade of entertainment from the Metropolitan Opera Company and Ice Capades to rock concerts and Billy Graham. Winston Churchill spoke here – without a microphone. But its main focus was ice hockey. No other building in the city – including Rogers Centre and the Air Canada Centre – captured sports fans' memories more intensely than The Gardens. It was a place of triumph and tragedy for the Toronto Maple Leafs. They played 24,522 games here. The first was in 1931 against the Chicago Black Hawks. They lost 2–1. The last, also against the Blackhawks, was on Saturday, February 13, 1999. They lost 6–2. Mercifully, between these two games, the Toronto Maple Leafs electrified the city by winning several Stanley Cups.

The latest kid on the block in this historic entertainment neighbourhood is a recently redesigned Dundas Square where overpowering outdoor advertising and suffocating architectural chaos seem more important than people. "Development in this city has now completely run amok," observed one critic. It would be interesting to hear what Oscar Wilde might have said.

Dundas Square **Experience:** Come to your own opinion about Dundas Square, then get away from it all and hide in St James Square.

MAP

17

Regent Park

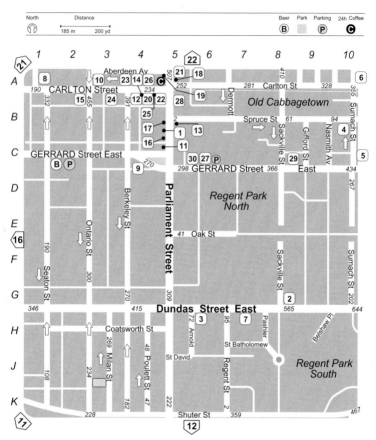

Places

Cabbagetown Community
Arts Centre, 4B **1**
Eastern Orthodox Church (1910),
8G **2**
Fire Hall #7, 6H **3**
Gerrard Street Methodist Church
(1878), 10B **4**
Ontario Medical College for
Women (1890), 10C **5**
Riverdale Farm, 10A **6**
St Batholomew's Church (1873)
Anglican, 7G **7**
St Peter's Church (1863)
Anglican, 1A **8**
Toronto Public Library, 4C **9**

Restaurants

Asahi *Japanese*, 3A **10**
Ben Wicks *British*, 4C **11**

Brass Taps *Pizza Pub*,
4A **12**
Cabbagetown *American*,
5B **13**
China Gourmet *Chinese*,
4A **14**
Cosmo *International*, 2B **15**
Flamingo House *Chinese*,
4C **16**
House on Parliament *Pub*,
4B **17**
Javaville *Espresso/Juice*,
5A **18**
Johnny G's *American*,
5A **19**
Margarita's *Mexican*, 4B **20**
Peartree *Continental*,
5A **21**
Town Grill *International*,
4B **22**
Two 26 *International*,
3A **23**

Accommodation

Amsterdam *Guesthouse*,
3B **24**

Shops

Antiques Collectibles
Antiques, 4B **25**
Daniel et Daniel
Fine food catering, 4A **26**
Double Take *Used Clothing*,
6C **27**
Epicure Shop *Bakery*,
5B **28**
Gerrard Glass *Mirrors*,
8C **29**
Goodwill *Used clothing*, 5C **30**

Regent Park **Profile**

During the 19th century, this neighbourhood is where women and the poor fought for a better place in Toronto society. Both groups are now doing much better.

 In the late 1800s, women were not allowed to enroll at the University of Toronto, or any other school, to study medicine. Tired of fighting this derision and injustice, Dr. Michael Barrett became the first dean of the Ontario Medical College for Women. He headed the medical school in a rented cottage around here and enlisted three students. Seven years later, in 1890, the Romanesque building you see today at 289 Sumach Street, a few metres north of Gerrard Street East, was opened with a staff of 25 lecturers and demonstrators. Its success forced the University of Toronto to accept female medical students in 1905.

This was not the only battle for equality that was fought around here. The area surrounded by Queen, Parliament, Gerrard and the Don Valley was looked down upon fifty years before Dr. Barrett set up shop. It was where the unskilled Irish workers first settled, to be followed by even poorer immigrants from other lands. After decades of steadily worsening conditions between the two World Wars, what is now known as Regent Park deteriorated into a major and highly controversial slum.

In the mid-1940s the city decided to knock down the entire complex of small, rat-infested houses and re-build. For people who had never had indoor plumbing or hot running water, the new development promised the dignity of equality. But the reconstructed neighbourhood turned out to be little more than a paternal, if not patronizing, concept. By 1949, within two years of the first residents moving in, there were confrontations with city fathers. People wanted to put up television aerials, but the mayor insisted this new form of entertainment was inappropriate for "the honest, though not entirely deserving, poor." One mother countered by saying that television in the home was necessary "to keep kids off neighbouring streets." The mayor threatened to have any aerials torn down.

By the mid-1980s it became obvious to everyone that all good intentions to rectify "poverty, alcoholism, disease and broken families" had irrevocably fallen apart. The largely Caribbean, Tamil and Asian poor found themselves living in a community rife with drug dealing and prostitution.

The historic derision toward this part of town, and the people it houses, has returned. Faced with this reality, the city is moving forward to completely redevelop the neighbourhood to make it a more livable environment.

Regent Park **Experience:** Expose yourself to earthy sights and sounds along Dundas Street East during daylight hours • take the kids to Riverdale Farm • see the historic medical college.

MAP

18

Little Italy

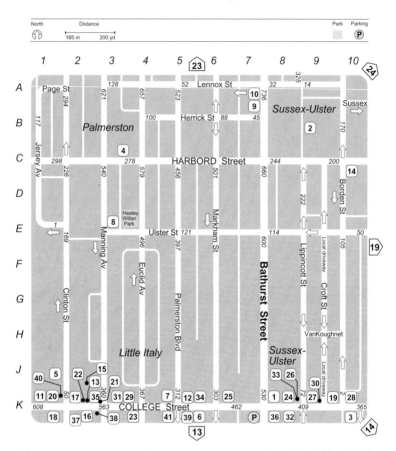

Places

Bank of Nova Scotia (1913), 8K **1**
Central Technical School, 9B **2**
Fire Station #8 (1878), 10K **3**
Harbord Collegiate Institute, 3C **4**
Holy Trinity Church
  Greek Orthodox, 1J **5**
Latvian House (1910), 5K **6**
Portuguese Seventh-Day
  Adventist Church
  (1888), 5K **7**
St Mary Magdalene Church
  (1888) Anglican, 3E **8**

Entertainment

Annex Theatre, 7B **9**
Bathurst Street Theatre, 7A **10**
Royal Cinema, 1K **11**

Restaurants

Airport Lounge International,
  5K **12**
Bar Italia Italian, 2K **13**
Boulevard Café Peruvian,
  10C **14**
Brasserie Aix French, 2K **15**
Butt'a International, 2K **16**
Café Diplomatico Italian,
  2K **17**
Capitol International, 1K **18**
Cloak and Dagger Pub, 9K **19**
Coco Lezzone Italian,
  1K **20**
College Street Bar Pub,
  3K **21**
Corso Italia Italian, 2K **22**
El Bodegon Peruvian, 4K **23**
El Rancho Latin, 8K **24**
Gamelle Bistro, 6K **25**

Hunan Palace Chinese, 8K **26**
Jing Peking Chinese, 9K **27**
Jun Jun Sushi Japanese,
  10K **28**
Kalendar Continental, 3K **29**
Maggie's Bistro, 9K **30**
Marlowe International, 3K **31**
Plaza Flamingo Spanish,
  8K **32**
Pomegranate Persian, 8K **33**
Pony International, 5K **34**
Riviera Bakery, 2K **35**
Sneaky Dee's Pub, 8K **36**
Sotto Voce Italian, 2K **37**
Southside Louie's Pub, 3K **38**
Teatro Italian, 5K **39**
Tempo Italian, 1K **40**
Xacutti Fusion, 5K **41**

Little Italy **Profile**

The South Annex was touted in the 19th century as being "situated in the most healthy and pleasant part of the city." That pleasantness has been redefined during the last 80 years nello spirito di Italia.

 The South Annex is known for a lot of things. First, it was promoted during the 19th century as being close to the new University of Toronto and the parliament buildings, both of which came into being in the mid-1800s. Salesmen at the time promoted its 'location, location, location'. It was a place for people setting out in life. And, running north-south through the midst of it all, there was Palmerston Boulevard. Stone and iron gateposts grace its College Street and Bloor Street West entrances and between these historic bookends you'll find the best of the neighbourhood's Victorian homes.

Between 1885 and 1925, the first wave of Italian immigrants settled just west along College Street and eventually took over most of the city's fruit markets. The second group came after World War II and made the area around Euclid Avenue and College Street their home. Bringing trade skills from the Old Country with them, they went on to make significant inroads into the construction business. Even today, it's almost impossible to find a construction crew anywhere around town that doesn't have a healthy Italian contingent.

Toronto now has one of the largest Italian communities outside Italy. To honour this distinction the area around Euclid Avenue and College Street was named 'Little Italy'. And you'll understand why if you pass by Café Diplomatico's sidewalk eatery on a sunny weekend afternoon. But, if you really want to party, come here when Italy next reaches World Cup soccer finals.

Few neighbourhoods in the city have as many schools as the South Annex. The most imposing is Central Technical School with a Norman-inspired tower rising above solid oak doors. Together with its playing fields, it occupies a city block. The second well-known school, though far less dramatic in appearance, is Harbord Collegiate Institute, built in 1931.

If you don't keep alert you most likely won't notice 148 Borden Street. It's a tiny worker's cottage that has survived as a reminder of times long gone. Another interesting discovery is St Mary Magdalene Church. Despite its name and location in a predominantly Italian-Catholic neighbourhood, it's Anglican. The church is notable for two things: First, it had the world-famous musician Healey Willan as its organist and choirmaster from 1921–1968. Second, Queen Elizabeth the Queen Mother unveiled a plaque on the front wall in his honour in 1989. It's one of few plaques in the city that bears her name.

Little Italy **Experience:** Get into the Italian spirit • sip a cappuccino • enjoy some live theatre • drop by St Mary Magdalene church • see the worker's cottage • eat your heart out.

MAP
19

University of Toronto

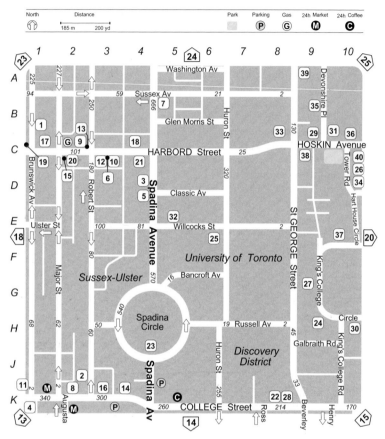

Places

First Narayever Synagogue
  (1890), 1B **1**
Hungarian Reformed Church
  (1892), 2J **2**
Knox Church *Presbyterian*
  (1907),4D **3**
St Stephen-in-the-Fields Church
  Anglican (1858), 1K **4**
Ukrainian Museum of Canada,
  4D **5**

Restaurants

93 Harbord *Middle Eastern*,
  3C **6**
Èlise *Café*, 5A **7**
Free Times *Café*, 2K **8**
Kensington Kitchen *Continental*,
  2C **9**

Latitude *International*, 3C **10**
Leao D'Ouro *Italian*, 1K **11**
Messis *International*, 3C **12**
Mo Mo's *Middle Eastern*,
  2B **13**
Oasis *Continental*, 3K **14**
Olive and Lemon *International*,
  2C **15**
Rancho Relaxo *Mexican*,
  3K **16**
Rowers *Pub*, 1C **17**
Splendido *Italian*, 4C **18**

Shops

Clay *Pottery*, 1C **19**
Harbord Bakery, 2C **20**
Toronto Women's Bookstore,
  4C **21**
University Bookstore, 8K **22**

U of T

1 Spadina Crescent, 4H **23**
Convocation Hall, 9H **24**
Earth Sciences Centre, 6E **25**
Hart House, 10 C **26**
Knox College, 9G **27**
Koffler Student Services Centre,
  8K **28**
Massey College, 9C **29**
Medical Sciences Building, 10H **30**
Munk Centre for International
  Studies, 10B **31**
New College, 5E **32**
Robarts Library, 8C **33**
Soldiers' Tower, 10D **34**
St Hilda's College, 9B **35**
Trinity College, 10C **36**
University College Chapel, 10E **37**
Whitney Hall, 9C **38**
Woodsworth College, 9A **39**
Wycliffe College, 10C **40**

University of Toronto **Profile**

An Ice Age relic stands erect in an area once dominated by the churches of England and Scotland.

The origins of Canada's largest university date back to 1827 when a Royal Charter was granted to King's College. It was the colony's first institution of higher learning and the following year it was granted over 91,000 ha of Crown land. The campus corner stone was laid in the middle of a forest on the site of the present-day provincial legislature. While the college was being built, lectures were held in the old parliament buildings near the corner of Front and Berkeley streets. In 1849 the government secularized the college from its Church of England origins and renamed it the University of Toronto. Construction of University College, the oldest building on campus, began in 1856.

Toronto's oldest newspaper, the *Globe and Mail,* once described the U of T this way: "The city has here a jewel, an eccentric but thoroughly charming mélange of architecture – Romanesque, Ruskinian, Oxbridgian, Arts and Crafts, high Victorian Gothic, late Gothic Revival, fussy Edwardian pomp (plus brutalism and the rest of the later stuff) – established 170 years ago in a sylvan, park-like setting designed to encourage spiritual and intellectual contemplation of the cosmos."

The campus is bounded by Spadina Avenue, Bloor Street West, College and Bay streets. A significantly re-styled St George Street, the official main street on campus, runs north-south proclaiming itself "at the heart of a great university." Everyone in town should visit the campus at least once, preferably on a summer weekend when there are fewer students around.

The university tends to overshadow lots of other interesting places in the neighbourhood. There's St Stephen-in-the-Fields, a Gothic Revival church, that was designed in 1858 by Thomas Fuller "who later gained renown in fashioning Canada's parliament buildings." If you keep an eye open, you'll discover a very rare igneous boulder left here by a 12,000 year-old glacier. It's at the west side of Spadina Circle on the south corner of Russell Avenue. Knox Presbyterian Church on Spadina Avenue currently occupies the second oldest site in this part of town. Its predecessor was built here in 1821 and was the first Presbyterian church in Toronto. The imposing old place at 1 Spadina Circle was built in 1844 as a Presbyterian seminary, then went on to become the Spadina Military Hospital and later the Connaught Medical Laboratories where insulin was first manufactured.

The *Globe and Mail* got it right regarding the spiritual and intellectual stuff.

University of Toronto **Experience:** Go out and take one of the nicest walks in the city • join students along St George Street • diabetics should see the building where insulin was first made.

MAP

20

Queen's Park

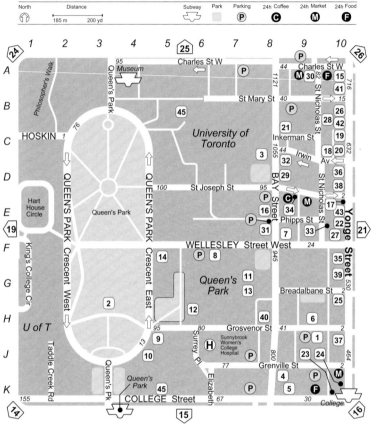

Places

Coroners Courts, 9H **1**
Provincial Legislature, 3H **2**
St Basil's (1854) *Catholic*, 8C **3**
Toronto Police HQ, 8K **4**
Toronto Police Museum, 9K **5**
YMCA, 9H **6**

Accommodation

Sutton Place Hotel, 8F **7**

Queen's Park

Ferguson Block, 6F **8**
Frost Building North, 4H **9**
Frost Building South, 4J **10**
Hearst Block, 7G **11**
Hepburn Block, 5H **12**
Macdonald Block
   First 2 floors, Hearst, Hepburn,
   Ferguson & Mowat blocks.

Mowat Block, 7G **13**
Whitney Block, 5F **14**

Restaurants

7 West *Café*, 10A **15**
Bistro 990 *Continental*, 8E **16**
Carrington's *Sports Bar*, 10E **17**
Ethiopian House *Ethiopian*,
   10C **18**
Friendly Thai *Thai*, 10C **19**
Europa Grill *Continental*,
   10C **20**
Foxes Den *Pub*, 8C **21**
Garlic Pepper *Szechuan*,
   10E **22**
Greek Islands *Greek*, 10K **23**
Hoops *Sports Bar*, 10K **24**
Hornero *Pizza*, 10G **25**
Living Well *International*,
   10B **26**
Mammina's *Italian*, 10F **27**
Matignon *French*, 10B **28**

Mullins *Irish Pub*, 8D **29**
Okonomi House *Japanese*, 9A **30**
Ruchiro *Café*, 8E **31**
Sage *Continental* 8C **32**
Segovia *Spanish*, 9E **33**
Tokyo Sushi *Japanese*, 8E **34**
What a Bagel *Café*, 10G **35**

Shops

A W Hockridge *China*, 10D **36**
Curry's *Art supplies*, 10J **37**
Gallery Boutique *Gallery*, 10D **38**
Gallery Hi Art *Gallery*, 10G **39**
Government Bookstore, 8H **40**
Metro Cigar *Cigars*, 10A **41**
Morningstar *Antiques*, 10B **42**
Northbound Leather *Adult*, 10E **43**

U of T

Banting Institute, 5K **44**
Victoria College, 5B **45**

Queen's Park **Profile**

For a long time, people have witnessed argument and opposition here. It's still popular public theatre. And Queen Victoria is not amused.

Queen's Park means different things to different people. It depends on who's talking. The northern extension of University Avenue is named Queen's Park. So is the southern extension of Avenue Road. The Provincial Legislature building has been called Queen's Park for so long that people, including some politicians, believe that's its real name. Bureaucrats refer to the civil service buildings to the east of the legislature as Queen's Park and they call the legislature building The Pink Palace. Journalists, among themselves, call everything The Park. For the record, the real Queen's Park is the park just north of the legislature building. And a sombre, if not sullen, Queen Victoria sits on her bronze throne to the right of the legislature's front steps and oversees everything named in her honour.

Despite her regal presence, the front steps of the legislature provide a stage for rebellious citizens to rail against the government of the day. Whenever the legislature is in session, you're almost certain to see a demonstration of some sort outside. The most famous of these free-for-all events took place in 1872 when 10,000 members of the Toronto Typographical Union protested on this site to get themselves a nine-hour workday. Their efforts led the then Canadian prime minister Sir John A Macdonald to pass a national law called *The Trade Union Act* that first established the legality of organized labour in the country.

But there was acrimony and screaming going on before the legislature was even built. It involved a competition for the building's design. A panel of judges couldn't agree on which concept to accept. In the end, and after many riotous debates, the award went to Richard Waite for the Romanseque Revival design you see today. The only problem was that Waite was not only a member of the adjudication panel – but he was also an American from Buffalo, NY.

Not even the discovery of insulin here was without rancour. It happened on College Street in 1922 when a University of Toronto research team consisting of orthopedic surgeon Frederick Banting, J J R Macleod, J B Collip and Charles Best found this elusive treatment for diabetes. Banting was credited with the discovery and won the Nobel Prize for medicine in 1923. Only then did he find out that he would have to share the honour with Macleod – with whom he was completely incompatible. Banting showed his indignation by giving half of his prize money to Best.

Dissent seems to be in the genes in this neighbourhood.

Queen's Park **Experience:** Attend Question Period when the legislature is sitting • walk around the university campus • catch up on famous local crimes at the Toronto Police Museum • join a demonstration • be surprised at how they've cleaned up Yonge Street.

MAP
21
Church-Wellesley Village

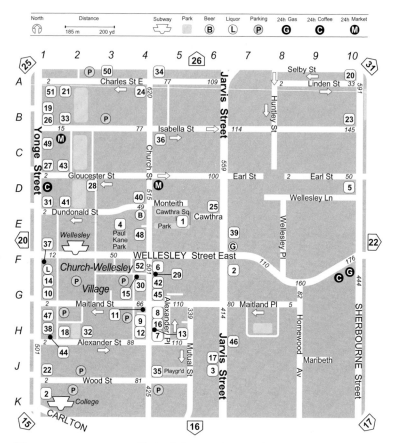

Places

AIDS Memorial, 5E **1**
CAA-AAA 1K **2**
National Ballet School, 6J **3**
Paul Kane House (1853), 3E **4**
Shrine of Our Lady of Lourdes
    Church, *Catholic*, 10D **5**

Gay

Bar 501 *Bar*, 4F **6**
Black Eagle *Leather bar*, 4H **7**
Churchmouse *Pub*, 4G **8**
Crews *Bar*, 4H **9**
O'Grady's *Pub*, 4H **11**
Play *Bar* 4H **12**
Priape *Adult clothing*, 4H **13**
St Marc *Sauna*, 1G **14**
Steamworks *Sauna*, 4G **15**
Woody's *Bar*, 4H **16**

Entertainment

Betty Oliphant Theatre, 6J **17**
Buddies in Bad Times Theatre,
    2H **18**
Panasonic Theatre, 1B **19**

Accommodation

Clarion Hotel, 10A **20**
Comfort Hotel, 2A **21**
Courtyard Marriott Hotel, 1J **22**
Hotel Isabella, 10B **23**
Town Inn Hotel, 4A **24**

Restaurants

Angelini's *Italian*, 6D **25**
Artful Dodger *Pub*, 1B **26**
Brown Stone *American*, 1C **27**
Bumpkin's *American*, 2D **28**
Byzantium *Continental*, 4F **29**
Cafe California *American*,
    4F **30**
Caffe Volo *Italian*, 1D **31**
Carman's *Steakhouse*, 2H **32**
Casa Mexico *Mexican*, 2B **33**
Croissant Tree *Café*, 4A **34**
Hair of the Dog *Pub*, 4J **35**
Java Jive *Café*, 4C **36**
Just Desserts *Café*, 1F **37**
Kathmandu *Nepalese,* 1H **38**
Keg Mansion *Steakhouse*, 7E **39**
Liban *Fusion*, 4D **40**
Local 4 *International,* 2D **41**
Lüb *Continental*, 4G **42**
Olympia 76 *Pizza*, 2C **43**
Pi Tom's *Thai*, 1H **44**
P J Mellon's *American*, 4G **45**
Red Lion *Pub*, 7H **46**
Red Planet *American*, 1G **47**
Slack Alice *American*, 4E **48**
Solo *International*, 1C **49**
Tokyo Kitchen *Japanese*, 3A **50**
W Wish *International*, 1A **51**
Zelda's *American*, 4F **52**

Church & Wellesley **Profile**

This is where the Union Jack flew over the city's first grand mansions. The red, white and blue is gone – and replaced with the Rainbow.

 The most striking examples of what this neighbourhood must have looked like well over a century ago can be seen near the northeast corner of Jarvis and Wellesley streets. The buildings are McMaster House and Chester Massey House, constructed in 1868 and 1887. They were home to the founders of the Massey-Ferguson farm equipment empire, film star Raymond Massey and Vincent, the country's first Canadian-born governor-general. McMaster House is now The Keg Mansion steak-house, and the original Massey house next door is being 'redeveloped'.

In the mid-1800s opulent estates dominated this part of town. William Jarvis, a provincial secretary of Upper Canada, owned a large tract of land here. The Home Wood Estate belonged to George Allen, a former mayor. And the Rideout family settled here after coming from Sherbourne in Dorsetshire, England. Street names are all that remain to remind us of them.

When the estates were sold and sub-divided, lesser homes were built. The best examples of these can be seen along Sherbourne and Jarvis streets, south of Wellesley. A few of these impressive residences, dwarfed by high-rise neighbours, have deteriorated and remain boarded-up.

The area was once known as 'Molly Wood's Bush', named after magistrate Alexander Wood. He was infamous in the early 1880s for personally examining the genitals of young male rape suspects. Once discovered, his crime was deemed 'too odious' to investigate. It was in this old neighbourhood that the core of our gay community openly emerged in the Sixties and developed it into today's vibrant Church-Wellesley Village.

The long-gone St Charles Tavern over on Yonge Street was the most prominent gay bar in town when the community took root. It soon became an annual flashpoint for homophobic disturbances each Halloween. Today, our open and successful gay and lesbian community has integrated seamlessly into downtown.

The 1882 mansion of Charles Gooderham, head of the Gooderham & Worts distillery empire, became a hotel in 1913. Ernest Hemingway lived there. "I would sit at my table in the Café Selby and let the good and true whiskey warm my spirit and my soul," he once remarked. It's now a Clarion Hotel. On Gay Pride Day, climaxing a week of activities at the end of June, thousands of people from Toronto's gay community join with visitors from all over to celebrate community achievement in a newly refurbished neighbourhood. On occasions like this, it seems the St Charles Tavern on Halloween was a very long time ago.

Church & Wellesley **Experience:** Look for the statue of Alexander Wood on the northwest corner of Church and Alexander • spend a reflective moment at the AIDS Memorial • enjoy the sights and sounds, both straight and gay, in the Village.

MAP
22

Old Cabbagetown

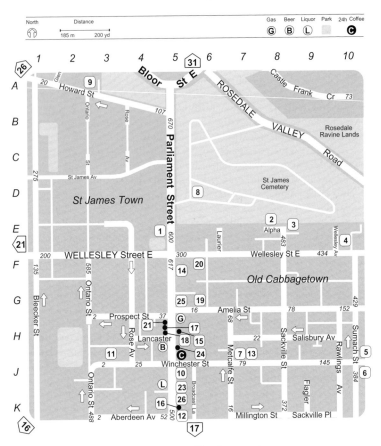

Places

600 Parliament Street, 4E **1**
Heritage houses, 8E **2**
Heritage houses, 8E **3**
Heritage houses, 10E **4**
Necropolis, 10J **5**
Riverdale Farm, 10J **6**
St Enoch's Gerrard Street Church (1878),
    7J **7**
St James-the-Less Chapel (1860), 5D **8**
St Simon the Apostle Church (1887)
    Anglican, 2A **9**
Winchester Hotel (1888), 5J **10**
Winchester Public School, 3J **11**

Entertainment

509 Dance
    Canadian Children's Dance Theatre, 5K **12**
Toronto Dance Theatre
    School of Toronto Dance Theatre, 7J **13**

Restaurants

Cranberries *American*, 5F **14**
Everybody *International*, 5H **15**
Jet Fuel *Café*, 5K **16**
Luciano's *Italian*, 5H **17**
Pelican *Fish & chips*, 5H **18**
Provence *French*, 6G **19**
Rashnaa *Southern Indian*, 5F **20**
Timothy's *Indian*, 5H **21**

Shops

Green's *Antiques*, 5J **23**
Menagerie *Pet shop*, 5H **24**
Patty's *Florist*, 5G **25**
Posterity *Prints*, 5K **26**

Old Cabbagetown **Profile**

We have nearly half a million residents of Irish descent. This is where many of their ancestors planted their roots – literally.

The original marshes at the mouth of the Don River were famous for three things: huge trees, disease-carrying mosquitoes and skunk cabbages. This is where the original Irish settlers built their homes and offered their unskilled labour to the Town of York's growing industries. It's possible that the skunk cabbages might have given the neighbourhood one of its derogatory names: 'Cabbage Town'. Others referred to it as 'Paddy Town'.

Because of famine and potato crop failures in Ireland in the 1840s, more Irish began to arrive. They settled north of the Don marshes in an area now bounded by the Don Valley, Parliament and Queen streets and St James Cemetery. It, too, became known as Cabbage Town – not because of skunk cabbages – but because the newcomers planted cabbages in their front gardens.

There's virtually nothing left of the original working class Cabbage Town south of Gerrard Street these days. What does remain, however, is the more affluent northern part of the old neighbourhood where the better-off residents built their homes. These old places got a new lease on life in the Seventies when upwardly mobile younger folk known as 'white painters' took over the densely wooded streets and spent a fortune on interior renovations. In recent years, a growing number of interesting restaurants and shops have opened in the area, adding to its fluid cultural mosaic.

The result is one of our proudest and most socially diverse communities. Local enthusiasts proclaimed it 'Old Cabbagetown' and boasted that it had "the largest number of occupied Victorian homes in North America." True, or not, it's peppered with heritage houses, with some of the most interesting on tiny Wellesley Avenue and out-of-the-way Alpha Avenue. These two enclaves give an insight into what the original Irish community must have looked like over 150 years ago.

To the northwest is St James Town, once the most densely populated area in Canada. When the old workers' houses were demolished to make way for the complex in the late 1960s, one resident stood firm against developers and refused to sell. That house is now a coin laundry at 600 Parliament Street.

This neighbourhood really shares its sense of community with the rest of us in September during the Old Cabbagetown Festival. But don't expect to see any cabbages growing in the front gardens.

Old Cabbagetown **Experience:** Go to the festival, tour the open houses and appreciate the wooded streets • stroll through St James Cemetery and count the number of historical figures laid to rest • roam around Riverdale Park • enjoy a diversity of world cuisine.

MAP
23

Korea Town

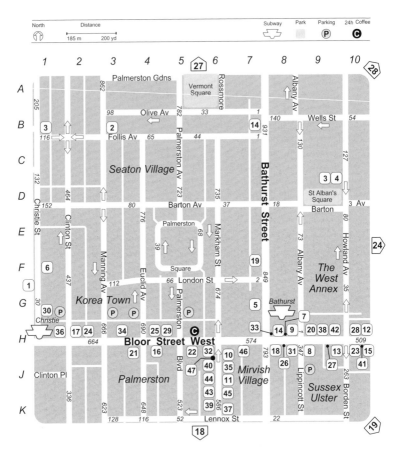

Places

Christie Pits Park, 1F **1**
Orthodox Church, 3B **2**
Royal St George College Chapel, 9C **3**
St Alban the Martyr Church Anglican, 9C **4**
St Peter's Church Catholic, 7G **5**
Ukrainian Cultural Centre, 1F **6**

Entertainment

Bloor Cinema, 8H **7**
Lee's Palace & Dance Cave Clubs, 8H **8**

Restaurants

Albany American, 8H **9**
Bordello Italian, 6J **10**
Butler's Café 6J **11**
By the Way Café, 10H **12**

Dooneys Continental, 9H **13**
Elixir Persian, 8H **14**
Future Café, 10H **15**
Happy House Korean, 4H **16**
Il Bun Ji Korean-Japanese, 2H **17**
Insomnia Cyber bar, 8H **18**
Island Thyme Caribbean, 7F **19**
Japan Sushi Japanese, 8H **20**
Jardin International, 3H **21**
Joons Korean, 5H **22**
Kilgour's American, 10H **23**
Korea House Korean, 2H **24**
Korean Village Korean, 4H **25**
Laila Lebanese, 8H **26**
Los Iguanas Mexican, 9H **27**
Mel's Delicatessen, 10H **28**
Moya Japanese, 4H **29**
Mul Rae Bang-A Korean-Japanese, 1G **30**
Paupers Pub, 8H **31**
Plum Tomato Italian, 6H **32**
Royal Thai Thai, 8H **33**

Se Jong Korean-Japanese, 3H **34**
Southern Accent Creole, 6H **35**
Tasty International, 1H **36**
Victory Café Eclectic, 6K **37**
Zizi Trattoria Italian, 9H **38**

Shops

Art Zone Stained glass, 5K **39**
Ballenford Books Architecture, 6J **40**
Book City Books, 10H **41**
Cheese Dairy Cheeses, 9H **42**
Cinema Shoppe Posters, 6J **43**
David Mirvish Art books, 6J **44**
Gallery Gabor Art, 6K **45**
Honest Ed's Bargain store, 7H **46**
Plantation Antiques, 6H **47**

Korea Town **Profile**

Toronto got its 'Hogtown' nickname from the slaughterhouses and pig farms that thrived here. Before then, prehistoric elephants used to nibble on the tasty plants. The cuisine has now switched to Korean.

 Many buildings constructed in Toronto in the early 1900s have a little bit of Christie Pits in them. This 3,000-year-old quarry provided the building trade with an almost inexhaustible supply of sand and gravel left behind by receding glaciers. It was vigorously mined to support a turn-of-the-century construction boom in the city. During early excavations a mammoth, or mastodon, was discovered buried in the pre-historic rubble. The pits have since been covered and landscaped to form the dish-shaped Christie Pits Park.

From the mid-Sixties to mid-Seventies, the first significant wave of Korean immigrants took place and new arrivals settled in and around Seaton Village. Although many of them have since taken up residence elsewhere in the city, the stretch of Bloor Street between Bathurst and Christie is still known as 'Korea Town'. This is where you'll find the best concentration of Korean restaurants in the city.

Although the Ukrainian community is better known further west along Bloor Street, the Ukrainian Cultural Centre on Christie Street remains the focus for those who had their Canadian roots in this area.

At the corner of Bloor Street West and Bathurst Street is one of our landmark stores. It's Honest Ed's, famed as much for its founder, Ed Mirvish, as it is for its flamboyant exterior and zany commercial signs. "Honest Ed's is the best place to find stuff you didn't know you needed!" is typical of what to expect.

A block-long section of Markham Street, south of Bloor, is known as 'Mirvish Village'. It came into being when the city planned to raze 24 little homes for a parking lot. Ed moved one step ahead of the city fathers and bought all the properties. He turned the place into a commercial colony for artists and things arty. Ed's son David owns one of the shops along here, David Mirvish Art Books. Together they own and operate the Princess of Wales and Royal Alexandra theatres, two of the city's premier stages. Ed also owned and refurbished London's historical Old Vic theatre before handing it back to the Brits.

If he ever finds out that hairy elephants wandered around here, he might just commission a life-sized model of one for his store. He'd probably have it nibbling on a plate of kimshee or bibimbab. His rationale would be: "If it made sense, we'd be out of business!"

Korea Town **Experience:** Humour yourself at Honest Ed's • have an unusual Korean meal • spend an interesting time wandering along Mirvish Village • play in Christie Pits Park • hang out in a sidewalk café and people watch.

MAP
24
The Annex

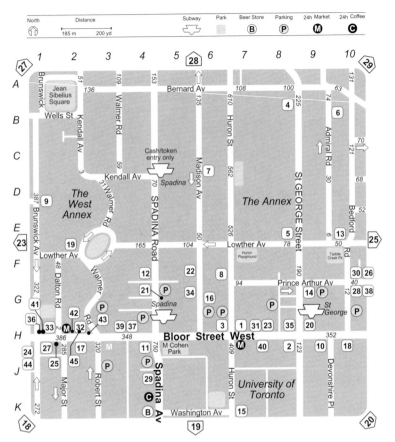

Places

Bahá'í Centre, 7H **1**
Bata Shoe Museum, 8H **2**
Bloor Street Church (1887) *United*, 6H **3**
Chinese Consulate General, 8B **4**
First Church of Christ Scientist, 8E **5**
German Consulate, 10B **6**
Heritage houses, 6C **7**
Italian Cultural Institute, 6F **8**
Loretto College, 1D **9**
Meteorological Office (1909), 9H **10**
Miles Nadal Jewish Centre, 4H **11**
Native Canadian Centre, 4F **12**
Quakers Meeting House, 10E **13**
Royal Canadian Yacht Club, 9G **14**
St Thomas Church (1893) *Anglo-Catholic*, 7K **15**
Tengye *Tibetan Buddhist*, 6G **16**
Trinity St Pauls *United*, 2H **17**
Varsity Stadium, 10H **18**
Walmer Road Church *Baptist*, 2E **19**
York Club, 9H **20**

Accommodation

Global *Guest house*, 4G **21**
Madison Manor *Boutique hotel*, 5F **22**
Quality Hotel, 8H **23**

Entertainment

Poor Alex Theatre, 1H **24**

Restaurants

350 Fahrenheit *International*, 2J **25**
Bedford Academy *Bistro*, 10F **26**
Brunswick House (1876) *Pub*, 1H **27**
Duke of York *Pub*, 10G **28**
Ferret & Firkin *Pub* 4J **29**
Fieramosca *Italian*, 10G **30**
Fox & Fiddle *Pub*, 7H **31**
Goldfish *International*, 2H **32**
James Joyce *Pub*, 1H **33**
Madigan's *Pub*, 5G **34**
Mercurio *Italian*, 8H **35**
Nataraj *Indian*, 1H **36**
Noodle Bowl *Asian*, 4H **37**
Opus *Italian*, 10G **38**
Real Thailand *Thai*, 4H **39**
Regal Beagle *Pub*, 7H **40**
Samraat *Indian*, 1H **41**
Serra *Italian*, 2H **42**
Shakespeare's *International*, 2H **43**
Tranzac *Pub*, 1J **44**
Via Oliveto *Italian*, 2H **45**

The Annex **Profile**

In 1877, the middle classes moved north to where noise and pollution wouldn't interfere with their sense of well-being. Then the Aussies and Kiwis moved in.

 It's known as 'The Annex' because it was annexed to the City of Toronto in 1887. To lure people here, north of the city limits, builders and developers of the day promised an idyllic subdivision where homes were "subject to reasonable building restrictions, so as to prevent the erection in the district of business places, inferior houses or terraces."

They did a good job. There is still virtually no commercial activity between Bloor Street West and the Davenport Road corridor and the elegance of a Victorian subdivision remains intact. A forest of maple and oak trees cloaks large and dignified homes under a canopy of green in the summer and a rainbow of colours in the fall. Here you'll find Admiral Road, which is one of the city's most genteel streets. There's a peppering of historic buildings and two of the city's most exclusive clubs.

By 1890 an electrified public transit line had replaced horse-drawn carriages. Bloor Street was linked with Sherbourne and King streets and Spadina Avenue to form what was known as 'The Belt Line'. This was when most of the streets in The Annex were paved with cedar blocks, although St George Street claimed at the time to be the only one paved with asphalt.

Defining The Annex depends on historical lore or present-day legal precision. The area was designated as follows when annexation took place: "Boundaries being the western edge of Yorkville, Dupont Street, Bloor Street and a line between Brunswick Avenue and Walmer Road." Purists say "the western edge of Yorkville" is Bellair Street (right in the middle of present-day Yorkville), while modernists prefer Avenue Road.

Many of the old mansions have been taken over by the University of Toronto, or converted into rooming houses for students. But it doesn't take much imagination to realize that this is how the neighbourhood must have looked during Victorian times.

Even Ye Olde Brunswick House is still here. It opened in 1876 and welcomed the first post-war wave of travelling Australians and New Zealanders who hit Toronto in the 1950s. The Brunswick became their pub of choice and the beer flowed freely.

The Tranzac Club they founded in 1961 is still here too. Predictably, it's just across the street – and it's a pub.

The Annex **Experience:** Wander around The Annex and down into the University grounds • try not to miss a visit to the Bata Shoe Museum • see if you can get someone who's very important to invite you to the York Club for dinner.

MAP

25

Yorkville

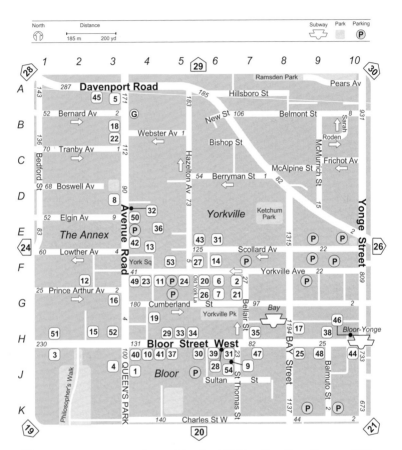

Places

Museum of Ceramic Art, 4J **1**
Paisley Garden (1867), 6G **2**
Royal Conservatory of Music (1881), 1J **3**
Royal Ontario Museum (ROM) 3J **4**

Restaurants

Arlequin *French*, 3A **5**
Bellini's *Italian*, 6G **6**
Bistro du Parc *French*, 6G **7**
Boba *International*, 3D **8**
Courtyard *Café*, 6J **9**
Dynasty *Chinese*, 4H **10**
Flow *Continental*, 4F **11**
Host *Indian*, 2F **12**
Il Posto Nuovo *Italian*, 4F **13**
Le Trou Normand *French*, 6F **14**
Lobby *Continental*, 2H **15**
Morton's *Steakhouse*, 3G **16**

Pangaea *International*, 8H **17**
Pink Pearl *Chinese*, 3B **18**
Prego Della Piazza *Italian*, 4G **19**
Remy's *American*, 6G **20**
Sassafraz *International*, 6G **21**
Sotto Sotto *Italian*, 3B **22**
Truffles (Four Seasons Hotel) *French contemporary*, 4F **23**

Shops

Arctic Bear *Native crafts*, 5F **24**
Birk's *Jewelry*, 8H **25**
Boss *Clothing*, 5G **26**
Budd Sugarman *Antiques*, 5F **27**
Bvlgari *Jewelry*, 6H **28**
Cartier *Jewelry*, 4H **29**
Chanel *Womenswear*, 5H **30**
Cole Haan *Shoes*, 6H **31**
Ferrari *Automobiles*, 3D **32**
Gucci *Accessories*, 5H **33**
Guerlain *Perfumes*, 5H **34**

Harry Rosen *Menswear*, 7H **35**
Hazelton Lanes *Mall*, 4E **36**
Hermès *Accessories* 4H **37**
Holt Renfrew *Clothing*, 9H **38**
Louis Vuitton *Accessories*, 6H **39**
Mont Blanc *Pens*, 4H **40**
Prada *Handbags*, 4H **41**
Rolls-Royce *Automobiles*, 3E **42**
Sable-Castelli Gallery *Art*, 5E **43**
Stollery's *Menswear*, 10H **44**
Stubbe *Chocolates*, 2A **45**
Swarkovski *Crystal*, 10H **46**
Tiffany & Co *Jewelry*, 7H **47**
William Ashley *China*, 9H **48**

Accommodation

Four Seasons Hotel, 4F **49**
Howard Johnson's Hotel, 4D **50**
Inter-Continental Hotel, 1H **51**
Park Hyatt Hotel, 3H **52**
The Hazelton Hotel, 5F **53**
Windsor Arms Hotel, 6J **54**

Yorkville **Profile**

Yorkville has gone from an isolated 19th century village to a 20th century 'hippie haven' to the 21st century's most upscale commercial district.

 It's hard to believe that this elegant part of town was once known as 'Haight Ashbury North'. The flower children of the Sixties, who made this neighbourhood a magnet for hippies from across North America, are long gone and so is the Mynah Bird that occupied the northeast corner of Hazelton and Yorkville avenues. It was the infamous club that tried to stage Toronto's first topless act.

This area, which was originally way north of the Town of York, was a forest until the 1830s when Joseph Bloor and Sheriff William Jarvis bought and subdivided a tract of land that was bounded roughly by today's Bloor Street, Avenue Road, Yonge Street and Marlborough Avenue. The Village of Yorkville was incorporated in 1853 and the first councillors were a brewer, butcher, carpenter, brick maker and blacksmith.

There are still a few reminders of those early days left. The 1867 house of John Daniels, the village constable, still stands at the corner of Yorkville Avenue and Bellair Street. It's now the Paisley Shop. A block further east is the 1876 fire hall that has been providing service to the neighbourhood for almost 135 years. On the corner of Hazelton and Yorkville avenues is the Olivet Congregational Church, built in 1876. It was converted into the Sable-Castelli Gallery. Next door is the 1909 Heliconian Club, once devoted to Women in the Arts. In 1883, Yorkville became the first village to be annexed by the City of Toronto.

After police moved the kids out of Yorkville during the summer of 1968, houses along Hazelton Avenue could be bought for $13,000. Today, most sell for a hundred times that. That's because the Bloor-Yorkville neighbourhood has become Canada's epicentre for expensive restaurants and some of the world's most prestigious stores. During the summer try to get a sidewalk table at a fashionable area restaurant so you can watch the Ferrari Folk trying to be unrecognizable behind dark glasses. Or, you can spend your life's savings on some baubles at the Bloor Street West marquees. If it's against your nature to be found inside Hermès, Gucci, Cartier, Bvlgari, or Tiffany & Co, there's always the refurbished Hazelton Lanes, hidden almost too discreetly between Hazelton Avenue and Avenue Road. But, whatever you do, get over to see the brilliantly re-designed exterior of the Royal Ontario Museum. David Libeskind's bursting crystal exterior is sheer architectural wonderment.

You won't need to be on a Sixties' high to groove on this masterpiece.

Yorkville **Experience:** Bring money and shop till you drop • see and be seen at Sassafraz • admire the heritage homes in The Annex • explore the new Royal Ontario Museum • treat yourself to an expensive dinner • think about buying a Rolls or Ferrari.

MAP

26

Bloor East

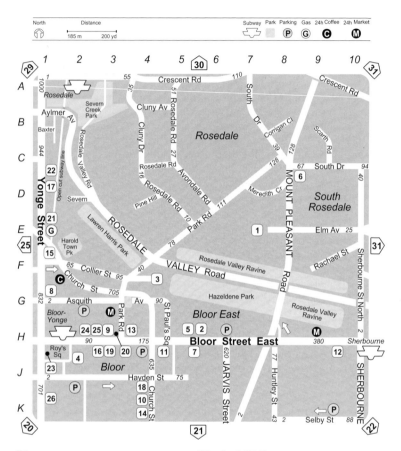

Places

Branksome Hall (1860), 7E **1**
Community, 5H **2**
Heritage houses, 4F **3**
Lotto Prize Office, 2J **4**
Manufacturers Life Building (1887), 5H **5**
Rosedale Presbyterian Church (1909), 8D **6**
St Paul's Church (1860), *Anglican*, 5H **7**
Toronto Reference Library, 1G **8**

Accommodation

Marriott Bloor-Yorkville Hotel, 2H **9**

Restaurants

Ashai Sushi *Japanese*, 4K **10**
Cultures *Salads & light meals*, 4H **11**
Groundhog *Pub*, 9H **12**
Ichiriki *Japanese*, 4H **13**
Indian Hut *Indian*, 4K, **14**
Indochine *French Vietnamese*, 1F **15**

Ithica *Greek*, 3H **16**
Romaris *Continental*, 1D **17**
Spirits *American*, 4J **18**
Spotted Dick *Pub*, 3H **19**

Shops

Boddington's *Bed & Bath*, 3H **20**
Canadian Tire *Automotive & household*, 1E **21**
Civello *Aesthetics*, 1C **22**
Condom Shack *Condoms*, 1H **23**
Hudson Bay Centre *Underground mall*, 2H **24**
Hudson's Bay Company (The Bay)
   Department store, 2H **25**
Kitchen Stuff *Kitchen needs*, 1K **26**

Bloor East **Profile**

Two influential men set a superior tone for the north side of the Rosedale Ravine 180 years ago. Then, and now, it's where the city's Old Money resides.

In the early 1800s Toronto extended no further north than Queen Street. The hinterland was nothing but forest and a deep ravine carved by the retreating glacial claws of the Wisconsin Ice Age. It was the north side of this isolated ravine that attracted William Jarvis, and especially a spot near the present corner of Cluny Drive and Rosedale Road. His wife Mary fell in love with the wild roses that grew in the forest and she named their 1821 country estate 'Rosedale'. Chief Justice William Draper built his residence on the south side of the ravine where Collier Street is today. The men joined their remote properties with a bridge.

Those residences are long gone, but Rosedale has retained its isolation and become one of the most prestigious places in Canada in which to live. Its mature, tree-lined streets and beautiful period homes bespeak the quiet respectability of Old Money, influence and power. The Rosedale Valley Ravine – filled with maple, oak, pine, beech, ash and basswood – provides a privacy wall to protect the moneyed scions of industry and commerce from those of us who are merely ordinary.

Bloor Street East, on the south side of the ravine, is the neighbourhood's stark divide. From here south is the much more mundane work-a-day world. Bloor East doesn't have the national *élan* attributed to Bloor West on the other side of Yonge Street, with its Louis Vuitton and Chanel storefronts. But it does run through an area filled with almost forgotten bits of interesting history.

The hundreds of thousands of us who use the Bloor-Yonge subway interchange each week, for example, are probably unaware that we're walking through an old burial ground known as 'Sandhill'. Just up the street, where Canadian Tire now stands, our first significant brewery came into being in 1835. About a kilometre further north a Mr. Richards opened an ice house in the 1840s. He was the first Black businessman to set up shop in Toronto.

St Paul's newly rejuvenated church on Bloor Street East is one of our most distinguished houses of worship. When the smaller church beside it, built in 1860, became inadequate to hold the congregation, the larger St Paul's was designed by architect E J Lennox to have the same seating capacity (2,500) as St Paul's Cathedral in London. It wasn't until renovations in 1991 that the seating was reduced to 1,700. Even so, it's the largest Anglican church in Canada and one of the most impressive churches in the country.

Bloor East **Experience:** Stroll through Severn Creek Park into the ravine • see Toronto's best kept lawn outside the Manufacturers Life Building • spend a moment in St Paul's church.

MAP
27

Davenport

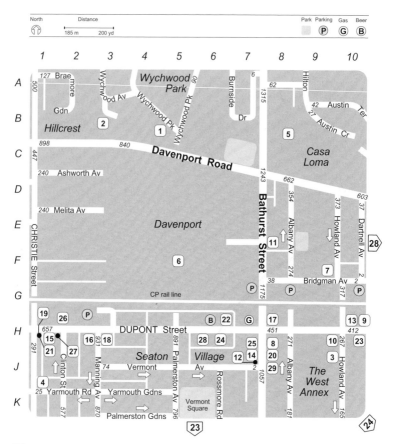

Places

6 Wychwood, 4B **1**
22 Wychwood, 3B **2**
Fire Station 23 (1910), 9J **3**
Korean Presbyterian Church (1914), 1J **4**
Rehabilitation Institute of Toronto, 8B **5**
TTC Hillcrest Yard, 5F **6**

Entertainment

Tarragon Theatre, 9F **7**

Restaurants

Annapurna *East Indian vegetarian*, 8H **8**
Bistro Tournesol *Continental*, 10H **9**
Choo Choo *Chinese*, 9H **10**
Dos Amigos *Mexican*, 8E **11**
Kos Café *American*, 7J **12**
Indian Rice Factory *Indian*, 10H **13**
Mayday Malone's *Pub*, 7J **14**

Mount Pinatubo *Filipino*, 1H **15**
Papamios *Italian*, 3H **16**
Vesta *Diner*, 8H **17**

Shops

55 Degreez *Motorcycle gear*, 3H **18**
Angus & Co *Furniture*, 1H **19**
Annex Books *Used & rare*, 8J **20**
Candy Machine *Candy*, 1H **21**
Cpused *Computers*, 6H **22**
Floor Works *Flooring*, 10H **23**
Kaolin *Gallery*, 6H **24**
La Parette *Print gallery*, 7H **25**
Loblaws *Supermarket* 1H, **26**
 Bakery
 Pharmacy
 Wine store
 Ziggy's deli
Marlene's *Baby needs*, 1H **27**
Residential Lighting *Fixtures*, 6H **28**
Triskelion *Used books*, 8J **29**

Davenport **Profile**

If you really want to take a nice long walk through pre-history, try Davenport Road. They say it's about 10,000 years old.

A very long time ago, the Iroquois used to travel along a trail that ran parallel to the shore of Lake Iroquois between the Humber and Don rivers. That was when the shores of Lake Iroquois (Lake Ontario) extended this far north. As the lake receded, leaving a plain on which the City of Toronto would eventually be built, the same path was used by missionaries and French fur traders. It appeared on maps for the first time with the settlement of Toronto's predecessor, the Town of York. That trail is now Davenport Road. It got its name from an isolated house built on the hill by John McGill in 1797.

The working class Davenport neighbourhood runs in a narrow swath between Davenport Road and the railway tracks west to past Dufferin Street. In this section the community is dominated by the Toronto Transit Commission's vehicle yards.

The land rises steeply from the north side of Davenport Road, giving homes on top of the hill a commanding view over the city and lake. Perched up here among a lot of trees is Wychwood Park. It's one of the most carefully hidden, intensely private and somewhat eccentric small neighbourhoods in the city.

Marmaduke Matthews, who was a landscape painter, wanted to start an artist's colony here in the 1870s. He named the tract of land after Oxfordshire's Wychwood Forest in England and set about creating one of the first planned communities in the area. Matthews' house is now number six Wychwood Park and that of his friend, Alexander Jardine, is number 22. They were built around 130 years ago.

Today, Ontario Heritage Conservation has designated the enclave an historic district. Each of the few dozen houses is listed in the Toronto Historical Board's inventory of heritage properties, even though some were built only 60 years ago.

Wychwood Park and the neighbouring Hillcrest and Casa Loma districts are in complete contrast to the much more modest residences of Seaton Village and the West Annex. Here, mansions give way to less pretentious Victorian duplexes with street-front verandahs and quiet, mature, leafy avenues. No executive council meets on this side of the railway tracks to oversee private roads and parkland. On this southern side of the neighbourhood, people much prefer life's less-pressing pleasures.

Davenport **Experience:** Say "hi" to folks sitting on their verandahs in Seaton Village • take a discreet peek at Wychwood Park • stroll with the locals along Dupont Street • take in a show at the Tarragon Theatre • enjoy a good meal around Dupont and Howland.

MAP
28

Casa Loma

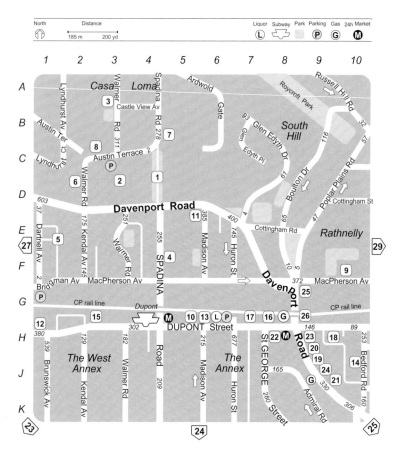

Places

Baldwin Steps, 4D **1**
Casa Loma (1913), 3D **2**
Casa Loma Stables (1905), 3A **3**
City of Toronto Archives, 5F **4**
George Brown College, 1E **5**
  Casa Loma Campus,
Lenwil (1915), 2D **6**
Spadina House Museum (1886), 4B **7**
The (Pellatt) Lodge (1905), 2C **8**
Toronto Hydro Sub Station H (1910),
  10F **9**

Restaurants

Annex Grill *International*, 5H **10**
Corner House *French*, 5D **11**
Dish *Café*, 1H **12**
Hey Good Cooking *Vegetarian*, 6H **13**
Le Paradis *French*, 10J **14**

News Café, 2G **15**
People's Foods *American*, 7H **16**
Pour House *Irish Pub*, 7H **17**
Praha *Czech,* 9H **18**

Shops

Davenport Art Gallery, 9H **19**
Designer's Walk #1 *Home design*, 9H **20**
Designer's Walk #2, *Home design*, 9J **21**
J S Bonbons *Chocolates*, 8H **22**
Ron's *Garden centre*, 9H **23**
Rug & Design *Persian carpets*, 9H **24**
Summerhill *Garden design*, 9G **25**
Woven Arts *Carpets*, 9G **26**

Casa Loma **Profile**

Toronto is pretty laid-back place, not known for any grandiose quirkiness, or outrageous eccentricities. Except for Casa Loma.

 On the hill overlooking this section of Davenport Road is a collection of residences that typify the personalities of three turn-of-the-century people with money and power. One of those residences is a castle.

Casa Loma was the fantasy of Sir Henry Pellatt. He rose to prominence as one of the founders of Ontario's vast hydroelectric system anchored at Niagara Falls. He also fancied himself as a military man. After being knighted in 1905 he decided to build himself a home that not only befitted a knight but also could serve as a place to entertain royalty royally. He toured the leading castles of Europe with local architect E J Lennox before deciding on a 17th century design that would be appropriate. It was the largest home built in Canada prior to 2002, even though Sir Henry went bankrupt trying to complete his project.

If the castle was a testament to Pellatt's ostentatious display of wealth, then The Stables attached to it through a 244 m tunnel attest to his bizarre venture into financial extravagance. They are the most lavish and expensive stables ever built in North America. Gauntly ornate vertical stone turrets rise above stalls handcrafted from mahogany. The floors are covered with Spanish tile and laid in a herringbone pattern so horses wouldn't slip. Windows are hinged at the bottom so the animals wouldn't experience annoying drafts.

It isn't known whether these architectural flourishes attracted the Royal Navy here in 1944, but this is where they assembled the forerunner to Sonar. It helped assure the Allies of victory at sea during World War II.

The castle intoxicated E J Lennox so much that he built his own house, Lenwil, across the street. His bedroom was designed to overlook Casa Loma so it would be the first thing he saw when he got up in the morning.

Just to the east of Casa Loma is Spadina House, the 1886 home of financier James Austin who introduced branch banking to Canada. The present structure, with its opulent interior and historic gardens, has undergone four expansions in the last century. It stands at the north end of Spadina Road, which was originally an old Aboriginal trail. The road was designed to be a grand thoroughfare leading from Queen Street to the residence site.

Perhaps Sir Henry Pellatt thought that if he couldn't have the equivalent of London's Mall, then he should at least have the palace.

Casa Loma **Experience:** Take a rewarding walk along Glen Edyth Drive and Admiral Road • climb the Baldwin Steps, read the plaques, and see the view • follow the trend and do the castle and stables ritual • have a nice dinner at the Corner House restaurant.

MAP

29

Summerhill

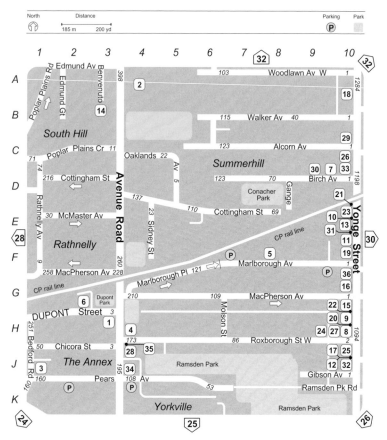

Places

Church of the Messiah (1891) *Anglican*, 3H **1**
De La Salle College, 4A **2**
Designers Walk Building 5, 1J **3**
Hare Krishna, 4H **4**
York Racquets Club, 8F **5**

Restaurants

Adriatico *Seafood*, 2G **6**
Avant Goût *Continental*, 10D **7**
Caffe Doria *International*, 10H **8**
Lakes *International*, 10H **9**
Musashi *Japanese*, 10E **10**
Pastis *French*, 10E **11**
Rebel House *American*, 10J **12**

Rosedale Diner *International*, 10E **13**
Scaramouche *French*, 3B **14**
Thai Magic *Thai*, 10G **15**

Shops

Absolutely *Antiques*, 10G **16**
Belle Epoque *Antiques*, 10J **17**
Braem & Minnetti *Antiques*, 10A **18**
Cadogan & Co *Prints*, 10F **19**
Constantine *Furniture*, 10H **20**
Conway & Gower *Table ware*, 10E **21**
Demarco Perpich *Home accents*, 10G **22**
Embros *Cook ware*, 10E **23**
French Country *Antiques*,10H **24**
Hollace Cluny *Home accents*, 10J **25**

Horse Feathers *Antiques*, 10C **26**
Hugo Quattrocchi *Antiques*, 10H **27**
Kamimura Gallery *Japanese antiques*, 3J **28**
L'Atelier *Antiques*, 10B **29**
Map Room *Antique maps*, 9C **30**
Matthew Berger *Antiques*, 10E **31**
Paul Hahn *Pianos*, 10J **32**
R G Perkins *Antiques*, 10C **33**
Roots *Home accents*, 4J **34**
Touch Wood *Furniture*, 4H **35**
Word of Mouth *Kitchen ware*, 10F **36**

Summerhill **Profile**

Here's one of the safest neighbourhoods in the city. And it's where a Canadian sports hero is remembered.

It's been about 125 years since the area between Avenue Road and Yonge Street, north of the train tracks, started to blossom with Victorian and Edwardian residences. By 1900, this was a well-established neighbourhood and the middle classes had settled themselves into a comfortable lifestyle.

About 12,000 years earlier, as the Ice Age was receding, waters of Lake Iroquois lapped the shores at the bottom of the Avenue Road hill. The hill remains as one of the very few steep grades in the city. Crowning its crest on the east side is an opulent old turreted mansion that's now part of De La Salle College.

Summerhill is not a grand place, but the mature homes along the magnificently treed Roxborough West and Woodlawn streets do create a sense of comfort and well-being. Scattered here and there are a few modern town homes that fit easily with the Victorian surroundings. Home décor and antique stores along Yonge Street cater to trendy and fastidious tastes.

Across Avenue Road, you'll find Edmund Gate. It's one of Toronto's many little streets that provides a discreetly up-scale address for its residents. The house at the end has one of the finest views in the city.

A rather ordinary green space called Lionel Conacher Park on Birch Avenue sits right in the middle of this western half of Summerhill. It memorializes a Toronto athlete who was known as the "greatest all-round athlete in Canada" for the first 50 years of the 20th century. Conacher could break 10 seconds for the 100-yard-dash. In 1921 he scored 15 of the points that gave Toronto a 23-0 victory over Edmonton in the Grey Cup final. He played hockey for the Chicago Black Hawks and won the Canadian light-heavyweight boxing championship. World heavyweight champion Jack Dempsey fought an exhibition with him.

Conacher died of a heart attack on the baseball field after hitting a triple. It happened on May 26, 1954, while he was playing a charity game on Parliament Hill in Ottawa. He was 54.

As Ontario's Athletic Commissioner, Lionel Conacher worked hard to provide recreational facilities in parks, especially in his hometown of Toronto.

Except for a tiny and seldom used softball area, the park that was dedicated to him by the city in 1967 is devoid of sports amenities.

Summerhill **Experience:** Browse the antique stores along Yonge Street • take a walk through Ramsden Park on a sunny day in the summer or fall • join the locals on the weekend for a coffee and snack at Caffe Doria.

MAP
30

Rosedale

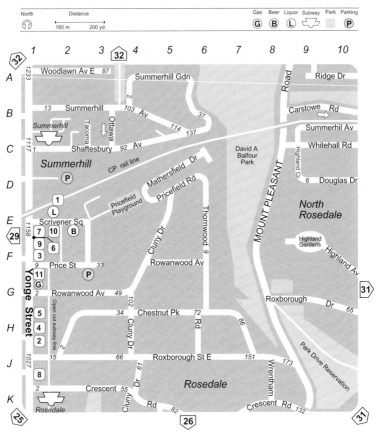

Map 30   **Map 31**

Places

North Toronto Railway Station (1913), 2D **1**

Restaurants

1055 *International*, 1H, **2**
Patachou *French coffee house*, 1F **3**
Quail and Firkin *Pub*, 1H **4**

Shops

Serendip *Antiques*, 1H **5**
All the Best *Fine foods*, 1E **6**
Harvest Wagon *Produce*, 1E **7**
House of Tea *Teas*, 1J **8**
Olliffe *Butcher*, 1F **9**
Pisces *Gourmet seafood*, 2E **10**
Sleep Country *Mattresses*, 1F **11**

Places

61 Bin-Scarth Road, 9E **1**
8 Castle Frank Road, 6L **2**
5 Drumsnab Road (1808), 9N **3**
44-66 Elm Avenue (1875), 1L **4**
89 Elm Avenue (1903), 5L **5**
1-7 Glen Road (1911), 1R **6**
6-8 Glen Road (1883), 2R **7**
9 Glen Road (1888), 1R **8**
55 Glen Road (1891), 3M **9**
64 Glen Road (1894), 3M **10**
65 Glen Road (1891), 3L **11**
66 Glen Road (1894), 3L **12**
87-89 Glen Road (1901), 4K **13**
92-94 Glen Road (1900), 3J **14**
97 Glen Road (1901), 4K **15**
2 Hawthorn Gardens, 7K **16**
Rosedale United Church (1867), 8B **17**

Rosedale **Profile**

A touch of old Venice was supposed to add a bit more class to this 180-year-old community. But, like Venice itself, things started falling apart.

 Here's where Rosedale really began. It's been said that Mary Jarvis, who gave this neighbourhood its name, was responsible for the meandering pattern of streets in the area. They are supposed to follow the various trails she carved out on the forest floor when she went horse back riding. Two of those trails are now Cluny Drive and Crescent Road, where there is a collection of century-old residences listed by the city as heritage properties.

The one thing that dominates this part of town today has less to do with horses and more to do with the 42-metre clock tower that rises above the old North Toronto Railway Station. It's a stately and classical spire made of stone and modelled after the Campanile in Venice's St Mark's Square. The Canadian Pacific Railway opened the station in 1916. King George VI and Queen Elizabeth got off the royal train here in 1939 when they visited the city. During the next few years, it was the major embarkation point for Canadian troops on their way to fight in World War II.

After the war, the venerable old landmark ceased operating as a railway station. Downtown's Union Station, built in 1927 and comparable to the grand stations in New York and Chicago, took over as the city's only railway terminal building. As a consequence, the North Toronto Railway Station became vacant and generally ignored except for the presence of a 65-year-old liquor store on the main floor. Old timers will tell you it's one of the best-known and oldest LCBO outlets in the city. As the years passed, the clock stopped working and the building started showing signs of premature age. It's no secret that the folk living in Rosedale found it embarrassing.

It wasn't the first time they'd been embarrassed. A long time ago, on the other side of Mt. Pleasant Road, they had to endure the lacrosse grounds. They have never quite forgotten the mayhem that ensued when the first Grey Cup game was played there. Sensitive and dignified feathers were truly ruffled.

In the spring of 1999 the large tract of vacant land immediately to the east of the old station came under residential development. To make the undertaking attractive to buyers and palatable to the old-time residents, developers have succeeded in bringing the old station back to within inches of its original glory. And that old clock in the Venetian tower has started ticking again.

Rosedale **Experience:** Shop for prime produce, meats and seafood around Scrivener Square • take a walk along Mary Jarvis' old riding trails • keep your eye on the clock • even if you don't drink, the beautifully restored Liquor Store is well worth a visit.

MAP
31   North & South Rosedale

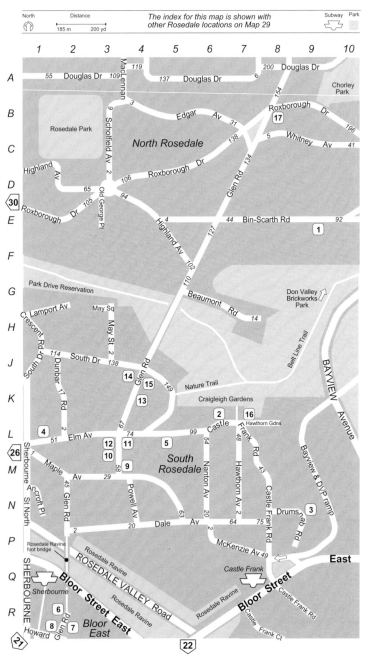

North & South Rosedale **Profile**

Vancouver's 'West Van' is impressive. Montreal's Westmount is also a coveted address. But our Rosedale still sets the standard as Canada's most respected and beautiful residential neighbourhood.

 One of the most eminent residential areas on the continent is detailed on maps 26, 30 and 31. Nowhere else in Canada could you come across a more impressively mature, quiet and historically significant place to live – or have such a selection of some of the country's most influential people as your neighbours.

The best way to see Rosedale is on foot. Start at the Rosedale subway station (map 26) and walk down the pathway through Severn Creek Park, along Rosedale Valley Road to Lawren Harris Park and on to the intersection of Park Road. You're now standing on the oldest road in the city. It was originally part of Davenport Road that followed a 10,000-year-old Aboriginal trail linking the Humber and Don rivers. Explorers, missionaries, fur traders and soldiers all came by here in the old days.

Go north along Park Road. Number 115 is the former home of Sir Ernest MacMillan, founder of the Royal Conservatory of Music and conductor of the Toronto Symphony Orchestra and Mendelssohn Choir. It contrasts with a controversial example of modern architecture at 111 Park Road. Near 30 Rosedale Road is where the original Rosedale House, owned by William Jarvis, stood. Continue up Park Road and go east along South Drive to Glen Road (map 31). Here you'll discover a cluster of Rosedale's historic homes.

In a neighbourhood drowning in splendid houses, you'll find 89 Elm Avenue, which was designed by the prolific social architect, E J Lennox. Five Drumsnab Road is the oldest continuously occupied house in the city. Built in 1808 on 81 ha (200 acres) of land, it has walls that are 76 cm thick. Eight Castle Frank Road, flanked along the front by five red maple trees, competes with the residence at 61 Bin-Scarth Road for being one of the most handsome houses in Rosedale. Each has one of the finest coach houses in the city. Another coach house can be found among the apartment residences at 2 Hawthorn Gardens.

All that's left of the famous old Osler Estate – home of financier Sir Edmund Osler – are the gates. He willed his massive residence to the city. It was then torn down and absorbed into Craigleigh Gardens. Ironically, Osler founded the Rosedale Association in 1905 to protect homes in the area from the 'progressive' ideas coming out of city hall.

North & South Rosedale **Experience:** Enjoy seeing an exquisite neighbourhood • walk south on Glen Road and over the Rosedale Ravine foot bridge. When you come out from under Bloor Street on the other side you'll experience the most dramatic social divide in the city. Within 150 m you'll go from abundant affluence straight into conspicuous poverty.

MAP
32
Yonge & St Clair

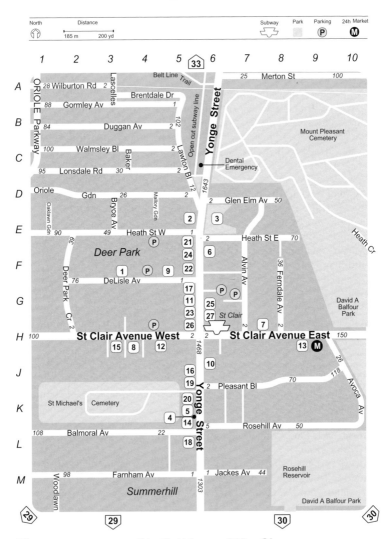

Places

Calvin Church *Presbyterian*, 3F **1**
Christ Church *Anglican*, 5E **2**
Yorkminster Park Church *Baptist*, 6E **3**

Restaurants

Bocconi *Deli*, 5K **4**
Caro *Italian*, 5K **5**
Circle *Thai*, 6E **6**

Edoya Sushi *Japanese*, 8H **7**
Fionn MacCools *Pub*, 4H **8**
Il Fornello *Italian*, 5F **9**
Passione Italiana *Italian*, 6J **10**
Rhodes *American*, 5G **11**
Scallywags *Sports bar*, 4H **12**
Simply Thai *Thai*, 8H **13**
Spiga *Italian*, 5K **14**
Sports Centre *Café*, 3H **15**
Sweet Rosie's *Café*, 5J **16**
Takara *Japanese*, 5G **17**
Terroni *Italian*, 5L **18**

Shops

Book City *Books*, 5J **19**
Crockery Barn *Homewares*, 5J **20**
Delisle Court *Mall*, 5E **21**
Gowans *Furniture*, 5F **22**
Prinziples *Prints*, 5G **23**
Reisman *Kitchenware*, 5F, **24**
Roots *Clothing*, 6G **25**
Saddle Bag *Handbags*, 5H **26**
St Clair Centre *Mall*, 6G **27**

Yonge & St Clair **Profile**

Aboriginal people called this place 'Mushquoteh'. It was where deer came to feed in a forest meadow.

 About 45 years after the founding of the Town of York in 1793, the Heath family ventured well north of the settlement and bought 16 ha of land. They named their new estate 'Deer Park'. In less than 20 years a small village emerged, complete with a racetrack. People who stayed at the Deer Park Hotel, on the present-day corner of Yonge and St Clair, could feed a roaming herd of deer.

Not least among the community's landmarks was an 80 ha tract of land purchased in 1873 for use as a Protestant cemetery. The Catholic church reserved another site close by for a burial ground. At the time, the combined plot capacity of these two cemeteries way outnumbered the total population of Toronto. Deer Park was indeed a place of eternal tranquility.

The community lost its rural identity when the City of Toronto annexed it in 1908. Country life around the old meadow changed dramatically as people of mainly British stock came north to live. By the mid-Thirties it was known as one of Toronto's best neighbourhoods.

There's still a distinct Anglo-Saxon feeling about the place that some locals refer to as 'The Hill'. It's one of the few communities in town that lacks a broad and noticeable cultural diversity. Its three main churches – Christ Church, Yorkminster and Calvin – underscore the Protestant background of those who live here. All were built within a few years of each other during the Twenties, but it's Calvin Presbyterian that is the most interesting.

It came about when a minority of Presbyterians decided not to join the 1925 unification of Methodist, Congregational and Presbyterian faiths into the United Church of Canada. They wanted to continue their Presbyterian traditions and built a Greek and Gothic styled church designed along practical lines because the congregation "didn't have silver to waste." The bitter church schism still lingers, albeit in a civilized way, after more than 75 years. But those who stood by their Scottish religious heritage have given us one of our most interesting places of worship.

This is a generally low-key, upper-middle-class neighbourhood. Mature condominiums around Rosehill Avenue and Pleasant Boulevard rank among the best high-rise addresses in the city. The old single-family homes are slowly disappearing as the demand for elevated living moves forward.

And the deer have found somewhere else to roam.

> *Yonge & St Clair* **Experience:** Spend time relaxing around the Rosehill Reservoir • join the locals along Yonge Street at the weekend • stroll through the old cemeteries • visit the churches.

MAP
33

Davisville

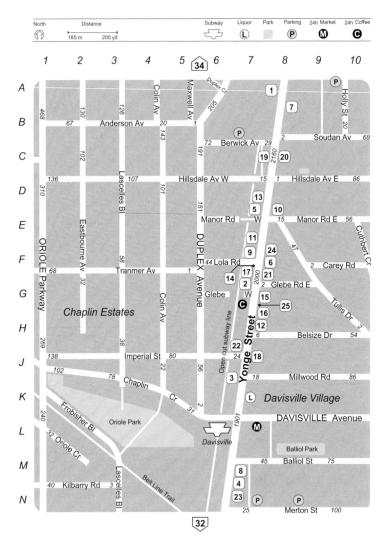

Places

TVOntario, 8A **1**

Entertainment

Limelight *Supper club,* 7F **2**

Restaurants

Bow & Arrow *Pub,* 6J **3**
Bull & Firkin *Pub,* 7M **4**
Esco-Pazzo *Italian,* 7D **5**

Grano *Italian,* 8F **6**
Hanna's Kitchen *Continental* 9A **7**
Izu *Japanese,* 7M **8**
Jaipur Grille *Indian,* 7F **9**
Manor Arms *Pub,* 8D **10**
Mariachi's *Mexican,* 7E **11**
Posticino *Italian,* 7H **12**
Quartier *French,* 7D **13**
St Louis *Sports bar,* 7F **14**
Stork on the Roof *Continental,* 7G **15**

Sushi Supreme *Japanese,* 7G **16**
Thai Thai *Thai,* 7F **17**
Vittorios Ristorante *Italian,* 7J **18**
Zucca Trattoria *Italian,* 7C **19**

Shops

Art Shoppe *Furniture,* 8C **20**
Au Lit *Bedding,* 7F **21**
Dell'Ernia *Lamp maker,* 7H **22**
Ethan Allen *Furniture,* 7M **23**
Indoors Out *Gard'n furniture,* 8E **24**
Paper Moon *Stationery,* 7G **25**

Davisville **Profile**

As Yonge Street runs alongside the open subway tracks, it loses the cachet that has been bestowed on its better-known sections around Eglinton and St Clair avenues. That changes when you go a block west.

 This area is a combination of two important tracts of land. To the east of Yonge Street was the modest farming community of Davisville Village. The settlement was named after John Davis, who came to this part of the world in 1840 from Staffordshire, England. He was the village's first postmaster and owned the pottery works that were the mainstay of the settlement's economy. It was a peaceful little place with no pretensions.

The top half, known as Davisville Glebe, was church property and it remained undivided until 1911. Davis owned the lower half around Davisville Avenue and it was first sub-divided in the 1860s. Many of the old homes built in this lower half have been replaced with commercial and residential high-density development along Merton Street.

While construction was underway in Davisville, the large, prestigious estate of William John Chaplin was being carved-up and promoted as a high-class residential district. Anyone who thought of living here was forced to abide by a lengthy and bureaucratic array of complex building codes and zoning bylaws. In the early Twenties the well-to-do were paying as much as $9,000 a lot.

Despite this – or because of it – Tudor, Georgian and English cottage architecture began to fill the empty lots until the place was turned into one of the most distinguished residential areas in the city.

You'll find an interesting old map imbedded in the sidewalk on the southwest corner of Yonge and Hillsdale Avenue West. It shows seven of the area's historic sites and the names of the original landowners. Curiously, the map is titled 'Southeast Part of York', which was actually the area around present-day Harbourfront.

Except for the high-rise complex on the south side of Oriole Park, Chaplin Estates remains one of our best and most sought-after addresses. To get the most out of this engaging neighbourhood, walk along Chaplin Crescent and north on Oriole Parkway to Hillsdale Avenue. Stroll through the streets south of Hillsdale, especially Colin and Tranmer avenues. This is definitely Mercedes territory.

And it has lots of cachet.

Davisville **Experience:** Browse around the furniture inside the Art Shoppe and Ethan Allen • enjoy some lively dinner theatre at the Limelight • introduce yourself to one of the last lamp makers in the city • take a nice long jog along the Belt Line Trail.

MAP
34

Yonge & Eglinton

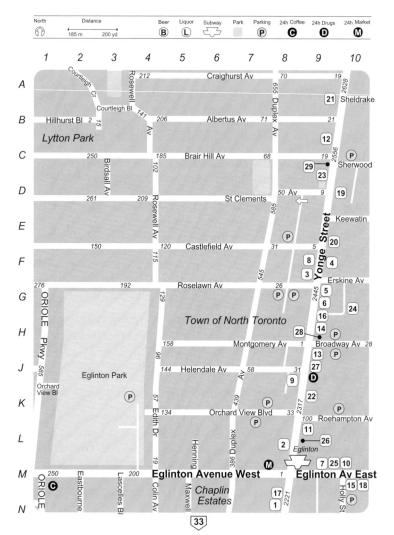

North	Distance	Beer	Liquor	Subway	Park	Parking	24h Coffee	24h Drugs	24h Market
	185 m 200 yd	Ⓑ	Ⓛ	⌄		Ⓟ	Ⓒ	Ⓓ	Ⓜ

Entertainment

Famous Players *Cinema*, 8N **1**
Silver City *Cinema*, 8L **2**

Restaurants

Acrobat *French*, 9F **3**
Alize *Italian*, 10F **4**
Amore *Italian*, 9G **5**
Bloor St Diner *Continental*, 9G **6**
Bombay Host *Indian*, 9M **7**
Centro *Canadian*, 9F **8**

Cheers *Pub*, 8J **9**
Cilantro *Continental*, 10M **10**
Duke of Kent *Pub*, 9K **11**
Gabby's *Pub*, 9C **12**
Grazie *Italian*, 9H **13**
Green Papaya *Vietnamese*, 9H **14**
Hooters *American* 10M **15**
La Vecchia *Italian*, 9G **16**
Mandarin *Chinese buffet*, 8M **17**
Melina's *Continental*, 10M **18**
North 44 *International*, 10D **19**

Redwood Grille *International*, 9E **20**
Roberto's *Italian*, 10A **21**
Rose & Crown *Pub*, 9K **22**
Sorn *Thai* 9C **23**
Spacco *Italian* 10G **24**
Summit Grill *American*, 9M **25**
Sunset Grill *American*, 9L **26**
Sushi Rock *Japanese*, 9J **27**
Valjean *Café*, 9H **28**
Zizi *Italian*, 9C **29**

Yonge & Eglinton **Profile**

One of Canada's most famous rebellions was hatched here. However, it was today's young urban professionals who eventually conquered the place.

Montgomery Avenue is named after the long-gone Montgomery Tavern that stood on the southwest corner of Yonge and Montgomery. It was the headquarters for William Lyon Mackenzie, who led the failed Upper Canada Rebellion of 1837. Despite the defeat, the disturbance precipitated the union of Upper and Lower Canada in 1841 that helped lead to the establishment of Canada as a nation.

Fifty years later, the energy of that anger had withdrawn into memory. The farm communities of Eglinton, Davisville and Bedford Park fused into a place they called 'New Toronto'. This was the northern terminal of the Metropolitan Street Railway that ran north on Yonge Street. And you could get here for five cents from downtown. Just before World War I, however, residents were getting fed-up with poor local services and voted to lose their independence and amalgamate with Toronto.

Except for the commercial corridors along Eglinton Avenue and up Yonge Street, this is largely a family-oriented neighbourhood. To the west of Yonge Street it's filled with mainly single-detached houses that were built between 1910 and 1940, even though development started here just before the turn of the century. Streets are lined with old trees that form leafy canopies over the sidewalks during the summer and fall.

It's in obvious contrast to the high-density buildings that have sprouted on the east side of Yonge. Some wry local folk point out that the wannabes with their tabby cats hang out in the high rises, whereas the dot.bomb crowd and their designer dogs continue to display an air of invincibility on the other side of the street.

The best time to experience the true flavour of Yonge and Eglinton is on a summer weekend. It's packed with local pedestrian traffic and dogs on leashes. Folk relax in coffee shops, browse the bookshelves at Indigo, behave with less than overt politeness to strangers, or wait for a brunch table at the Mandarin restaurant. When the stars come out they can choose from two of Toronto's top five restaurants – North 44° and Centro – for dinner. There's a confidently aloof taste of success in the air.

The last thing on their minds is rebellion.

Yonge & Eglinton **Experience:** Splurge a bit on dinner at a good restaurant • see what all the fuss is about at Hooters • have Sunday brunch at the Mandarin • watch the canines walking their human pets on a summer weekend • above all, look successful.

MAP
35

North York Centre

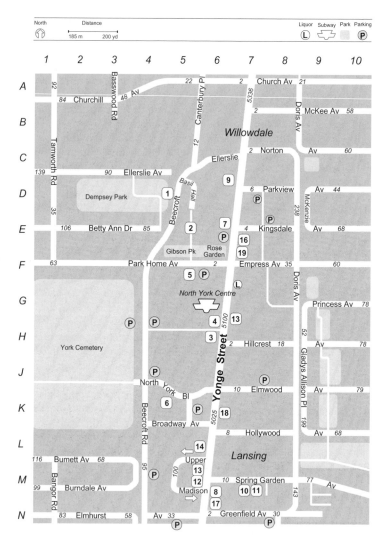

Places

Dempsey Store, 4D **1**
Gibson House (1851), 5E **2**
Mel Lastman Square, 6H **3**
North York Centre, 6G, **4**

Accommodation

Novotel North York, 5F **5**

Entertainment

Toronto Centre for the Arts,
4K **6**
  George Weston Recital Hall
  Main Stage

Restaurants

Asian Legend *Asian*, 6D, **7**
Black Sheep *Pub*, 6M **8**
Cuisine of India *Indian*, 6C **9**

Ichiban Fish House *Japanese*,
  7M **10**
Kiyomizu *Japanese*, 7M **11**
Mazzoni's *Italian*, 5M **12**
Milestone's *International*, 6G **13**
Moxie's *International*, 5L **14**
Mr Greek *Greek*, 5M **15**
Seashell *Seafood*, 7E **16**
Smokey Joe's *American*, 6N **17**
Taste of Spain *Spanish*, 6K **18**
Thai Mango *Thai*, 7E **19**

North York Centre **Profile**

North York came into being when two isolated rural communities - Lansing and Willowdale - finally grew into each other. Fast forward to Mel Lastman and his rule that lasted for decades.

 Jacob Cummer came to Lansing from Pennsylvania around 1797 to find a new life. The settlement was barely a year old when he built a modest log cabin near the present intersection of Church Avenue and Yonge Street. Thirty-five years later he erected what became known as 'Cummer's Chapel' – "a place where Divine services were to be held forever" in the Methodist Episcopalian tradition.

The chapel and its services no longer exist. In their place is a tiny cemetery on the north east corner of Yonge and Church with headstones going back more than 165 years. It's one of three sites that links North York to its past.

The other two are Gibson House and the old Dempsey Store. A Scot named David Gibson built himself a Victorian farmhouse here in 1851 and then went on to become deputy land surveyor and an ardent political force. The house remains intact today as a popular museum.

The old Dempsey Store now sits in Willowdale after being hauled up Yonge Street in 1996 from its original 1860 Lansing site at Yonge and Sheppard. It was built by Joseph Shepard, and housed a thriving hardware business for over 75 years. Shepard was one of the area's first residents and built his original home – a log cabin – on the northwest corner of present day Yonge and Sheppard.

A lot has changed since the days of Cummer, Gibson and Shepard. This is the only area in Toronto that boasts a soaring condo-cluttered skyline to rival the downtown core. It was no accident. The rivalry between Toronto and North York, before they joined into one city in January 1998, raised civic political theatre into an art form. The lead character, who never missed a performance for almost a quarter-century, was Mel Lastman, North York's mayor.

It is fair to say that Lastman single-handedly created what is now uptown. The handsome Mel Lastman Square rivals downtown's Nathan Phillips Square as the place for us to be seen on New Year's Eve. The carillon atop the North York Centre is known all over town as 'Mel's Bells'.

And, if all this wasn't enough, in December 1997 we elected him as the first mayor of the newly amalgamated City of Toronto, a job he held until he finally retired in 2003.

North York Centre **Experience:** Hear the great acoustics inside George Weston Recital Hall • join one of the annual celebrations in Mel Lastman Square • explore what the neighbourhood was like in the old days • see all of Mel's 11 portraits inside the North York Centre.

Neighbourhoods Street index, maps 1 – 35

Street name followed by **page** number.

A

Aberdeen Ave, 56.66
Adelaide St East, 26,44
Adelaide St West, 38, 40, 42
Admiral Rd, 70, 78
Aitken Pl, 36
Albany Ave, 68, 76
Albert St, 42, 52
Albertus Ave, 90
Alcorn Ave, 80
Alexander Pl, 64
Alexander St, 64
Alpha Ave, 66
Alvin Ave, 86
Amelia St, 66
Ancroft Pl, 84
Anderson Ave, 88
Andrews Pl, 48
Ardwold Gt, 78
Armoury St, 52
Arnold Ave, 56
Ashworth Ave, 76
Asquith Ave, 74
Atlantic Ave, 26
Augusta Ave, 40, 50, 60
Austin Cr, 76
Austin Terr, 76, 78
Avenue Rd, 72, 80
Avoca Ave, 86
Avondale Rd, 74
Aylmer Ave, 74

B

Baker Ave, 86
Baldwin St, 50
Balliol St, 88
Balmoral Ave, 86
Balmuto St, 72
Bancroft Ave, 60
Bangor Rd, 92
Barnaby Pl, 52
Barton Ave, 23
Basil Hall, 68
Basswood Rd, 92
Bathurst St, 28, 38, 48, 58, 68, 76
Bay St, 32, 42, 52, 62, 72
Bayview Ave, 84
Baxter St, 74
Beaumont Rd, 84
Bedford Rd, 70, 78, 50
Beecroft Rd, 92

Bellair St, 72
Bellevue Ave, 48
Bellwoods Ave, 38, 48
Belmont St, 72
Belshaw Pl, 56
Belsize Dr, 88
Benvenuto Pl, 80
Berkeley St, 46, 56
Bernard Ave, 70, 72
Berti St, 44
Berryman St, 72
Berwick Ave, 88
Betty Ann Dr, 92
Beverley St, 40, 50, 60
Bin-Scarth Rd, 84
Birch Ave, 80
Birdsall Ave, 90
Bishop St, 72
Bishop Tutu Blvd, 28
Bleecker St, 66
Bloor St East, 66, 74, 84
Bloor St West, 68, 70, 72
Blue Jays Way, 30, 40
Bond St, 44, 54
Bonnycastle St, 36
Borden St, 58, 68
Boswell Ave, 72
Boulton Dr, 78
Braemore Gdns, 76
Brant St, 40
Breadalbane St, 62
Bremner Blvd, 30, 32
Brentdale Dr, 86
Briar Hill Ave, 90
Bridgman Ave, 76, 78
Bright St, 46
Britain St, 44
British Columbia Dr, 26
Broadcast La, 66
Broadway Ave, 90
Brunswick Ave, 60, 70, 78
Bryce Ave, 86
Bulwer St, 40
Burnett Ave, 92
Burndale Ave, 92
Burnside Dr, 76

C

Camden St, 40
Cameron St, 40, 50
Canada Blvd, 26
Canterbury Pl, 92

Carey Rd, 88
Carlton St, 54, 56, 64
Carlysle St, 48
Carr St, 48
Carstoe Rd, 82
Casimir St, 48
Castle Frank Cres, 66
Castle Frank Ct, 84
Castle Frank Rd, 84
Castle View Ave, 78
Castlefield Ave, 90
Cawthra Sq, 64
Cecil St, 50
Centre St, 52
Chaplin Cr, 88
Charles St East, 64
Charles St West, 62, 72
Charlotte St, 40
Cherry St, 36, 46
Chestnut Park, 82
Chestnut St, 52
Chicora St, 80
Christie St, 68, 76
Church Ave, 92
Church St, 34, 44, 54, 64, 74
Churchill Ave, 92
Claremont St, 38, 48
Clarence Sq, 40
Classic Ave, 60
Clinton Pl, 68
Clinton St, 48, 58, 68, 76
Cluny Ave, 74
Cluny Dr, 26, 74, 82
Coatsworth St, 56
Colborne St, 11??
Colin Ave, 88, 90
College St, 50, 52, 58, 60, 62
Collier St, 74
Cooper St, 34
Corktown La, 46
Corrigan Cl, 74
Cottingham Rd, 78
Cottingham St, 78, 80
Court St, 44
Courtleigh Bl, 90
Courtleigh Cr, 90
Craighurst Ave, 90
Crescent Rd, 74, 82, 84
Crocker Ave, 38
Croft St, 58
Cumberland Ave, 72
Cuthbert Cr, 88

94

D

D'Arcy St, 50
Dale Ave, 84
Dalhousie St, 44, 54
Dalton Rd, 70
Dartnell Ave, 76, 78
Davenport Rd, 72, 76, 78
David St, 56
Deer Park Cr, 86
DeLisle Ave, 86
Denison Ave, 38, 40, 48, 50
Dennison Sq, 50
Derby St, 46
Dermott Pl, 56
Devonshire Pl, 58, 70
Doris Ave, 92
Douglas Dr, 82, 84
Draper St, 40
Drumsnab Rd, 84
Dufferin Street, 26
Duggan Ave, 86
Duncan St, 42
Dunbar Rd, 84
Dundas St East, 54
Dundas Sq, 54, 56
Dundas St West, 48, 50, 52
Dundonald St, 64
Duplex Ave, 90
Duplex Cr, 88
Dupont St, 76, 78, 80

E

Earl St, 64
Eastborne Ave, 88, 90
Eastern Ave, 46
Eden Pl, 48
Edgar Ave, 84
Edith Dr, 90
Edmund Ave, 80
Edmund Gt, 80
Edward St, 52
Eglinton Ave East, 90
Eglinton Ave West, 90
Elgin Ave, 72
Elizabeth St, 52, 62
Ellerslie Ave, 92
Elm Ave, 74, 84
Elm St, 52
Elmhurst Ave, 92
Elmwood Ave, 92
Emily St, 42
Empress Ave, 92
Erin St, 46
Erskine Ave, 90
Euclid Ave, 8, 38, 48, 58, 68

F

Farnham Ave, 86
Ferndale Ave, 86
Flagler St, 66
Fleet St, 26, 28
Follis Ave, 68
Foster Pl, 52
Fraser Ave, 26
Frederick St, 34, 44
Freeland St, 34
Frichot Ave, 72
Frobisher Bl, 88
Front St East, 44, 46
Front St West, 28, 38, 40, 42

G

Galbraith Rd, 60
Gardiner Expy, 28, 30, 32, 34, 36
Garrison Rd, 26, 28
George St, 34, 44, 54
George St South, 44
Gerrard St East, 54, 56
Gerrard St, West, 52
Gibson Ave, 80
Gifford St, 56
Gilead Pl, 46
Gladys Allison Pl, 92
Glasgow St, 50
Glebe Rd East, 88
Glebe Rd West, 88
Glen Rd, 66, 84
Glen Edyth Dr, 78
Glen Edyth Pl, 78
Glen Elm Ave, 86
Glen Morris St, 60
Gloucester St, 64
Gore St, 48
Gormley Ave, 86
Gould St, 54
Granby St, 54
Grange Ave, 50
Grange Pl, 50
Grange Rd, 50
Greenfield Ave, 92
Grenville St, 62
Grosvenor St, 62

H

Hagerman St, 52
Hahn Pl, 36
Harbord St, 58, 60
Harbour St, 32
Hart House Cir, 60, 62
Hawthorn Ave, 84
Hawthorn Gdns, 84
Hayden St, 74

Hayter St, 52
Hazelton Ave, 72
Heath St East, 86
Heath St West, 86
Helendale Ave, 90
Henderson Ave, 48
Henning Ave, 90
Henry La Ter, 34
Henry St, 50, 60
Herrick St, 58
Hickory St, 48
Highland Ave, 82, 84
Highland Cr, 82
Hillcrest Ave, 92
Hillhurst Bl, 90
Hillsboro St, 72
Hillsdale Ave East, 88
Hillsdale Ave West, 88
Hilton Ave, 76
Holly St, 88, 90
Hollywood Ave, 92
Homewood Ave, 64
Hoskin Ave, 60
Housey St, 28
Howard St, 66, 84
Howland Ave, 68, 76
Huntley St, 74
Huron St, 50, 60, 64, 70, 78

I

Imperial St, 88
Inkerman St, 62
Irwin Ave, 62
Isabella St, 64

J

Jacques Ave, 86
James St, 42
Jarvis St, 44, 54, 64, 74
Jefferson Ave, 26
Jersey Ave, 58
John St, 40
John McKenzie Gt, 92
Jordan St, 42

K

Keewatin Ave, 90
Kendal Ave, 70, 78
Kensington Ave, 50
Kilbarry Rd, 88
King St East, 44, 46
King St West, 38, 40, 42
King's College Cir, 60, 62
King's College Rd, 60
Kingsdale Ave, 92

L

Lake Shore Blvd East, 6, 7??
Lake Shore Blvd West, 28, 30, 32
Lamport Ave, 84
Lancaster Ave, 66
Laplante Ave, 52
Larch St, 50
Lascelles Blvd, 88, 90
Laurier Ave, 66
Lawton Blvd, 86
Leader La, 44
Leonard Ave, 48
Lennox St, 58, 68
Linden St, 64
Lippincott St, 48, 58, 68
Little Norway Ct, 28
Lola Rd, 88
Lombard St, 44
London St, 68
Longboat Ave, 36
Lonsdale Rd, 86
Lother Ave, 72
Lower Jarvis St, 34, 44
Lower Sherbourne St, 34, 44
Lower Simcoe St, 32
Lower Spadina Ave, 30
Lowther Ave, 70
Lyndhurst Ave, 78
Lyndhurst Ct, 78

M

MacLennan Ave, 84
MacPherson Ave, 78, 80
Madison Ave, 70, 78
Major St, 60, 70
Maitland Pl, 64
Maitland St, 64
Mallory Gdns, 86
Manning Ave, 38, 48, 58, 68, 76
Manor Rd East, 88
Manor Rd West, 88
Mansfield Ave, 48
Maple Ave, 84
Market St, 6, 44
Maribeth Ave, 64
Marlborough Ave, 80
Marlborough Pl, 80
Markham St, 38, 48, 58, 68
Mathersfield Dr, 82
Maud St, 38, 40
Maxwell Ave, 88, 90
May Sq, 84
May St, 84
McAlpine St, 72

McCaul St, 40, 42, 52
McGill St, 54
McKee Ave, 92
McKenzie Ave, 84
McMaster Ave, 80
McMurrich St, 72
Melinda St, 42
Mercer St, 40
Meredith Cr, 74
Merton St, 86, 88
Metcalfe St, 66
Michener Ct, 38
Milan St, 56
Mill St, 46
Millington St, 66
Millwood Rd, 88
Mitchell Ave, 38
Molson St, 80
Monteith St, 64
Montgomery Ave, 90
Morrison St, 40
Mount Pleasant Rd, 74, 82
Mowat Ave, 26
Murray St, 52
Mutual St, 44, 54, 64

N

Nanton Ave, 84
Nasmith Ave, 56
Nassau St, 48, 50
Navy Wharf Ct, 30
Nelson St, 40, 42
New St, 72
Newfoundland Dr, 26
Niagara St, 38
North York Bl, 92
Norton Ave, 92
Nunavut Rd, 26

O

Oak St, 56
Oaklands Ave, 80
Oaklawn Gdns, 86
Old George Pl, 84
Old York La, 72
Olive Ave, 68
Ontario Dr, 2???
Ontario St, 46, 56, 66
Orchard View Bl, 90
Orde St, 52
Ordnance St, 26
Oriole Cr, 88
Oriole Gdn, 86
Oriole Pkwy, 86, 88, 90
Ottawa St, 82
Oxford St, 48, 50
Oxley St, 40

P

Page St, 58
Palmerston Ave, 38, 48, 68, 76
Palmerston Blvd, 58, 68
Palmerston Gdns, 68, 76
Palmerston Sq, 68
Park Rd, 74
Park Home Ave, 92
Parliament St, 36, 46, 56, 66
Parkview Ave, 92
Pashler Ave, 56
Passmore Rd, 68
Pearl St, 9, 42
Pears Ave, 72, 80
Pembroke St, 54
Peter St, 40
Phipps St, 62
Phoebe St, 40, 50
Pine Hill Rd, 74
Piper St, 42
Pleasant Blvd, 86
Polson St, 36
Poplar Plains Cr, 80
Poplar Plains Rd, 78, 80
Portland St, 28, 38
Portugal Sq, 38
Poulett St, 56
Powell Ave, 84
Power St, 46
Price St, 82
Pricefield Rd, 82
Prince Arthur Ave, 70, 72
Prince Edward Island Cr, 26
Princes' Blvd, 26
Princess Ave, 92
Princess St, 36, 46
Prospect St, 66

Q

Quebec St, 26
Queen St East, 34, 36, 44, 46
Queen St West, 38, 40, 42
Queen's Park, 62, 72
Queen's Park Cres East, 62
Queen's Park Cres West, 62
Queen's Quay West, 28, 30, 32

R

Rachael St, 74
Ramsden Park Rd, 80
Rathnelly Ave, 80
Rawlings Ave, 66
Rees St, 30
Regent St, 56

Remembrance Dr, 26, 28
Renfrew Pl, 40
Richardson St, 34
Richmond St East, 44, 46
Richmond St West, 38, 40, 40
Ridge Dr, 82
Robert St, 60, 70
Robertson Cr, 30
Robinson St, 48
Roden Pl, 72
Roehampton Ave, 90
Rose Ave, 66
Rosedale Rd, 74
Rosedale Valley Rd, 66, 74, 84
Rosehill Ave, 86
Roselawn Ave, 90
Rosewell Ave, 90
Ross St, 50, 60
Rossmore Rd, 76
Rowanwood Ave, 82
Roxborough Dr, 82, 84
Roxborough St East, 82
Roxborough St West, 80
Roy's Sq, 74
Russell Ave, 60
Russell Hill Rd, 78
Ryerson Ave, 8, 48

S

Sackville Pl, 66
Sackville St, 46, 56, 66
Salisbury Ave, 66
Saskatchewan Rd, 26
Scadding Ave, 46
Scarth Rd, 74
Scollard Ave, 72
Scott St, 44
Scrivener Sq, 82
Seaton St, 46, 56
Selby St, 64, 74
Severn St, 74
Schofield Ave, 84
Shaftsbury Ave, 82
Sheard St, 54
Sheldrake Blvd, 90
Sheppard St, 42
Sherbourne St, 44, 54, 64, 74, 84
Sherbourne St North, 74, 84
Sherwood Ave, 90
Shuter St, 46, 54, 56
Simcoe Pl, 52
Simcoe St, 42, 52
Small St, 36
Soho St, 40, 50
Soudan Ave, 88

South Dr, 72, 84
Spadina Ave, 30, 38, 50, 60, 70
Spadina Cir, 60
Spadina Rd, 70, 78
Spring Garden Ave, 92
Spruce St, 56
St Andrew St, 50
St Bartholomew St, 56
St Clair Ave East, 86
St Clair Ave West, 86
St Clements Ave, 90
St George St, 60, 70, 78
St James Ave, 66
St Joseph St, 62
St Mary St, 62
St Nicholas St, 62
St Patrick St, 42, 52
St Paul St, 46
St Paul's Sq, 74
St Thomas St, 72
Stadium Road, 28
Stanley Ave, 38
Station St, 32
Stephanie St, 50
Stewart St, 38
Strachan Ave, 26
Sullivan St, 50
Sultan St, 72
Sumach St, 46, 56, 66
Summerhill Ave, 82
Summerhill Gdn, 82
Surrey Place, 62
Sussex Ave, 60
Sussex St, 58
Sydenham St, 46

T

Tacoma Ave, 82
Taddle Creek Rd, 62
Tamworth Rd, 92
Tecumseth St, 38
Temperance St, 42
The Esplanade, 34, 44, 46
Thornwood Rd, 82
Toronto St, 44
Tower Rd, 60
Tranby Ave, 72
Tranmer Ave, 88
Trefann St, 46
Treford Pl, 48
Trinity St, 46
Tullis Dr, 88

U

Ulster St, 58, 60
University Ave, 42, 52
Upper Madison Ave, 92

V

Vanauley St, 40
VanKoughnet St, 58
Vermont Ave, 76
Victoria St, 44, 54

W

Wales Ave, 48, 50
Walker Ave, 80
Walmer Rd, 70, 78
Walmsley Blvd, 86
Walnut Ave, 38
Walton St, 52
Washington Ave, 60, 70
Webster Ave, 72
Wellesley Ave, 66
Wellesley La, 64
Wellesley Pl, 64
Wellesley St East, 64, 66
Wellesley St West, 62
Wellington St East, 44
Wellington St West, 38, 40, 42
Wells St, 68, 70
Whitaker Ave, 38
Whitehall Rd, 82
Whitney Ave, 84
Widmer St, 40
Wilburton Rd, 86
Wilkins Ave, 46
Willcox St, 60
Willis St, 38
Wilton St, 34, 44
Winchester St, 66
Windsor St, 40
Wolseley St, 38
Wood St, 64
Woodlawn Ave East, 82
Woodlawn Ave West, 80, 86
Wrentham Pl, 82
Wychwood Ave, 76
Wychwood Pk, 76

Y

Yarmouth Gdns, 76
Yarmouth Rd, 74
Yonge 32, 34, 42, 44, 52, 54, 62, 64, 72, 74, 80, 82, 88, 90, 92
York Sq, 72
York St, 32, 42
Yorkville Ave, 72

Neighbourhoods Origins of street names

Many of Toronto's downtown streets were named after personalities of the day. Here's an introduction to some of them.

Bathurst Street
The third Earl of Bathurst was Secretary of War for the Colonies from 1812-1827 under George IV. He never visited Canada.

Bloor Street
Joseph Bloore, despite his strong Methodist leanings, built one of York's first breweries near Sherbourne Street. The 'e' is now missing from the street.

Carlton Street
Guy Carleton, Lord of Dorchester, fought the French in Québec in 1759 and later became Lt-Gov of Québec from 1766-1768.

Cumberland Street
One of Yorkville's first councillors, James Wallis, was born in the former county of Cumberland, England.

Danforth Avenue
Asa Danforth was the American contractor who built the road from the Town of York to Kingston.

Dufferin Street
This formed the early western side of the city and was known as the Side Line. It was re-named in 1876 after Governor General Lord Dufferin, who opened the first Canadian National Exhibition here in 1878.

Dundas Street
John Graves Simcoe had this built as a military road in case the Americans attacked York. It was named after the Right Honourable Henry Dundas, who was British Home Secretary at the time.

Gardiner Expressway
Frederick Goldwin Gardiner became the first chairman of Metropolitan Toronto when it was formed in 1953. He pressed vigorously for construction of the expressway in 1955.

Longboat Avenue
Thomas Charles Longboat was born on the Six Nations Reserve near Brantford. He won the Boston Marathon in 1907 and the World's Professional Marathon Championship in 1909.

Richmond Street
Charles Lennox was the fourth Duke of Richmond, who came to Canada in 1818 from England to become governor-in-chief of British North America.

Wellesley Street
The first Duke of Wellington was Arthur Wellesley, who defeated Napoléon at the Battle of Waterloo.

Accommodation

First, check out the neighbourhoods below to see where you want to stay. Then select a place that suits your budget. All accommodation listed comes recommended.

Hotels, motels, backpackers, **99**   Bed & breakfast, **103**

Accommodation **Hotels, motels, backpackers**

Suburban Toronto - map *Toronto*

CROWNE PLAZA HOTEL TORONTO-DON VALLEY
1250 Eglinton Avenue East • 416-449-4111• **ichotelsgroup.com** • room rate $98 • all major credit cards.

DELTA TORONTO EAST
2035 Kennedy Road • 416-299-1500 • **www4.deltahotels.com** • room rate $200 • all major credit cards.

VALHALLA INN
1 Valhalla Inn Road • 416-239-2391 • **valhalla-inn.com** • room rate $130 • all major credit cards.

WESTIN PRINCE HOTEL
900 York Mills Road • 416-444-2511 • **princehotels.co.jp/toronto** • room rate $180.00 • all major credit cards,

Harbourfront Park - map 4

RADISSON PLAZA HOTEL ADMIRAL TORONTO-HARBOURFRONT
249 Queen's Quay West • 416-203-3333 • **radisson.com/torontoca_admiral** • room rate $130 • all major credit cards.

RENAISSANCE TORONTO DOWNTOWN
1 Blue Jays Way • 416-341-7100 • **marriott.com** • room rate $170 • all major credit cards.

Harbourfront Centre - map 5

WESTIN HARBOUR CASTLE HOTEL
1 Harbour Square • 416-869-1600 • **westin.com/harbourcastle** • room rate $200 • all major credit cards.

Queen's Quay East - map 6

NOVOTEL TORONTO CENTRE
45 The Esplanade • 416-367-8900 • **novotel.com** • room rate $220 • all major credit cards.

Queen's Quay West - map 8

TRAVELODGE TORONTO DOWNTOWN MOTEL
621 King Street West • 416-504-7441 • **travelodgetorontodowntown.com** • room rate $120 single, $130 double • all major credit cards.

Fashion District - map 9

CANADIANA BACKPACKERS INN
42 Widmer Street • 416-598-9090 • **canadianalodging.com** • $25 dorm bed • Visa and Mastercard.

GLOBAL VILLAGE BACKPACKERS
460 King Street West • 416-703-3884 • **globalbackpackers.com** • $28 single in four-bed mixed dorm • Visa and Mastercard.

HOLIDAY INN ON KING
370 King Street West • 416-599-4000 • **hiok.com** • room rate $160 • all major credit cards.

HOTEL LE GERMAIN
30 Mercer Street • 416-345-9500 • **germaintoronto.com** • room rate $225 • all major credit cards.

SOHO METROPOLITAN TORONTO
318 Wellington Street West • 416-599-8800 • **metropolitan.com/soho** • room rate $250 • all major credit cards.

Financial District - map 10

FAIRMONT ROYAL YORK HOTEL
100 Front Street West • 416-368-2511 • **fairmont.com/royalyork** • room rate $180 • all major credit cards.

HILTON TORONTO
145 Richmond Street West • 416-869-3456 • **hilton.com** • room rate $190 • all major credit cards.

HOTEL VICTORIA
56 Yonge Street • 416-363-1666 • **hotelvictoria-toronto.com** • room rate $115 • all major credit cards.

INTERCONTINENTAL TORONTO CENTRE
225 Front Street West • 416-597-1400 • **ichotelsgroup.com** • room rate $190 • all major credit cards.

SHERATON CENTRE HOTEL TORONTO
123 Queen Street West • 416-361-1000 • **sheratontoronto.com** • room rate $170 • major credit cards.

STRATHCONA HOTEL
60 York Street • 416-363-3321 • **thestrathconahotel.com** • room rate $110 • all major credit cards.

St Lawrence - map 11

CAMBRIDGE SUITES HOTEL
15 Richmond Street East • 416-368-1990 • **cambridgesuitestoronto.com** • room rate $210 • all major credit cards.

LE ROYAL MERIDIEN KING EDWARD HOTEL
37 King Street East • 416-863-9700 • **toronto.lemeridien.com** • room rate $180 • all major credit cards.

Room rates quoted can change. You usually get the best price by phoning a hotel directly.

QUALITY HOTEL DOWNTOWN
111 Lombard Street • 416-367-5555 • **toronto.com/qualityhoteldowntown** • room rate $120 • all major credit cards.

Discovery District - map 15

DELTA CHELSEA HOTEL
33 Gerrard Street West • 416-595-1975 • **deltahotels.com** • room rate $170 • all major credit cards.

METROPOLITAN HOTEL TORONTO
108 Chestnut Street • 416-977-5000 • **metropolitan.com/toronto** • room rate $135 • all major credit cards.

TORONTO MARRIOTT DOWNTOWN EATON CENTRE
525 Bay Street • 416-597-9200 • **marriott.com** • room rate $210 • all major credit cards.

Dundas Square - map 16

BOND PLACE HOTEL
65 Dundas Street East • 416-362-6061 • **bondplacehoteltoronto.com** • room rate $90 (low season) • all major credit cards.

COMFORT SUITES CITY CENTRE
200 Dundas Street East • 416-362-7700 • **toronto.com** • room rate $110 • all major credit cards.

DAYS HOTEL TORONTO DOWNTOWN
30 Carlton Street • 416-977-6655 • **dayshoteltoronto.ca** • room rate $95 • all major credit cards.

GRAND HOTEL & SUITES
225 Jarvis Street • 416-863-9000 • **grandhoteltoronto.com** • room rate $170 • all major credit cards.

NEILL-WYCIK COLLEGE HOTEL
96 Gerrard Street East • 416-977-2320 • **neill-wycik.com** • open to the public from May through September • room rate $40 single, $60 double • Visa and Mastercard.

PANTAGES SUITES HOTEL & SPA
200 Victoria Street • 416-362-1777 • **pantageshotel.com** • room rate $190 • all major credit cards.

PRIMROSE BEST WESTERN HOTEL
111 Carlton Street • 416-977-8000 • **torontoprimrosehotel.com** • room rate $190 • all major credit cards.

RAMADA HOTEL & SUITES
300 Jarvis Street • 416-977-4823 • **ramadahotelandsuites.com** • room rate $90 • all major credit cards.

Regent Park - map 17

AMSTERDAM GUEST HOUSE
209 Carlton Street • 416-921-9797 • **ca.geocities.com/amsterdamreservations@rogers.com** • room rate $85 • Visa and Mastercard.

Queen's Park - map 20

SUTTON PLACE HOTEL
955 Bay Street • 416-924-9221 • **toronto.suttonplace.com** • room rate $160 • all major credit cards.

Church-Wellesley Village - map 21

CLARION HOTEL & SUITES SELBY
592 Sherbourne Street • 416-921-3142 • **hotelselby.com** • room rate $100 • all major credit cards.

COMFORT HOTEL DOWNTOWN
15 Charles Street East • 416-924-1222 • **toronto.com** • room rate $110 • all major credit cards.

ISABELLA HOTEL & SUITES
556 Sherbourne Street • 416-922-2203 • **tours.travelhero.com** • room rate $80 • Visa and Mastercard.

MARRIOTT COURTYARD TORONTO DOWNTOWN
475 Yonge Street • 416-924-0611 • **marriott.com** • room rate $140 • all major credit cards.

TORONTO TOWN INN SUITES HOTEL
620 Church Street • 416-964-3311 • **towninn.com** • room rate $140 • all major credit cards.

The Annex - map 24

GLOBAL GUEST HOUSE
9 Spadina Road • 416-923-1208 • room rate $60 single, $70 double • Visa and Mastercard.

MADISON MANOR BOUTIQUE HOTEL
16 Madison Avenue • 416-922-5579 • **madisonavenuepub.com** • room rate $120 • all major credit cards.

QUALITY HOTEL MIDTOWN
280 Bloor Street West • 416-968-0010 • **choicehotels.ca** • room rate $120 • all major credit cards.

When you book a hotel room, remember that most establishments have non-smoking rooms for your comfort. Check out any special weekend packages they might have that will save you money. Also, see if they have high-speed Internet facilities in their rooms.

Yorkville - map 25

FOUR SEASONS HOTEL
21 Avenue Road • 416-964-0411 • **fourseasons.com/toronto** • room rate $340 • all major credit cards.

HOWARD JOHNSON DOWNTOWN TORONTO-YORKVILLE
89 Avenue Road • 416-964-1220 • **hojo.com** • room rate $90 • all major credit cards.

INTERCONTINENTAL TORONTO
220 Bloor Street West • 416-960-5200 • **toronto.intercontinental.com** • room rate $200 • all major credit cards.

PARK HYATT TORONTO
4 Avenue Road • 416-925-1234 • **parktoronto.hyatt.com** • room rate $270 • all major credit cards.

THE HAZELTON HOTEL
5 Hazelton Avenue • 416-928-1859 • this hotel opens early in 2007.

WINDSOR ARMS HOTEL
18 St Thomas Street • 416-971-9666 • **windsorarmshotel.com** • room rate $300 • all major credit cards.

Bloor East - map 26

TORONTO MARRIOTT BLOOR-YORKVILLE
90 Bloor Street East • 416-961-8000 • **marriott.com** • room rate $270 • all major credit cards.

North York Centre - map 35

NOVOTEL TORONTO NORTH YORK
3 Park Home Avenue • 416-733-2929 • **novotel.com** • room rate $150 • all major credit cards.

Accommodation Bed & breakfast

You can either Google your way around to find an individual establishment that looks interesting, or you can contact one of the reservation services below. These services have been in business for years, and each has a good reputation for matching guests with private hosts. Before you go searching for a B&B, take time to look through the Toronto neighbourhood section to get an idea of where you might want to stay. Remember that downtown locations are usually more expensive than those in the suburbs. Also, try to find a place close to a bus stop or, better still, a subway station.

DOWNTOWN TORONTO ASSOCIATION OF BED AND BREAKFAST GUEST HOUSES
416-410-3938 • **bnbinfo.com**

TORONTO BED AND BREAKFAST RESERVATION SERVICE
705-738-9449 • **torontobandb.com**

Places

The city has an exceptional diversity of places. A gold skyscraper grabs your attention in the Financial District. An enormous bursting crystal encases a major museum. There's a genuine castle up on a hill, and a house built in 1794. Toronto is a city where you can browse through street markets, get close to history and the arts, or stroll through one of 2,000 parks and wooded ravines. Wherever you decide to go, the world's tallest building will always be looking down on you.

Buildings, **104**

Historical sites & churches, **113**

Markets, **123**

Museums, galleries & public art, **126**

Parks, beaches, squares & zoos, **136**

Places **Buildings**

The CN Tower is only one of the impressive buildings in Toronto. For over 200 years, architects from around the world have come here to create distinctive structures that are constantly changing the skyline and capturing the imagination of the city.

CASA LOMA
1 Austin Terrace • map 28 • 416-923-1171 • **casaloma.org** • open daily, 9:30 AM – 4:00 PM • admission $ • subway: Spadina and take Davenport 127 bus.

Not too many cities in North America can boast they have a genuine castle on their tax rolls. Toronto happens to be lucky in this regard. Casa Loma is designed in massive Norman, Gothic and Romanesque styles, towering over 2.4 ha of gardens and woodland overlooking the western part of the city. The Casa Loma Stables, just north on Walmer Road, and accessible through a tunnel from the castle, are worth a visit. The whole set-up is a bit odd to say the least, but the castle has manufactured a slightly insane history for itself, plus a touch of quasi-Medieval grandeur. Justifiably, it's a top attraction for tourists and locals alike.

CITY HALL
100 Queen Street West • map 15 • 416-338-0338 • **city.toronto.on.ca** • open weekdays during office hours • subway: Queen and take Queen streetcar west to Bay Street.

Before the CN Tower came along, city hall was Toronto's signature building. Finnish architect Viljo Revell won an international competition to design the complex from among 500 entries from 40 countries. Governor General Georges Vanier opened the building on September 13, 1965, ten months after Revell's death. It's one of the best pieces of modern architecture downtown, with two concave towers enclosing an oyster-shaped council chamber. A stylized version of the building forms the city's official logo.

CN TOWER
301 Front Street West • map 4 • 416-868-6937 • **cntower.ca** • open daily • admission
$ • subway: Union and take the Skywalk.

At 553 m, this is the world's tallest building. When it opened in 1976 the
Guinness Book of Records noted it was the "world's tallest free-standing structure," but gave it the 'world's tallest building' designation in later editions.
Even when the new 541 m World Trade Centre is built in New York City, the
CN Tower will still retain its record height. Six glass-walled elevators whisk
passengers to the top in a dizzying 58 seconds. The tower wasn't built primarily for tourists, even though it welcomes over 2,000,000 visitors each year.
Its main function is to consolidate and improve the city's vast electronic communications systems. Originally, CN meant 'Canadian National'. It now
means 'Canada's National'.

COMMERCE COURT NORTH
25 King Street West • map 10 • 416-861-3475 • **emporis.com** • open daily • subway:
King.

Esthetically, the main 57-storey CIBC tower, built in 1972, is secondary to the
old bank building next door that it replaced. This aging landmark near the
corner of King and Bay streets is known as Commerce Court North and
served as the headquarters of the Bank of Commerce when it opened in 1931.
Later, the Commerce amalgamated with the Canadian Imperial Bank to form
the CIBC. The old architectural icon once held the distinction of being the
tallest building in the British Empire and its observation deck 34 floors above
ground was the CN Tower of its day. The inside has been preserved and
offers one of the most beautiful examples of corporate interior restoration in
the city.

EATON CENTRE
Yonge Street between Dundas & Queen streets • map 15 • 416-598-8700 •
torontoeatoncentre.com • open daily • subway: Dundas or Queen.

With the exception of the PATH underground walkway, more people go
through the Toronto Eaton Centre each weekday than through any other
place in the city. It's also believed to be our top tourist attraction. The vast
four-level atrium, built in 1979 and housing nearly 300 stores, was inspired
by Milan's galleria. A few years ago the Yonge Street side and main west
entrance were re-designed to make the complex more accessible from the
street. The north end was then completely rebuilt to accommodate changes to
Dundas Square. Outside the northwest entrance is the historical Trinity
Square that few of us even know exists. Without doubt, it's one of the most
pleasant and historical squares in the city. The Eaton Centre was named after
Timothy Eaton, whose first department store opened at the southern end of
the complex back in 1869. Eaton's went on to become a Canadian merchandising monolith, but went into receivership and was taken over by Sears
Canada in the fall of 1999. However, the centre retained the Eaton name.

FIRST CANADIAN PLACE
100 King Street West • map 10 • 416-862-8138 • **firstcanadianplace.com** • open
daily • subway: King.

105

The 72-floor complex, clad in white marble and built in 1976, is the highest office tower in Canada. When you add the mechanical rooms at the top, the building is 298 m high. Italian crystal chandeliers light its impressive white Italian marble main lobby. The building's main tenant is the Bank of Montreal. First Canadian Place arrived in the Financial District at a time when the major banks seemed determined to out-build each other with ever more impressive structures. Together with other large bank complexes at this intersection, it forms a major component of the PATH underground walkway system.

HERITAGE SQUARE
161-181 Bay Street (BCE Place interior) • map 10 • 416-777-6480 • bceplacetoronto.com • open daily, 7:00 AM – 2:00 AM • subway: King or Union.

This dramatic indoor space, completed in 1993, was the brainchild of Spanish architect Santiago Calatrava. His design was in response to the city's 1986 edict that any commercial building over 20,000 sq m should devote 1% of its total cost to art. Rather than scatter some expensive sculpture around, he conceived that the galleria itself would be designed as a self-standing piece of art. The result is an inwardly inclined parabolic structure 130 m long, 14 m wide and 27 m high. It's one downtown building that should not to be missed. The Heritage Square galleria in BCE Place is understandably one of the most photographed indoor sights in the city. Several television commercials and movies have used this location because of the spectacular vaulted glass ceiling that arches above a dramatic pedestrian mall, showering everything in natural light.

NATIONAL BALLET SCHOOL
372 Jarvis Street • map 21 • 416-640-1595 • nbs.enb.on.ca • subway: Carlton.

In June 2003 work began to convert two historic buildings on Jarvis Street, previously used as the English network headquarters of the Canadian Broadcasting Corporation, into the new National Ballet School. The $87.5 million project, under the direction of architect Phil Goldsmith, refurbished Havergall Ladies' College (1898) and Northfield House (1856) and joined them with the school's existing Betty Oliphant theatre next door. Havergall College is now the school's Margaret McCain Academic Building and Northfield House has become the Celia Franca Centre. The late Ms Franca was the founder of the National Ballet School back in 1959, turning it into one of the continent's most prestigious ballet schools.

NATIONAL TRADE CENTRE – NTC (DIRECT ENERGY CENTRE)
100 Princes Boulevard, Exhibition Place • map 2 • 416-263-3000 • ntc.on.ca • open during events • admission $ included in event • subway: Union and take the 509 Harbourfront streetcar west.

Just in case you might be confused, the Direct Energy Company gave the City of Toronto $7-million so it could put its name on the National Trade Centre. It's new name is the Direct Energy Centre. When the city-owned NTC at Exhibition Place opened in the late 1990s it was the biggest in the country and now ranks as the 6th largest in North America. Its modern curved design, with four signature cylindrical glass turrets, encloses almost 93,000 sq m of connectable space, plus that of the refurbished Automotive Building next door, which is connected through a tunnel. Within the complex is the Ricoh Coliseum, a $38-million multi-purpose sports complex with a seating capacity for 10,000 people. It can be turned into the world's largest indoor lake after being flooded with 4,500,000 litres of water. This is probably the only indoor facility in North America that can hold a major international boat show on water. Two of the city's largest indoor annual events, the Royal Agricultural Winter Fair and the Sportsman's Show, are held here.

NORTH TORONTO RAILWAY STATION
10 Scrivener Square • map 30 • subway: Summerhill, walk one block south on Yonge Street.

There was a railway station here back in the 1880s that provided employment to the residents of the small community of Summerhill. It was demolished and replaced in 1916 with the Venetian-looking structure you see today. The plan by the Canadian Pacific Railway was to make Summerhill the line's main terminal for Toronto. However, work was underway in 1914 to build another major rail terminal at the bottom of Yonge Street for the Grand Trunk Railway. In 1927, after the demise of the Grand Trunk and the emergence of Canadian National Railways, the southern terminal, called Union Station, dominated passenger traffic to and from Toronto. The North Toronto Railway station was then abandoned and remained virtually boarded up until the turn of this century. The station has now been renovated to its original state, and the 60-year-old liquor store there is one of the most up-scale in the country.

ONE KING WEST
1 King Street West • map 10 • emporis.com • 416-363-7399 • subway: King.

Technically speaking, this complex, completed in 2005, is the slimmest occupied building in the world. It sits on a sidewalk frontage less than 9 m wide, yet soars 259 m skyward. Look closely as you walk by, otherwise you'll miss it completely. The 48th floor was turned into a single condominium residence that sold for $6,000,000. After clearing the old Dominion Bank building next door, it spreads in width slightly to become a combined hotel-condominium address and the first of three such luxury multi-use buildings approved for the downtown Financial District. One is the Sapphire Tower at Sheppard and Temperance streets that will reach 80 storeys and become an instant glittering blue landmark. The other is the 68-storey titanium-topped Trump International Hotel and Tower on the southeast corner of Bay and Adelaide Streets.

ONTARIO SCIENCE CENTRE
770 Don Mills Road • map Toronto and in detail on the following page • 416-696-3127 • ontariosciencecentre.ca • open daily, 10:00 AM – 5:00 PM • admission $ • subway: Eglinton and take the 34 Eglinton East bus to Don Mills Road.

The 2006 renovation of this venerable science playground cost $40-million dollars and has transformed the complex into one of North America's most interesting places for kids and adults. You're really encouraged to touch stuff, get involved, and be amazed. There are now over 600 exhibits spread among 10 exhibition halls, plus the ever-popular IMAX DOME theatre. The centre was our ambitious project for Canada's centennial year in 1967. The building, which opened two years late and cost six times the estimated $5,000,000 budget, has a brand new forecourt called the Exploration Plaza. The centre seems nothing more than a wide, low-rise building from the outside, but once you step inside you'll find it cascading down into a wooded ravine. Architect Raymond Moriyama, who created the building, also designed the Bata Shoe Museum and Toronto Reference Library.

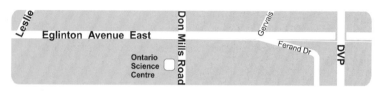

PATH UNDERGROUND WALKWAY
From Front Street West north to Dundas Street West, and from Yonge Street west to John Street • map Underground walkways, page 21 • city.toronto.on.ca/path • subways: Union, King, Queen, Dundas and St Andrew.

This enormous underground city system, which is technically a building, connects 371,600 sq m of commercial spaces with 27 km of climate controlled walkways. Five thousand people work here and the number of pedestrians who use the facility is estimated to be in excess of 150,000 each weekday. The first underground public passage opened in 1900 and joined Eaton's main store at Yonge and Queen streets to its annex. Today's PATH began modestly in the Sixties when some underground shops around the Richmond-Adelaide and Sheraton centres were joined. In 1973 these two complexes were connected underground with others and the idea, based on isolating pedestrians from traffic and bad weather, took flight. It's now believed to be the longest continuous urban underground walkway in the world and the world's largest underground shopping mall. A labyrinth of passageways connects major hotels, transportation terminals, arenas, residential towers and commercial complexes throughout the inner city. Therefore, it's theoretically possible to live downtown and never have to go outside.

PROVINCIAL LEGISLATURE OF ONTARIO
Queen's Park • map 20 • 416-326-1234 • gov.on.ca • weekdays, 8:30 AM – 4:30 PM. Security may be in effect • subway: Queen's Park.

This is the seat of government in Ontario. The building houses the legislative chamber, offices of the speaker, premier, leaders of the opposition parties and press gallery. When the house is sitting you can attend Question Period each weekday at 2:00 PM. For people not acquainted with a parliamentary system of government, Question Period gives the opposition parties an opportunity to question members of the government on any issue of the day. Passes are available in the lobby. For details on the history of the legislature building, see the *Queen's Park Profile* on page 63.

ROYAL BANK PLAZA
200 Bay Street • map 10 • 416-974-3940 • emporis.com • open daily • subway: Union.

No other building in the world had more glass used in its construction than these twin towers – and no other building in modern times has used more gold. In fact, 70,875 g of 24-karat gold was used to coat the inner panes of 14,000 double-glazed windows. This works out to $70 for each window, or over a million dollar's worth of gold for the building. The reason for this seeming extravagance was to improve insulation. Don't try to get rich quick by trying to scrape any gold off the windows because it has been rendered worthless during the coating process. A dramatic banking hall that rises inside to 39 m connects the 40-floor South Tower to the North Tower. The complex cost $100,000,000 by the time it opened in 1979. The fountain outside was then the largest of its kind in North America.

ROYAL YORK HOTEL
100 Front Street West • map 10 • 416-368-2511 • fairmont.com • free access to public areas • subway: Union.

The 1,365-room Fairmont Royal York, the most venerable of our hotels, sits on land that has seen a lot of changes. The first building here was a log cabin built in 1812. Thirty-two years later, Sword's Hotel was erected and 18 years after that the Queen's Hotel took over the site. During the 1880s circuses pitched their tents on this site. It wasn't until June 1929 that the Canadian Pacific Railway opened the doors of its latest jewel in the national hotel chain. The Royal York boasted en suite bathrooms and radios in every room. It even had its own 12-bed hospital and a 12,000-volume library. An in-house concert hall contained a 50-ton pipe organ that was put together with 300 miles of copper wire, making it the largest in the country. There was more than 6,000 sq m of public spaces. The kitchen bakery was capable of turning out 15,000 French rolls every day. The hotel's 20 m long switchboard was manned with 35 operators. It quite simply dominated the city's skyline in both height and width to become the largest hotel in the British Empire. Over the years, the Royal York has cared for guests ranging from royalty and presidents to pop stars and just ordinary, plain folk – and there's now a broadband Internet connection in every room.

SAPPHIRE TOWER
66 Temperance street • map 10 • sapphiretower.com • subway: Queen.

The city's skyline will change in 2006 when construction begins on the Sapphire Tower at the corner of Temperance and Sheppard streets in the Financial District. This dramatic twin cylindrical building, clad in sapphire blue glass, rises 80 storeys from a 15-storey base of Jerusalem gold limestone. On top is a landmark prismatic sphere suspended in a stainless steel frame. The building is designed to house a luxury hotel – the Sapphire Tower Hotel – and upscale condominiums. A full-floor condominium penthouse is believed to cost around $7,000,000. No other occupied building in the country comes close to matching this one in height. It was no secret that local developer Harry Stinson was determined to trump Donald Trump who had previously announced his own 'tallest building in Canada' – the Trump International Hotel and Tower – only two short blocks away. Trump's original plan called for a 68-storey structure, housing a five-star hotel and an upscale condominium property. It is to be completed in 2009. Whoever ends up winning the skyscraper challenge, Toronto's skyline is undergoing an impressive realignment.

SCARBOROUGH CIVIC CENTRE
150 Borough Drive • map Toronto and in detail below • 416-338-0338 •
city.toronto.on.ca • subway: Kennedy & transfer to the LRT for Scarborough Town
Centre.

Raymond Moriyama was the architect for many of our prominent public buildings including the award-winning Scarborough Civic Centre. It's more than 25
years since this dramatic piece of modern architecture was built to house the
municipal offices of the City of Scarborough and the Scarborough Board of
Education. People in neighbouring Toronto were aghast at the time that
'Scarberia' would finally have a building worth more than a passing glance.
Since then, Scarborough has become part of Toronto and its prized city hall
demoted to a civic centre. Moriyama's idea was to design a building around a
soaring interior central public meeting space, placing citizens at its centre.
Circled above, and looking downwards, are the centre's open plan offices.

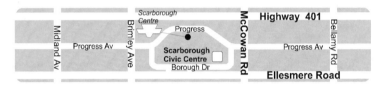

St PAUL'S ANGLICAN CHURCH
227 Bloor Street East • map 25 • 416-961-8116 • **stpaulsbloor.org** • Monday –
Friday, noon – 2:00 PM; Sunday services • subway: Bloor-Yonge and go one and a
half blocks east on Bloor Street East.

St Paul's has a seating capacity close to 3,000 and is one of the largest churches in Canada. It represents the second oldest Anglican parish in the city after
St James' cathedral. The first church on this site was a wooden structure built
in 1842. In 1860 it was moved west to the corner of Bloor Street and Avenue
Road and replaced by the more substantial small stone building that remains
in place today. St Paul's church, designed by prolific local architect E J
Lennox, opened in 1913 to replace the smaller church to its right. Lennox
based his plans for this new building on London's historic St Paul's cathedral. Toronto's St Paul's is washed with history, having stone relics from
British churches dating back to 563 AD displayed just inside its front door on
the north wall. It is a dramatic introduction to the longevity of Christianity.
The focal point of St Paul's is the magnificent Rose Window, set above seven
cusped windows, and believed to be one of the largest of its kind. A stylized
version of it is used as St Paul's logo. This is a popular place to drop into at
lunch time and spend a quiet moment of contemplation.

TORONTO CONVENTION CENTRE
255 Front Street West • map 10 • 416-585-8000 • **mtccc.com** • open to public when
events not scheduled • subway: Union or St Andrew.

Canada's largest convention facility was built in two stages, finally cascading
down an embankment south from the main entrance on Front Street West to
Bremner Boulevard. There are 185,800 sq m of space available and the complex can be re-arranged into 70 fully-equipped meeting rooms ranging in size

from 46 sq m to 4,600 sq m. The 1,330-seat John Bassett Theatre, with a full orchestra pit, forms part of the complex. An underground parking area holds 1,700 vehicles and a further 17,000 spaces are available within easy walking distance. The centre attracts dozens of local and international events annually, including the Canadian International Auto Show each February which attracts well over 300,000 visitors.

TORONTO DOMINION CENTRE (TD CENTRE)
55 King Street West • map 10 • 416-869-1144 • tdcentre.ca • open daily • subway: King.

Internationally-acclaimed Dutch architect Mies Van Der Rohe designed the complex that began a massive redevelopment of the city's Financial District back in 1967. Originally, there were two towers; a 56-storey headquarters for the Toronto Dominion Bank and another for the Royal Trust. Since then the complex has expanded to include a total of six similar buildings for other major corporations. It represents the largest collection of Mies Van Der Rohe buildings in the world and incorporates the façade of the old Toronto Stock Exchange into the eastern wall of the complex. On the ground floor of each building there is a permanent display of Canadian art, some of which is easily visible from outside. When it was built, the TD Centre formed the beginnings of the PATH underground walkway system in the Financial District. Above ground the area is laced with swaths of open green space that is peppered with whimsical statuary, providing a popular summer lunchtime spot for local office workers.

TORONTO REFERENCE LIBRARY
789 Yonge Street • map 26 • 416-393-7131 • tpl.toronto.on.ca; virtual library vrl.tpl.toronto.on.ca • Monday – Thursday, 10:00 AM – 8:00 PM; Friday & Saturday, 10:00 AM – 5:00 PM; Sunday, 1:30 PM – 5:00 PM • subway: Bloor-Yonge.

This is the main library of the Toronto library system and is the largest in Canada. The building, designed by Raymond Moriyama and opened in 1977, houses both the Sir Arthur Conan Doyle and Audubon collections. The Doyle collection consists of 5,000 books and assorted memorabilia housed in a replica of Sherlock Holmes' study at 221B Baker Street in London. The Audubon collection has a four-volume folio of 435 hand-coloured, life-sized birds that was originally published between 1827 and 1838. The Baldwin Room specializes in Canadian history, and the Genealogy and Local History section has a fine collection of modern and historic maps of the local area and around the world. Library staff answers about 9,000,000 questions annually and encourages you to log on to the Virtual Reference Library (**vrl.tpl.toronto.on.ca**) for an amazing source of information.

TORONTO STOCK EXCHANGE (TSX)
130 King Street West • map 10 • 416-947-4700 • tse.com • open each business day • subway: St Andrew.

Since 1983, when the Exchange moved here from around the corner on Bay Street, hundreds of billions of investment dollars have raced at computerized speed through North America's fourth largest and most modern stock exchange. It all happens quietly. You won't find any Hollywood drama on the trading floor because the TSX was the first exchange on the continent to get rid of all that Tinseltown hype and confetti. However, "friendly, nicely-dressed guides" will be delighted to tell you stories about the old-fashioned way of doing business back over on Bay Street and, when you've been told everything you want to know, you can go away and play with the interactive games and exhibits. Just give them a call and they will tell you when is the best time to pay them a visit.

TRINITY COLLEGE CHAPEL
6 Hoskin Avenue • map 19 • 416-978-3288 (Chaplain's office) •
trinity.toronto.edu/divinity/chapel • daily, 7:00 AM – 10:00 PM • subway: Museum.

Sir Gilbert Scott, architect of Liverpool's Gothic cathedral, created this chapel for the University of Toronto's Trinity College. It was a gift from Gerald Larkin of the Salada Tea Company to a college that traces its Anglican ancestry back to 1851. The modified Gothic interior, built by Italian stonemasons, is over 30 m long and rises more than 14 m at the vault bosses. Sir Gilbert was also famous for designing the British Post Office's distinctive red telephone booths. The chapel is one of the finest examples of traditional architecture in the country and among the city's best acoustic spaces.

TRUMP INTERNATIONAL HOTEL AND TOWER
325 Bay Street • map 10 • 416-214-2800 (during development) • trumptoronto.ca •
subway: King.

Thirty years ago, Canada's five major banks competed with each other to build the most impressive skyscrapers in the Financial District. Nowadays, the race is on to build the tallest and best hotel-condominium towers. New York developer, Donald Trump, was the first to announce his "breathtaking 68-storey landmark for Toronto" and his first such development outside the United States. "The thing that excites me most is the architecture," Trump declared. Indeed, the building's impressive needle spire will demand attention. When The Donald first announced his plans for the 2009 opening in Toronto back in 2003, he had hoped his project would be the tallest residential tower in the country. However, a local Toronto developer is building the Sapphire Tower just around the corner that will open earlier and be 12 storeys higher.

UNION STATION
67 Front Street West • map 10 • city.toronto.on.ca/union_station • open daily •
subway: Union.

The block on Front Street West from Bay to York streets is home to the largest and busiest passenger rail terminal in Canada. It is the major station for Via Rail, GO Transit and the TTC subway. Over 150,000 passengers pass through here every business day, which is more than those who go through Pearson International airport. Union Station, originally intended to serve the Grand Trunk Railway before it went bankrupt, was completed in 1927 by Canadian National Railways which became the Trunk's successor. The station's dramatic Great Hall – measuring 76 m long, 27 m wide and 27 m high – takes its place among other great architectural triumphs by railways throughout many major cities of North America. The *beaux-arts* style uses 22 Doric exterior columns, each weighing 22 tons and rising 12 m from the sidewalk. John M. Lyle, who created the Royal Alexandra Theatre, was the architect most responsible for Union Station's design. Plans are underway to proceed with the station's first major refurbishment in over half a century.

Places Historical sites and churches, 1794 - 1899

The city's oldest building is Scadding cabin, built in 1794. Scores of other old structures also survived the Fifties when a demolition derby seemed determined to erase Toronto's architectural heritage. Now there's a sudden fervor to preserve what's left.

BANK OF UPPER CANADA
252 Adelaide Street East • map 11 • subway: King and take the 504 King streetcar east to George Street, then walk north to Adelaide Street East.

This is one of the oldest buildings in the city and one of three consecutive buildings along this block on Adelaide Street East that distills Toronto's early days. Outside its rather sombre and lonely exterior, a plaque reads: "Chartered in 1821, the Bank of Upper Canada, was until its demise in 1866, one of British North America's leading banks. It played a significant role in the development of Upper Canada – supplying currency, protecting savings and making loans – and aided Toronto's rise as the commercial centre of the colony. This building, opened in 1827, was the second home of the bank. Its design reflects the image of conservative opulence favoured by financial institutions of the time. The portico, designed by John G. Howard, a leading architect of the period, was added about 1844." There's no doubt that this bank was an impressive financial player in its day. The building's rear extension north along George Street now houses private offices.

BLACK CREEK PIONEER VILLAGE
Steeles Avenue West at Murray Ross Parkway • map Toronto and in detail on the following page • 416-736-1733 • blackcreek.ca • daily, except December 25 & 26 • admission $ • subway: Jane and transfer to bus 35 going north.

Daniel and Elizabeth Stong were the original owners of this site back in 1816 when they set about establishing a farm from hundreds of acres of forested wilderness. Before long they had succeeded in building a grain barn, piggery and smokehouse. These buildings now form the heart of Black Creek Pioneer Village where smoke still curls from the chimneys and their home still welcomes visitors. With over 35 carefully restored 1860s shops and homes, the settlement re-creates the life and times of Upper Canada. Here's where you can talk to the blacksmith, the cabinetmaker and others about their crafts. Costumed guides take you around original buildings giving you an opportunity to explore village crafts, which make unusual gifts, and are available

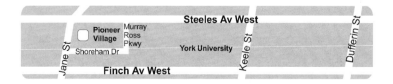

in some of the homes and workshops. The best times to experience the true flavour of the site are during the annual Pioneer Festival held in mid-September, or around the Yuletide season. This is when the village comes into its own and warmly embraces the fall and winter seasons.

CHURCH OF St STEPHEN-IN-THE-FIELDS
103 Bellevue Avenue • map 19 • 416-921-6350 • saintstephens.on.ca • open during services • subway: College and take the 506 bus west to Bellevue Avenue.

St Stephen's was built in a field surrounded by dense forests in 1857. The land was part of the old Bellevue Homestead that included much of what is today's Kensington Market. St Stephen's heritage is that of a 'People's Church' because it was one of the first churches in Toronto to be operated on the principle of a 'free' gospel. Almost everywhere else, parishioners had to pay for their seat in a pew. Here, though, "every sitting was absolutely free to any one, and, you may choose your own place and you will be heartily welcome to occupy it." The building was destroyed by fire in 1865 and rebuilt exactly like the original. Twenty-five years later it was enlarged to its present dimensions. In 1927, St Stephen's became the first Canadian church to broadcast its services via radio to Europe.

CHURCH OF THE HOLY TRINITY
10 Trinity Square, Eaton Centre • map 14 • 416-598-4521 • toronto.anglican.ca/parish/ht • daily, 11:00 AM – 3:00 PM • subway: Dundas.

The church was well north of the city when it was built in 1847 on land donated by John Simcoe Macauley. In those days, like St Stephen's above, it was common practice for the Church of England to charge pew fees. Mary Lambert Swale of Yorkshire, England, paid for the construction and stipulated that "it be free and unappropriated forever" so that working-class parishioners would not be burdened with financial obligations. The building's bricks were made locally in the Don Valley, timbers were taken from the surrounding forest and the roof slate came from England as ballast in British sailing ships. When the Eaton Centre was being built, serious thought was given to demolishing the church and its two adjacent historic church buildings. Sanity finally prevailed and the church, now part of one of the most pleasant squares in the city, continues its 150-year-old work of supporting underprivileged people of all cultures in the inner-city.

DANIEL BROOKE BUILDING
150-154 King Street East • map 11 (area 6F) • subway: King and take the 504 King streetcar east to Jarvis Street.

Here is one of the few surviving commercial buildings from Toronto's days as the Town of York. There's a plaque outside that reads: "This building was first constructed in 1833 for owner Daniel Brooke, a prominent merchant in the Town of York. It was substantially rebuilt between 1848 – 49 prior to the great fire of April 1849 which started in a next door stable. While much of the business district was destroyed, this building escaped major damage. It housed a variety of commercial enterprises over the years, including the prosperous wholesale grocery business of James Austin and Patrick Foy in the 1840s. Austin went on to become a president of the Consumers' Gas Company and of the Dominion Bank. His home, Spadina (page 79), became a museum in 1984. During the mid-19th century, the Daniel Brooke Building contained the offices of *The Patriot*, an influential conservative newspaper."

DE LA SALLE INSTITUTE
258 Adelaide Street East • map 11 • subway: King and take the 504 King streetcar east to George Street and walk north to Adelaide Street East.

Four years after the Bank of Upper Canada collapsed in 1870, the building next door at 252 Adelaide Street East was bought by the Christian Brothers, a Roman Catholic teaching order, to house the De La Salle boys' school. Prior to the move, the school was occupying temporary premises two blocks away at what are now Jarvis and Lombard streets. Two years later the Brothers built an extension to their new property that took it as far east as the old York Post Office, now known as the First Post Office of Toronto. This extended building is one of the earliest surviving reminders of the Roman Catholic Church's entry into what was a dominant Church of England colony. The school remained at this location until 1913 when it moved to Bond Street, beside St. Michael's Cathedral.

ENOCH TURNER SCHOOL
106 Trinity Street • map 12 • **enochturnerschoolhouse.ca** • open daily when private events not being held • subway: King and take the 504 King streetcar east to Trinity Street.

This little-known historical gem is the oldest surviving schoolhouse in Ontario. Enoch Turner established a school for immigrant children here in 1849, just behind Little Trinity Church, and it served this purpose until 1859 when it was converted into the church's Sunday school. The West Hall was added that year and 30 years later was to become a recruiting centre for Canadians wanting to sign up for the Boer War. During both World wars it continued the tradition of being allied with servicemen and was turned into a 'home away from home' for members of the armed forces. During the Great Depression the schoolhouse was converted into a soup kitchen and served about 1,500 meals every week to destitute residents. Beginning in 1970, the schoolhouse was restored to its original condition and declared a Heritage site 30 years later. These days, the classroom is still there, complete with its original desks, ink wells, chalkboard and a pot-bellied stove. It's not hard to sit among this memorabilia and imagine all the stories this place could tell. For those not interested in history, the old school makes a wonderful setting for wedding receptions.

FLATIRON BUILDING
49 Wellington Street East • map 11 • open during business hours • subway: King and walk east along King Street East and south on Church Street.

On this corner, in 1832, a dead man was found lying in the mud. He was the first case of cholera that was about to affect more than a quarter of the population of the Town of York. Across the street, along then Henrietta Lane, were the town's notorious brothels that ended up being blamed as the crucible for the epidemic. This is also the spot where the city's first street gaslight was illuminated in 1841. The Romanesque-Gothic building standing here today, and built in 1892, is more correctly named the Gooderham Building and was the corporate headquarters for the Gooderham and Worts' distillery empire. Even though it was built ten years earlier, it has more than a passing resemblance to New York's famous Fuller (Flatiron) Building on a triangular block at Fifth Avenue, Broadway and W 23rd Street. But the one here in Toronto distinguishes itself by being the first building in the city to have had an electric passenger elevator. It has become one of the most photographed pieces of architecture in town, especially its western wall overlooking Berczy Park which displays the mesmerizing work of artist Derek Besant. In 1998, Michael and Anne Tippin completely renovated the building in the belief that Toronto's architectural heritage should be preserved intact for future generations.

FORT YORK
100 Garrison Road • map 3 • 416-392-6907 • **city.toronto.on.ca** • open daily, 10:00 AM – 5:00 PM, but closed during the Christmas season • admission $ • subway: St Andrew and take a 504, or 508 streetcar west to Strachan Avenue.

When Lieutenant Governor John Graves Simcoe arrived at the future site of Toronto in 1793, one of his first priorities was to construct a fort to house a military garrison. With the help of the Queen's Rangers, the Loyalist Regiment he commanded in the Revolutionary War, he chose a site two miles west of the original Town of York. His instincts about a potential American attack on the new colony proved accurate and American troops invaded and occupied York twice during the War of 1812, destroying most of it in the process. After the war the fort was rebuilt, but fell into disrepair towards the end of the 19th century. In 1909 the city bought Fort York and restored eight of its original buildings as part of Toronto's centennial celebrations. The present buildings are a combination of these restored original structures from the 1813 – 1815 period and replica buildings of the same era. The fort comes alive with explosive charm on the first Monday in August (Simcoe Day) when soldiers put on a display of musketry. During the rest of the year this national historic site re-creates conditions during the earliest days of the Town of York and its defence against the Americans during the War of 1812.

GOODERHAM AND WORTS HISTORIC DISTILLERY DISTRICT
55 Mill Street • map 12 • 416-364-1177 • **thedistillerydistrict.com** • open daily • subway: Union and take the 72A bus to Mill Street.

This complex of old Victorian industrial buildings, regarded as being among the finest in North America, has become one of the city's most popular destinations. It all started in 1832 when William Gooderham and his brother-in-law, James Worts, built a wind-driven gristmill to convert surplus grain into whiskey. The windmill that powered the operation was later to be used as the pivotal survey point for laying out the city. A quarter century later they had parlayed this fledgling operation into Toronto's largest employer housed within the province's largest industrial complex. It soon became internationally renowned for its brand of Canadian whiskey. The present buildings, dating from 1859 till the end of the 19th century, are the result of a re-building program that took place after a fire destroyed most of the original complex in 1859. In 1926 the company merged with Hiram Walker Co. and manufacturing operations finally came to an end in 1990. After lying dormant and boarded-up for a decade, the 45 buildings emerged in 2000 as the object of a major restoration effort that has resulted in a stunningly handsome mixture of restaurants, art spaces, retail outlets and performance stages. The cobblestone streets and alleys once again echo with human activity and the area has been declared a national historical site.

GREAT FIRE OF 1849
166 King Street East • map 11 (area 7F) • subway: King and take the 504 King streetcar east to Jarvis Street.

At about one o'clock in the morning on April 7, 1849 a fire broke out in a stable behind Covey's Inn, a popular tavern on King Street. No one knows exactly what caused it, but it went on to consume the town's commercial district. Witnesses said the flames could be seen across the lake as far away as St Catharines. The tolling of the bell at St James church, which was used as the town's fire alarm, woke up the population. Within minutes, flames had reached the church and the bell melted. The water company building was burned to the ground, leaving people no alternative but to form hastily organized bucket brigades. Virtually everything from Adelaide Street, south to Front Street and from Church Street to Parliament Street was razed to the ground. Incredibly, there was only one casualty. A reporter working for *The Patriot* newspaper next door to Covey's Inn was overcome by smoke and died. Equally amazing is the fact the building in which he died survived with little damage and stands today on the northeast corner of King and Jarvis streets.

HENRY SCADDING HOUSE
6 Trinity Square, Eaton Centre • map 15 • subway: Dundas.

In a small and little known open space off the northwest side of the Eaton Centre is Trinity Square. Here, you'll find three historical buildings linking the city with its past: Holy Trinity Church (1847), the Old Rectory (1861), and next to that is Henry Scadding House, built in 1860, and the home of the Rev. Henry Scadding. The historic plaque on this building reads: "Scadding was born in Devonshire, England in 1813, and came to Upper Canada in 1821. Educated at Upper Canada College and Cambridge University, he was ordained to the Anglican priesthood at St. James Church, Toronto, in 1838, and the same year became Master of Classics at Upper Canada College. In 1847 Scadding was appointed first rector of the nearby Church of the Holy Trinity, where he served until 1875. He lived in this town house from its completion in 1862 until his death. Here Scadding, a noted scholar, wrote numerous religious, literary, and historical works, including his best-known book, *Toronto of Old* in 1873."

LITTLE TRINITY CHURCH
417 King Street East • map 12 • 416-367-0272 • littletrinity.on.ca • open during services • subway: King and take the 504 King streetcar east to Trinity Street.

This is the oldest surviving church building in Toronto. Its cornerstone was laid on July 20, 1843 and its first service was held only seven months later. The building was largely financed through donations from William Gooderham, James Worts and Enoch Turner, all prominent local distillers and brewers. Local craftsmen gave their time freely during construction and bricks were donated from clay mined in the Don Valley. The architect was Henry Bowyer Lane, a twenty-five-year-old immigrant from England who drew up plans for the church in a neo-Gothic tradition that virtually copied an 1839 church on Gem Street in Birmingham, England. Little Trinity was best known in its heyday as the church that welcomed the first wave of immigrants from Ireland.

McMASTER HALL
270 Bloor Street West • map 25 • 416-408-2825 • rcmusic.ca • open weekdays, but phone ahead for admission • subway: St George.

The plaque outside this imposing old reddish Victorian building, just past the Royal Ontario Museum, reads as follows: "This building was designed by the Toronto firm of Langley, Langley and Burke, specialists in church architecture, to house Toronto Baptist College. The structure typifies the High Victorian style popular in the 1880's. Its chief characteristics include rock-faced masonry, decorative stone and brick patterns, massive dormers and chimneys, and facades with projecting bays and recessed panels. Senator William McMaster financed the construction of the College, which opened in 1881. After plans for federation with the University of Toronto were abandoned, the College was united in 1887 with Woodstock College to form McMaster University, which moved to Hamilton in 1930. This building was acquired by the University of Toronto and has housed the Royal Conservatory of Music since 1963."

METROPOLITAN UNITED CHURCH
56 Queen Street East • map 10 • 416-363-0331 • metunited.org • subway: Queen and take the 501Queen streetcar east to Church street.

Metropolitan has a long history of worship and service that began in 1818 in what is now the commercial heart of Toronto. The first building housing the congregation was a small Methodist chapel located on nearby King Street. Membership grew, along with population, so in 1831 another site was acquired on Adelaide Street, and a Georgian-style building was opened in 1833 that could accommodate 1,000 people. In 1868 the Methodist Church bought the present property and built Metropolitan Wesleyan Methodist Church, which was dedicated in 1872. The building seated 2,000 and was described as Canada's 'cathedral of Methodism.' This is the grandest of the original Methodist churches in the city. The respected Casavant organ makers of Québec built over 8,000 pipes into the church's instrument in 1930. Organ and carillon recitals are held during the church's Music at the Metropolitan series from May through October. Today, the church is part of the United Church of Canada.

OLD CITY HALL
60 Queen Street West • map 10 • city.toronto.on.ca • open during business hours with security in effect • subway: Queen and walk one block west to Bay Street.

Torontonians refer to the dark beige building with the big clock tower, facing down Bay Street from Queen Street West, as "old city hall". E J Lennox, the architect who was famous for designing Casa Loma and other prestigious buildings around town, spared no expense when he received the commission in 1887. The final bill was $2,500,000, up considerably from the budgeted $600,000. He created the building from carved stone brought in from the Credit River valley and New Brunswick and managed to get his face carved into the west side of the central arch. When it opened on September 18, 1899, it was hailed as "one of the most magnificent municipal buildings in North America" and one of Canada's most important examples of monumentally scaled city halls. The historic plaque reads: "In one structure, these municipal buildings combined a City Hall, in the east portion, and Court-House, in the west. Massive, round-arched, and richly carved, it is in the Romanesque Revival style, then popular in expanding cities throughout North America. The interior, as complex and monumental as the exterior, includes a large stained glass window by Robert McCausland." The building, which is now used primarily as a court house, was designated as a national historical site in 1989. The Cenotaph is at the bottom of the front steps.

OLD GARRISON BURYING GROUND
Victoria Memorial Park • map 8 (area 9H) • fortyork.ca • subway: King and take the 504 King streetcar west to Portland Street and walk south.

This is the oldest marked burial site in the city, dating back to 1794 when the British army established it here. It lies diagonally across Victoria Memorial Park and is believed to be the resting place for many of those who fell in the defence of Fort York during the War of 1812. The cemetery occupies an area of no more than 38 m by 91 m. Some of the original tomb stones lie at the base of a memorial statue that rises from the centre of a treed green space. The first person buried here was the infant daughter of Lt-Governor John Graves Simcoe. The last of the known burials was that of Private James McQuarrick who passed away in 1863. It's possible that the first person to commit suicide in this early colonial era was also buried here. He was Lt Zachariah Mudge, private Secretary to Sir John Colborne, and his demise was reported to "have shaken the Colony."

OSGOODE HALL
130 Queen Street West • map 10 • 416-947-3300 (Law Society of Upper Canada) • osgoodehall.com • open during court hours with security in effect • subway: Osgoode.

This building is the historical epicentre of the law profession in Ontario and is one of the city's earliest architectural gems. A plaque on the property reads: "In 1829-32 the Law Society of Upper Canada erected the east wing of this imposing building. Named after William Osgoode, the province's first chief justice, the Regency structure housed law courts and judicial offices, and provided accommodation for lawyers and students. It was severely damaged during the six years in which provincial troops were stationed here following the Rebellion of 1837. Henry Bowyer Lane, an accomplished Toronto architect, drew up plans for its construction and, in 1844 – 46, the west and central portions were erected and the east wing remodeled."

PAUL BISHOP HOUSES
353-355 Adelaide Street East • map 11 (area 10E) • subway: King and take the 504 King streetcar east to Sherbourne Street and walk north to Adelaide Street East.

As far as anyone knows, these two houses at 353 and 355 Adelaide Street East were the only private residences to have survived the path of the Great Fire of 1849. Archival evidence seems to support the possibility that they were built in 1840. Paul Bishop, a French-Canadian, was the town's leading wheelwright and blacksmith and he bought the two properties from Sheriff Jarvis in 1842. A couple of years later, Bishop went out of business and sold them to Malachy O'Donohue. Since then, the dwellings have had a rather uninspiring life and it wasn't until December 1998 that Toronto city council realized their historical worth and kept them spared forever from the wrecker's ball. In 2005 they were gutted, restored and sold as "freehold homes, circa 1842."

SCADDING CABIN
Exhibition Place • map 2 • **doorsopen.org** • open weekends 10:00 AM – 4:00 PM • subway: Dufferin and take the 29 Dufferin bus south to Exhibition Place.

This was the first house built in the Town of York and was the residence of John Scadding, clerk to Lieutenant-Governor John Graves Simcoe. The one-room structure, built in 1794 of squared white pine logs with dovetailed corners, represents the only clue we have of how the original British settlers first made homes for themselves. In 1879 the York Pioneer Society moved the cabin from its original site on the east bank of the Don River to its present location at Exhibition Place, an act now recognized as the city's earliest example of architectural preservation. Scadding cabin is furnished as a typical settler's first house, with artifacts dating from the 1790s to the 1850s.

St JAMES' CATHEDRAL CHURCH
65 Church Street • map 11 • 416-364-7865 • **stjamescathedral.on.ca** • open daily, 7:30 AM – 5:30 PM; Saturdays, 9.00 AM - 3.00 PM; Sunday services • subway: King and take the 504 King streetcar east to Church Street.

Arguably, this is one of the most significant historical sites in the city. In 1803 soldiers at Fort York started to build the colony's first church on this corner. It was completed in 1807 and became known as the Church at York. Ten years later, on a visit to this remote corner of his diocese, Bishop Stewart of Québec dedicated the building to the Apostle St James. In 1830, it was replaced with a larger stone structure that opened in 1832, but burnt down in 1839. The third building was able to seat a congregation of 2,000 people. It was built in the neo-classical style used by Sir Christopher Wren for St. Paul's Cathedral and other churches in London. However, this building also burned down, together with much of Toronto, during the Great Fire of 1849. In fact, it was the church's tolling bell that alerted the population to the early morning start of the conflagration. The church you see today, designed by Frederick Cumberland and made with Toronto brick and Ohio sandstone, is in the Gothic Revival style that was the ecclesiastical architecture of choice in England at the time. Cumberland's other buildings in town included Osgoode Hall and University College. St James Cathedral Church held its first service in 1853; the tower was finished in 1865; and the spire in 1874. Today, St. James is the cathedral for the Anglican Diocese of Toronto and the spiritual hub of 235 parishes and missions in Greater Toronto and the surrounding areas.

St LAWRENCE HALL
157 King Street East • map 11 • 416-392-7130 • **stlawrencemarket.com** • open weekdays during business hours • subway: King and take the 504 King streetcar east to Jarvis Street.

This is one of the most elegant old landmarks in the city. It was designed by architect William Thomas and built in 1850 to replace commercial buildings destroyed here during the Great Fire of 1849. The idea of the hall was to provide a public meeting place and a covered market extending from the back of the building down to Front Street. In its heyday it was the venue for many important social occasions, cultural events and lectures. People like Jenny Lind, the 'Swedish Nightingale', sang here to packed houses in 1851, and Tom Thumb attracted lots of fascinated spectators. Around the end of the 19th century the old hall fell on hard times when no one seemed particularly interested in repairing its failing infrastructure and it was generally disregarded. It was almost torn down during the late Fifties when the city seemed immune to saving anything of historical significance. Then, just before Canada's Centennial Year in 1967, council put it on its list of centennial projects and the grand old St Lawrence Hall was restored to its former self, thus regaining its historical importance and social status.

St MICHAEL'S CATHOLIC CATHEDRAL
200 Church Street • map 16 • 416-364-0234 • ca-catholics.net • open Monday - Saturday before 6:00 PM and for Sunday services • subway: Dundas and take the 505 Dundas streetcar east to Bond Street (two blocks) and walk south to Shuter Street.

William Thomas, who also designed St Lawrence Hall, adapted the cathedral's cruciform shape from a 14th century Neo-Gothic style inspired by England's Yorkminster cathedral. The cornerstone was laid on May 8, 1845 and consecration was celebrated on September 29, 1848. The church was built to serve a mainly immigrant population of 3,000 Catholics from Ireland who came here to escape the potato famine. They made up about a quarter of the town's population of 13,000. Despite all good intentions at the time, the church's location was considered my many to be "too far away" from the town. The Great Chancel Window, designed by French artist Etienne Theuenot, was installed ten years after the church was built and nine years before the tower spire.

St PAUL'S CATHOLIC BASILICA
83 Power Street • map 12 • 416-364-7588 • ca-catholics.net • open Sundays 7.30 AM – noon; Saturdays 4:00 PM – 6:00 PM • subway: Queen and take the 501 Queen streetcar east to Power Street.

The Roman Catholic Church built on this site in 1826 represented the first presence of formal Catholicism in Toronto. In 1842, when Toronto separated from the older Kingston diocese, it served as an informal cathedral. The present Italian Renaissance structure, based on Rome's St Paul-Against-the-Wall, opened in 1889. The city's first Catholic cemetery, which is now unmarked, was just to the east of this building. The Pietà, sitting to the left of the main entrance, is in memory of victims who died during the 1847 typhoid epidemic that swept the city after a water pipe burst and became contaminated with water from the harbour. St Paul's was elevated to minor basilica status in August, 1999.

THE GRANGE
317 Dundas Street West (at the rear) • map 14 • 416-979-6610 • ago.on.ca • open Tuesday – Friday, noon – 9:00 PM; weekends, 10:00 AM – 5:30 PM • admission $ • subway: Dundas and take the 505 Dundas streetcar west to McCaul Street.

This is the oldest surviving brick house in the city. It dates back to the days of the Town of York when the colonial governor gave vast lots of land to people of influence along what is now Queen Street. At the time, Queen Street was appropriately named Lot Street. D'Arcy Boulton Jr was one of the fortunate recipients of this largesse and his 15-room Georgian mansion, built in 1817, has been restored to the elegance of the 1830s. Its symmetrical five-bay façade and central pediment reflect the conservative influence of the British classical tradition of the 18th century. The west wing represents two later additions. The house was given to the Art Museum of Toronto in 1911 and now forms part of the Art Gallery of Ontario.

UNIVERSITY OF TORONTO – St GEORGE CAMPUS
Maps 19, 20 and 24 • 416-978-2011 • utoronto.ca • subway: Spadina, St George and Queen's Park.

On March 15, 1827, a Royal Charter was bestowed on King's College in the Town of York and 22 years later the college became the University of Toronto. Over the years, three federated universities and four constituent colleges merged with the U of T to form Canada's largest university. The federated universities are Victoria University (Methodist, 1836), University of Trinity College (Church of England, 1851) and the University of St Michael's College (Roman Catholic, 1852). Each of these entities brought with it some of the city's finest original buildings and blended them into a campus that has perhaps the highest concentration of major historical buildings in the city. The best way to enjoy this extensive, rewarding and beautiful setting is to get a free copy of the *University of Toronto St George Campus Map* from the university bookstore, 214 College Street on the northwest corner of St George Street. The shop is open Monday - Friday, 9:00 AM - 6.00:PM; Saturday, 10:00 AM - 5:00 PM; and Sunday, noon - 5:00 PM. Telephone: 416-978-7900

VICTORIA HOSPITAL FOR SICK CHILDREN
67 College Street • map 15 • 416-813-1500 • sickkids.on.ca • subway: College and walk two blocks west along College Street.

In this former hospital building on January 23, 1921, a 14 year-old boy named Leonard Thompson received the world's first insulin treatment for diabetes. The history of the Hospital for Sick Children goes back to early 1875 when a group of Toronto women, led by Elizabeth McMaster, rented an 11-room house in downtown Toronto for $320 a year. They set up six iron cots and declared open a hospital "for the admission and treatment of all sick children." On April 3rd that year, Maggie, a scalding victim, became the institution's first patient. The demand for services was so great that the hospital moved in 1876 to a larger building. But even the new quarters, with its 16 beds, soon proved to be too small. In 1891, under the leadership of John Ross Robertson, publisher of the *Evening Telegram* and chairman of the Hospital's Board of Trustees, the hospital moved to an impressive new four-story, 320-bed facility that still stands today at the corner of Elizabeth and College Streets. Designed by the architectural firm of Darling and Curry and built of red sandstone, the Victoria Hospital for Sick Children opened in May 1892. It was the first hospital in Canada designed exclusively for pediatrics. Among its many accomplishments was the introduction of milk pasteurization some 30 years before it became generally accepted; the use of x-rays in 1896; and the first use of Pablum baby food. Even though the building has 'Victoria

Hospital for Sick Children' carved in stone above the entrance, the name was never officially recognized. These days, the Hospital for Sick Children – or 'Sick Kids' as it's more commonly known – has moved around the corner and occupies a major block along University Avenue. It is internationally regarded as one of the world's major centres for pediatric treatment and research. This old building is currently occupied by Canadian Blood Services.

YORK (FIRST) POST OFFICE
260 Adelaide Street East • map 11 • 416-865-1833 • tha.on.ca/firstpo • open weekdays, 9:00 AM – 4:00 PM; weekends, 10:00 AM – 4:00 PM. Closed on statutory holidays • subway: King and take the 504 King streetcar east to George Street and walk north to Adelaide Street East.

This is the oldest functioning post office in Canada. Originally, all post offices in Upper Canada were owned by appointed Imperial postmasters and administered by the British Post Office. Postmaster James Scott Howard was the first to occupy this building, which was constructed in 1833 in the Town of York. This was York's fourth post office building and, in 1834, it became the 'first post office' in the newly minted city of Toronto. Howard held his position from 1833 to 1837 before being fired. It was rumoured that he was a reform sympathizer during the Upper Canada Rebellion of 1837. He appealed his dismissal "with much eloquence" but never got his job back. These days the post office operates as both a post office and museum, enabling visitors to step back in time and learn about postal history. If a genuine quill pen and sealing wax are on your shopping list, then this is where you can buy them. It's also the only post office in the country where you can buy American and British postage stamps.

Places Markets

Toronto's two major downtown markets have a long and distinguished history. Each is the major focal point of its respective neighbourhood, and both attract lively crowds from across the city. Here's where you can mix with a truly cosmopolitan array of merchants and indulge in a seemingly endless variety of international foods.

KENSINGTON MARKET
Baldwin Street at Augusta Avenue • map 14 • toronto.com • open daily, but best and busiest on Saturday • subway: Dundas and take the 505 Dundas streetcar west to Augusta Avenue. Then walk north on Augusta into the market.

There is no other place in the city that offers such a dizzy assortment of funky sidewalk shops, used clothing merchants and food stalls than Kensington Market. It's where you go to buy great cheeses from around the world, exotic fresh fruits from far away places, pastries and breads you'll find nowhere else, and an abundance of seafood, meats and poultry. This is a disordered, often untidy, but always intriguing kind of place. And, regardless of the language you speak, chances are you'll find someone here to chat with you over coffee.

Kensington Market can trace its beginnings back to the 18th century. The area wasn't originally designed to be anything like it is today. On the contrary. In the 1820s, large building lots along Spadina Avenue, between Queen and Bloor streets, were being promoted to only the most prosperous of the early British settlers. The tone of the proposed new community could be seen in street names like Essex, Kensington, Oxford and Wales. Fifty years later, with no more than about 20 homes gracing the avenue, it became obvious that the moneyed folk were putting their roots down elsewhere around town. As the gentry started to move away in the late 1880s, an unannounced and curiously foreign mix of immigrant people started to move in, and especially those from Eastern Europe of Jewish heritage. Before long that Jewish element was the principal ethnic group in the neighbourhood. By the early Thirties their numbers had increased to the point where Kensington was the epicentre of Toronto's Jewish population.

Because Jewish people were still shunned within this city of predominately Angle-Saxon power and influence, few had any opportunities to prosper. So they banded together to help each other mainly through drawing on their tradition of open-air markets. They set up stalls in the front, back and side yards of their houses and created their own, independent micro-economy. Very quickly this whole area became known as the Jewish Market. Over the years, as their fortunes and social status improved, they - like the British before them – moved away and took their families to better neighbourhoods. After World War II the vacuum was filled with immigrants from Hungary, Romania, Italy and Portugal. Within the next 40 years they were joined by waves of people from places as diverse as Vietnam, China, India, Ethiopia and the Caribbean.

Today, Kensington Market retains lively evidence of all these competing cultures and traditions. It's evident among a hundred shops crammed along narrow streets and cluttered sidewalks. It is a heady brew of organized chaos, alien sights and aromas, cheap merchandise, indulgent foods and the occasional terrific bargain. Bring your adventurous spirit and a desire for the unexpected.

St LAWRENCE MARKET
92 Front Street East • map 11 • 416-392-7120 (Market); 416-392-7605 (Gallery) • stlawrencemarket.com • South market: Tuesday – Thursday, 8:00 AM – 6:00 PM; Friday, 8:00 AM – 7:00 PM; Saturday, 5:00 AM – 5:00 PM. **Farmer's Market:** Saturday, 5:00 AM – 4:00 PM. **Gallery:** Wednesday – Friday, 10:00 AM – 4:00 PM; Saturday, 9:00 AM – 4:00 PM; Sunday, noon – 4:00 PM • subway: King and take the 504 King streetcar east to Jarvis Street and walk one block south.

There are lots of people who get up before 5 o'clock on a Saturday morning to go shopping – and they head straight for the St Lawrence Market. Under one big roof covering the two storey South Market block there are scores of fish mongers, butchers, grocers, produce merchants, sellers of exotic spices and herbs, bakers, and assorted purveyors of just about anything you might want to put on your dinner table. Across the street, in the Farmer's Market, about 80 of Ontario's growers and producers will greet you as if you're a long lost friend. Here's where to get fresh eggs, flowers and plants, homemade deli treats, gourmet teas and coffees, organically grown produce, honeys and yogurts, bulk foods and general groceries. There is no better single place in town than the St Lawrence Market to get caught up in the sensory delights of shopping for food. Even the city's finest chefs have been seen elbowing each other out of the way to grab the very freshest meats and produce for that evening's menu. Their dinner customers appreciate the devotion.

The St Lawrence Market goes back a very long way. Over two hundred years ago, Governor Peter Hunter issued a proclamation that all the land north of Front Street, south of King Street, and bounded by Jarvis and Church streets, would be designated as the Town of York's Market Block. When the City of Toronto was incorporated in 1834, thereby eliminating York, council members met in temporary quarters in an old market building on the south-west corner of King and Jarvis streets where the St Lawrence Hall stands today. However, this brick structure, built in 1831, was burnt down like most other buildings during the Great Fire of 1849.

With the city's population now nearing 40,000, council members were able to sponsor a competition for the construction of a city hall. It was to have a multi-purpose function: municipal offices, a market and a police station. Henry Bowyer Lane, the energetic young English immigrant who designed Little Trinity Church, won the competition and built the complex on a 43 m site on Front Street, previously occupied by the Home District Farmer's Storehouse. It opened in 1845. His original design, modified over the years to accommodate the changing nature of the building, was in the Georgian tradition of contrasting red brick and white stone. Above the three-storey centre block was a pediment topped by a cupola and a clock, and two wings extending from either side. Police Station Number One was located on the main floor in the centre of the building with the jail cells in the basement. Directly above, on the second floor was the council chamber. Along the corridor in the west wing were the offices of the mayor, the city clerk and his assistants. In the east wing were the offices of the chamberlain, General Inspector of Licenses, city engineer and the Board of Works. On the ground floor of both wings were various shops.

Within little more than five years, John George Howard, the city engineer, tabled complaints that the shops were too small and that flooding in the basement forced prisoners to be knee-deep in water. The following year, new shops were designed for the wings, keystones were added to the arched windows and cells in the police station were rearranged. From 1868 until 1872, Henry Langley was responsible for yet another renovation. Finally, in 1899, the over-crowded civic offices were transferred to the imposing new city hall, designed by E J Lennox, located at Bay and Queen streets. These days, on the second floor of the South Market building, you'll find historical exhibits including the original council chamber that was once part of Toronto's first city hall from 1845 to 1899. This is a great place to browse through all sorts of interesting old stuff and get in touch with a fascinating city block.

So, if you don't want to get up at 5 o'clock on a Saturday morning to go shopping, just drop by any other day from Tuesday to Saturday at a more civilized hour. All you need to bring is your curiosity and a hearty appetite.

Places Museums, galleries and public art

 Toronto is distinguished from other North American cities by the wealth of art on its streets. Added to this civic taste for beautiful things is the high international standard of our 61 art galleries and museums. Putting it all together has made Toronto the cultural hub of the country.

AIDS MEMORIAL
Cawthra Square Park • map 21 • **the519.org/programs** • subway: Wellesley and walk east along Wellesley Street and north on Church Street.

Like all big cities, Toronto has felt the toll of the HIV-AIDS epidemic. On June 19, 1993, this memorial, designed by Patrick Fahn and set in Cawthra Park, was unveiled before 400 people standing in light rain. The purpose of the celebratory concrete and stainless steel columns is "to acknowledge the need for private meditation and remembering. It should in some way be able to function as a focus for public gatherings – in mourning, anger or celebration. It should take its place in the everyday life of the park." Hundreds of names and dates appear on the columns. They are arranged chronologically from 1984 when HIV-AIDS first started to take its toll on the community.

ART GALLERY OF ONTARIO (AGO)
317 Dundas Street West • map 14 • 416-979-6648 • **ago.on.ca** • Tuesday – Friday, noon to 9:00 PM; weekends, 10:00 AM – 5:30 PM • admission $ • subway: St Patrick and take the 505 Dundas streetcar west to McCaul Street.

Canadian born architect Frank Gehry, creator of Spain's Guggenheim Museum in Bilbao, is also the architect for the $200-million redesign of the Art Gallery of Ontario. The rejuvenated gallery, entered through a sweeping foyer, comes complete with Gehry's signature titanium and glass exteriors and will expand the gallery's exhibition space by almost half. The 2007 official opening unveils an outstanding 'baroque' staircase rising through the rear southern wall. Founded in 1900 by a group of private citizens as the Art Museum of Toronto, the AGO, before its renovation, was the 10th largest art museum in North America. It has more than 38,000 works in its collection, spanning from the 11th century to the present day. A little more than half the works represent those of Canadian artists. Ambitious visiting collections from around the world find their way here every year to supplement outstanding permanent exhibits. There's a rental and sales gallery, plus the AGO Gallery Shop for books, jewelry and reproductions.

BATA SHOE MUSEUM
327 Bloor Street West • map 24 • 416-979-7799 • **batashoemuseum.ca** • open Tuesday – Sunday. Hours vary • admission $ • subway: St George.

This is where you'll find everything you ever wanted to know about shoes and shoe making. Ten thousand exhibits trace the history of shoes for over 4,000 years and include everything from chestnut crushing clogs and Chinese bound-foot shoes, to footwear belonging to people as diverse as Pope Leo XIII, Queen Victoria, Imelda Marcos and Elton John. Special exhibitions are constantly changing, bringing visitors fresh insights into something we have taken for granted since the dawn of civilization. This strikingly modern, five-storey museum was designed by prolific Toronto architect Raymond Moriyama and is the leading one of its type. Do you know what percentage of all the bones in the human body are found in the foot? Drop by the museum to find out.

CAMPBELL HOUSE MUSEUM
160 Queen Street West • map 10 • 416-597-0227 • **advsoc.on.ca** • open Monday – Friday, 9:30 AM – 4:30 PM; Saturday and Sunday, May through September, noon – 4:30 PM • admission $ • subway: Osgoode.

Queen Elizabeth the Queen Mother opened this museum in 1972. Built in 1822, it is the earliest surviving example of formal Georgian domestic architecture from the Town of York. Over 30 years ago it was moved here from the intersection of Adelaide and Frederick streets in the old town. The historic plaque reads: "Sir William Campbell, 1758-1834, was born near Caithness, Scotland. He fought with the British forces during the American Revolution and was taken prisoner at Yorktown in 1781. Three years later he was practicing law in Nova Scotia where, in 1799, he was elected to the House of Assembly. In 1811, Campbell moved to Upper Canada where he had accepted a judgeship on the Court of King's Bench. He was made chief justice of the province and speaker of the Legislative Council in 1825. Four years later he received the first knighthood awarded a judge in Upper Canada."

CANADIAN AIRMEN'S MEMORIAL
University Avenue at Dundas Street West • map 15 • subway: St Patrick.

University Avenue is the closest thing Toronto has to a *grand allée*. As it goes north from Queen Street to Queen's Park, its handsome median is sprinkled with commemorative statues. One of them is the once highly controversial Canadian Airmen's Memorial designed by Oscar Nemon that was dubbed 'Gumby Goes to Heaven' after its unveiling. Other war-related works in the area include The Great War memorial by Charles Adamson on University Avenue at Elm Street; the Cenotaph fronting the old city hall on Queen Street West at Bay Street; and a memorial to the 48th Highlanders of Canada at the north end of Queen's Park.

CITY PEOPLE
Front Street West at Bay Street in front of the Royal Bank Plaza • map 10 • subway: Union.

This area of town, in the middle of the Financial District, is constantly buzzing with business types on cell phones seemingly having the deal of a lifetime within their grasp. Catherine Widgery's multi-piece cutout sculpture is one of our most whimsical pieces of public art and captures this frenzied human activity perfectly. It depicts a cartoonish mix of hurried and harried folk dashing off up the stairs to who knows where. There are days when you can't tell what's art and what's for real. The sculpture is part of the Royal Bank of Canada's art collection.

COLBORNE LODGE MUSEUM
Colborne Lodge Drive, High Park • map Toronto • 416-392-6916 •
city.toronto.on.ca/culture/colborne • open Tuesday – Sunday, noon – 5:00 PM •
admission $ • subway: Keele and walk one block west to Colborne Lodge.

Finding an historic museum in the city that's not smothered by close neighbours is quite an achievement. This one, centered in High Park, is a notable
exception. It's a Regency-style cottage, built in 1837, complete with period
artifacts and furnishings. It belonged to John and Jemima Howard who
founded what is now one of the largest parks in the city. John Howard was
among Toronto's first architects as well as a city engineer and surveyor. He
was an avid amateur painter and some of his watercolours, depicting images
of early Toronto, are on display. The lodge's extensive ornamental and
kitchen gardens have recently been restored and provide a period setting for
the annual Harvest Festival and Christmas celebrations.

FLATIRON MURAL
West wall of the Flatiron building overlooking Berczy Park • map 11 • subway:
Union and go two blocks east along Front Street.

Derek Besant's 1980 *Flatiron Mural* is one of the city's most photographed
works of street art. It's best viewed from the west end of Berczy Park through
the trees and across the gardens. It's an absorbing and fascinatingly illusion-
al piece that draws even more attention to the historic Flatiron building
which, in itself, is one of the city's architectural icons. The plaque underneath
says precious little about the mural or the artist, but manages to say a lot
about the politicians who made it possible. For the record, Besant was born
in Fort Macleod, Alberta, in 1950 and his public works have appeared
throughout the world, including large-scale projects in New York.

FLIGHT STOP
Inside the Eaton Centre • map 15 • subway: Dundas or Queen.

Down the inside length of the Eaton Centre there's a suspended flock of Canada geese coming in for a landing before continuing the flight south for the
winter. Lucky for us these birds, designed by Michael Snow, have decided to
remain in town regardless of the season. The centre is one of the busiest
places in the city, so the geese have lots of admiring company.

GALLERY OF INUIT ART
79 Wellington Street West, ground level, Aetna Tower, TD Centre • map 10 • 416-
982-8473 • tdcentre.ca/tourist • Monday – Friday, 8:00 AM – 6:00 PM; Saturday &
Sunday, 10:00 AM – 4:00 PM • subway: King.

Canada's Native art is one of the things that sets this country apart from others. The two major contributors are the west coast First Nations' peoples and
the Inuit of the northern Arctic regions. This gallery, housed within dramatic
Mies Van Der Rohe architecture, was originally conceived in 1960 and provides a permanent home for the TD Bank's renowned collection of over 200
pieces of Inuit art. The gallery, which has been created to foster an appreciation of that art, provides a museum environment for the works on display.

GIBSON HOUSE MUSEUM
5172 Yonge Street • map 35 • 416-395-7432 •
city.toronto.on.ca/culture/gibson_house • open Tuesday - Friday, 9:30 AM – 4:30

PM; weekends and holidays, noon – 5:00 PM • admission $ • subway: North York Centre and walk one block north on Yonge Street and west along Park Home Avenue.

Gibson House Museum is an elegant Georgian farmhouse built by Scottish émigré David Gibson in 1851. He was a land surveyor who mapped early Toronto and helped prepare the surrounding wilderness for settlement. A participant in the Upper Canada Rebellion of 1837, Gibson was forced to flee to the United States where he remained in exile for 11 years. This home was built to celebrate his return to Toronto. Costumed guides explain the home's interior furnishings and relate what country life north of Toronto must have been like during the mid-1800s. Activities include hearth-cooking classes and a guided exploration of the museum.

GROUP OF SEVEN – St ANNE'S CHURCH
270 Gladstone Avenue inside St Anne's church • map Toronto (area 8M) and in detail below • 416-536-1202 • **stannes.on.ca** • open during the day • subway: Dufferin and take a 29 bus south to Gladstone Avenue.

St Anne's is the only Byzantine-style Anglican church in Canada. It's one of those places you've probably heard about, but haven't bothered to visit. This is a quiet neighbourhood church, tucked away from busy Dundas Street on Gladstone Avenue. Famous for its interior art, St Anne's has 11 imposing canvas panels painted by three members of celebrated Canadian Group of Seven: J.E.H. MacDonald, Frank Carmichael and Frederick Varley. The church's spire rises 23 metres above the spacious and imposing nave, giving the interior an unexpected feeling of openness and grandeur in all directions.

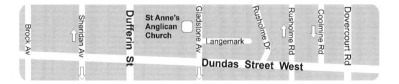

HARBOURFRONT CENTRE CRAFT STUDIO
235 Queen's Quay West in the York Quay building • map 5 • 416-973-3000 • **harbourfrontcentre.on.ca** • open February – December, Tuesday, 10:00AM – 6:00 PM; Wednesday – Saturday, 10:00 AM – 8:00 PM; and Sunday, 10:00 AM – 6:00 PM • subway: Union and take the Harbourfront 509 streetcar.

The centre is one of the busiest cultural venues in the city. Its one-of-a-kind Craft Studio gives you the opportunity to watch close up as working professionals design works in glass, metal, textiles and ceramics. Eight display cases, situated at the south end of the building, are dedicated to the exhibition of fine contemporary Canadian craft, featuring artists' expressions of present day, historical and culturally diverse ideas.

HENRY MOORE SCULPTURES
Maps 14 & 15 • subways: St Patrick (AGO) and Osgoode or Queen (city hall).

We have two large public bronzes by Henry Moore. His impressive *Large Two Forms* is outside the Art Gallery of Ontario. Inside the gallery, you'll find the world's largest collection of his works including his *Draped Reclining Woman* in the entrance foyer. Moore's other outdoor bronze, *The Archer* (1966), is a centrepiece in Nathan Phillips Square fronting city hall.

J M BARNICKE ART GALLERY
7 Hart House Circle inside Hart House, University of Toronto • map 20 • 416-978-8387 • **utoronto.ca/gallery** • Monday – Friday, 11:00 AM – 7:00 PM; weekends, 1:00 PM – 4:00 PM. Closed Sundays during July & August • subway: Queen's Park.

Toronto has 30 public art galleries and this is the only one devoted to including Canadian artists in the early stages of their careers. The works date from 1921 to the present. There is also a coveted collection of historical, contemporary and recent acquisitions. These include paintings by Emily Carr, Tom Thomson and J W Beatty. However, some of the gallery's most prized exhibits include those from celebrated Group of Seven artists Lawren Harris, J E H MacDonald, Frank Carmichael, A Y Jackson and Fred Varley. The principal aim of the Hart House Art Committee is "to preserve and develop the Hart House Permanent Collection, for the benefit of the University Community, the Toronto region and for Canada."

MACKENZIE HOUSE MUSEUM
82 Bond Street • map 16 • 416-392-6915 • **city.toronto.on.ca/culture/mackenzie_house** • open Tuesday – Sunday, noon – 5:00 PM during summer; Tuesday – Friday, noon – 5:00 PM in the fall; and weekends, noon – 5:00 PM during winter • admission $ • subway: Dundas and walk two blocks east along Dundas Street East and south on Bond Street.

Just around the corner from bustling Dundas Square there's a two-storey Greek Revival row house that was bought by the community for the Town of York's first mayor. That man was William Lyon Mackenzie. He was born in Dundee, Scotland, and left his homeland for Canada in 1820. He arrived first in Montréal and after working on the Lachine Canal, and as a journalist for the *Montreal Herald*, he moved to Upper Canada and settled in the thriving community of the Town of York. Mackenzie, as colourful a person as you might find in any era, quickly became involved in the affairs of the day. He led the unsuccessful 1837 Upper Canada Rebellion, and was five times expelled from the Legislative Assembly of Upper Canada for 'libel' - and five times re-elected by his constituency. He was also renowned in his day as the influential publisher of the *Colonial Advocate* and his old print shop is still in working condition. In fact, kids can spend 90 minutes learning how to typeset and print their own creations on an 1845 flatbed press. The museum is a good place to explore and discover what all the fuss was about.

MONTGOMERY'S INN MUSEUM
4709 Dundas Street West • map *Toronto* and in detail below • 416-394-8113 •**montgomerysinn.com** • open Tuesday – Friday, 9:30 AM – 4:30 PM; weekends, 1:00 PM – 5:00 PM • admission $ • subway: Islington and take the 37 bus to Dundas Street West.

Built around 1830, the inn was a going concern for about 25 years until the last guest departed around 1850. The building is one of the last examples of late Georgian or Loyalist architecture we have in the city. You'll be treated to an authentically restored building of the period 1847 - 1850 staffed by folk dressed in attire of that much less hurried day. The inn is well worth visiting for its fine collection of British, Canadian and American antiques. You can also get involved in making your own bread jewelry, or taking part in an old-fashioned cooking class.

MUSEUM OF CERAMIC ART
111 Queen's Park • map 25 • 416-586-8080 • gardinermuseum.on.ca • open Tuesday – Sunday, hours vary • admission $ • subway: Museum.

The Gardiner Museum of Ceramic Art is Canada's only museum set aside exclusively for the collection and display of ceramic art. It is also one of the finest of its type in the world. Philanthropists George and Helen Gardiner founded it in 1984 to house their personal collection and make it available to the public. In 2005 the museum reopened after completing a $15-million expansion program that increased its exhibition areas by 940 sq m. An Asian porcelain gallery has been added, as has space for international touring exhibits. Here's where you can get involved in clay classes, browse through over 3,600 exhibits, or find something unique to take home from the Gardiner Shop.

MUSEUM OF CONTEMPORARY CANADIAN ART (MOCCA)
952 Queen Street West • map Toronto (area 7N) and in detail below • 416-395-7430 • mocca.toronto.on.ca • Tuesday – Sunday, noon – 5:00 PM • subway: Osgoode and take the 501Queen streetcar west to Shaw Street.

The museum was formed in 1999 from the former Art Gallery of North York and has retained its mandate to exhibit, research, collect, and promote innovative art produced by Canadians whose works address the challenging themes and issues of our times. In addition, MOCCA exhibits work by international artists to complement those from Canada to create a global context for the Canadian cultural voice. In September 2004, MOCCA relocated from the Toronto Centre for the Arts in North York to the heart of the city's Queen West design district "to broaden its ability to address contemporary Canadian and international art."

ONTARIO COLLEGE OF ART AND DESIGN (OCAD)
100 McCaul Street • map 14 • 416-977-6000 • ocad.ca • subway: St Patrick.

This is not so much a building to visit, as it is a piece of arresting street art. Raucous debate over the college's hotly controversial Sharp Centre building is still going on, long after its opening. It was one of six buildings honoured in 2004 with the first ever Royal Institute of British Architects Worldwide Award. It looks like a suspended checkerboard hovering like a tabletop over the neighbourhood. The structure was designed by British architect Will Alsop and described by the RIBA judges as "courageous, bold and just a little insane." Many would say this is an understatement. It's right behind Frank Gehry's re-design of the Art Gallery of Ontario, giving you an architectural perspective that ranges from the sublime to the ridiculous.

POWER PLANT
231 Queen's Quay West • map 5 • 416-973-4949 • **thepowerplant.org** • Tuesday –
Sunday, noon – 6:00 PM; Wednesdays, 5:00 PM - 8:00 PM • admission $, but free on
Wednesdays • subway: Union and take the Harbourfront 509 streetcar.

The art gallery with the strange name is Toronto's main public gallery for innovative contemporary art. The various forms include photography, sculpture, painting and new media. The Power Plant is a non-collecting gallery
specializing in often stunning solo and group exhibitions from across Canada
and around the world. A great place to visit in a fun environment.

PRINCESS OF WALES THEATRE MURALS
Pearl Street • map 9 (area 10E) • **mirvish.com** • subway: St Andrew.

When Ed Mirvish built the Princess of Wales Theatre in 1993 for the Canadian
première of *Miss Saigon*, he commissioned contemporary American artist
Frank Stella to provide 930 sq m of murals. One of the largest of these is displayed on the exterior Pearl Street wall of the theatre. Inside, Stella's work
graces the hall, foyers and ceilings. There was some consternation at the time
about Mirvish commissioning an American to embellish the new theatre with
art, but that soon faded away.

REDPATH SUGAR MUSEUM
95 Queen's Quay East • map 6 • 416-366-3561 • **redpath.com** • phone ahead for
days and times of admission • subway: Union and take the 6 bus east to Cooper
Street.

The museum is an informal place that traces the history of sugar production
through exhibits and a video presentation. You'll find it at the back of the
Redpath Sugar Refinery, which was opened on June 29, 1959, by Queen
Elizabeth II. Wyland's whale mural is on the outside wall of the raw sugar
shed facing Queen's Quay East.

ROSE WINDOWS
St Paul's Anglican church, 227 Bloor Street East • map 26 • 416-961-8116 •
anglican.ca • noon hour weekdays and services on Sunday • subway Yonge-Bloor.

St Paul's could be described as the church of choice for Toronto's downtown
Anglicans of influence. Recent renovations to this 145-year-old structure have
only enhanced the Rose Windows in each transept, which are believed to be
among the largest of their kind. Other stained glass windows that are
outstanding are on the east wall. They're dedicated to those in the congregation who gave their lives in World War I.

ROYAL ONTARIO MUSEUM (ROM)
100 Queen's Park • map 25 • 416-586-8000 • **rom.on.ca** • open Monday – Saturday,
10:00 AM – 6:00 PM; Sundays, 11:00 AM – 6:00 PM • admission $ • subway: Museum.

In 2004 the world-renowned Polish born architect David Libeskind, who won
the competition to design New York's new World Trade Centre, began his
dramatic transformation of the ROM into what is likely to become one of the
city's iconic buildings. The old building, which opened in 1914 and was
declared an historical property in 1973, will be partially encased by an enormous bursting crystal design. It's a stunning concept based on interlocking
prismatic forms embracing six new galleries overlooking Bloor Street West.
The ROM is one of the continent's leading museums, specializing in an exten-

sive collection of decorative arts, archaeology and science. There are 6,000,000 objects and artifacts in over 40 permanent galleries. The Chinese collection is one of the world's best. Special changing exhibits year-round. It's a place where you can get your hands on 4.6-billion years of history and still find enough time to gaze at the 193-carat Star Sapphire.

SALMON RUN
Southeast corner of Rogers Centre • map 4 • subway: Union and take the Skywalk.

There's so much activity around the base of the CN Tower and the Rogers Centre that people who go there tend to miss what is surely one of the most engaging pieces of public sculpture in the city. Take time to look at the cascading waterfalls as they splash over two-dimensional salmon swimming and jumping upstream on their way to spawn. Susan Schelle created the work in 1991 for this location.

SCULPTURE GARDEN
115 King Street East • map 11 • 416-485-9658 • city.toronto.on.ca/parks • open dawn to dusk • subway: King.

This is a small park on the east side of the La Maquette restaurant. Exhibits change regularly and portray a wide range of themes from 'flying saucers' to animals and contemporary pieces. It was once the site of historic Oak Hall that was demolished in 1938 to make way for a tiny parking lot. The garden was opened in 1981 after the civic fathers finally realized that historical buildings were more important than parking cars.

SPADINA HOUSE MUSEUM
285 Spadina Road • map 28 • 416-392-6910 • city.toronto.on.ca/culture/spadina • open Tuesday – Sunday, noon – 5:00 PM • admission $ • subway: Dupont and walk north to the intersection of Spadina Avenue and Davenport Road.

Located beside Casa Loma, this is the third Spadina House on the site. The original owner of the property was William Warren Baldwin, a prominent early resident of York who was a lawyer, doctor and sometimes architect. Baldwin's grandson sold the 32 ha estate to financier James Austin in 1866, who erected the present building. It has undergone some major renovations over the years, including the addition of a third floor in 1912. The Austin family remained at Spadina House until 1980, when the building and 2.5 ha of the original estate were donated to the city as a museum. An unusual feature of Spadina House is that most of the furnishings and artwork were donated along with the building, giving it an air of authenticity and integrity. The property has 2.4 ha of Victorian and Edwardian gardens with 300 varieties of flowers and vegetables. It's one of the top spots in town for taking wedding photos. Incidentally, Spadina House is pronounced 'Spa-dee-na', whereas Spadina Avenue is pronounced 'Spa-dine-a"

TEXTILE MUSEUM OF CANADA
55 Centre Street • map 15 • 416-599-5321 • museumfortextiles.on.ca • open Tuesday – Friday, 11:00 AM – 5:00 PM; Wednesdays, 11:00 AM – 8:00 PM; weekends, noon – 5:00 PM • admission $ • subway: St Patrick and walk one block east along Dundas Street and south on Centre Street.

According to the museum's publicity, its permanent collection contains more than 10,000 textiles and spans almost 2,000 years and 190 world regions. This diverse collection includes fabrics, ceremonial cloths, garments, carpets, quilts and related artifacts which reflect the ethnographic, cultural and aesthetic significance that cloth has held over the centuries. This museum, which is tucked away on a quiet street in Chinatown, is internationally recognized for its collection of over 8,000 artifacts. It's the only museum in Canada devoted to the collection, exhibiting and documentation of textiles from around the world.

THE AUDIENCE
North exterior wall of Rogers Centre • map 3 • rogerscentre.com • subway: Union and take the Skywalk.

There are two parts to this conspicuous 1989 Michael Snow sculpture: Audience 1 on the east side of the north wall shows gargoyles cheering; Audience 2 on the west side of the north wall depicts jeering fans - including Fat Man and Muscle Man. The works, which are made of fibreglass and painted to look like bronze, dominate the north side of the stadium. Not everyone was enamoured with them when they appeared, but time has mellowed any initial controversy. Snow's other well-known public sculpture is the far less controversial Flight Stop inside the Eaton Centre.

TODMORDEN MILLS MUSEUM
67 Pottery Road • map Toronto and in detail below • 416-396-2819 • city.toronto.on.ca/todmorden • open Tuesday - Friday, 11:00 AM – 4:30 PM; weekends noon – 5:00 PM • subway: Broadview and take the 87 bus north to Pottery Road.

In 1796 Lieutenant Governor John Graves Simcoe directed that one pair of mill stones and a set of grist mill irons be given to Isaiah and Aaron Skinner to build the first grist mill on the Don River. The place was named Todmorden Mills and the following year a sawmill was built to ensure a supply of lumber for the growing Town of York. About 24 years later the Don Valley became home to a thriving brewery that manufactured beer for town residents and people living around the Great Lakes. Together with the brewery, the site soon supported a distillery and a second grist mill. In 1827, the Don Mills were converted into the York Paper Mill, the second paper mill in Upper Canada. The mill worked away on the Don River during Victorian times and has been restored as an example of local industry in the 19th century.

TORONTO POLICE MUSEUM
40 College Street in the Toronto Police Headquarters building • map 20 • 416-808-7020 • torontopolice.on.ca/cos/cpsmuseum • museum open daily, 9:00 AM – 9:00 PM; Gift Shop open, Monday – Friday, 9:00 AM – 3:30 PM • admission $ • subway: College and walk one block west along College Street.

Despite Toronto being one of the safest major cities in North America, we have had our share of notorious crimes over the years. The Toronto Police

Museum catalogues some of the more infamous of these, along with artifacts and displays that reflect the history of Toronto policing. You'll find interesting displays of uniforms, police equipment and interactive displays with actual dispatch calls. You can also select videos from the media library to watch in the Museum Theatre. There's also a sobering exhibit, visible from the street, showing the remains of a car salvaged from a drunken driving incident. Friendly members of the Toronto Police help you find almost everything you need to know about the force and how it operates.

UNTITLED (MOUNTAIN)
Simcoe Place, Front Street • map 10 (area 1J) • city.toronto.on.ca/culture • subway: Union.

A lot of street art is emerging in this part of town. Anish Kapoor's metallic sculpture of ribbed, triangular mountain peaks stands just back from Front Street and dominates other pieces of sculpture and fountains around Simcoe Place and Metro Square. It isn't hard to find. All you have to do is head for the crowd of camera-happy tourists. After a while you realize that Kapoor's work has an uncanny resemblance to the signature mountain at Paramount Canada's Wonderland north of the city.

WOODPECKER COLUMN
Toronto Convention Centre's south entrance • map 5 • city.toronto.on.ca/culture • subway: Union and take the Skywalk.

There are a few pieces of street art around town that really reach out and grab you. The 30 m high Woodpecker Column, by Dai Skuse and Kim Kozzi outside the Bremner Boulevard entrance to the Toronto Convention Centre, is one of them. It's a thick black pole dominated by a pileated woodpecker and a yellow-bellied sapsucker. The 1997 work, which does not appear to have a plaque acknowledging the artists, joins Salmon Run, just to the west, as one of many sculptures around downtown devoted to Canada's native animals.

YORK (FIRST) POST OFFICE MUSEUM
260 Adelaide Street East • map 11 • 416-865-1833 • tha.on.ca/firstpo • open weekdays, 9:00 AM – 4:00 PM; weekends, 10:00 AM – 4:00 PM. Closed on statutory holidays • Subway: King and take the 504 King streetcar east to George Street and walk north to Adelaide Street East.

This is the oldest functioning post office in Canada. Originally, all post offices in Upper Canada were owned by Imperialy-appointed postmasters and administered by the British Post Office. Postmaster James Scott Howard was the first to occupy this building, which was constructed in 1833 in the Town of York. This was York's fourth post office building and, in 1834, it became the 'first post office' in the newly minted city of Toronto. Howard held his position from 1833 to 1837 before being fired. It was rumoured that he was a reform sympathizer during the Upper Canada Rebellion of 1837. He appealed his dismissal "with much eloquence" but never got his job back. Today the post office operates as both a post office and museum, enabling visitors to step back in time and learn about postal history. If a genuine quill pen and sealing wax are on your shopping list, then this is where you can buy them. It's also the only post office in the country where you can buy American and British postage stamps.

Places Parts, beaches, squares and zoos

Places **Parks, beaches, squares and zoos**

 Toronto is renowned for the tree-lined streets and wooded ravines that are woven into its urban fabric. In the fall, the place is transformed into one magnificent palette of blazing colour. Check it all out – and, please, DO walk on the grass.

ALBERT CAMPBELL SQUARE
Scarborough Civic Centre • map Toronto (area 17F) and in detail below • 416-396-7111 • **city.toronto.on.ca/parks** • open daily • subway: Kennedy and take the LRT to Scarborough Centre.

This relaxing 9,300 sq m public square, complete with art and a cascading waterfall, won the Vincent Massey Award for urban design. It forms an impressive entry to the Scarborough Civic Centre, which was designed by acclaimed architect Raymond Moriyama. The centre is one of our best examples of modern architecture, both inside and out. Three large pines in the square are turned into illuminated Christmas trees during the Yuletide season.

ALLAN GARDENS – PALM HOUSE
19 Horticultural Avenue • map 16 • 416-392-1111 • **city.toronto.on.ca/parks** • park open daily; Greenhouses open daily, 10:00 AM – 5:00 • subway: College and take the Carlton streetcar east along Carlton Street to Jarvis Street.

The highlight of Allan Gardens is the conservatory. It's comprised of six greenhouses, covering nearly 1,500 sq m, housing the best collection of tropical plants in the city. The Palm House, erected in 1910, was modeled after similar structures in the United States and England. In 2004 another city greenhouse was moved here to become the Children's Conservatory. Historically, you could say that Allan Gardens might be the place where Toronto's formal parks system was born. The Prince of Wales, later King Edward VII, opened a 2 ha space here in 1860 at the behest of the Toronto Horticultural Society. It later became known as Allan Gardens in 1901. It's best to avoid the park at night.

BEACHES

People start to get serious about swimming around Victoria Day, the third Monday in May. After the Labour Day weekend, on the first Monday in September, lifeguards no longer protect the beaches. For years the polluted condition of the city's swimming holes had been the source of ridicule and

136

fierce public debate. But, things have changed dramatically. City officials now check the water quality of all beaches on a daily basis during the season. And, in 2004, Toronto was the first North American city to apply for Blue Flag certification, a rating system widespread in Europe and the Caribbean, which recognizes beaches that are safe for swimming. The following is a small selection of some of the beaches you might want to check out. Just keep your eyes open for that blue flag. The best Web site is **torontobeach.ca**

Bluffer's Park

Bluffer's is the focal point of summer activity for people living in the east end of the city. The beach forms part of the much larger Bluffer's Park complex with its marinas, picnic sites and walking trails. This is where you go for a tan if you want to see the imposing Scarborough bluffs. There's no public transit into the park and walking down Brimley Road to the lakefront from Kingston Road is not recommended because of the heavy summer traffic.

Cherry Beach & Clarke Beach

A bit confusing, but these two beaches are really the same. They are in the middle of the two worlds that have dogged the Toronto waterfront for more than 200 years. Is this industrial land, or is it parkland? To get to the beach at the bottom of Cherry Street you have to go through abandoned industrial wasteland and uninspiring port facilities to get to the water. Once there, Tommy Thompson Park beckons you from across the Toronto Inner Harbour. It's on a man-made peninsula extending five kilometres out into Lake Ontario. One of the most significant features of the park is the colonization of various plant communities. These wetlands, meadows and forests now support many threatened and unusual species. Lying on Cherry/Clarke beach you can look over at all this and enjoy swimming in one of the safest beaches in the city. Take the 72A bus from Union Station, get off at Commissioners' Street, and walk down Cherry Street.

Hanlan's Point Beach

This historical beach, named after the Hanlan family who settled here in 1862, is unique because it was declared 'clothing optional' by city council back in 1894. Since then, no one has been brave enough to get the law changed, though many puritans over the years have tried. The beach, secluded along the west shore of Centre Island, is one of three popular swimming spots along the west and southern shores of the Toronto Islands. It could be said that the name 'Toronto' originated here. Iroquois called the extensive sand bar that gave birth to the islands 'Taronto', which meant 'a meeting place near trees in the water'. Take the Hanlan's Point ferry at the foot of Bay Street across to the islands and follow the signs.

Kew Beach

Kew is just a few blocks east of Woodbine beach and is part of the Kew gardens complex at the bottom of Lee Avenue, off Queen Street East. This is a good summer location if you want to combine lying in the sun, having a swim, playing ball, or just looking around a well-kept park spread over 8 ha. The 501 Queen Street East streetcar drops you right at the door.

Sunnyside Beach

History notes that this beach was one of those places during the Twenties and Thirties that proved to be an irresistible magnet for singles and families. These days, the inflatable rubber tubes and long, striped bathing costumes have gone, giving way to laptop computers, cell phones and barely-legal attire. The pedestrian walkway along the sand is a competing mix of joggers and cyclists weaving their way along the Martin Goodman Trail and through more sedentary folks relaxing under umbrellas. Across the sand and over the lake you can see the Palace Pier towers close by on the western city skyline. The beach is at the bottom of Parkside Drive, off Lake Shore Boulevard East. Take the 501, 508 or 80 transit line along the Queensway and walk about five minutes south.

Woodbine Beach

Woodbine beach is part of the multi-purpose Ashbridge's Bay recreation area. This popular summertime spot goes way back to the Empire Loyalist Ashbridge family who settled here when the Town of York was founded in 1793. Sarah Ashbridge was a Quaker widow and her two sons, John and Jonathan, fought in the War of 1812 and were involved in the Rebellion of 1837. One of their later homesteads still stands only a short distance away at the corner of Queen Street East and Connaught Avenue. Woodbine beach, which is very popular with local residents, sits in a curve along the shore of Ashbridge's Bay park opposite the Ashbridge's Bay Yacht Club, and forms the western end of a continuous coastal greenbelt. Vehicles can enter Ashbridge's Bay park from Lakeshore Boulevard East, just east of Coxwell Avenue. TTC routes include the Queen 501 streetcar east from the Queen subway; the 92 bus south from Woodbine subway; and the 22 bus south from Coxwell subway.

BLUFFER'S PARK
South end of Brimley Road • map Toronto and in detail below • 416-396-7111 • bluffersparkmarina.com • open daily • there's no public transit into the park complex.

When Elizabeth Simcoe, wife of the first lieutenant-governor of Upper Canada, saw this area she said it reminded her of Scarborough Bluffs in Yorkshire, England. The name 'Scarborough' has remained and so have the bluffs. Before Simcoe arrived, they were known as the Toronto Highlands – high cliffs that rose sheer from Lake Ontario to give Toronto its most dramatic topographical feature. Bluffer's Park is the largest and most accessible of many parks along the bluffs and includes a large marina, beaches, walking trails, impressive views and picnic sites. Joining it to the east and west are Cathedral Bluffs park and Scarborough Bluffs park. Together, they provide a

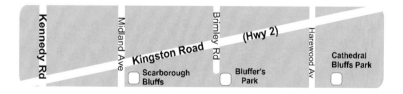

perfect spot for thousands of Torontonians living the eastern end of the city to go and relax when the sun is shining.

CENTENNIAL PARK
256 Centennial Park Road • map Toronto • 416-338-6754 (Ski information) • city.toronto.on.ca • admission $ to some facilities • subway: Kipling and take the Rathburn 48 bus.

This is one of our largest and best all-season recreational parks and the favourite spot in town for organized winter skiing. If you haven't brought downhill and snowboard gear, you can rent some with no problem. Facilities in the 212 ha area include ski and toboggan hills and cross-country trails, a skating arena, golf, picnic sites, an Olympic-sized pool and baseball diamonds, tennis courts and a 2,200 seat stadium. At the end of Elmcrest Road, off Rathburn Road, you'll find the Centennial Park Conservatory. The gardens, which house a wide variety of plants, consist of three glass houses covering 1,100 sq m.

DISCOVERY WALKS
City-wide • 416-392-8186 • city.toronto.on.ca and look under 'Discovery Walks.'

When you want to escape the downtown concrete, you can enjoy a network of self-guided walks that have been designed by the city's Parks Department. Just log on to Toronto's Web site (city.toronto.on.ca). Here's something they had to say there: "On these walks you will enjoy nature, learn about local area natural and social history, and during the warmer weather, see the many beautiful floral displays at our feature park sites." That said, it's amazing what you can accomplish. In fact, it's possible for you to walk from the lake to the city's northern boundary without ever leaving a park or ravine. We've given 'taking a walk in the park' a whole new meaning.

DUNDAS SQUARE
Yonge Street at Dundas Street • map 16 • 416-979-9960 • ydsquare.ca • subway: Dundas.

Back in the late 1990s, the city – and just about everyone else – decided that Dundas Square needed to be cleaned-up and totally re-designed. The goal was "to create a strong, dynamic area, bringing Yonge Street back to its former glory." This precipitated a frenzy of building in the square and around its perimeter. In 2000, when it was starting to take shape, *Architecture Magazine* awarded the square a Progressive Architecture citation for "pushing the limits for invention and originality." Some would say this is an understatement. The result is the most heavily concentrated outdoor advertising gallery in the country, outdone on the continent only by Las Vegas and New York's Times Square. The square itself is designed to hold a crowd anywhere from 1,000 to 12,000 people for public celebrations, or private rentals. There have been caustic comments about its design by everyone from suburbanites and sophisticates to the homeless and disabled. The city fathers think it's wonderful, and people who have to stumble over its seemingly pointless steps and stairs really don't agree. Best to judge for yourself. Go after sundown when the razzle-dazzle effect is even more overpowering.

EDWARDS GARDENS

777 Lawrence Avenue East at Leslie Street • map Toronto (area 12H) • 416-397-8186
• city.toronto.on.ca • open daily, dawn to dusk • subway: Eglinton and take the
Lawrence East 54 bus to Leslie Street.

A lot of us regard this former estate, originally belonging to Alexander Milne, as the best of the city's three formal public gardens. Milne began milling operations here shortly after he bought the property in 1812. In 1944 Rupert Edwards bought 11 ha of the property which, by now, had become overgrown and ignored. Although he had virtually no knowledge of landscaping and gardening, he managed to turn his property into what you see today. The gardens are renowned for perennials, roses and wildflowers. Make a visit in spring, when the magnolias, azaleas and more than 200 rhododendron varieties are in full bloom. It's one of the top city attractions for gardeners. The Civic Garden Centre, one of the country's top gardening education facilities, uses the gardens as its base. As a bonus, you can see three apple trees here that are over 150 years old.

HARBOURFRONT PARK

Queen's Quay West at Rees Street • map 4 • city.toronto.on.ca • subway: Union and
take the 509 streetcar to Rees Street.

Harbourfront Park has spawned more plans, public consultations and committee meetings than any one can recall. For many years, the lake's edge immediately to the south of Rogers Centre has been awash in promises by all levels of government "to do something." The general idea has been "to transform Toronto's central waterfront into a destination for international tourism, national celebration and local enjoyment." While all this has been going on, developers have forged ahead building a wall of high-rise condominiums along the north side of Queen's Quay West. Apart from the Toronto Music Garden, this thin strip of the waterfront between the lake and Queen's Quay West yawns for attention. Apparently, the transformation is finally underway regarding the 'international tourism, national celebration and local enjoyment' thing. Just don't hold your breath too long.

HIGH PARK

Bloor Street West at Parkside Drive • map Toronto and in detail below •
city.toronto.on.ca • subway: Keele.

From the corner of Bloor Street West and Parkside Drive (the extension of Keele Street), the park extends south to the Queensway and west halfway to South Kingsway. John George Howard, who built a lodge here in 1873, once owned most of this land. Since then the space has become one of the largest multi-use parks in the city. Where else could you set up your own community garden, go fishing, swoosh down a toboggan hill, become part of the audience for a play by Shakespeare, or let Fido run around without a leash? You could also play tennis, check out a llama, or even get all enthused over a sculpture symposium. Rounding all this out is historical Colborne Lodge, John Howard's original home. High Park's main feature is Grenadier Pond, which forms most of the park's western boundary. Those of us who live nearby make it a focal point for year-round outdoor activities.

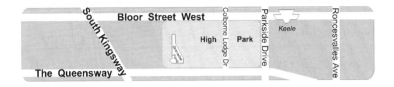

HUMBER ARBORETUM
205 Humber College Boulevard • map *Toronto* (area 1C) and in detail below •
416-675-5009 • humberc.on.ca • open daily, 9:00 AM – 3:30 PM • subway: Finch and
take 36C bus west to Humber College Boulevard.

Up in the northwest corner of the city, situated on the west branch of the
Humber River, there's 96 ha of green space that includes an extensive collection of over 5,000 trees, shrubs and herbaceous plants in a natural environment. It provides a walk with nature along the banks of the Etobicoke Creek
and reflects a different view of nature as the seasons change. The arboretum,
which opened in the fall of 1982 and is maintained by Humber College students, offers over three kilometres of bike and walking trails, a nature club for
kids, an area where you can get ideas for landscaping, and ways to explore
wetlands, meadows and forests.

HUMBER BAY PARK
Lake Shore Boulevard West at Park Lawn Road • map Toronto • 416-392-8186 •
city.toronto.on.ca • subway: Old Mill and take the 66D bus.

This is where Mimico Creek enters the lake after curling through the biggest
waterfront park in the city's west end. There are two yacht clubs here, together with a marine unit of the Toronto Police. The three scenic lookout points
will give you a perfect view of the city skyline. This park surrounds you with
water, gives you a glimpse of an historic lighthouse and pampers you with
an adventurous set of pathways, including the Waterfront Trail. Developed
by the former Metropolitan Toronto and Region Conservation Authority with
5.1 million cubic metres of lakefill, at a cost of $6.56-million, Humber Bay
Park was opened by Lieutenant-Governor John Black Aird on June 11, 1984.
Several habitat restoration projects have been initiated here including the
planting of Carolinian trees and shrubs, the establishment of wildflower
meadows and the creation of a warm-water fish habitat and wetland on the
east peninsula. It's also a great spot for bird watching. You can walk from this
point on Lake Ontario up to Steeles Avenue on the northern side of the city
without ever leaving ravine parkland – which is quite a challenge!

MEL LASTMAN SQUARE
5100 Yonge Street, fronting North York Civic Centre • map 35 • 416-395-7584 •
toronto.com • subway: North York Centre.

When North York was a city, it created a square in front of city hall to rival
Toronto's Nathan Phillips Square. When the cities amalgamated in 1998,
competition came to an end. Even though North York is now uptown
Toronto, Mel Lastman Square remains this area's lively focal point for celebrations and general good times. During the summer there's usually a
farmer's market, several festivals and lots of outdoor concerts taking place.

141

Of the city's five civic squares, this one is considered to be among the most attractive. Mel Lastman, after whom the square is named, was the last mayor of North York and the first mayor of Toronto after the cities amalgamated. The square is both wheelchair and scooter accessible.

MOUNT PLEASANT CEMETERY
375 Mount Pleasant Road • map 32 • 416-485-9129 • mountpleasantgroupofcemeteries.ca • open 8:00 AM – dusk • subway: Eglinton and take the 103 bus.

Here is one of Canada's most historical public cemeteries. Since 1876 it has become the final resting-place of many prominent Canadians, including former prime minister William Lyon Mackenzie King; Jennie Smillie-Robinson, Canada's first female surgeon; and celebrated concert pianist, Glenn Gould. Other famous folk include Nobel Prize winner, Dr. Frederick Banting, co-discoverer of insulin, and nationally-known families like the Masseys and Eatons. An example of practically every kind of tree that grows around Toronto can be found here. Hundreds of varieties include everything from Oriental elm and Babylon willow to oak trees that were mature when the cemetery opened. This arboreal diversity could be the largest in a single place in North America. Like nearly all the cemeteries in Toronto, Mount Pleasant welcomes the public to drop by and spend a few relaxing hours just roaming around and exploring interesting things in peace and quiet.

NATHAN PHILLIPS SQUARE
100 Queen Street West • map 10 • 416-392-1111 • city.toronto.on.ca • subway: Queen or Osgoode.

When we go out to celebrate something like New Year's Eve, we usually descend in our tens of thousands on Nathan Phillips Square in front of city hall. It's one of the most photographed places in town with the Freedom Arches raised over a reflecting pool in the summer and a hugely popular skating rink in the winter. A piece of the Berlin Wall lays flat at the base of the centre freedom arch on the south side. In the middle of the square is The Peace Garden consisting of a simple cube with a pitched roof, an eternal flame, a pool and stone platform walls. The roof has a damaged appearance, which signifies conflict and evokes the theme of civilization's frailty. Nathan Phillips Square, which will soon receive some fresh design elements, is where you'll see the winter ice sculpture competition, July's Toronto Outdoor Art Exhibition, plus countless demonstrations, welcoming ceremonies, cultural displays and open-air concerts. Two pieces of sculpture – Henry Moore's Three-way Piece #2 (commonly called 'The Archer') and a defiant Winston Churchill – let the square pay homage to two British icons from totally different spheres. After serving 40 years in city politics, Nathan Phillips became mayor of Toronto from 1955 to 1962, and is the person most responsible for building the new city hall. The "mayor of all the people" died in 1976.

QUEEN'S PARK
Queen's Park Crescent at Wellesley Street East • map 20 • subway: Queen's Park and walk north along Queen's Park Crescent East to the northern side of the legislative buildings.

The Prince of Wales named this park in honour of Queen Victoria in 1860, thirty-two years before the provincial legislative buildings opened at its southern end. It seems that just about everything in the immediate vicinity is associated with the Queen in some way or another. Of special interest here is the statue of a mounted King Edward VII which was given to Canada by the Indian government after their independence from Britain. It sits in the middle of this heavily wooded enclave, surrounded on three sides by the University of Toronto. The university owns the park and the city leases it from them for one dollar a year. At the park's northern end is a tribute to the 48th Highlanders of Canada, a militia infantry regiment based in Toronto and founded in 1891. It has served in every major conflict since.

RIVERDALE FARM
201 Winchester Street • map 22 • 416-392-6794 • city.toronto.on.ca • open daily 9:00 AM – 5:00 PM (January – April and November - December); 9:00 AM – 6:00 PM (May – October) • subway: College and take the 506 streetcar east to Sumach Street and walk north.

Not many large cities have a fully operational farm in their downtown core, especially one depicting rural life at the end of the 19th century. The Riverdale Farm sits within the historic community of Cabbagetown and gives people, especially children, an idea of what stoic rural life was like and what it's all about. This site goes way back to 1856 when the city bought it for a park. That prospect was never fully realized because they then decided to open the city's first zoo here in 1894. It remained the city's only zoo until 1974 when all the animals were moved to the new Toronto Zoo out in Scarborough. If your kids have never been to a farm, a visit here will keep them fascinated.

ROSETTA McCLAIN GARDENS
Kingston Road at Fishleigh Drive • map Toronto (area 16L) and in detail below • city.toronto.on.ca • open daily, dawn to dusk • subway: Warden and take the 69 bus south.

Just west of the Scarborough Bluffs parks complex is one of the most secluded and attractive public gardens in the city. It's one of the few, if any, places along the eastern lake shore that is free of Canada Geese, bikes, dogs and people having picnics. The gardens, on a 16.2 ha site donated by Robert McClain in 1959, are a place for strolling among summer flower beds and leafy trees, or just sitting near a waterfall and looking out over the lake. It's one of many parks that has a site map in Braille.

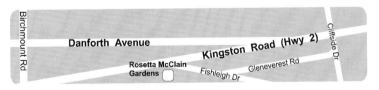

ROUGE PARK
Sheppard Avenue East at Twyn Rivers Drive • map Toronto and in detail on the following page • 416-287-6843 • rougepark.com • subway: Kennedy and take an 86 Zoo bus to Sheppard Avenue East, then walk east along Sheppard and down Twyn Rivers Drive.

This is the largest urban park in North America. It's now all but forgotten that here, at the mouth of the Rouge River, from 1655 to 1687, there was a Seneca village called Ganatsekywagon and it hosted the first European residence in the Toronto area. It was also the site of the province's first school, which was built in 1669. This magnificent valley has survived repeated attempts by developers to turn it into prime residential property. A frustrated local developer once put up a notice along the busy highway stating: "If it wasn't for the white-tailed deer, you'd be home by now." Local residents battled hard to keep the deer in and developers out. Then they launched a massive campaign against the federal government's plans to build a new airport nearby. Their efforts to preserve the valley in pristine condition were finally rewarded when the government finally protected it as a wilderness area. In 1994, after considering the recommendations of the Rouge Valley Park Advisory Committee, the Province of Ontario announced that the Rouge River watershed would become the home of the largest park ever created within an urban area in North America. The ravine lands cover 5,400 ha, making them four times larger than the Toronto Islands and seven times bigger than New York's Central Park.

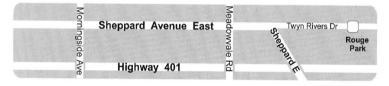

St JAMES' CEMETERY AND CREMATORIUM
635 Parliament Street • map 22 • 416-964-9194 • stjamescathedral.on.ca • open daily, 8:00 AM – 8:00 PM • subway: Castle Frank and go west along Bloor Street East and south on Parliament Street.

John G Howard, one of the most respected architects of his day, began laying plans for the cemetery in 1842 at the behest of the Church of England. St James is the oldest public cemetery in Toronto and contains the burial sites of many of the city's prominent historical figures. In 1857, the architectural firm of Cumberland and Storm was selected to prepare plans for a burial chapel just inside the Parliament Street entrance. The chapel was built of Georgetown stone and white brick with Ohio stone trim. In 1860, the Chapel of St James-The-Less was consecrated and is now listed as a national historical site. The heavily wooded burial ground, although not officially a park, is a favourite place for neighbourhood strolls and is a treasure trove of interest for history buffs.

St JAMES SQUARE
Entry off Gould Street, or Gerrard Street East, east of Yonge Street • map 16 • ryerson.ca • subway: College and walk south to Gerrard Street.

In 1850, Egerton Ryerson founded public education in Ontario and set up shop on a parcel of semi-rural land known as St. James Square. The land was bought from the city and used to build what became known as the 'Normal School', which was Canada's first teacher's college. Since then, this plot of land has been the site of the city's first museum, Toronto's first art school and, during World War II, the Royal Canadian Air Force's headquarters for training men and women in trades for the war industry. The museum moved away and became the Royal Ontario Museum and the art school found a new home and called itself the Ontario College of Art and Design. Bits of the old Normal School remain standing in the square, which is virtually unknown to anyone except the faculty and students at Ryerson University. These days it's a quadrangle within the university's grounds and you get into it through gates on both Gerrard Street East and Gould Street. Peace and quiet are guaranteed.

THE CENTRAL DON
Eglinton Avenue East at Leslie Street • map Toronto and in detail on the following page • 416-392-8186 • city.toronto.on.ca/parks • subway: Eglinton and take the 34 bus east to Leslie Street.

In the geographical centre of the city there's a magnificent series of inter-connected parks known collectively as the Central Don. Anchored by Edwards Gardens in the north, the Central Don includes the popular Sunnybrook Park together with Serena Gundy, Wilket Creek and Ernest Thompson Seton parks. Sunnybrook is home to the Toronto Police Central Don Stables, sporting fields and lots of picnic sites in a mature forest setting. You can drive through the park complex, but it's much better to get out of your vehicle and stay awhile. This is a great place to take a nice long walk during any season, but particularly during the fall when this entire area is awash in a sea of magnificent colours. In the winter, bring the whole family for cross-country skiing and tobogganing.

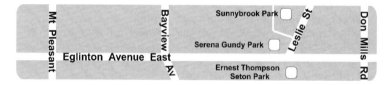

TORONTO ISLANDS PARK
The southern side of Toronto harbour • map 1 • city.toronto.on.ca • subway: Union and take the 509 streetcar west to Bay Street and the ferry terminal.

People have been coming here for centuries to relax and enjoy themselves. This is the site for everything from the hugely popular Caribana picnic, to the Royal Canadian Yacht Club and the city's only clothing-optional beach. On Centre Island the kid's will enjoy the low-key amusement park and petting zoo, while adults will find lots to explore among the marinas and leafy parks. If you're a photography wonk, here's where you'll get some great shots of the city skyline. The Toronto Islands were not always islands but actually a series of continuously moving sand bars originating from the Scarborough Bluffs and carried west by Lake Ontario currents. The peninsula and surrounding sand bars were first surveyed in 1792 by Lieutenant Bouchette of the British Navy. A report in 1813 noted that "the long beach, or peninsula, which affords a most delightful ride, is considered so healthy by the Indians that they resort to it whenever indisposed". On January 1, 1956 the 230 ha Toronto Islands Park and its wildlife reserves were designated as a regional park. It has been estimated that more than 1,225,000 people pay it a visit every year.

TORONTO MUSIC GARDEN
475 Queen's Quay West at Lower Spadina Avenue • map 4 • 416-338-0338 • city.toronto.on.ca/parks • subway: Union and take the Harbourfront streetcar west along Queen's Quay West to Lower Spadina Avenue.

When it opened to the public in June 1999 the garden was hailed as being one of the most creative uses of open space in the city. Julie Messervy designed the waterfront project in collaboration with landscape architects from the city's Parks and Recreation department. The garden design interprets in nature Bach's *First Suite for Unaccompanied Cello,* with each dance movement within the suite corresponding to a different section in the garden. Tom Tollefson fabricated the Music Pavilion and Anne Roberts designed the Maypole. Internationally renowned concert cellist, Yo-Yo Ma, worked with the landscapers to help translate Bach's music into a garden.

TORONTO ZOO
Two kilometres north of Sheppard Avenue East on Meadowvale Road • map Toronto and in detail below • (416) 392-5929 • **torontozoo.com** • open daily: Spring and Fall, 9:00 AM – 6:00 PM; Summer, 9:00 AM – 7:30 PM; Winter, 9:30 AM – 4:30 PM. Closed Christmas Day • subway: Kennedy and take the Zoo bus.

The Toronto Zoo is one of the largest and most respected zoos in the world. It occupies 287 ha of land on the edge of the extensive Rouge wilderness park in the north-eastern section of the city and is divided into what's called six 'zoogeographic' regions: Indo-Malaya, Africa, the Americas, Australasia, Eurasia and the Canadian Domain. Over 6,000 animals, representing 460 species, are displayed indoors in tropical pavilions and outdoors in simulated natural environments. The zoo opened on August 15, 1974, after a committee was formed back in 1949 "to look into construction of a major new zoo." The zoological park has over 10 km of walking trails that weave among the pavilions, picnic sites, gardens and waterfalls. Almost 40,000,000 people have visited the zoo since it opened more than three decades ago.

TRINITY SQUARE
Northwest side of the Eaton Centre • map 15 • 416-598-4521 • holytrinitytoronto.org • open daily • subway: Dundas.

No square in town holds quite the history of Trinity Square. Three of our oldest buildings can be found here: Holy Trinity church (1847), Scadding House (1860) and the Old Rectory (1861). It seems unbelievable now, but it was seriously considered that these historical landmarks should be demolished to make way for the building of the Eaton Centre. The square has developed into one of most the pleasant and restful places in the downtown core, despite the fact that it's only just across the street from raucous Dundas

Square. It's a great place to brown-bag your summer lunch and catch up on the next chapter of that book you're reading. In 2000, the city decided to create a labyrinth here, made of turf grass, and copied from the 13th century stone labyrinth at Chartres Cathedral in France. Walking the labyrinth involves the creative and intuitive mind. Unlike a maze that can become frustrating, the labyrinth can be calming and unifying. It is not possible to get lost in a labyrinth. The only decision needed is to enter and walk and relax.

VILLAGE OF YORKVILLE PARK
Cumberland Street at Bellair Street • map 25 • 416-392-1111 • crave.com/yorkville
• subway: Bay and use the Bellair Street exit.

What you see is the result of an international design competition launched by the city in 1991. Several objectives were set for the project, including a desire "to provide a variety of spatial and sensory experiences..." In reality, it has 13 separate sections for plant life and a rock. According to the landscape team: "We designed the park to reflect the Victorian style of collecting. In this case we were collecting landscapes of Canada – pine grove, prairie, marsh, orchard, rock outcropping and so on – and arranging them in the manner of the nineteenth-century row houses." But it's that 19 x 15 m slab of rock that caused all the controversy. It's over a billion years old, weighs 650 tonnes, and it took 20 flatbed trucks to haul it in pieces from the northern town of Gravenhurst. Once in place, the bits were flame treated around the edges to create almost invisible seams. It's not polite to ask how much all of this cost.

Entertainment

Few cities offer the extensive diversity of entertainment that's available year-round in Toronto. It's been estimated that one in nine Torontonians is employed, directly or indirectly, in the entertainment business. The result of their endeavours deserves nothing less than sustained applause.

Annual events, **148**
Ballet & dance, **160**
Cinema, **161**
Clubs & bars, **163**
Family entertainment centres, **164**

Opera & classical music, **166**
Sport, **169**
Stage companies, **172**
Theatres, concert halls & stadiums, **175**

Entertainment **Annual events**

Throughout the year, the city's streets and stages provide a never-ending supply of events and festivals to keep us involved, enthralled, interested and amused. From Gay Pride and the Great Salmon Hunt, to Chinese New Year and Caribana, here's an idea of what's happening throughout the year.

*Events in **bold** type below are reviewed alphabetically following this schedule.*

JANUARY
Chinese New Year
Toronto International Boat Show

FEBRUARY
Antiques Canada Show
Canadian International Auto Show
Chinese New Year
WinterCity Festival

MARCH
Canada Blooms
Canadian Music Week
International Home & Garden Show
Toronto Model Railway Show
Toronto Sportsmen's Show

APRIL
Creative Sewing & Needlework Festival
Images Festival
National Home Show
Toronto Wine & Cheese Show

MAY
Fashion Cares
Inside Out Film & Video Festival
MILK International Children's Festival

JUNE
Canada Dance Festival
Festival of Fire
Gay Pride Parade
Toronto Downtown Jazz Festival
Toronto Dragon Boat Race Festival
Toronto International Festival Caravan

JULY
Beaches International Jazz Festival
Canada Day
Caribana
Celebrate Toronto Street Festival
CHIN International Picnic
Corso Italia Toronto Fiesta
Festival of Fire
Great Salmon Hunt
Molson Indy Toronto
Toronto Downtown Jazz Festival
Toronto Fringe Theatre Festival
Toronto International Festival Caravan
Toronto Outdoor Art Exhibition

AUGUST
Breeder's Stakes
Canadian National Exhibition (CNE)
Caribana Parade
Great Salmon Hunt
Rogers Cup
Taste of the Danforth

SEPTEMBER
Canadian International Air Show
Canadian National Exhibition (CNE)
Cabbagetown Cultural Festival

Todmorden Mills Harvest Festival
Toronto International Film Festival
Toronto In-water Boat Show
Vegetarian Food Fair
Word on the Street

OCTOBER
Canadian International Marathon
International Festival of Authors
Toronto Ski Show
Toronto Trails Festival

NOVEMBER
Canadian Aboriginal Festival
One-of-a-kind Craft Show
Royal Agricultural Winter Fair
Santa Claus Parade

DECEMBER
One-of-a-kind Craft Show
New Year celebrations

ANTIQUES CANADA SHOW
February, last week • Toronto Convention Centre, north building • map 10 • 1-800-667-0619 • **antiqueshowscanada.com** • admission $ • subway: Union and walk two blocks west along Front Street.

A few years back, when the old Antique Market on Queen's Quay West was torn down to make way for condominiums, it left quite a hole in the lives of those folk who enjoy pottering around dusty corners in search of something old and unusual. Now, for a few days anyway, those folk can get an annual fix. So, should you be looking for anything from antique maps to vintage wedding dresses, or from original Québec pine furniture to militaria and old tins, here's where you should be. Dealers from across Canada descend on the Toronto Convention Centre to bring you Canada's largest exposition of premier, in-demand antique and collectible merchandise. To make it even better, you can browse around an antiquarian book fair.

BEACHES INTERNATIONAL JAZZ FESTIVAL
July, third week • Kew Gardens and Queen Street East between Woodbine and Beech avenues • map Suburbs & neighbourhoods and in detail on the following page • 1-888-277-0796 • **beachesjazz.com** • subway: Woodbine and take a 92 bus to Queen Street.

The Beach(es) is a trendy part of town, filled with old homes and occupied by a closely-knit community. Musicians, locals and tens of thousands of other people turn out to make the festival one of the city's top summer music attractions. They take over a two-kilometre section of Queen Street East during the four-day blowout, packing bistros, street corners, rooftops and the main stage at Kew Gardens. The festival has been wowing everyone for close to 20 years and there are usually pre-festival performances outside the neighbourhood as far away as the downtown Distillery District.

CABBAGETOWN CULTURAL FESTIVAL
September, first or second week • Parliament Street south of Wellesley Street East • map 22 • 416-921-0857 • oldcabbagetown.com • subway: Wellesley and take a 94 bus east along Wellesley to Parliament Street

Become part of the neighbourhood as one of our most distinctive communities stages what it calls "the best fall festival in downtown." Who cares if it's the only one. Pancake breakfasts, street dancing, garage sales, plus a parade and restaurant/pub crawl are just some of the things you can enjoy. The festival also gives homeowners the opportunity to showcase their renovated Victorian houses to those of us who want to peep inside. It's a good idea to case the neighbourhood beforehand to make a list of houses displaying a small plaque indicating that the owners will be happy to welcome you at festival time. If all this isn't enough, the neighbourhood has its own film festival.

CANADA BLOOMS
March, second week • Toronto Convention Centre, South Building • map 10 • 416-447-8655 • canadablooms.com • admission $ • subway: Union and go two blocks west along Front Street West.

Canada Blooms, or the Toronto Flower and Garden Show as it is often known, is the largest flower and garden show in the country. This feast for gardeners and flower-lovers alike is a show that promotes and enhances the awareness of horticulture by featuring the best designs, products and services of the amateur and professional horticultural community. This very popular show has received national and international recognition. The *New York Times* referred to it as one of the top three shows of its kind in North America. Close to a thousand volunteers get together to make sure everything is just right before the public gets a chance to shed their winter blahs and enjoy the promise of spring. Proceeds go to the Garden Club of Toronto and Landscape Ontario to support educational projects promoting horticulture and civic landscaping.

CANADA DAY
July first • various locations around the city.

Most of the city closes for the national holiday. The biggest celebrations are at Ontario Place, Nathan Phillips Square, Centre Island, Mel Lastman Square and Queen's Park. Catch the Festival of Fire at Ontario Place, or watch the Toronto Harbour Parade of Lights. Centre Island has the country's oldest and biggest canoeing and rowing regatta that day. Official greetings, good times and music abound in Nathan Phillips Square, or you can relax with your kids during activities at Queen's Park. The International CHIN Picnic kicks off for four days at Exhibition Place. In the evening, families turn out for local fireworks in parks across the city. The best uptown venue is Mel Lastman Square where fireworks are mixed with a concert featuring Canadian talent. Both East York and Scarborough hold local community parades.

CANADIAN INTERNATIONAL AIR SHOW
September, Labour Day weekend • Exhibition Place • map 2 • 416-393-6061 • cias.org • admission $ included with CNE admission • subway: Union and take the Harbourfront 509 streetcar to Exhibition Place.

The air show has entered its second half-century as the grand finale to the Canadian National Exhibition. The thunderous display takes place over Lake

Ontario and the best vantage points are Exhibition Place, Ontario Place and the immediate lakefront. The show starts around 1:00 PM and lasts about three hours with a mix of military and civilian aircraft, plus the Canadian Forces Snowbirds aerobatics team. The Snowbirds were formed back in 1970 and consists of nine Canadair CT-114 Tutor aircraft. Tickets to the air show are included in your admission price for the CNE.

CANADIAN INTERNATIONAL AUTO SHOW
February, third week • Toronto Convention Centre and Rogers Centre • maps 10, 4 • 416-585-3660 • **autoshow.ca** • admission $ • subway: Union and walk two blocks west along Front Street.

The show is one of the biggest names on the worldwide auto exhibition circuit, closely following Paris, Detroit and Tokyo in international prominence. Within the last few years, Toronto's auto show has concentrated on putting itself on the leading edge of automobile design. Its aim is to provide a new generation of designers with a spectacular stage to showcase their work and to offer the car-buying public a stunning presentation of what the future holds. This is one of the world's five official international auto shows. More than 46,500 sq m of floor space in the Convention Centre are given over to a dreamland of four-wheeled horse power. What's left over fills the infield of the Rogers Centre. Promoted as the "total automotive experience, "the auto show lets you see what nearly 150 exhibitors and manufacturers have to offer in the way of new, concept and vintage vehicles, plus lots of automotive gear. It's the ultimate tire-kicking experience.

CANADIAN INTERNATIONAL MARATHON
October, mid month • start at Mel Lastman Square • map 35 • 416-972-1062 • **runtoronto.com** • entry fee $.

The marathon has huffed and puffed its way through more than a decade. Participants have four muscle-aching choices: the full marathon, a half-marathon, a half-marathon walk and a 5 km marathon. After leaving Mel Lastman Square, the runners make their way in a general southerly direction to the Queen's Park finishing line. This means that motorists will find sections of these thoroughfares closed that day: Yonge Street, Steeles Avenue, Dufferin Street, Sheppard Avenue, Bayview Avenue, Rosedale Valley Road, Spadina Road, Lake Shore Boulevard, Front Street and University Avenue. It might be a good idea for Sunday drivers to stay home and watch the event on television and wonder why people would pay as much as $80 each to go through all this agony.

CANADIAN NATIONAL EXHIBITION (CNE)
Mid August through Labour Day • Exhibition Place • map 2 • 416-393-6090 (Tickets) • **theex.com** • admission $ • subway: Union and take the Harbourfront 509 streetcar to Exhibition Place.

'The Ex' has been a Toronto summer experience for well over 100 years and has a place in most everyone's memory. The midway, candy floss, Food Hall and exhibitors from more than 40 countries combine to make this a traditional family summer outing. It's believed to be the oldest continuing exhibition of its type in the world. In 1882 the Exhibition Grounds became the first in the world to be lit by electricity. Two years later Canada's first electric railway was introduced, making it the second operational system in the world. In 1888 a young Thomas Edison recorded a message by Lord Stanley (of Stanley Cup fame) to the President of the United States. The recording was made at the Exhibition and today remains the oldest existing sound recording. Much later, Canada's first television broadcast originated here. The name of the Exhibition was changed in 1912 from the Toronto Industrial Exhibition to the Canadian National Exhibition in order to reflect its rapidly expanding scope and importance. The historical significance of this part of Toronto goes back even further. If you go down to the CNE's western waterfront, just west of the band shell, you'll see a tall monument, a memorial plaque and a concrete outline in the grass. This is the spot where the French built little Fort Rouillé in 1748 to protect the first European settlement in the area.

CARIBANA PARADE
August, first weekend • Exhibition Place start, then along Lake Shore Boulevard West • maps 2, 3, 4 • 416-465-4884 • caribana.com • admission $ to seated area, otherwise free • subway: Union and take the Harbourfront 509 streetcar to Exhibition Place for the parade.

This is North America's largest celebration of Caribbean culture. Two weeks of events, food and festivities climax with the lavishly costumed parade that attracts large crowds of people from all over the world. The next two days are spent partying on Centre Island. Together with Mardi Gras in New Orleans, the Caribana parade is North America's most lavish street extravaganza. Don't expect everything to start on time, but be prepared to be caught up in the party-like atmosphere. Thousands of brilliantly costumed masqueraders and dozens of trucks carrying live soca, calypso, steel pan, reggae and salsa artists jam the 1.5 km parade route all day. If you're coming to town for this event, book your hotel room well in advance.

CELEBRATE TORONTO STREET FESTIVAL
July, second weekend • Yonge Street at Eglinton Avenue, St Clair Avenue, Bloor Street and Dundas Street intersections • times: Saturday, 11.00 AM – 11.00 PM; Sunday, 11.00 AM – 5.00 PM • maps: Toronto, 34, 32, 25, 16 • 416-338-0338 • city.toronto.on.ca • subways: Eglinton, St Clair, Yonge-Bloor & Dundas.

Big bands, jazz groups, dance, kids' stuff, family fun and star acts take over four of the city's main Yonge Street intersections. There's an official kick-off to the weekend on Friday night, usually at Dundas Square. All intersections are closed to traffic. Check out the Web site for details, join about a million other people, get into the mood – and party!

CHIN INTERNATIONAL PICNIC
July 1 • Exhibition Place • map 2 • 416-531-9991 • chinradio.com • subway: Union and take the Harbourfront 509 streetcar to Exhibition Place

Following its modest beginning about 30 years ago, the picnic has become the world's biggest free international party for adults and kids. More than 2,000 performers entertain an estimated crowd of 250,000 people during the four days of festivities. Be prepared for non-stop cultural and contemporary song and dance entertainment, a circus, amusement park rides, games, a beer garden, dozens of food concessions, major sports events, and an international shopping bazaar. Then, to top it all off, get ready for the Mr. and Miss CHIN bikini pageants. CHIN, founded by the late Johnny Lombardi, is Toronto's multi-lingual radio station.

CHINESE NEW YEAR
End of January, or early February, depending on the date for Chinese New Year • the city's three major Chinatowns: Dundas at Spadina (map 14); Gerrard at Broadview (map Toronto, area 12M and in detail below); and around Sheppard Avenue East at Midland Avenue (map Toronto, area 17E and in detail below) • 416-299-9092 (Chinese Business Promotion Centre) • admission: $ for restaurant meals and free for street festivities.

This is the best time of the year to go to a Chinese restaurant. Chefs pull out all the stops with lots of special dishes to make you drool during a two-week culinary extravaganza. Take in the noise and fun of dragon dances and fire crackers around the Dundas Street West and Spadina Avenue neighbourhood in the downtown core.

CORSO ITALIA TORONTO FIESTA
July, second week • St Clair Avenue West between Dufferin Street and Lansdowne Avenue; Earlscourt Park • map Toronto (area 8K) and in detail on the following page • 416-658-0901 • torontofiesta.com • subway: Lansdowne and take a 47 bus north to St Clair; Dufferin and take a 29 bus north to St Clair.

Here's your opportunity to join the Italian community while it puts on a two-day multi-cultural street experience along St Clair Avenue West in the middle of Corso Italia. The festival provides a good opportunity to really get into the Italian spirit, peoplewatch, take advantage of sidewalk sales, eat enormous amounts of Italian food and relax with a cappuccino. If Italy should get to the final of the soccer World Cup again, this is where you should head for the festivities.

FASHION CARES
May, last week • Toronto Convention Centre, South Building • map 5 • fashioncares.org • subway: Union and walk two blocks west along Front Street.

Nowhere else in the country will you be able to attend such a spectacular fashion gala. Here's where the local and international fashion and design industries come together to put on a memorable event that commands the hottest ticket in town. Since its beginning in 1986, each and every Fashion Cares gala has been a success critically, artistically and financially. With its first 17 years bringing in over 44,000 guests and raising more than $6,000,000 for HIV-AIDS, there's little wonder that tickets usually sell out well in advance. If you plan to come, book early. The event is put on by the AIDS Committee of Toronto (ACT), a charitable organization devoted to HIV-AIDS support, prevention and education. The show reaches a worldwide television audience numbering well over a million viewers and enjoys the support of many of Canada's foremost businesses.

GAY PRIDE PARADE

June, last weekend • starts downtown at Bloor Street East and Church Street, goes west along Bloor, south on Yonge, then east on Gould to Church • maps 26, 21, 16 • 416-925-9872 (Xtra! Gay Infoline) • pridetoronto.com • subway: Bloor, Wellesley, College.

The televised parade is the largest pride outing in Canada. Although estimates vary considerably, it's generally conceded that upwards of around 700,000 people line the main parade route. Much lesser numbers turn out for the Dyke March the day before. These two events climax a week of gay and lesbian cultural activities centred in the Church-Wellesley Village neighbourhood where the immediate area is blocked to traffic from Friday night till early Monday morning for one non-stop street party. If you are coming to town for the celebrations, and want a nearby hotel, book well in advance.

GREAT SALMON HUNT

July, second week - end of August • Lake Ontario from Wellington to St Catharines • 416-695-0311 • sportsmensshows.com • registration $.

It wasn't long ago that many people thought that the polluted waters of Lake Ontario would destroy the salmon stock. Those days are gone and now almost $1,500,000 in prize money awaits anglers, especially the one who hauls in the specially tagged salmon. Ten prizes are awarded each week, with total cash amounting to nearly $300,000 for those landing the heaviest fish. You have to register to be eligible for the riches, but don't get really excited until your catch weighs at least 9 kg. Once you've netted one this big you'll be entered into a special prize draw. If you catch anything less than 7 kg you might as well throw it back and prepare another line. Close, but no cigar.

MILK CHILDREN'S FESTIVAL OF THE ARTS

May, last week • Harbourfront Centre • map 5 • 416-973-4000 • harbourfrontcentre.com/milk • admission $ • subway: Union and take the LRT to Harbourfront Centre.

Here's something specifically designed to attract the kids. For eight days, Harbourfront Centre is alive with the world's best professional contemporary performing arts groups for youngsters. The festival's promoters are quick to point out that "We have searched the globe to bring you the most creative and diverse productions, many presenting in Canada for the very first time. These amazing mainstage productions showcase our belief that art and cultural experiences are essential for the development, enrichment, creativity and imagination of children, students, teachers, and adults of all ages."

MOLSON INDY TORONTO

July, second week • Exhibition Place & Lakeshore Boulevard West • map 1 • 416-872-4639 (tickets) • molsonindy.com • admission $ • subway: Union and take the Harbourfront 509 streetcar to Exhibition Place.

Top racing drivers from around the world compete with Canadian champions in events that offer lots more than just the roar of engines. The Indy is part of the 20-race FedEx championship that includes events in Australia, Brazil, Japan and the United States. Races highlight a week-long celebration, known as Indyfest, that revs up over 300,000 race fans, Champ Car drivers, celebrities, sponsors, media and the community at large. It is designed to create awareness for the race and raise funds for children's charities.

NEW YEAR CELEBRATIONS
December 31 • various locations.

The biggest bash in town is at Nathan Phillips Square in front of city hall. This is where tens of thousands of people brave the temperature and settle down for a huge televised pop concert. Other organized locations include Dundas Square and Mel Lastman Square. These are liquor-free events and have a history of being great places to let your hair down and enjoy the safe and friendly atmosphere. If you're looking for something more intimate, check out what's planned around town at **nowtoronto.com** and **eye.net**

ONE-OF-A-KIND CRAFT SHOW
November, last week; December, first week • National Trade Centre • map 2 • 416-960-4513 • **oneofakindshow.com** • admission $ • subway: Union and take the 509 streetcar.

For over 30 years, the show has been an unforgettable pre-Christmas shopping experience for thousands of people in search of the unique, the fantastic, and just plain different. Every year, almost 800 artisans, artists and designers from across the country converge on Toronto to offer the locals something special and unique. After all, this is a "one-of-a-kind" shopping event, so what you buy is always a talking point. Choose from art pieces, furniture, fashions, stunning home décor ideas, toys and food. There's really nothing else quite like it.

ROYAL AGRICULTURAL WINTER FAIR
November, first two weeks • National Trade Centre • map 2 • 416-263-3400 • **royalfair.org** admission $ • subway: Union and take the Harbourfront 509 streetcar.

As they say, this is part of local tradition. Simply put, it's the largest indoor combined agricultural, horticultural, canine and equestrian event in the world. Those who run the event like to say: "It's the place where entertainment meets education and where the thrill of competition meets the pride of accomplishment. Where the country shows the city a thing or two." Since 1922, the fair has been a celebration of Ontario's rural and agricultural traditions. Attractions include the Agricultural Show, the Royal Horse Show and the Winter Garden Show. The Royal Horse Show features top equestrians and attracts socialites and visitors from across Canada and around the world. It's certainly one of the annual events in town where you come to see and be seen.

SANTA CLAUS PARADE
November, third week • route starts at Christie Street (map 23), goes east along Bloor Street West, south on University Avenue, east on Queen Street West, south on Yonge Street, then east on Front Street East to Church Street • 416-599-9090 #500 • **thesantaclausparade.com** • subway: Museum, Queen's Park, Osgoode, Queen, or King.

The first Santa Claus Parade took place back in 1905 as a bit of a publicity stunt by the Eaton department store. Mr and Mrs Timothy Eaton went down to the railway station to meet Santa on his arrival in town and walked him a few blocks up Yonge Street to their store on Queen Street. The stunt, which took place on December 2nd, wasn't even mentioned in the paper until the previous day so only a few hundred onlookers bothered to turn up. The Eaton department store is long gone, but the parade has developed into a century-old city institution. The television audience at home, and as far away as New Zealand, attracts millions more than the half-million folks who line the parade route in often freezing weather. Santa's float is usually last, but well worth waiting for. Don't forget to wear warm clothing.

TASTE OF THE DANFORTH
August, second week • Danforth Avenue between Broadview Avenue and Jones Avenue • map Toronto (area 13L) • 416-469-5634 • tasteofthedanforth.com • subway: Broadview, Chester, Pape and Donlands • admission free, but small cost for food samples.

Each year, for well over a decade, this annual festival seems to get just bigger and better. Danforth Avenue is home to the largest Greek community in North America and the organizers of the festival take over twelve blocks of the neighbourhood to put on a massive outdoor smorgasbord. Everywhere you look is food and they claim it's the "largest food festival in Canada." Almost a million people go to take in the sights, entertainment and food during a three-day period. There are beer gardens, waiter races, fashion shows, concerts and special events for kids. Go along and join in the fun while casting your eyes over possibly more food than you've ever seen before in one place. One or two dollars get you a taste of anything you like and net proceeds go to charity.

TODMORDEN MILLS HARVEST FESTIVAL
September, third week • Broadview Avenue at Pottery Road • map Toronto and in detail below • 416-396-2819 • city.toronto.on.ca/todmorden • admission $ • subway: Broadview and walk three blocks north on Broadview Avenue to Pottery Road.

This mill was one of the first industrial complexes on the banks of the Don River. These days, Todmorden Mills has become a heritage museum and arts centre that celebrates the fall season each year in a really old-fashioned way. Visitors are invited to tour the site's two historic houses while costumed staff take on the seasonal work of preserving fruits and vegetables for the winter in the same way they did back in Victorian times. You can also watch demonstrations such as cedar shingle-making, flax-processing and pioneer tin smithing. Don't forget to catch Dr. Zonk's Museum of Curiosities and a hands-on experience with the amazing technology of the Camera Obscura, a prelude to today's photo imaging.

TORONTO DOWNTOWN JAZZ FESTIVAL
June, starting during the last week • various venues • 416-363-8717 • tojazz.com • admission $ for some locations, free in others.

It all started in 1987 as du Maurier Downtown Jazz. The government stepped in and cigarette manufacturers weren't allowed to sponsor such things anymore. Anyway, that first year headlined Oscar Peterson, Canada's greatest gift to jazz, at Roy Thomson Hall. Dizzy Gillespie was also on hand, as was the United Nations Festival Superband which included Monty Alexander, Paquito d'Rivera, James Moody, Sam Rivers, Jon Faddis and a guest appearance by Canada's 'Swinging Shepherd', Moe Koffman. Since then, the festival has continued to attract big names from across the continent. These days, more than 2,000 jazz artists play it up for devoted crowds during ten days of concerts at nearly 50 locations around the downtown area. Some of the performances take place in concert halls, while others can take over street corners, bars and local parks.

TORONTO DRAGON BOAT RACE FESTIVAL
June, last weekend • Marilyn Bell Park • map 2 (area 1E) • 416-598-8945 • dragonboats.com • subway: Dufferin and take the 29 bus south.

This three-day re-enactment of an ancient Chinese legend pits 6,000 athletes in 200 competitive crews against each other to delight 200,000 cheering people. It all goes back to the story of Qu Yuan, the Chinese poet and philosopher. In the fourth century BC, disgruntled with the ruler and the state of affairs in China, he jumped into the Mei Lo River. According to legend, local fishermen, upon seeing their beloved poet's act of courage, raced out with their boats in an attempt to save him. To their dismay, they arrived too late. To stop his body from being eaten by fish, they beat the waters with their paddles and threw rice dumplings wrapped in silk into the river to divert the fish to tastier morsels. People in over 40 countries re-enact this moment in history every year and Toronto does it with more spectacle than any place outside Asia.

TORONTO FRINGE THEATRE FESTIVAL
July, first two weeks • various stages throughout town • 416-966-10629 • fringetoronto.com • admission $.

One really has to wonder what Shakespeare unleashed when he wrote the line: "The play's the thing." Apparently he got all caught up in his own words and went on to write 37 of them. Little did he know that one day the Toronto Fringe Theatre Festival would put on over three times that amount without batting an eyelid. Therefore, if you're into live theatre, there's probably no other place to be in July than here. The festival is going on almost 20 years and provides you with a dizzying selection of over 130 plays, spread over nearly 1,000 performances in 20 venues during 12 days. If it sounds exhausting, it is. On the upside, most tickets are under $10 and your fellow theatre patrons are a chatty and friendly lot. Just about everything about this festival is unusual, so check out their Web site for all the rewarding details. This theatrical *tour de force* is often called 'Toronto's biggest stage blowout' for good reason.

TORONTO INTERNATIONAL BOAT SHOW
January, third week • National Trade Centre • map 2 • **torontoboatshow.com** •
admission $ • subway: Union and take the 508 streetcar west.

Outside, the lakes are frozen over. Inside the National Trade Centre the
world's largest indoor lake is all warm and inviting and dotted with everything from ultra-luxurious yachts to kayaks and sports boats. More than a
thousand watercraft just beg to be looked at, admired, boarded and bought.
There are antique boats, a live trout fishing tank, stuff for kids and cottagers,
marine gifts and accessories, to say nothing of the latest outboard and inboard
motors. If it floats, it's here. The show's slogan is "Put some summer in your
winter!" and more than 100,000 people decide to go along and do just that.

TORONTO INTERNATIONAL FESTIVAL CARAVAN
June, last week; July, first week • various locations • 416-977-0466 • admission $.

This popular festival started more than 30 years ago to salute the growing
cultural diversity of the city. Over the years, dozens of countries and foreign
cities have hosted pavilions around town to promote their food, culture and
heritage. It's a lot of fun to roam around town to find out what's going on and
get involved with something completely different. If you want to have a beer
in an Aussie pub, or experience the finer points of Japanese table etiquette
while munching on sushi, then Caravan is well worth exploring with friends.
The idea is to pick up a 'passport' to visit all the pavilions as many times as
you want. There's also an unlimited single day pass.

TORONTO INTERNATIONAL FILM FESTIVAL
September, second week • various downtown cinemas • 416-967-7371 •
bell.ca/filmfest • admission $.

Over 250,000 stars and lesser folk come from all over to see more than 300
movies and generally strut their way from gala to gala. It's the largest film festival in North America and generally regarded as the most important in the
world next to Cannes. Readers of the *Los Angeles Times* went a step further and
voted it the number one film festival anywhere, period. Needless to say, it's
media-frenzy-time in town as limos force their way through hordes of fans, trying not to knock over TV lights or run down overly-enthralled showbiz reporters. Don't even think of trying to get a reservation at a smart restaurant. But,
if you want to casually walk past the Bistro 990 on Bay Street, you might just see
'someone' sitting in the sidewalk café. Don't tell anyone you read about it here.
All this glitz goes back to 1976 when someone decided to put on a few movies
and give it the utterly pretentious title: 'Festival of Festivals'. Little did we know
then that the festival would indeed live up to its original name, or get a new corporate Festival Centre headquarters on the King and John street's corner.

TORONTO OUTDOOR ART EXHIBITION
July, second week • Nathan Phillips Square • map 10 • 416-408-2754 •
Torontooutdoorart.org • subway: Queen or Osgoode.

This popular exhibition, which is a fresh-air alternative to conventional art
shows and galleries, has been a city fixture for over 40 years. It's the largest
of its kind in Canada and one of the largest in North America. During a three-
day exhibition you can stroll around the square and take in the work of established artists, undiscovered talents and assorted craftspeople. It's not

158

surprising that around 100,000 visitors take time to attend this exhibition because the extent and diversity of the artistic talent is quite remarkable. Don't be surprised if you see a few well-known art dealers snooping around either. This is serious business and the Toronto Outdoor Art Exhibition's Award Programme gives out nearly $40,000 in prizes to deserving artists. If you're in the market for something unusual to hang on your wall, spending time here is time well spent.

TORONTO SPORTSMEN'S SHOW
March, second week • National Trade Centre • map 2 • 416-695-0311 • sportsmensshows.com • admission $ • subway: Union and take the 509 streetcar to Exhibition Place.

Since its inception nearly 60 years ago, the show has attracted more than 10,000,000 visitors. That statistic, in itself, shows the tremendous amount of interest people have in this annual event. This is where you'll find everything to do with hunting, camping, hiking, boating and fishing. More than 6 ha of exhibition space are now set aside for the show and in 2005 an entire exhibit hall was opened as the headquarters for the avid hunter and outdoorsman. The Hunting Hall features major gun, bow and related accessory manufacturers, hunting specialists and retailers. Even if you're a couch potato and hate hunting, you'll be amazed by the Gold Whistle Retriever Trials, demonstrating the amazing bond between a handler and his dog.

TORONTO TRAILS FESTIVAL
October, each Sunday • torontotrailsfestival.theplatformgroup.net • various locations throughout the city.

The folks who put on this event have a mission: "To encourage Torontonians and tourists to enjoy the many health and social benefits of walking and hiking on the world-class system of trails in Toronto." There's little doubt that the city's parks and ravine system is unchallenged anywhere for its diversity and natural beauty, and the best time to enjoy it all is in the fall when the trees burst forth in an over-abundance of rich colours. Walkers have a choice of nearly 30 different areas to explore and enjoy throughout the city. However, online registration is required so the organizers can round-up enough guides for each location. In partnership with the City of Toronto, The Platform Group developed the Toronto Trails Festival and on Sunday September 21, 2003, they took Toronto for a walk with the very first annual celebration of the joys of walking.

WORD ON THE STREET
September, last Sunday • Queen's Park • map 20 • 416-504-7291 • thewordonthestreet.ca • subway: Queen's Park.

A day to celebrate the joy of reading with authors, publishers and tens of thousands of other like-minded spirits. The area around Queen's Park, from the ROM down to Wellesley Street West, is closed to traffic and lined with close to 200 booths full of books and magazines, lots of places for author readings, general literary activities and family fun spots. This is the country's biggest public book bash with similar events staged in Vancouver, Calgary, Halifax and Kitchener. Even the kids get special attention with their very own KidStreet section that's devoted entirely to fun, games and their favourite books.

Entertainment **Ballet and dance**

When summer activities come to a close, several renowned Canadian companies start unveiling their new productions. Joining them on the city's stages are visiting international companies that have captured the attention and applause of audiences around the world.

CANADIAN CHILDREN'S DANCE THEATRE
Season: check Web site • for performance venue check Web site • 416-924-5657 • ccdt.org • admission $.

The company was founded in 1980 "to provide a creative home for young bodies, minds and spirits." During the last quarter century these gifted young artists, whose ages range from 13 to 19, have roamed the world presenting well over a thousand critically acclaimed performances. The company's founders, Deborah Lundmark and Michael deConinck Smith, conceived the modern repertoire to showcase and develop some of the country's most outstanding young dancers. Only limited performances are available for the hometown audience.

DANCEMAKERS
Season: September – May • Premier Dance Theatre, Harbourfront Centre • map 5 • 416-367-1800 • dancemakers.org • admission $ • subway: Union and take the streetcar to Harbourfront Centre.

Dance magazine has called Dancemakers "Toronto's pre-eminent contemporary troupe." In 1974, a group of independent dancers joined together to create and perform new choreography. In the 70's and 80's, artistic directors such as Anna Blewchamp, Carol Anderson and Bill James led the company in pushing the boundaries of creation. It has now been around for three decades, and yet Dancemakers is still on the leading edge of contemporary dance in Canada. Under the artistic direction of Serge Bennathan since 1990, the company's reputation has continued to spread as it travels throughout Canada, the Americas and Europe, winning acclaim wherever it performs. Bennathan's choreography is charged with beauty and risk. Its dynamic energy conveys the extremes, the lyricality and the tenderness of human existence.

DANNY GROSSMAN DANCE COMPANY
Season: Check Web site • Premier Dance Theatre, Harbourfront Centre • map 5 • 416-531-8350 • dgdance.org • admission $ • subway: Union and take the streetcar to Harbourfront Centre.

During the last 30 years, Danny Grossman has moulded his troupe into a Toronto institution that's noted for its *avant-garde* interpretations of social themes through dance. The unique style of his choreography, maintained throughout about 30 works, has found its way into the repertoires of companies around the world. "I want to use my company to present dance that, like my own, is about humanity", Grossman says. "Dance that is clear, concise, daring and universal – not afraid of subject matter. I believe in art that expresses values. My repertoire and my company reflect my personal values of equality, pacifism, honesty, courage, social responsibility, sympathy for the underdog and a willingness to reveal the demons."

NATIONAL BALLET OF CANADA
Season: Fall - Spring • Four Seasons Centre • map 10 • 416-345-9595 (tickets) • national.ballet.ca • admission $ • subway: Osgoode.

Celia Franca founded the company in 1951 and, as it enters its second half-century, its performance venue has moved from the venerable Hummingbird Centre. Several years ago the National Ballet joined with the Canadian Opera Company to spearhead a drive that would give Toronto a ballet-opera house specifically designed for their needs. That dream was realized in 2006 with the opening of the Four Seasons Centre for the Performing Arts. The company has also been successful in building its new corporate headquarters and ballet school on Jarvis Street in a mix of new and historic buildings. Critics have been generous to the National Ballet over the years, giving rave reviews to dancers, choreographers and set designers. The company concentrates on a solid repertoire of classical works while encouraging new ballets and Canadian choreographers. The season highlight is a lavish production of *The Nutcracker*, which is traditionally performed during the festive season to sold-out audiences.

TORONTO DANCE THEATRE
Season: check Web site • Premier Dance Theatre, Harbourfront Centre • map 5 • 416-967-1365 • tdt.org • subway: Union and take the streetcar to Harbourfront Centre.

The company has had a profound influence on Canadian dance. Christopher House has been the artistic director since 1994, which moved the *New York Times* to say: "Christopher House trusts movement and its power to delight the eye, pique curiosity and stimulate thought. No wonder Toronto Dance Theatre is always a welcome visitor to New York." The company, founded in 1968 by Peter Randazzo, Patricia Beatty and David Earle, has become internationally recognized for intelligent, visually stunning contemporary performance. It is dedicated to the creation of original works that celebrate the power of the human imagination.

Entertainment Cinema

On a per capita basis, Torontonians go to the movies more than anyone else in North America. In fact, Hollywood's first great movie star, Mary Pickford, was born here. It's little wonder that the city hosts one of the world's most prestigious film festivals. Toronto is the third largest film and television production centre on the continent, adding over $1.4 billion annually to the local economy.

ALLIANCE ATLANTIS
See newspapers or Web site for movie times and locations • 416-646-0444 • allianceatlantiscinemas.com

The company, which is headquartered in Toronto, is one of the biggest film, video and general entertainment companies around these days. In Canada,

Alliance Atlantis is the largest distributor of motion pictures, DVDs and videos. It has a picture library of more than 6,000 titles that, if screened one after the other, would take about 14,000 hours to see. In partnership with Famous Players, there are three Alliance Atlantis cinemas dotted around town in the form of upscale multi-screen locations.

AMC
See newspapers or Web site for movie times and locations • amctheatres.com

Here is a company that can trace its roots way back to the glory days of the silent screen. The organization's history goes way back to 1920 when American Edward D Durwood opened his Durwood Theatre. This humble beginning evolved into AMC, which credits itself with inventing the multiple-theatre concept in 1963 in Kansas City. It also touts its introduction of the coffee cup holder arm rest and advance ticket sales. AMC is one of the world's largest theatrical exhibition companies, with more than 3,500 screens. In Toronto, its main location is at Kennedy Commons, on Kennedy Road just south of highway 401.

CINEPLEX ODEON
See newspapers or Web site for movie times and locations • cineplex.com

Loews Cineplex Entertainment was founded in 1998 with the merger of Loews Theatres and Cineplex Odeon Corporation. Loews was the oldest motion picture exhibitor in North America, having been started in 1904 by Marcus Loew. He then joined with Louis B Mayer and Samuel Goldwyn in 1924 to launch MGM. Cineplex Odeon was once a Canadian company, created by Garth Drabinsky. It opened Canada's first multi-screen cinema complex in April, 1979 at the Eaton Centre. On March 13, 2001, the site closed due to financial reasons.

FAMOUS PLAYERS
See newspapers or Web site for movie times and locations • famousplayers.com

N.L. Nathanson owned the now long-gone Majestic Theatre on Adelaide Street and used it to begin the Regent chain. In 1929 he installed the country's first movie sound system in Montreal's Palace Theatre. Famous Players is the oldest movie exhibition company in the country and has more screens here than any of its competitors. But it's Canadian no longer. Viacom, the American entertainment mega-giant, has taken over.

IMAX
See newspapers or Web site for movie times and locations • imax.com

Few people remember that the IMAX film system was developed in Toronto back in 1967. The large format screen came into its own during Montreal's Expo '67 when several exhibitors produced some stunning technical breakthroughs in terms of visual and audio effects. In 1971 IMAX opened its first permanent theatre, named Cinesphere, at Ontario Place. It is still in operation after more than 30 successful years. By 1983, IMAX had entered the theme park business with a permanent site at Disney's Epcot Centre in Florida. Since its initial launch, the IMAX format has developed 3D imagery. More than 850,000,000 people in 35 countries have had an IMAX experience in more than 250 theatres. Needless to say, those IMAX theatres are well represented throughout their hometown here in Toronto.

INSIDE OUT LESBIAN AND GAY FILM AND VIDEO FESTIVAL
May, last two weeks • see Xtra! weekly newspaper or Web site for movie times and
locations • 416-977-6847 • insideout.on.ca • admission $.

Close to 25,000 keen movie buffs have made this festival one of the largest of
its kind. Spread over 11 days, the event is crowded with parties, directors'
talks, panel discussions and screenings of more than 275 films and videos
from Canada and around the world. It all started back in 1991 at the Euclid
Theatre on the assumption that a film and video festival of this kind would
attract established artists while providing opportunities for audiences to
view the best and most diverse work of interest to the gay and lesbian community. In 1998, the Queer Youth Digital Video Project was added to the mix
so emerging young producers, directors, editors and writers might benefit
from a series of workshops to teach them everything from development to
editing to final post-production within in a queer-positive environment.
Their resultant work is premiered at the festival alongside the professionals.

TORONTO INTERNATIONAL FILM FESTIVAL
September, second week • various downtown cinemas • 416-967-7371 •
bell.ca/filmfest • admission $.

Over 250,000 stars and lesser folk come from all over to see more than 300
movies and generally strut their way from gala to gala. It's the largest film
festival in North America and generally regarded as the most important in
the world next to Cannes. Readers of the *Los Angeles Times* went a step further and voted it the number one film festival anywhere, period. Needless to
say, it's media-frenzy-time in town as limos force their way through hordes
of fans, trying not to knock over TV lights or run down overly enthralled
showbiz reporters. Don't even think of trying to get a reservation at a smart
restaurant. But, if you want to casually walk past the Bistro 990 on Bay Street,
you might just see 'someone' sitting in the sidewalk café. Don't tell anyone
you read about it here. All this glitz goes back to 1976 when someone decided to put on a few movies and give it the utterly pretentious title: 'Festival of
Festivals'. It awaits its new Festival Centre building at King and John streets
in 2008.

Entertainment Clubs and bars

There are probably more than 6,000 places in town where you can
settle down for a drink. Of these, there are almost 120 clubs and
lounges catering to everyone from the permanently cool to
sophisticated socialites. Typing yourself is entirely up to you.

The club, live music, bar and jazz scenes change almost daily. This is such a
fluid part of Toronto life that unexpected surprises crop up every week.
However, here's the best way to keep abreast of what's happening and
where: Get a copy of either *eye* (**eye.net**) or *NOW* (**nowtoronto.com**) weekly
newspapers. They're free, come out every Thursday, and you can get a copy
from street boxes, coffee shops, bars, convenience stores and restaurants anywhere downtown. The most popular club areas in the city core are on maps

8, 9, and 10, but there's lots of fun outside the middle of downtown as well. If you're wired, the following two Web sites will have most of the information you need:

pubclub.com/toronto

This Web site fills you in on the current club and bar scenes and gives some insider chatter about what's hot and what's not. It breaks down the venues into districts and types, makes suggestions that could help you decide where to go, and gives the low down on after-hours haunts. No matter if you're a well-dressed clubbie, or just into a mindless night on the town, this site has a bit of everything for everyone. Just as hip night spots come and go, the same holds true for Web sites. It always helps to Google around a bit to see what's new.

xtra.ca

Pink Triangle Press, publishers of the gay and lesbian bi-weekly newspaper *xtra!*, has put this site together. From the home page, click on *Bottoms Up*. If you're not on-line, you can get a copy of the paper just about anywhere around the intersection of Church Street and Wellesley Street East in the gay village. Incidentally, Woody's on Church Street is reputed to sell more beer than any other bar in the city.

Entertainment Family entertainment centres

There are about half a dozen major areas around town that have been built for enjoyable family outings. Together, they represent a diverse mix of fun and education. And that's a pretty good way of spending the day.

BLACK CREEK PIONEER VILLAGE
Steeles Avenue West at Murray Ross Parkway • map Toronto and in detail below • 416-736-1733 • **blackcreek.ca** • daily, except December 25 & 26 • admission $ • subway: Jane and transfer to bus 35B.

Here's somewhere for you and the kids to go to see how great-great-Grandma lived all those many years ago. Daniel and Elizabeth Stong were the original owners of this site back in 1816 when they set about establishing a farm from hundreds of acres of forested wilderness. Before long they had succeeded in building a grain barn, piggery and smokehouse. These buildings now form the heart of Black Creek Pioneer Village where smoke still curls from the chimneys and their home still welcomes visitors. With over 35 carefully restored 1860s shops and houses, the settlement re-creates the life

Steeles Av West

Jane St

Pioneer Village   Murray Ross Pkwy

Shoreham Dr

York University

Keele St

Dufferin St

Finch Av West

and times of Upper Canada. Here's where you can talk to the blacksmith, the cabinetmaker and others about their crafts. Costumed guides take you around original buildings giving you an opportunity to explore a fascinating bygone time.

CENTREVILLE AMUSEMENT PARK
Ward's Island, Toronto Islands ? map 1 • 416-203-0405 • centreisland.ca • daily, June – Labour Day; weekends, May & September • admission $ • take the Ward's Island ferry from the foot of Bay Street.

The park's summer charm lies in it being away from downtown in 250 ha of parkland, yet close enough to get a great view of the city. Centreville is best for younger kids who can have fun on an assortment of 30 rides of various descriptions, get involved in lots of attractions and satisfy their appetites at any one of 14 food outlets. Mum and Dad can take some impressive shots of the downtown skyline while strolling around and enjoying the island's natural charm. The ferry ride there and back is an added bonus.

EXHIBITION PLACE
100 Princes' Boulevard • map 2 • 416-263-3600 • explace.on.ca • open daily • events admission $ • subway: Union and take the 510 streetcar.

Some 192 acres of parkland were set aside about 130 years ago to provide an impressive civic recreation and entertainment centre. Today, Exhibition Place houses the National Trade Centre and Ricoh Coliseum complex as well as 24 historical structures that include Scadding Cabin, the oldest building in the city. Over 4,500,000 people visit here during the year for the Canadian National Exhibition (CNE), Molson Indy, Royal Agricultural Winter Fair, CHIN Picnic, Caribana and the Toronto International Boat Show.

HARBOURFRONT CENTRE
235 Queen's Quay West • map 5 • 416 973-3000 • harbourfrontcentre.com • open daily • subway: Union and take the 509 streetcar to York Street.

There are probably more things going on here during the year than almost any place else in the city. Someone once estimated that over 4,000 events of various kinds take place here throughout any given year. You can learn to skate during the winter, attend summer camps, get involved in the Milk International Children's Festival of the Arts, or take in countless pop concerts, poetry readings and theatre performances year round The on-site Power Plant is one of Toronto's most intriguing art galleries. If you want to watch professional artisans at work, crafting from textiles, glass, ceramics and metal, then head for the Craft Studio. The centre, which is situated on four ha of waterfront parkland, never disappoints in living up to its purpose of exploring new and bold frontiers in the arts and creative expression.

ONTARIO PLACE
South of Exhibition Place • map 2 • 416-314-9900 • ontarioplace.com • open May - September; Cinesphere daily • admission $ • subway: Union and take the 509 streetcar to Exhibition.

Over 30 years ago, the provincial government decided to build a permanent entertainment complex on three man-made islands in Lake Ontario just off the southern shore of Exhibition Place. It did not escape peoples' notice at the time that this could be Toronto imitating Montreal's hugely successful island venue in the St Lawrence River for Expo 67. Toronto's site was a little less ambitious and covers 39 ha with parkland, inter-connecting bridges, the iconic geodesic dome of Cinesphere (which, incidentally, mimics Buckminster Fuller's Expo 67 centrepiece), and has more rides and attractions than any kid could ask for. Cinesphere, by the way, was the world's first permanent IMAX theatre and it continues to show an impressive range of mega-screen productions. Ontario Place has a motto proclaiming "Kids wanna have fun!" and it has no problem living up to its promise. The complex opened in May 1971 at a cost of $29,000,000 and every year since then the site is tweaked to make sure it's kept right up to date.

Entertainment Opera and classical music

 Toronto has three orchestras, two internationally-renowned ensembles, two opera companies and four honoured choirs. And each year the city hosts an impressive array of international soloists. The other good news is that we have some of the finest performance venues in North America.

CANADIAN CHILDREN'S OPERA CHORUS (CCOC)
Performances in various locations • 416-366-0467 • canadianchildrensopera.com • April - December • admission $.

For nearly 40 years members of this highly acclaimed group of youngsters have appeared in productions by the Canadian Opera Company, the Toronto Symphony Orchestra, the University of Toronto Faculty of Music and the National Ballet of Canada. This is Canada's only permanent children's opera chorus, and it also develops and produces new operas for children. Since its inception in 1968, the CCOC's performances have grown from 14 to over 50 per season. The core of choristers consists of 80 girls and boys under the artistic direction of Ann Cooper Gay.

CANADIAN OPERA COMPANY (COC)
227 Front Street East (Tanenbaum Opera Centre) • map 12 • 416-363-6671 • coc.ca • open during business hours • subway: Union and take the 65A bus.

Canada's premier opera company is now into its second half-century. To celebrate this milestone, its productions are moving into its new 'opera house', the Four Seasons Centre for the Performing Arts, in 2006. Before 1961 the COC performed at the University of Toronto's Hart House, the Royal Conservatory of Music – with which it was associated – and the Royal Alexandra Theatre. After that date, productions moved into the O'Keefe Centre (now the Hummingbird Centre). The COC's administrative, workshop and rehearsal space is housed in the Joey and Toby Tanenbaum Opera Centre, which includes the 450-seat Imperial Oil Theatre. The building, situated in the old Town of York, was constructed in 1885 for the Consumers Gas Company in the style of an early Christian basilica.

ELMER ISELER SINGERS
Performances in various locations • 416-971-4839 • elmeriselersingers.com • October - May • admission $.

The late Elmer Iseler, known as 'the Dean of choral conductors' by his peers across Canada, founded the choir in 1979. It is one of the few professional choirs in the world and currently enjoys its status as the choir-in-residence at the University of Toronto's Faculty of Music. The 20-voice ensemble, now under the direction of Lydia Adams, is renowned for its purity of tone and vocal colour. It travels extensively, giving around 100 concerts annually in North America and Europe.

OPERA ATELIER
Performances in various locations • 416-925-3767 (information); 416-872-1212 (tickets) • operaatelier.com • season usually Spring and Fall • admission $.

The internationally acclaimed Opera Atelier fits no particular mould. The company specializes in historically precise performances of opera, ballet and drama in a mix that invites a unique theatrical experience. Exquisite costumes and stylistic gesturing are trademarks that have been researched at the Bibliothèque Nationale and the Paris Opéra, the Juilliard School in New York and at London's Royal Academy of Dancing. The company tours worldwide to give its audiences and media critics an enjoyable and entertaining experience rooted in Baroque traditions. When at home, productions usually take place at the Elgin Theatre.

SCARBOROUGH PHILHARMONIC ORCHESTRA
Performances in various locations • 416-261-0380 • spo.ca • season November - May • admission $.

In 1980 a group of Scarborough musicians, under the direction of the legendary Canadian pianist and educator Clifford Poole, formed the Scarborough Philharmonic Orchestra. A quarter century later it has established itself as one of the finest and most forward-thinking community orchestras in the country. It usually gives a half-dozen concerts each year, mainly in the auditorium at Birchmount Park Collegiate, and divides its repertoire among classical, pop, opera and children's programs. Each concert features at least one Canadian composition.

TAFELMUSIK
Trinity-Saint Paul's United Church Centre • map 24 • 416-964-9562 • tafelmusik.org • season September - May • admission $ • subway: Spadina and walk half a block west on Bloor Street.

More properly named the Tafelmusik Baroque Orchestra and Chamber Choir, this internationally acclaimed ensemble of over 40 performers brings us the seldom-heard sounds of classical Baroque instruments and period choral music. The season schedule usually offers around 50 concerts in town and overseas. The award-winning group was founded in 1979. Most of its home appearances take place at Trinity-St Paul's United Church Centre, but other venues in Toronto include the George Weston Recital Hall in North York, and the Royal Ontario Museum (ROM) for its *ROM Friday Nights* series.

TORONTO CHILDREN'S CHORUS
Performances in various venues • 416-932-8666 • torontochildrenschorus.com • season November, February & May • admission $.

Places like New York's Carnegie Hall and London's Barbican Centre are no strangers to this group of young choristers whose ages range from six to 17.

Although the chorus consists of 320 voices, most performances usually rely on about a third of the total company. The repertoire is taken from works written between the Renaissance and the 20th century and contains Canadian compositions.

TORONTO CONSORT
Trinity-Saint Paul's United Church Centre • map 24 • 416-966-1045 (administration); 416-964-6337 (tickets) • **torontoconsort.org** • season October - March • admission $ • subway: Spadina and walk half a block west on Bloor Street.

The Toronto Consort is Canada's leading chamber ensemble specializing in the music of the Middle Ages, Renaissance, and early Baroque. Some of this country's leading early music specialists have come together to form this highly praised group, whose members include both singers and instrumentalists. The Consort was founded in 1972 and its performances have garnered critical acclaim across Canada and throughout the United States and Europe.

TORONTO MENDELSSOHN CHOIR
Roy Thomson Hall • map 10 • 416-598-0422 • **tmchoir.org** • season September - May • admission $ • subway: St Andrew.

This is one of the oldest and most respected performing arts groups in Canada. Dr Augustus S Vogt formed the choir in 1894 as an extension of his Jarvis St. Baptist Church choir. It gave its first concert in Massey Hall, as part of the hall's inaugural season, on January 15, 1895. The choir's name was chosen to honour the composer Felix Mendelssohn Bartholdy who had died just a half-century before its founding. Today, the choir has a membership of 160 volunteer choristers. Apart from its four annual concerts in Roy Thomson Hall, the Mendelssohn joins with the Toronto Symphony Orchestra during the performance of major choral works. The choir's annual highlight is a sold-out performance of Handel's *Messiah*.

TORONTO OPERETTA THEATRE
Jane Mallett Theatre, St Lawrence Centre • map 11 • 416-465-2147 • **torontooperetta.com** • season October – April • admission $ • subway: Union.

Toronto Operetta Theatre is Canada's premier professional operetta company. It was founded in 1985 to produce classical operetta, light opera and musical theatre featuring professional Canadian artists of exceptional talent. Each season the company stages about four major productions to critical acclaim. Operettas in the repertoire include those by Gilbert and Sullivan to Franz Lehar and Jacques Offenbach.

TORONTO PHILHARMONIA ORCHESTRA
George Weston Recital Hall, Toronto Centre for the Arts • map 35 • 416-499-2204 • **torontophil.on.ca** • season September – May • admission $ • subway: North York Centre.

Before changing its name to the Toronto Philharmonia, the orchestra was known as the North York Symphony. It was founded in 1971 and is the orchestra-in-residence at the highly acclaimed George Weston Recital Hall, where it gives about a dozen concerts annually. The repertoire, under the direction of conductor Kerry Stratton, is based on the classics and contemporary Canadian works. Stratton is used to rave reviews. The *Washington Post* once wrote about the conductor's appearance in the American capital this way: "The music expertly played by the Moscow Symphony Orchestra, Kerry Stratton conducting, is a delight throughout."

TORONTO SYMPHONY ORCHESTRA (TSO)
Roy Thomson Hall • map 10 • 416-593-7769 (administration); 416-593-4828 (tickets) • tso.on.ca • season September - May • admission $ • subway: St Andrew.

The orchestra was founded in 1922 by a group of Toronto musicians and Viennese-born conductor Luigi von Kunits. The New Symphony Orchestra, as it was then called, gave its first performance in April 1923 at Massey Hall. The name Toronto Symphony Orchestra was adopted four years later. Some of the renowned conductors who have led the TSO during its more than 80 years of residency in Toronto have included Sir Ernest MacMillan, Walter Susskind and Seiji Ozawa. The orchestra gives about 125 concerts each season that often include outstanding international soloists. The TSO has toured extensively to cities across Canada, the United States, Europe, Japan and Australia.

Entertainment Sport

 When it comes to professional sports, Toronto fans turn out in droves to boost the local team. Over the years, we have won the World Series, Stanley Cup and the Grey Cup more than once.

AMERICAN LEAGUE BASEBALL – TORONTO BLUE JAYS
Rogers Centre • map 4 • 416-341-1111 (ticket information); 416-341-1234 (ticket order by credit card); 416-341-1000 (administration) • bluejays.com • games during the scheduled baseball season • admission $ • subway: Union and take the Skywalk.

The Blue Jays faced their fans for the first time on April 7, 1977, at Exhibition Stadium against the Chicago White Sox. For trivia buffs, the first pitcher was Bill Singer and Doug Ault scored the first home run. The Jays won the game 9–5. Since then, the club has won the World Series twice and is always anxious to have another taste of fame. However, gone are the 45,000+ crowds at the Rogers Centre (formerly the SkyDome) since the long-gone but not forgotten baseball strike. The good news is that there are always good seats available any time you care to show up at the gate. Although the stadium abounds with food outlets inside, die-hard fans are attracted to the hot dog vendors outside who seem to offer tastier fare and much cheaper prices.

CANADIAN FOOTBALL LEAGUE – TORONTO ARGONAUTS
Rogers Centre • map 4 • 416-341-ARGO (tickets) • argonauts.on.ca • games during the scheduled CFL season • admission $ • subway: Union and take the Skywalk.

Founded more than 130 years ago, the Argos is the oldest professional sports team in North America. After their Grey Cup win in 2004, all is forgiven and the club is again a crowd pleaser. Having spent over 15 years playing at the spectacular and climate-controlled Rogers Centre (formerly SkyDome), the team considered moving out to a new open-air, 25,000-seat stadium at York University. However, the deal fell through and those fans who had hoped to sit outside in the snow like real Canadians will now have to put up with all the interior comforts of home for another few years.

CANADIAN OPEN TENNIS – ROGERS CUP, MASTERS SERIES
Rexall Centre • map Toronto • 416-665-9777 • tenniscanada.com • first week in August • admission $ • subway: Keele and take the 41 bus north to Steeles Avenue West.

This is Canada's top international tennis event. It's shared with Montréal so that men's matches in Toronto are held on even-numbered years and the women's program on odd-numbered years. This is a Masters Series event on the world professional circuit and is sandwiched between the classic Wimbledon and the US Open tournaments. Consequently, it attracts big names. Total prize money is around $US 3,000,000. American M. Farnum won the first men's singles in 1883.

HOCKEY HALL OF FAME
BCE Place, 30 Yonge Street • map 10 • 416-360-7765 • hhof.com • open daily, though times vary • admission $ • subway: Union, or King and go through the PATH walkway to BCE Place.

This is Canada's shrine to ice hockey, housed in the reputedly haunted 1885 Bank of Montreal building. It is, in effect, a museum commemorating Canada's obsession with the game. Play goalie against virtual reality shooters, or browse through the most comprehensive collection of hockey stuff anywhere. And, best of all, you can have your picture taken standing next to the Stanley Cup, which is on permanent exhibition here. The Spirit of Hockey store is the place for mementos and gear.

MOLSON INDY
Exhibition Place • map 2 • 416-966-6213 (administration); or 416-872-INDY (tickets) • molsonindy.com • mid July • admission $ • subway: Union and take the Harbourfront 509 streetcar to Exhibition Place.

Top racing drivers from around the world compete with Canadian champions in events that offer lots more than just the roar of engines. The Indy is part of the 20-race FedEx championship that includes events in Australia, Brazil, Japan and the United States. Races highlight a week-long celebration, known as Indyfest, that revs up over 300,000 race fans, Champ Car drivers, celebrities, sponsors, media and the community at large. It is designed to create awareness for the race and raise funds for children's charities.

NATIONAL BASKETBALL ASSOCIATION – TORONTO RAPTORS
Air Canada Centre • map 5 • 416-366-3865 • nba.com/raptors • games during the scheduled NBA season • admission $ • subway: Union and take the PATH walkway south.

As the Toronto Raptors approached their scheduled home opener at the Sky-Dome on November 3, 1995, club President John Bitove could congratulate himself on having pulled off a remarkable achievement. The NBA's expansion into Toronto was unique because it marked the league's first step beyond the borders of the United States. The young club is still intent on winning the championship and we're filling the seats in their permanent home at the Air Canada Centre. Be prepared for lots of hoopla both on and off the court. In the first game played at the Air Canada Centre on Sunday, February 21, 1999, the Raptors defeated the Vancouver Grizzlies 102-87.

NATIONAL HOCKEY LEAGUE – TORONTO MAPLE LEAFS
Air Canada Centre • map 5 • 416-977-1641 • torontomapleleafs.com • games during the scheduled NHL season • admission $ • subway: Union and take the PATH walkway south to the Air Canada Centre.

A team named the St Patricks won its first Stanley Cup back in 1927 against the Vancouver Millionaires. It was after this game that the St Patricks changed its name to the Toronto Maple Leafs. In 1931 the Leafs moved into the new, $1,500,000 Maple Leaf Gardens on the corner of Church and Cartlton streets and began a long and exciting history that captivated fans, not only in Toronto, but across the country. The Gardens was an architectural wonder of its time, being built in less than six months. On opening night, seat prices ranged from 95 cents to $2.95. The team won its first Stanley Cup there in 1932 and went on to win it a total of 11 times. Maple Leaf Gardens has seen its last NHL game and is destined to live out its days as a supermarket. The blockbuster Toronto v Montreal games once played there have become legend. But the die-hard fans have quickly adapted to the Air Canada Centre. And no fan can compete with a Leaf's fan. The team mightn't have won the Stanley Cup since May 2, 1967, but the Leafs know how to fill a stadium and subject its rafters to deafening cheers. For trivia fans, the Leafs defeated the Montréal Canadiens 3-2 in overtime on Saturday, February 20, 1999, during the first game played at the Air Canada Centre.

OLYMPIC SPIRIT
35 Dundas Street East • map 16 • 1-888-466-9991 • olympicspirit.ca • open daily, 10.00 AM - 6.00 PM • admission $ • subway: Dundas.

On the southeast corner of Dundas Square you'll find the world's first and only permanent entertainment complex themed around the Olympic Games. At a cost of $40,000,000, the 4,800 sq m facility offers visitors a state-of-the-art, five-level sporting experience. When it opened in the summer of 2004, CEO Peter Doyle said: "There is nothing in the world like Olympic Spirit Toronto. When visitors leave our complex they will be awed, inspired, impressed and entertained." Juan Antonio Samaranch, Honourary President of the International Olympic Committee, stated that, "Olympic Spirit is an important project for the International Olympic Committee. It gives more people a chance to experience the Olympic Games and discover the courage and the stamina it takes to become an Olympic athlete." The building is topped with a 47 m media tower in the stylized shape of an Olympic torch.

THOROUGHBRED HORSE RACING: QUEEN'S PLATE AND BREEDERS' STAKES
Woodbine Racetrack • map Toronto • 416-675-7223 • ojc.com • Queen's Plate run during the last weekend in June; Breeders' Stakes in mid-August • admission $ • subway: Islington and take the 37A bus.

The Queen's Plate is the oldest continuously run thoroughbred race in North America. It's the first Triple Crown event and carries a purse of about $500,000 for the winner. The Breeders' Stakes, also run at Woodbine, and the Prince of Wales Stakes held at Fort Erie, round out the Triple Crown events.

Entertainment **Stage companies**

 Toronto has often been promoted as the third-largest live theatre centre in the English-speaking world after London and New York. This could be true, considering the city has 91 professional theatre companies performing on 79 stages.

The following are some of the highly-acclaimed major theatre companies that provide us with a diversity of stage productions.

BUDDIES IN BAD TIMES
12 Alexander Street • map 21 • 416-975-9130 (administration); 416-975-8555 (tickets) • **buddiesinbadtimestheatre.com** • season throughout the year • admission $ • subway: College.

Buddies has been characterized as the most controversial, influential and vital theatre in the country. It was founded in 1979 and had its modest beginnings in a dilapidated building on George Street. Some years ago it moved into a new space on Alexander Street, close to the gay community. The only full-time gay stage in North America, its productions cover a full spectrum of *avant-garde* material that has garnered over 30 national prizes, including three coveted Governor General's Awards. The Chamber, which seats 300, and the much smaller Tallulah's Cabaret, have been the launching pads for dozens of now successful playwrights, directors, technicians, actors and designers.

CANADIAN STAGE COMPANY
St Lawrence Centre • map 11 • 416-367-8243 (administration, 26 Berkeley Street); 416-368-3110 (tickets) • **canstage.com** • season year round • admission $ • subway: Union.

The Canadian Stage Company was created in 1987 as a not-for-profit, community supported organization through the merger of the Toronto Free Theatre and CentreStage. It earns over half its $7.2-million budget from seat sales. Using the St Lawrence Centre, the Berkeley Street Theatre and the thousand-seat amphitheatre in High Park as its venues, Canadian Stage produces a full season of mainly Canadian works. Occasionally, they'll perform internationally contemporary plays such as the acclaimed *Angels in America*.

FAMOUS PEOPLE PLAYERS
110 Sudbury Street • map Toronto, area 8N and in detail on the following page • 416-532-1137 • **fpp.org** • season year round • admission $ • subway: Osgoode and take the 501 Queen streetcar west to Dovercourt Road.

Famous People Players has impressed audiences around the world with such great theatre and great food that Tom Cruise described the experience as "nothing like it on earth." The group is a non-profit organization that gives people with developmental disabilities an opportunity to entertain a live audience in the unique comfort of a dinner theatre. The black light productions, featuring amazing puppetry, have received rave reviews from people as diverse as Bill Cosby and Paul Newman to Liberace who hired the company for his Las Vegas show. When it played the Lyceum Theatre on

Broadway, Famous People Players elicited this review from the *New York Times*: "Iridescent spectacle that drenches the senses in light and sound. It is something for the kids and also for the grown-ups. The magic of the theatre, the magic of diversion, the magic that compels one to say 'That's Entertainment'."

MIRVISH PRODUCTIONS

Princess of Wales Theatre (map 9); Royal Alexandra Theatre (map 10) • 416-593-0351 (administration for both theatres); 416-872-1212 (tickets for both theatres) • mirvish.com (includes on-line ticket sales) • season year round • admission $ • subway: St Andrew.

'Honest' Ed Mirvish and his son David are two theatrical entrepreneurs who have made one of the city's major theatre districts their own. Ed is more than a theatrical person known for his marketing genius. He's one of the city's icons. Literally rising from rags to riches, he has gone from working as a kid in his parents' modest shop to starting his own flamboyant department store (Honest Ed's), and once owning London's Old Vic theatre. The Mirvishes own both the historical Royal Alexandra and the modern Princess of Wales theatres on King Street West, and used to run most of the restaurants in between before they were disbanded. Bus-loads of patrons from western New York and cities throughout southern Ontario commute to Mirvish's stage offerings imported from Broadway and London's West End. The shows include everything from mega-musicals such as *Miss Saigon* and *The Lion King* to award-winning dramas like *Art* and super-spectacles including *Lord of the Rings*.

SOULPEPPER THEATRE

Young Theatre (map 12) and Harbourfront Centre (map 5) • 416-203-6264 • soulpepper.ca • season varies • admission $ • subway: (Young Theatre) Union and take the 72A bus.

Many theatre professionals believe that the Soulpepper Theatre Company, founded as an actors' theatre in 1998, has changed the face of theatre in Canada. The company has a three-tiered mandate: to present vital Canadian interpretations of the world's classics; to provide professional development in the classics to young theatre artists; and to reach a young audience with classical theatre. The company is also committed to developing emerging Canadian talent as well as spearheading instruction and workshops aimed at a variety of disciplines including design, directing and acting. In association with George Brown College, the company will be a major player in the Young Centre for the Performing Arts in the historic Distillery District. Too many theatre critics, both here and abroad, have praised this company for you not to experience its truly exceptional talent.

TARRAGON THEATRE
30 Bridgman Avenue • map 27 • 416-536-5018 • **tarragontheatre.com** • season: September through June • admission $ • subway: Dupont and one black west to Howland Avenue.

Bill Glassco founded this critically acclaimed theatre in 1970 as "a play-wright's theatre." Over the last 35 years it has undertaken hundreds of productions and established itself as a leading venue for the creation and development of new works. Although the company doesn't produce with touring in mind, it has sent its productions to theatres across Canada and beyond. It has appeared at the Edinburgh Festival, Glasgow's Mayfest, Expo 86 and the Festival des Ameriques in Montreal. The theatre has two areas: the 205-seat MainSpace and the 100-seat ExtraSpace.

(LORRAINE KISMA) THEATRE FOR YOUNG PEOPLE
165 Front Street East • map 11 • 416-363-5131 (administration); 416-862-2222 (tickets) • **lktyp.ca** • season: October through April • admission $ • subway: Union or King.

LKTYP is Canada's largest professional theatre for young people and the city's first not-for-profit theatre. Its productions cater to a wide spectrum, running from classic to contemporary theatre and shows with a distinctly Canadian theme. The company has strong links to the educational system and remains an integral and important part of the artistic and cultural life of our changing and socially diverse city. There are two performing spaces: one with 468 seats, the other with 300.

THEATRE PASSE MURAILLE
16 Ryerson Avenue • map 8 • 416-504-8988 (administration); 416-504-7529 (tickets) • **passemuraille.on.ca** • season: usually September through May • subway: Osgoode and take the Queen Street 501 streetcar west to Ryerson Avenue.

The theatre was founded on the radical intention of creating a distinctly Canadian voice in theatre. Now into its fourth decade, that voice has been heard. Passe Muraille has acted as mentor for emerging theatres across Canada, from Newfoundland's CODCO and Saskatoon's 25th Street Theatre to our own Buddies in Bad Times. Passe Muraille is often regarded as English Canada's national theatre, a distinction that artistic director Layne Coleman views as an important responsibility: "Passe Muraille is a theatre driven by a need to engage its audiences. It is a dream come true and a dream worth pre-serving." There are two spaces: Mainstage and Backstage.

TORONTO FRINGE FESTIVAL
Various stages throughout downtown • 416-534-5919 • **fringetoronto.com** • season: first 11 days of July • admission $.

The Fringe is a Canadian theatre phenomenon that embraces many cities across the country. The Toronto Fringe audience has continued to develop and grow and now more than 42,000 enthusiastic Fringers attend Toronto's largest theatre festival each summer. These patrons have come to embrace the Fringe philosophy and the fun of discovering some of the most exciting and entertaining theatre in the city. With their support The Toronto Fringe Festival has grown to include 11 venues and more than 120 theatre compa-nies from Ontario, across Canada and around the world and is now the third-largest Fringe in Canada. Tickets are usually under $10, or you can get a 10-show pass for $60.

Entertainment **Theatres, concert halls and stadiums**

 With four major professional sports teams, two symphony orchestras, plus one ballet, two opera and numerous theatre companies, it's little wonder the city is more than adequately served with entertainment spaces. Here are some of the major venues.

AIR CANADA CENTRE (ACC)
40 Bay Street • map 5 • 416-815-5500 • **theaircanadacentre.com** • open for events and tours year round • admission $ • subway: Union and take the PATH walkway south.

The ultra-modern centre opened in February, 1999, on the site of an old postal building and became home to the Toronto Maple Leafs and Toronto Raptors. Despite being known as 'The Hangar', it's considered North America's premier arena for basketball and ice hockey. With seating for up to 19,800 game fans, or over 20,000 concert-goers, the building is famous for the 640 television screens scattered throughout the complex. You won't miss a play or a song even if you're in a washroom. Another sport's venue – Maple Leaf Square – will soon emerge on the west side of the building. The Leafs and Raptors each won their opening game in the ACC.

CANON THEATRE
263 Yonge Street • map 16 • 416-872-2222 (tickets) • **mirvish.com** • season varies • admission $ • subway: Dundas.

Most people remember this magnificent theatre as the Pantages. However, after a generous donation by a corporate benefactor in 2001, the company was able to get its corporate name on the marquee. An extraordinary amount of money was spent in 1989 to refurbish this once decaying 2,200-seat theatre for the opening of *Phantom of the Opera.* Few theatres in the world can boast such restored turn-of-the-century elegance as this gem on Yonge Street. Sweeping staircases, rich woods and ornate décor have given us as much to applaud as anything that might happen on stage.

ELGIN AND WINTER GARDEN THEATRES
189 Yonge Street • map 11 • 416-872-5555 (tickets); 416-314-2901 (tours) • **toronto.com** • tours Thursdays 5.00 PM and Saturdays 11.00 AM • admission $ • subway: Queen.

During the great vaudeville period people like Burns and Allen, Edgar Bergen and 'Charlie McCarthy', Milton Berle and Sophie Tucker played here. Those were the glory days, but now these houses are the last operating double-decker theatres left on the continent. They were completed a couple of months apart during the winter of 1913–14. When vaudeville lost its charm, they were turned into trendy movie houses of their day. Then, after many years in the dark, the theatres were declared a national historical site in 1982 and completely refurbished at a cost of $29,000,000 to return them to their original décor and style.

FOUR SEASONS CENTRE FOR THE PERFORMING ARTS
University Avenue at Queen Street West • map 10 • **fourseasonscentre.ca** • subway: Osgoode.

It had been a long time coming. For decades the Canadian Opera Company, later in league with the National Ballet of Canada, had been planning for an opera house all its own. Their performance space at the Hummingbird Centre was always derided as second best. The modern Toronto Centre for the Arts was dismissed as being too far away from downtown. The COCs dream will all come together at this central downtown corner in the form of the 2,000-seat Four Seasons Centre for the Performing Arts in September 2006. Local architect, Jack Diamond, designed the $181,000,000 house around a horseshoe auditorium (R Fraser Eliott Hall), fronted along the west exterior wall by a vast glass enclosed City Room that overlooks one of the least impressive vistas in the downtown core. There's growing agreement the building will not become an architectural icon. Some have ventured to say it mirrors Toronto's genetic predisposition for pedestrian architecture. However, it is touted as the "first purpose-built opera house in Canada," even though the Grand Opera House had its glory days only a few blocks away on Adelaide Street in 1874. The COC opens its first season at the new centre with opera's most challenging production – Wagner's *Ring Cycle.*

GEORGE WESTON RECITAL HALL
5040 Yonge Street, Toronto Centre for the Arts • map 35 • 416-733-9388 • **tocentre.com** • subway: North York Centre.

This intimate concert hall is blessed with an acoustical quality that is probably unmatched anywhere in Canada. It is part of the Toronto Centre for the Arts, a major theatrical complex in the north end of the city. The space is a fully equipped, 1,036-seat, world-renowned concert hall, and home to The Toronto Philharmonia Orchestra and Amadeus Choir. It was specifically designed for large orchestras, choirs and soloists and has a boldly modern, if somewhat sterile interior. If you crave great sound, you owe it to yourself to attend a performance here.

HARBOURFRONT CENTRE THEATRE
231 Queen's Quay West • map 5 • 416-973-4000 • **harbourfrontcentre.com** • subway: Union and take the 509 streetcar to Simcoe Street.

Originally, this building was an ice house built on the harbour over 80 years ago. These days it has been transformed into a multi-purpose, 425-seat performance space that is favoured by most of the local dance companies and visiting *avant-garde* ballet troupes. The theatre opened in 1992 as a sleek, three-storey facility encased by glass on three sides and equipped with dressing rooms, high quality sound and lighting equipment, acoustical devices, and a sophisticated heating, ventilation and air conditioning system. The Harbourfront Centre complex, of which the theatre is part, has been exploring new and bold frontiers in the arts and creative expression for years while introducing Toronto audiences to artists and art forms that would not normally be seen in commercial venues.

HUMMINGBIRD CENTRE FOR THE PERFORMING ARTS
1 Front Street East • map 11 • 416-872-2262 (tickets) • **hummingbirdcentre.com** • subway: Union.

On this site, over 160 years ago, a pier jutted out into Lake Ontario and welcomed Charles Darwin as he disembarked on May 4, 1842, for his only visit to Toronto. That was Act 1. During Act 2 the 3,155-seat O'Keefe Centre was built and staged the world première of Lerner and Loewe's *Camelot*. Next morning the *Toronto Star's* theatre critic panned it unmercifully. Nathan Cohen stood by his original evaluation of the show until the day he died. Since then the theatre has seen more than its fair share of glitzy Broadway and West End productions, plus many of the world's leading solo acts. It was re-named the Hummingbird Centre after a software company came up with a corporate grant of $5,000,000. For years this had been home stage for the Canadian Opera Company and the National Ballet of Canada. However, their aspiration to have a ballet-opera house all their own was finally realized in 2006 when they moved into the new Four Seasons Centre for the Performing Arts. Now the city fathers are murmuring about "doing something" with the Hummingbird Centre, like building condominiums on the site. Guess we have to wait for Act 3.

MASSEY HALL
178 Victoria Street • map 16 • 416-872-4255 (tickets) • **masseyhall.com** • subway: Dundas, or Queen.

In 1892, industrial baron Hart Massey (1823-96) bought land at Shuter and Victoria Streets and hired architect Sidney Badgley to design a memorial to his son Charles Albert Massey. Massey intended his gift "to aid in the development of the arts" to be "an auditorium – spacious, substantial and comfortable, where public meetings, conventions, musical and other entertainments, etc., could be given." When the hall opened in 1894 with a performance of Handel's *Messiah*, it was obvious this was a space with stunning acoustics. The 2,750-seat red brick facility was, for many years, the venerable home of the Toronto Symphony Orchestra. Now well into its second century, it can look back on having welcomed a daunting international list of classical and pop artists to its stage, as well as eminent story-tellers like G K Chesterton, Arthur Conan Doyle, John Masefield, J B Priestly and Grey Owl.

MOLSON AMPHITHEATRE
Ontario Place • map 2 • 416-260-5600 • **hob.com** • season: May through September • subway: Union and take the Harbourfront 509 streetcar.

A lot of folk will remember this stage when it was called the Ontario Place Forum. Its rebirth in 1995 as the Molson Amphitheatre made it a magnet for summer pop concert-goers who want to relax outdoors. There are now 5,500 reserved seats under its modern roofline, another 3,500 seats out in the open and a further 7,000 general admission places on surrounding lawns. It is one big place to chill out during the summer and take in some of the greatest acts around. Despite its size, the state-of-the-art sound system allows patrons on the lawn to hear as well as those in reserved seating. And there's always those two giant video screens to make stuff on stage seem more close and personal.

PANASONIC THEATRE
561 Yonge Street • map 21 • subway: Bloor-Yonge

In this day and age, corporate sponsorships are all the rage when it comes to getting your name on a theatre or stadium. In 2005, the old New Yorker theatre that most people didn't notice as they passed by it on Yonge Street, became the Panasonic Theatre. It has been transformed into a state-of-the-art theatrical and technological showpiece. The lobby alone has been outfitted with up to $250,000 worth of Panasonic's next-generation audio-visual and display equipment, including its 65" high definition plasma TV. Clear Channel Entertainment, which owns the venue, invested close to $15,000,000 for interior renovations. The Blue Man Group highlighted the new opening.

PRINCESS OF WALES THEATRE
300 King Street West • map 9 • 416-872-1212 (tickets) • **mirvish.com** • (Information and tickets) • subway: St Andrew.

The Princess of Wales Theatre, which opened in May 1993, is a 2,000-seat playhouse built by the father and son producing team of David and Ed Mirvish, who also own and operate Toronto's old Royal Alexandra Theatre. The Princess of Wales was the first privately owned and financed theatre built in Canada since 1907, and the first anywhere in North America in over 30 years. The stage is one of the widest and deepest on the continent and large enough to accommodate the most spectacular theatrical productions like *Lord of the Rings*. It's also one of the most technically state-of-the-art theatrical venues. Frank Stella created over 900 sq m of murals for the foyer, auditorium and exterior rear wall. It's believed to be the largest mural commission of this century. The first production staged here was *Miss Saigon*.

REXALL CENTRE
4700 Keele Street at Steeles Avenue West • map Toronto and in detail below • 416-665-9777 • **tenniscanada.com** • subway: Keele and take the 41C bus.

This new, 12,500-seat stadium is set in over 6 ha of parkland on the campus of York University. In 2002 it was identified as Canada's new National Tennis Centre. It has 6,000 premium seats, 150 President's Club Suite seats, 48 exclusive Skylounge suites and 5,500 upper seat stands. There are 16 tennis courts built adjacent to commercial and retail units and the community has use of the facilities outside of scheduled tournament play. The $30-million centre is home to the Rogers Cup (the Canadian Open) and hosts the major international ATP event sandwiched between Wimbledon and the US Open. The first person to win a singles event at the Canadian Open was American Delano Osborne in 1892.

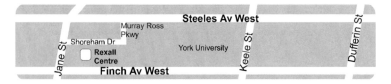

RICOH COLISEUM ENTERTAINMENT CENTRE
100 Princes' Boulevard, National Trade Centre, Exhibition Place • map 2 •
416-263-3001 • ricohcoliseum.com • subway: Union and take the 509 streetcar.

The Ricoh Coliseum, which opened in November, 2003 inside the vast National Trade Centre, is one of the city's newest general-purpose entertainment centres. Its principle feature is a 10,000-seat stadium. The $38,000,000 structure entirely transformed the previous Coliseum building that had been a landmark for over 80 years. The Coliseum is home ice for the Toronto Road Runners of the American Hockey League. Fans appreciate not only the high-tech environment inside, but also the 7,000 parking spaces just outside the door.

ROGERS CENTRE
1 Blue Jays Way • map 4 • 416-341-3663 (information); 416-870-8000 (tickets); 416-341-2770 (tours) • **rogerscentre.com** • tour admission $ • subway: Union and take the Skywalk.

This landmark facility started its life as the SkyDome when it opened in May, 1987 at a cost of $628,000,000, which was $478,000,000 over the original budget. It was designed to host the Toronto Blue Jays baseball team and the Toronto Argonauts football club. A private consortium bought the place for $151,000,000 in 1994 and four years later the enterprise went bankrupt. Sportsco took over the stadium in 1999 for $85,000,000 and five years later the Blue Jays, now owned by Rogers Communications, bought the place for $25,000,000. On February 2, 2005, the SkyDome was renamed the Rogers Centre in deference to its new owner. These days, it has been re-branded as an 'entertainment centre' but the Jays and the Argos are still the main attraction here, as is a large portion of the Canadian International Auto Show. The old Jumbotron has been replaced with a new giant LCD screen and lots of dazzling new scoreboards abound. A special reconfiguration of the interior can transform the stadium into a gigantic concert hall for visiting artists. The Rogers Centre was the first multi-purpose stadium to have a retractable roof. The facility has 1,280 toilets, three-quarters of which are for women. The 11,000-ton roof, which spans 3.2 ha, takes about 20 minutes to open or close. The Eaton Centre, St Paul's Cathedral in London, or Rome's Coliseum could fit easily inside the 32-storey structure. Seating capacity is just over 50,000 for games and 67,000 for concerts. The Jays went down 5–3 to the Milwaukee Brewers on opening day, June 5, 1989, and the biggest crowd was assembled here in 2002 when 68,237 fans turned up for Wrestlemania.

ROY THOMSON HALL
60 Simcoe Street • map 10 • 416-872-4255 (tickets and information) • **roythomsonhall.com** • admission free, except for performances • subway: St Andrew.

Arthur Erickson's design for a $57,000,000 concert hall raised eyebrows when it opened in 1982. The circular glass-clad concrete structure caused added concern when acoustics didn't match those of the venerable Massey Hall that had been a distinguished home for concert-goers during previous generations. Even its name raised people's hackles. Canada's late press baron, Roy Thomson (Lord Thomson of Fleet) after whom it was named, was reputed never to have willingly attended a symphony concert. There wasn't much that could be done about the name, but the acoustics drew ever louder boos from both sides of the stage. So, "to ensure seamless and elegant integration of the acoustical modifications with the functional and aesthetic enhancements to the Hall" the place was shut down for 22 weeks in 2002 so about $20,000,00 could be spent on a major acoustical fix. These days, the members of the Toronto Symphony Orchestra can actually hear themselves play.

ROYAL ALEXANDRA THEATRE
260 King Street W • map 10 • 416-872-1212 (tickets) • **mirvish.com** • subway: St Andrew.

Helen Hayes, John Gielgud, Edith Evans and the Barrymores have all played the 'Royal Alex" during the theatre's staging of more than 3,000 productions. When it opened in 1907 it was hailed as a technological triumph of its day. It was the first fireproof theatre built on the continent and is now the oldest legitimate theatre in Toronto. In 1962 the Alex was scheduled for demolition. Just before the wrecking ball was brought in, entrepreneur Ed Mirvish bought the property and launched a theatrical career that reached a pinnacle when he purchased London's Old Vic. The top balcony of the Royal Alex betrays the theatre's age: stairs are steep and seating is cramped, so it is recommended only to mountain climbers. By the way, it is rumoured that a deceased stagehand occasionally appears up here from out of nowhere to keep you company.

ST LAWRENCE CENTRE FOR THE ARTS
27 Front Street East • map 11 • 416-366-7723 (tickets) • **stlc.com** • subway: Union.

With over 30 years under its belt, the St Lawrence Centre has provided us with a unique mix of theatre, music and social consciousness. The 876-seat Bluma Appel Theatre is home for the Canadian Stage Company and was chosen as the venue for the world première of *Kiss of the Spiderwoman*, which went on to spend a Tony Award-winning season on Broadway. The smaller 497-seat Jane Mallett theatre is best for intimate music recitals, small theatre and public debates on issues of the day.

TORONTO CENTRE FOR THE ARTS
5040 Yonge Street • map 35 • 416-733-9388 (administration) • **tocentre.com** • subway: North York Centre.

When North York was a separate city, it made a conscious effort to compete with Toronto's downtown theatre district. Mayor Mel Lastman and entrepreneur Garth Drabinsky teamed-up as the driving forces behind building the North York Centre for the Performing Arts, consisting of the Apotex Theatre, George Weston Recital Hall and the Studio Theatre. Its name changed to the Ford Centre and then to the Toronto Centre for the Arts. During the late 1990s the Apotex Theatre, with 1,800 seats and one of the city's largest stages, held the world premières of *Showboat, Ragtime* and *Fosse* – all of which originated in Toronto before their award-winning runs on Broadway. The Apotex is now called the Main Stage. The George Weston Recital Hall shares the best acoustics in the city with Massey Hall.

WOODBINE RACETRACK
**555 Rexdale Boulevard • map Toronto and in detail below •1-888-675-RACE •
woodbineentertainment.com • subway: Islington and take the 37A bus.**

Woodbine is the most famous name in Canadian racecourse history. The track is home to the $1 million Queen's Plate, North America's oldest continuously run stakes race; the $1 million ATTO Mile; the $1.5 million Canadian International and the $1 million North America Cup for Standardbreds. The original Woodbine opened in 1874 on the then far-eastern outskirts of Toronto, which is now virtually downtown. The name of the original track was changed to Old Woodbine in 1956 and it became Greenwood in the spring of 1963. Live racing at Greenwood was terminated at the end of 1993. The present Woodbine, which has undergone several multi-million-dollar expansions and upgrades, was opened on June 12, 1956, amid 640 acres in the northwestern section of the city. Woodbine is the only racetrack in North America capable of conducting standardbred and thoroughbred racing on the same day. It boasts a seven-eighths-mile harness racing surface, a one-mile dirt track and the spectacular 1.5 mile E P Taylor Turf Course encircling both tracks.

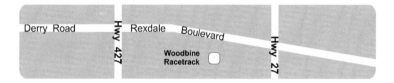

Restaurants

Toronto is where you can put the world on your plate. Our multi-cultural neighbourhoods burst with interesting places where you can discover all sorts of great cuisine. In fact, there are about 18,000 places to eat in the city – including 1,500 sidewalk cafés and patios. *Bon appétit!*

Restaurants General information

 Dining out around town ranges from very classy establishments and intimate patios to family-run neighbourhood eateries and trendy thirtysomething places. Fast food outlets and fashionable coffee shops abound. Restaurant competition is so intense in some areas that any momentary lapse in the kitchen could doom a place to extinction quicker than you could order a bottle of designer water.

The best concentrations of good, expensive restaurants are in Yorkville, the Entertainment District and on Yonge Street in midtown. Trendy folk hang out around the Fashion District, or head for little places along Queen Street West. The Greek community dominates The Danforth, which exudes Mediterranean sights and aromas. The Bay Street élite keep close to their skyscrapers for power lunches. Baldwin Street, between McCaul and Beverley streets, is a small hidden treasure. Theatre crowds stay near their seats around Yonge and Front streets, along King Street West near John Street and on Elm Street between Yonge and Bay streets. Italian restaurants are everywhere. Chinatown looks more like Vietnam these days, but the old, established Chinese places are still well in evidence and hard to beat for atmosphere.

DRESS

If you're going out to splurge on a meal, a general rule is to dress for dinner in what's known as 'smart casual' attire. This ranges from Versace in Yorkville and midtown to Tommy Hilfiger and the Gap around the Entertainment and Fashion districts. Business people dress conservatively when clients are around. If you're not looking for a high-end place, then dress as casually as you please.

TIPPING

Tips for waiters are generally about 15% of the food bill before taxes. A quick way to do the math is add the two taxes (7% + 8%) on the bill. If the service is bad, tip less or, in extreme cases, not at all. The maître d'hôtel should be offered $5.00 – $10.00, depending on the tone of the establishment. (Don't confuse this fellow with a person who just points you in the general direction of a dirty table at Joe's Greasy Spoon.) The sommelier gets 10% of the before-tax price of wine.

CREDIT CARDS

Make sure ahead of time that the restaurant you choose accepts your credit card or traveller's cheques. This saves possible embarrassment later. In the *Restaurant Reviews* section the term 'all major credit cards' is used. This refers to American Express, Mastercard and Visa credit cards. American visitors should be aware that restaurants here do not usually accept the Discover Card.

HEALTH NOTICES

The Toronto Public Health Food Premises Inspection and Disclosure system regularly updates all eating establishments and assigns ratings for cleanliness. These notices are clearly posted for you to see. A green notice is a 'pass'; a yellow one is 'conditional', while a red one means the place has been closed. If you want more information, log on to **toronto.on.ca** and look under 'health'.

Restaurants Listings by cuisine

This list of restaurants is arranged according to the type of food they serve and each establishment is shown with a map reference for your convenience. However, these groupings should be taken with a grain of salt. Many restaurants these days don't adhere strictly to their chosen category and often wander off into fusion experiments without telling anyone. Some steakhouses, on the other hand, are also renowned for their seafood. The establishments in **bold type** below are discussed in the following *Restaurant Reviews* section.

---

*Restaurant name followed by **map** number, or reference to the **Toronto** map.*

---

24 HOUR
24h restaurants are shown on maps 10, 11, 13, 14 and 20 by the black **Food** logo.

AFRICAN
Boujadi, Toronto
Ethiopian House, 20
Sultan's Tent, 11

AMERICAN
Albany, 23
Armadillo, 10
Boiler House, 12
Brown Stone, 21
Bumpkin's, 21
Cabbagetown, 17
Café California, 21
Canary, 12
Cranberries, 22
Graffiti's, 14
Hard Rock Café, 4, 16
Hooters, 9, 34

Hughie's, 15
J J Muggs, 15
Johnny G's, 17
Kilgour's, 23
Kos, 27
Left Bank, 8
Montana, 9
P J Mellon's, 21
People's Foods, 29
Planet Hollywood, 9
Rebel House, 29
Red Book, 14
Red Planet, 21
Remy's, 25
Rhodes, 32
Rock 'n Roll, 16
Senator Diner, 16
Sightlines, 4

Slack Alice, 21
Smokey Joe's, 35
Southern Accent, 23
Spirits, 26
Summit Grill, 34
Sunset Grill, 34
Superior, 16
VOX, 12
Zelda's. 21

ASIAN
Asean, 14
Asian Legend, 35
Indochine, 15
Noodle Bowl, 24
Rain, 9
The One, 15

BISTRO
Bedford Academy, 24
Biff's, 11
Bouchon, 11
Gamelle, 18
Maggie's, 18

BUFFET
Mandarin, 34
Town-Country, 6

CAFÉ
7West, **20**
Balzac's, 12
Baroli, 16
Berkeley, 12
Berkeleys, 12
Bulldog, 16
Butler's, 23
By the Way, 23
Courtyard, 25
Croissant Tree, 21
Dish, 28
Eggstacy, 16
Élise, 19
Epicure, 8
Free Times, 19
Future, 23
Irie, 8
Java Jive, 21
Just Desserts, 21
Just Fuel, 22
Kos, 27
Le Gourmand, 9
Lettieri, 9
News, 27
Patachou, 30
Portobello, 8
Portuguese, 13
Ruchiro, 20
Sports Centre, 32
Sweet Rosie's, 32
Tuscany, 14
Valjean, 34
Victory, 23
What a Bagel, 20

CANADIAN
Canoe, 10
Centro, 34
Mill Street Brewery, 12
Wayne Gretzky's, 9

CHINESE
China Gourmet, 17
Choo Choo, 27
Dragon Dynasty,
   Toronto

Dynasty, 25
Flamingo House, 17
Forestview, 14
Garlic Pepper, 20
Gold Stone, 14
Happy Seven, 14
Hong Shin, 15
Hunan Palace, 18
Jing Peking, 18
Kim Sang, 15
King's Garden, 10
Lai Wah Heen, 15
Lee Garden, 14
Lucky Dragon, 14
Mandarin, 34
New Sky, 14
Pink Pearl, 25
Ruby, *Toronto*
Shanghai Lily, 14

CONTINENTAL
Avalon, 9
Avant Goût, 29
Bistro 990, 20
Bistro Tournesol, 27
Bloor St Diner, 34
Bravi, 11
Byzantium, 21
Carlu, 15
Cilantro, 34
Dooneys, 23
Europa Grill, 20
Far Niente, 10
Flow, 25
Habitat, 8
Hanna's Kitchen, 33
Hemispheres, 15
Kalendar, 18
Kensington Kitchen, 19
Lobby, 25
Lüb, 21
Melina's, 34
Mövenpick, 10
Mövenpick Marché, 10
Oasis, 19
Palavrion, 9
Pear Tree, 17
Pegasus, 15
Romaris, 26
Sage, 20
Schmooze, 9
Sen5es, 9
Stork on the Roof, 33
Verona, 9

DELICATESSEN
Bacconi, 32

Mel's, 23

FRENCH
Acrobat, 34
Arlequin, 25
Auberge du Pommier,
   Toronto
Bistro du Parc, 25
Brasserie Aix, 18
Corner House, 28
Herbs, Toronto
La Bodega, 14
La Palette, 14
Le Papillon, 11
Le Paradis, 28
Le Select, 9
Le Trou Normand, 25
Matignon, 20
Pastis, 29
Provence, 22
Quartier, 33
Sauvignon, *Toronto*
Scaramouche, 29
Truffles, 25

FUSION
Liban, 21
Xacutti, 18

GREEK
Greek Islands, 20
Ithica, 26
Mr Greek, 35
Pappa's, *Toronto*
Penelope, 11
Tommy's Backyard, 13

GRILL
Annex, 28
Courthouse, 11
Duncan Street, 10
Europa, 20
Summit, 34
Sunset, 34

INDIAN
Annapurna, 27
Bombay Host, 34
Bombay Palace, 11
Cuisine of India, 35
Host, 25
Indian Flavour, 15
Indian Hut, 26
Indian Rice Factory, 27
Jaipur, 33
Jodphore, 14
Karma, 10
Nataraj, 24

184

Rashnaa, 22
Rasosee, 9
Saffron Tree, 15
Samraat, 24
Sangam, 15
Timothy's, 22

INTERNATIONAL
350 Fahrenheit, 24
360, 4
1055, 30
Airport Lounge, 18
Annex, 28
Azul, 8
Boathouse, 5
Boba, 25
Brassai, 9
Butt'a, 18
Bymark, 10
Caffe Brasiliano, 12
Caffe Doria, 29
Capitol, 18
Chocolate, 11
Cocoberry, 5
Cosmo, 17
Everybody, 22
Fat Cat, *Toronto*
Fig Leaf, 11
Frisco's, 9
Goldfish, 24
Jardin, 23
Jump, 10
La Maquette, 11
Lakes, 29
Latitude, 19
Lemon Meringue,
    Toronto
Living Well, 20
Local 4, 21
Loft, 8
Marlowe, 18
Messis, 19
Milestones, 9, 35
Moxie's, 35
Musa, 13
North 44°, 34
Old Mill, *Toronto*
Olive Lemon, 19
Pangaea, 25
Peter Pan, 9
Pony, 18
Redwood, 34
Rivoil, 9
Rosedale Diner, 29
Rosewater, 11
Sassafraz, 25

Shakespeare's, 24
Solo, 21
Spoon, 9
Susur, 8
Taro, 8
Tasty, 23
Tequilla Bookworm, 8
The Docks, 7
Toba, 11
Town Grill, 17
Two 26, 17
Urban, 9
W Wish, 21
Waterfall, 9
Windows on Sightline, 4

ITALIAN
Acqua, 10
Alice Fazooli's, 9
Alize, 34
Amalfi, 16
Amore, 34
Angelinis, 21
Bar Italia, 18
Bellini's, 25
Biagio, 11
Bordello, 23
Café Diplomatico, 18
Caffe Volo, 21
Caro, 32
Casa di Georgio, 6
Coco Lezzone, 18
Coppi, *Toronto*
Corso Italia, 18
Donatello, 15
East Side Mario's, 10
Esco-Pazzo, 33
Fieramosca, 24
Frascatti, 15
Giovanna, 8
Grano, 33
Grazie, 34
Hot House, 11
Il Fornello, 32
Il Posto Nuovo, 25
Innocenti, 8
Joe Badali's, 10
John's, 14
La Vecchia, 34
Leao D'Ouro, 19
Leoni's, 9
Little Anthony's, 10
Living Well, 20
Luciano's, 22
Mammina's, 20
Mazzoni's, 35

Mercurio, 24
Milano, 9
Noona's. 8
Opus, 24
Oro, 15
Paese, *Toronto*
Papamios, 27
Passione, 32
Piazza Manna, 5
Plumb Tomato, 23
Posticino, 33
Prego Della Piazza, 25
Roberto's, 34
Romagna Mia, 11
Serra, 24
Sotto Sotto, 25
Sotto Voce, 18
Spacco, 34
Spiga, 32
Spinello, 11
Splendido, 19
Teatro, 18
Tempo, 18
Terroni, 32
Toulà, 5
Via Allegro,
    Toronto
Via Oliveto, 25
Vittorios, 33
Zizi, 23, 34
Zucca, 33

JAPANESE
Asahi, 17, 26
Diao, 16
Edo, *Toronto*
Edoya Sushi, 32
Fujiyama, 14
Hiro Sushi, 11
Ichiban Fish House, 35
Ichiriki, 26
Izu, 33
Japan Sushi, 23
Japango, 15
Jun Jun Sushi, 18
Kabuki, 11
Kiyomizu, 35
Moya, 23
Musashi, 29
Nami, 11
Okonomi, 20
Oyshi, 5
Sakura, 11
Sushi Kaji, *Toronto*
Sushi Rock, 34
Sushi Supreme, 33

185

Takara, 32
Takesushi, 10
Tokyo Kitchen, 21
Tokyo Sushi, 20
Toshi Sushi, 8

KOREAN
Happy House, 23
Il Bun Ji, 23
Joons, 23
Korea House, 23
Korean Village, 23
Mul Rae Bang-A, 23
Se Jong, 23

MALAYSIAN
Asean, 14
Mata Hari, 14

MEXICAN
Casa Mexico, 21
Dos Amigos, 27
El Trompo, 14
Jalapeño, 8
Los Iguanas, 23
Margarita's, 14, 17
Mariachi's, 33
Rancho Relaxo, 19

MIDDLE EAST
93 Harbord, 19
Elixir, 23
Laila, 23
Mo Mo's, 19
Pomegranate, 18

MISCELLANEOUS
Ben Wick's, *British,* 17
Cugini, *Sandwiches,* 15
Cultures, *Salads,* 26
Dufflet, *Pastries,* 8
Fez Batic, *Eclectic,* 9
Furama, *Desserts,* 14
Hornero, *Pizza,* 20
Insomnia, *Cyber bar,* 23
Island Thyme,
    Caribbean, 23
Jamie Kennedy,
    Wine bar, 11
Javaville, *Espresso,* 17
Kathmandu, *Nepalese,* 21
Little Tibet, *Tibetan,* 8
Medieval Times,
    Ancient, 2
Mount Pinatubo,
    Filipino, 27
Olympia 76, *Pizza,* 21
Pelican, *Fish & chips,* 22

Praha, *Czech,* 28
RD's, *Ribs,* 10
Riviera, *Bakery,* 18
Vesta, *Diner,* 27

PERUVIAN
Boulevard Café, 18
El Bodegon, 18
El Rancho, 18

PORTUGUESE
Adega, 15
Amadeu's, 14
Benfica Aguia, 13
Chiado, *Toronto*
Churrasqueira, 13

PUBS
*Note: Not all pubs serve
food.*
Artful Dodger, 21
Banknote, 8
Black Bull, 9
Black Sheep, 35
Bow & Arrow, 33
Brunswick House, 24
Bull & Firkin, 33
Cheers, 34
Churchmouse, 21
Cloak & Dagger, 18
College Street, 18
Duke of Kent, 34
Duke of York, 24
Ein-stein, 14
Ferret & Firkin, 24
Fionn MacCool's, 9, 32
Foggy Dew, 8
Fox & Fiddle, 24
Foxes Den, 20
Gabby's, 34
Groundhog, 26
Hair of the Dog, 21
Imperial, 16
James Joyce, 24
Madigan's, 24
Manor Arms, 33
Mayday Malone's, 27
Mick E Flynn's, 16
Monarch, 13
Mullins, 20
O'Grady's, 21
Paddy Murphy's, 8
Paupers, 23
Pour House, 28
Quail & Firkin, 30
Queenshead, 8
Red Lion, 21

Regal Beagle, 24
Rose & Crown, 34
Rowers, 19
Sneaky Dee's, 18
Southside Louie's, 18
Spotted Dick, 26
Tranzac, 24
Village Idiot, 14
Wheat Sheaf, 8
Winchester, 22

SEAFOOD
Adriatico, 29
Captain John's, 6
Filet of Sole, 10
Ichiban, 35
Pure Spirits, 12
Rol San, 14
Seashell, 35
Sen Ming, 14
Starfish, 11
Wah Sing, 12
Xam Yu, 14

SPANISH
Casa Barcelona, *Toronto*
La Hacienda, 8
Plaza Flamingo, 18
Segovia, 20
Taste of Spain, 35

SPORTS BARS
Carrington's, 20
Harbour Sports, 5
Hoops, 20
Scallywags, 32
St Louis, 33
Wayne Gretsky's, 9

STEAKHOUSES
Barberian's, 15
Carman's, 21
Harbour Sixty, 5
Keg, 11
Keg Mansion, 21
Le Bifthéque, 10
Morton's, 25
Ruth's Chris, 10
Tom Jones, 11

THAI
Ban Vanipha, 14
Bangkok, 14
Bangkok Garden, 15
Circle, 32
Coco Rice, 8
Friendly Thai, 8, 20
Golden Thai, 11

HungAry Thai, 14
Pi Tom's, 21
Real Thailand, 24
Royal Thai, 23
Simply Thai, 32
Sorn, 34
Spice Thai, 4
Spring Rolls, 15
Thai Magic, 29
Thai Mango, 35
Thai Princess, 9

Thai Thai, 33
Young Thailand, 9

VEGETARIAN
Annapurna, 27
Commensal, 15
Hey Good Cooking, 28
Imagine, 9
King's, 14
Lotus Garden, 14
Woodlands, 14

VIETNAMESE
Ginger 2, 16
Green Papaya, 34
Indochine, 26
Kim Bo, 13
Peach, 16
Pho Hu'ng, 14
Rainbow, 14
Saigon, 14

Restaurants **Reviews**

 All restaurants listed on maps in the *Inner-city neighbourhoods* section of this book enjoy popular local support. Those of special interest are highlighted in **bold type** in the previous *Listings by cuisine* section and are reviewed alphabetically on the following pages. If a restaurant isn't reviewed here, it doesn't mean you shouldn't check it out. But, if you're really into doing your own research, get a copy of the monthly magazine *Toronto Life*. Its reviews are a bit obscure, lack practical information, and let style dominate substance. But affluent patrons and chefs alike do read them. You'll also find the red and white *Toronto Life* annual seal of approval on many restaurant doors around town. The free weekly newspapers *eye* and NOW have pithy restaurant reviews, designed primarily for the trendy set, and highlight lesser known places. For quick and current information check out one of these Web sites: **toronto.com** or **torontolife.com** or **nowtoronto.com** Prices change, so use those below as a guide only.

360 *International*
301 Front Street West in the CN Tower • map 4 • 416-362-5411 • cntower.ca • lunch daily • dinner daily • dinner $215 for two • all major credit cards • reservations required.

This revolving room is higher off the ground than any restaurant in the world, and prices match the altitude. Food is taken very seriously up here. A change took place around the mid-1990s when the revolving room decided to stop packing the tourists in and become an upscale place for Torontonians. There's a varied menu from Arctic char to paté, and from pasta dishes to memorable desserts. Don't be surprised if you find more than a hint of Canadian fusion. The wine list, which represents 70 vintages, is extensive.

ACQUA *Contemporary Italian*
10 Front Street West • map 10 • 416-368-7171 • acqua.ca • lunch Monday – Friday, dinner Monday – Saturday • dinner $150 for two • all major credit cards • reservations suggested.

There's a certain style about this room that's attracting business tycoons and ordinary folk alike to the corner of Front and Yonge streets. Operating under a culinary premise somewhere in between *nouvelle cuisine* and New Age, the menu has a tempting array of selections that even cater to diabetics and vegetarians. There are seasonal changes in a menu that sometimes includes masterful classic Italian dishes using seafood and chicken. This is one place where you should pay special attention to the dessert menu.

ADEGA *Portuguese*
33 Elm Street • map 15 • 416-977- 4338 • **torontolife.com** • lunch Monday – Friday, dinner Monday – Saturday • dinner $130 for two • all major credit cards • reservations advisable.

The appearance of Adega has brought fine Portuguese cuisine to this busy part of town. For years Elm Street has been known as one of downtown's most varied restaurant districts and this room adds yet another choice. Fish and seafood dominate the menu, as might be expected, and the servers are polite, professional and willing to help folk in the pleasantries of Portuguese food and a fine selection of wine. There's a wine cellar, an upstairs bar, lots of ports and Madeiras, and a cigar room available until the city says otherwise.

ANGELINI'S *Italian*
504 Jarvis Street • map 21 • 416-922-5811 • **toronto.com** • lunch Monday – Friday, dinner Monday – Saturday • dinner $95 for two • all major credit cards • reservations advisable.

Angelini's is one of a handful of upscale restaurants housed in historical homes. In this case, it's the former 1891 residence of Toronto's once-richest man, Charles Gooderham. True to this pedigree, the menu bespeaks tradition and the service sometimes borders on Old World. During the summer, you can relax outside on a large patio under tall shade trees. Despite all these attributes, paying the check might not require your bank manager's approval. The dress code suggests that you wear something appropriate, such as a jacket and tie for men. As a critic once remarked: "It's a good place to take your grandparents once a year."

ANNAPURNA *Indian Vegetarian*
1085 Bathurst Street • map 27 • 416-537-8513 • **toronto.com** • lunch Monday – Saturday, dinner Monday – Saturday (Wednesday till 6:30 PM) • dinner $35 for two • Mastercard and Visa • reservations recommended for more than four people.

This unassuming room is nearing its quarter-century in the West Annex, which makes it the oldest vegetarian restaurant in Canada. The menu mixes western touches with a basic southern Indian tradition to produce such apparent contradictions as French onion soup alongside masala dosai. This is a place for people serious about vegetarian food that packs a delicious punch at a very affordable price.

ARLEQUIN *French*
134 Avenue Road • map 25 • 416-964-8686 • **toronto.com** • lunch Monday – Saturday, dinner Monday – Saturday • dinner $120 for two • Mastercard and Visa • reservations recommended for weekends.

For about 20 years, Arlequin has been a welcome fixture at Avenue and Davenport roads. Here's a place that can juggle over 4,000 bottles in its wine cellar. Front counter take-out and a sit-down clientele consist mainly of the arty folk who abound in this part of town. Despite its name, Arlequin doesn't clown around in the kitchen. This is a serious and rather sparse room with time-honoured credentials and a revamped décor to boot.

188

AUBERGE DU POMMIER *French contemporary*
**4150 Yonge Street • map Toronto • 416-222-2220 • aubergedupommier.com •
lunch Monday – Friday, dinner Monday – Saturday • dinner $205 for two • all major
credit cards • reservations recommended.**

The *auberge* is almost hidden among trees on the west side of Yonge Street,
just north of York Mills Road, in two renovated century cottages. It provides
a rewarding dining experience in the competitive midtown area, while offering a unique location away from city noise. The relaxing 160-seat restaurant
is noted for its high-class cuisine, tasteful appointments, faultless presentation and professional service. Fireplaces add an intimate atmosphere in winter and the terrace is just right for summer dining. The wine list, which
complements the menu superbly, relies on French and Californian vintages.
In 2000, the room received a Four Diamond AAA rating. If you want to check
this restaurant out on the Web, you might prefer to find it at **torontolife.com**.
The restaurant's own Web site is quite difficult to read.

AVALON *Continental*
**270 Adelaide Street West • map 9 • 416-979-9918 • avalonrestaurant.ca • lunch
Wednesday – Friday, dinner Monday – Saturday • dinner $210 for two • all major
credit cards • reservations recommended.**

Avalon, situated in the middle of the Theatre District, is one of the classiest and
most sought-after rooms in the city. However, you would be well-advised to
stay awhile and fully enjoy this room, rather than rush off to catch a show. You
may choose from a daily *á la carte* menu, the Chef's Gastronomic Menu, or
even the Adventure Menu that will set you back $175 per person - including
drinks, of course. These choices are predicated on the freshest and finest of
ingredients. It comes as no surprise that Avalon has one of the best wine cellars in Toronto, usually topping 300 vintages. The room has an island fireplace,
soft minimalist décor and is staffed with sophistication. It earns the top vote of
several media critics and definitely should be investigated by serious diners.

BAN VANIPHA *Laotian - Thai*
**638 Dundas Street West • map 14 • 416 340-0491 • canada.com • dinner Monday –
Saturday • dinner for two $85 • Mastercard and Visa • reservations recommended
for weekends.**

These are the relatively new digs for this highly respected kitchen just down
the street from where it stood for years at 193 Augusta Avenue. The place is
now larger and a bit more upscale than it was before, but the Laotian-Thai
cuisine made the journey successfully in March of 2001. The establishment
still has no pretensions and newcomers might think they've landed in the
wrong part of town. Make no mistake, Ban Vanipha has an unusually creative
and dedicated kitchen that weaves magic with soups, appetizers and main
dishes. For those who delight in devouring intense spices, try the chicken in
coconut curry.

BANGKOK GARDEN *Thai*
**18 Elm Street • map 15 • 416-977-6748 • torontolife.com • lunch Monday – Friday,
dinner daily • dinner $125 for two • all major credit cards • reservations
recommended for dinner late in the week.**

It's been a long time since Thai restaurants first made their appearance in Toronto. Nowadays, Thai cuisine influences more chefs around town than you

could possibly imagine. Bangkok Garden was one of the country's first in this genre, setting down roots on Elm Street which has since become a nest for interesting restaurants. Today, Bangkok Garden retains its tried and proven upscale appearance and menu, catering to moneyed folk who still know their way around the subtle and spiced delicacies of southeast Asia. It's also one of the few restaurants in the city that has a fake river running through lush tropical gardens. If the Thai style is your thing, and you want to spend a bit more than usual on ambience and discreet service, Bangkok Garden is just your cup of green tea.

BIAGIO *Northern Italian*
155 King Street East • map 11 • 416-366-4040 • torontolife.com • lunch and dinner Monday – Saturday • dinner $160 for two • all major credit cards • reservations advisable, especially at weekends.

This establishment has more than held its own for well over a decade in an area where competition is often fierce. There's a nice patio for summer business lunches and a comprehensive wine list with half bottles available. The setting in St Lawrence Hall couldn't be more 'Toronto' and the theme of the old city is reflected on walled photographs. The menu is influenced by Northern Italian traditions and meals are executed with welcome professionalism. Be confident of this choice in this part of town.

BISTRO TOURNESOL *Continental*
406 Dupont Street • map 27 • 416-921-7766 • toronto.com • dinner Monday – Saturday • dinner $115 for two • Visa • reservations recommended for the Tarragon pre theatre crowd.

Here's a place that relies on mainly local ingredients, often of organic origin. You can choose from *prix fixe* and *à la carte* combinations, with the former giving a choice from about 10 appetizers and one main dish. Although 'continental' with its overall offerings, a distinctly French touch prevails. The bright sunny room truly reflects *un tournesol* and the staff reflects an additional sunny disposition. This is one of the most popular places in the East Annex and often the first choice among Tarragon Theatre patrons.

BOBA *International fusion*
90 Avenue Road • map 25 • 416-961-2622 • torontolife.com • dinner Monday – Saturday • dinner $170 for two • all major credit cards • reservations essential on weekends.

The menu here can skip from Asia to the shores of the Mediterranean without losing a beat. How about throwing in an ostrich loin for good measure? Grilled quail, roasted sea bass and chicken breast wrapped in rice paper are only some of the items to challenge your ability to make decisive judgements. A solid wine cellar (mandatory in this part of town) has about 120 labels, making it competitive. It goes all the way from New Zealand and France to California. This is a decidedly upscale place for upscale people.

BOMBAY PALACE *Southern India*
71 Jarvis Street • map 11 • 416-368-8048 • toronto.com • lunch and dinner daily • dinner $50 for two • all major credit cards • reservations advisable for weekends and Hindi festivals.

Lots of folk in the know will tell you that this is one of their favourite Indian restaurants. Menu items are influenced by the flavours of southern India, which means a good assortment of chili sensations and coconut sauces. The atmosphere is informal and it's becoming a good and inexpensive place to go for families and their kids. The daily 25-item all-you-can-eat lunch buffet, for example, sets you back about $10.

BOUJADI *African - Moroccan*
999 Eglinton Avenue West • map Toronto • 416-440-0258 • boujadi.com • dinner Wednesday - Sunday • dinner $60 for two • Mastercard and Visa • reservations accepted, except on Saturdays.

Boujadi is a small town in the Atlas region of Morocco and it's where the local folk take time to live their lives at leisure. This restaurant reflects this heritage and is consistently ranked among some of the best restaurants in town, regardless of cuisine. Its expertly executed culinary delights seem to have made an unusual number of converts within the neighbourhood and across the city. It's a small and modest family-run place and menu items are prepared in the traditional tagine slaoui. If you've wanted to venture into Moroccan food, but didn't quite know what to ask for, try the marhaba. It's a collection of all sorts of different food samples and a good introduction to the well-run kitchen. Don't be surprised if you think about a second visit. The establishment charges a mandatory 15% gratuity for parties of eight or more. And, just a reminder, it's traditional here not to serve milk-based foods.

BOULEVARD CAFÉ *Peruvian*
161 Harbord Street • map 18 • 416-961-7676 • toronto.com • lunch and dinner daily • dinner $85 for two • all major credit cards • reservations recommended.

This café on the corner of Borden Street is one of the most likeable places around. The menu is chock full of tantalizing Peruvian fare that takes its genesis from African, Spanish and Incan flavours. The accent is on yellow foods, such as squash and corn, which have their special place in Incan agriculture. The room is charming and the patio is a delight during the summer, even though there's usually a wait to go there. Never mind, the staff will let you nibble on free cornbread and sip sangria until your table is ready. The spicy seafood stew is worth investigating, as is the rack of lamb with zucchini and eggplant. Peruvian wines are well represented.

BYMARK *International*
66 Wellington Street West • map 10 • 416-777-1144 • lunch Monday – Friday, dinner Monday – Saturday • dinner for two $220 • Visa and Mastercard • reservations required.

On the southern edge of the lawn in the Toronto Dominion Centre you'll notice a low, starkly square building with a discreet downstairs entrance off the Wellington Street sidewalk. Inside, the design is by Yabu Pushelberg and it honours the soaring Mies Van der Rohe architecture that dominates this part of downtown. Bymark suddenly became a mainstay of the financial crowd who appreciates its quietly intimate and reassuring ambience. There aren't many places in North America where a hamburger can set you back $35, but this is one of them. However, expect it to be accompanied by richly battered onion rings, porcini mushrooms and melted Brie. Regrettably, there is no Kobe steak inside. Seared fois gras with caramelized mango wins discreet applause as a less bourgeois alternative. How about throwing caution to the winds in favour of the flourless chocolate cake with liquid chocolate filling when it comes to choosing dessert? It's like seeing your portfolio go up a notch. What more could one ask for?

CANOE *Canadian*
66 Wellington Street West, 54th floor • map 10 • 416-364-0054 • oliverbonacini.com • lunch and dinner Monday – Friday • dinner $220 for two • all major credit cards • reservations for lunch and dinner are essential.

In such a multicultural city, defining Canadian cuisine becomes a challenge. Canoe literally rises above it all (to the 54th floor of the TD Bank tower) and boldly offers traditional local fare such as Arctic char, Ontario pheasant and roast of caribou. Therefore, it defines 'Canadian' as creating the finest meals from our indigenous harvests and wildlife. By using as many Ontario ingredients as possible in the kitchen, it refuses to appease fashionable fusion tastes that seem to abound around town. The chef's creative flair truly enhances all the best aspects of dining out. Many believe it's the best truly Canadian restaurant in the country. Renowned service, a praised wine list favouring local vintages and great view from two rooms. Little wonder that this is a prime place for Bay Street tycoons to relax away from merger stress. The restaurant is closed to the public on Saturday evenings.

CASA BARCELONA *Spanish*
2980 Bloor Street West • map Toronto • 416-234-5858 • toronto.com • lunch and dinner daily • dinner for two $120 • all major credit cards • best to reserve a month ahead for dinner on Friday and Saturday nights.

It's worth a trip to the west end of the city just to spend a night saturated in all things Spanish. Located in a low-rise red brick building, spotlighted with its familiar yellow and red exterior, this establishment has been highly rated for over seven years. There are more than 30 main dishes on hand, supplemented with the largest Spanish wine cellar in North America. Ever had tripe soup? No? Well, here's your chance. This is a family place, loaded with happy folk being serenaded by strolling guitarists. If you can't get a reservation for Saturday night, come back on Sunday at noon and go crazy trying to select something from the 140-item tapas bar.

CENTRO GRILL AND WINE BAR *Canadian*
2472 Yonge Street • map 34 • 416-483-2211 • centrorestaurant.com • dinner Monday – Saturday • dinner $150 for two • all major credit cards • reservations are usually essential.

This is a highly respected restaurant that has had a committed international following for years. You can choose the main room on the second floor, or the sushi and oyster bar on the main level. There are over 800 labels on the wine list and only Rosenthal china on the table. Foie gras is made from ducks organically raised in Québec. Roasted rack of Ontario lamb has a honey mustard crust. But continental and Asian presentations will not escape you. Service and attention to detail are both impeccably executed. Centro lists over a dozen achievements from independent organizations, including *Wine Spectator* and *Gourmet Magazine*, as well as a four diamond citation from AAA/CAA.

CHIADO *Portuguese*
864 College Street • map Toronto • 416-538-1910 • torontolife.com • dinner Monday – Saturday • dinner $175 for two • all major credit cards • reservations advised.

The Portuguese community is the fourth largest cultural group in Toronto. Therefore, it comes as no surprise that Portuguese cuisine is treated with respect in the city. Never a year passes without Chiado being listed among the city's best restaurants, regardless of the type of cuisine. The room has a relaxing and elegant atmosphere with service provided by some of the finest waiters in town. Food tends to concentrate on the lighter side with no heavy overtones. There's no hiding the fact that many of the wines hail from Portugal and servers are pleased to help you with any vintages that could be unfamiliar. If you could choose only one Portuguese restaurant, this is the one.

COPPI *Italian*
3363 Yonge Street • map Toronto • 416-484-4464 • torontolife.com • dinner Monday – Saturday • dinner $150 for two • all major credit cards • reservations are advisable.

A lot of care is taken in this kitchen, with special attention given to seafood. There's a noticeable freshness to the ingredients and a regard for the traditions of coastal Italian cuisine. The wine list is comprehensive with a dominance of Italian vintages and a smattering of bottles from other countries. In this upscale area of town there are lots of good places to choose and Coppi will not turn into a disappointment. Just in case you want to know the name of the person shown in the big photo, it's the famed Italian cyclist Fausto Coppi.

CORNER HOUSE *French*
501 Davenport Road • map 28 • 416-923-2604 • torontolife.com • dinner Tuesday – Saturday • dinner $150 for two • all major credit cards • reservations advisable.

In the shadow of Casa Loma there's an unobtrusive little corner house that's become the favourite destination of Forest Hill's upper class when they go out for dinner. Five small rooms provide the privacy and ambience that's expected in this part of town. But it's the food that's really the big attraction. Here's where you can indulge in a creatively designed mélange of dishes with accents of the traditional culinary arts of France. There's either the full menu, or a reasonable *prix fixe*. This is just the right little hideaway where you can get away from the irritations of the city and indulge yourself in an evening of excellent food and uniquely pleasant surroundings.

CUISINE OF INDIA *Indian*
5222 Yonge Street • map 35 • 416-229-0377 • torontolife.com • lunch Monday – Thursday, dinner daily • dinner $80 for two • all major credit cards • reservations are a good idea for close to the weekend.

The papadums arrive before you can get comfortably seated and this kind of service continues throughout your stay. The same kind of attention is evident in the kitchen where chefs grind their own spices to make sure that flavour is always at an optimum level. One of the things you'll notice here is a cultural mix of people and a near absence of traditional Indian décor. If you're inquisitive, you can always peep into the glassed-in kitchen to check out the tandoori ovens. Don't forget the mango or saffron ice cream. And don't deprive yourself of this highly respected and sought-after place when you want to indulge in the best of Indian food.

DRAGON DYNASTY *Chinese*
2301 Brimley Road • map Toronto • 416-321-9000 • torontolife.com • lunch and dinner daily • dinner $120 for two • all major credit cards • dinner reservations essential.

Ever heard the sage advice that you can judge a Chinese restaurant by the number of Chinese people it attracts? Those in the know will tell you that Scarborough is the place to go when you want to treat the family to authentic Chinese food served in a room filled with people who originated in Hong Kong, Taiwan, or China. At the Huntingwood intersection of Brimley Road is a typical strip mall and a very untypical restaurant. So untypical, in fact, that people lining up to get in are often more smartly dressed than the crowd you'd find downtown. This is a high-class room catering to an increasingly well-to-do Chinese community. Table servers are patient and polite with those of us who might be uninitiated into the finer points of Chinese cuisine. The food is so well prepared that Dragon Dynasty has been singled out as one of the most sought-after fine dining restaurants in the city's prospering suburban Chinese neighbourhoods.

DYNASTY *Chinese - Cantonese*
131 Bloor Street West, 2nd floor • map 25 • 416-923-3323 • torontolife.com • lunch and dinner daily • dinner $140 for two • all major credit cards • reservations accepted.

On the second floor of the old Colonnade building you'll find one of the most respected and long-standing Chinese restaurants in the Bloor-Yorkville neighbourhood. It's certainly not an overly ornate place, or even remotely trendy by Yorkville standards, but it does attract Asian visitors who seem to be in the know about where to go when they're in town. The cuisine is Cantonese and getting past the great array of starters is a challenge as you contemplate more substantial fare. The chicken wings here are boned and soaked in wine. This will give you an idea of how the chef's culinary mind wanders away from the ordinary.

EDO *Japanese*
484 Eglinton Avenue West • map Toronto • 416-322-3033 • torontolife.com • dinner daily • dinner for two $120 • all major credit cards • reservations strongly advised.

Edo follows the characteristics of other fine Japanese rooms by providing guests with an elegant and serene atmosphere. Barely audible light jazz reflects off softly lit walls. Attentive and courteous servers are always conscious that your visit here must be memorable. The sushi bar is certainly a favourite place for those not intent on exploring Edo's more substantial dinner offerings. The fish exude a special freshness and it will be awhile before you forget the subtle delicacy of the shrimp and seaweed appetizer gently fried in tempura batter. The selections of sake and beer are more than adequate and many items on the wine list are available by the glass. All round, this is one restaurant you'll be telling friends about.

EL BODEGON *Peruvian*

537 College Street • map 18 • 416-944-8297 • **torontolife.com** • lunch and dinner Wednesday – Sunday • dinner $50 for two • all major credit cards • reservations suggested for late week dinner.

There's a distinct feeling that you've landed in South America the moment you walk through the door. The décor and music are both unashamedly Latin and the service is just as sunny. But do be patient with your server when the room gets crowded. Menu portions are almost too generous. Favourite dishes include seafood, chicken and red meats served with available salads and bean concoctions. The wine list is modest with vintages well-suited to the cuisine. The summer patio is a local attraction, alive with good-natured folk.

FAT CAT *International*

376 Eglinton Avenue West • map Toronto • 416-484-4228 • **fatcat.ca** • dinner Monday – Saturday • dinner for two $180 • all major credit cards • reservations advised.

It's easy to miss the small entrance, but it's well worth keeping your eyes open. Inside, those eyes quickly get accustomed to candlelight flickering over an intimate room and revealing a distant and discreet open kitchen. The menu changes with the season, but expect surprises like a new version of haggis, perhaps a venison chop, or even some sesame crusted scallops. If the spirit moves you, there's always the seven-course starter menu for $75. The wine list gives an excellent balance to your meal. One local food critic described this place as "a gourmet's paradise."

HAPPY SEVEN *Chinese*

358 Spadina Avenue • map 14 • 416-971-9820 • **torontolife.com** • daily till 5:00 AM • dinner $70 for two • Mastercard and Visa • reservations not accepted.

Seems that virtually everything about this place is designed to make you happy. For instance, virtually any time you get a craving for fish in black bean sauce, Happy Seven will be there to calm your addiction. After a daily late-morning opening it goes all the way through till 5:00 AM which means you'll meet a cross-section of the city's most interesting folk when the rest of the people in town are asleep. The place is constantly in motion with swift service, lots of customers and a super clean, brightly-lit environment. The only problem with Happy Seven is making up your mind. A happy problem to have! The menu lists an astounding number of dishes, even for Chinatown, with well over 200 selections, including 14 soups and 30 seafood concoctions. And, if you think the chefs can't possibly deliver quality with this much on their plates, think again!

HERBS *French*

3187 Yonge Street • map Toronto • 416-322-0487 • **herbsrestaurant.com** • lunch Monday – Friday, dinner daily • dinner $150 for two • all major credit cards • reservations for dinner advised late in the week.

Herbs pioneered an *haute* form of cuisine and presentation in midtown before others moved into the neighbourhood. It still ranks among the preferred places to go for finicky folk who need a fix of French food with an expanded Continental twist. Duck, seafood and sweetbreads are given special care in the kitchen and you should give them serious thought if they turn up on the menu the night you're there. If you're considering dessert, make sure not to get your blood checked for a few days. The wine selection is above average, including half bottles, and there's a small patio where you can graze.

HIRO SUSHI *Japanese*
171 King Street East • map 11 • 416-304-0550 • torontolife.com • lunch and dinner Tuesday – Saturday • dinner $115 for two • all major credit cards • reservations needed.

In a city where sushi has become a fad, Hiro Sushi has elevated it to an art form. Chef Hiro Yoshida is a master who provides surprising little innovations blended with more traditional tricks to make your meal something to remember. There's little doubt that here is a place for connoisseurs of subtle and meticulous tastes to enjoy the foremost in freshness and execution. The room is low-key and minimalist so as not to distract from presentation. For added authenticity, and a great evening in the gracious traditions of Japan, it's worth your while to dine here omakase-style.

HOST *Indian*
14 Prince Arthur Avenue • map 25 • 416-962-9224 • toronto.com • lunch buffet daily, dinner daily • dinner $60 for two • all major credit cards • reservations suggested towards the end of the week.

This Prince Arthur address has seen reputable kitchens come and go over the years, but the Host looks like it will be laying claim to 14 Prince Arthur for sometime to come. Its faithful client base assures it of a long and happy life here. The pleasant surprise is not so much the excellent Indian food, or comfortable surroundings and fine service, but the relatively modest price – a rarity in Yorkville. So, if you blanch when you get your bill on checkout at either the Four Seasons or Hyatt Park, you can save a few dollars at Host. The menu is top-notch with virtually everything portraying culinary authenticity.

IL BUN JI *Korean - Japanese*
668 Bloor Street West • map 23 • 416-534-7223 • lunch and dinner daily • dinner $50 for two • all major credit cards • no reservations.

Although the Japanese incursions into Korea a century ago are a painful chapter of history, the period gave birth to a hybrid cuisine of significant interest. And this fascinating Korean-Japanese mix of dishes has made Il Bun Ji one of Koreatown's favourite places. A pleasant staff makes you feel right at home and an inexhaustible supply of roasted rice tea is always on the table. Apart from the standard sushi, sake and Japanese beer, it's worth exploring the elegantly prepared wakame salad, donburi and sunomono. To make the experience more authentic, try to get a private booth. Well worth the trip to this section of Bloor West.

IL POSTO NUOVO *Italian*
148 Yorkville Avenue in York Square • map 25 • 416-968-0469 • toronto.com • lunch and dinner, Monday – Saturday • dinner $170 for two • all major credit cards • reservations invited.

The well-to-do who inhabit Yorkville have made this room one of their favourites for over two decades. It's where you can get a perfectly prepared magret of duck positioned over a ragoût of wild mushrooms and savory cabbage. Even the ravioli is a thing to be remembered. A well-chosen cellar highlights a changing assortment of bottles from France, Italy and California.

Expect those at the next table to be ladies lunching or influential business people lingering over an after dinner cognac.

INDIAN FLAVOUR *Indian*
595 Bay Street • map 15 • 416-408-2799 • torontolife.com • lunch and dinner daily • dinner $80 for two • all major credit cards • reservations might be a good idea at weekends.

Samosas, tandoori chicken, lamb tikka and chicken kesar malai are available on a menu that has proven to be successful with lunch hour business types and evening family groups. Although you can order from a menu, it's the regular buffet here that has made the room a permanent favourite with people interested in Indian food that's a cut above the ordinary. There's minimal traditional décor in this split-level room and it can get a bit crowded at times, due mainly to the busy location in the Atrium on Bay.

INDOCHINE *French Vietnamese*
4 Collier Street • map 26 • 416-922-5840 • torontolife.com • lunch Monday – Saturday, dinner daily • dinner for two $130 • all major credit cards • reservations accepted and advisable at weekends.

Just across the street from the northern end of the Toronto Reference Library is a little restaurant that you could easily pass by. If you enjoy superior Vietnamese food with other south Asian accents, try not to miss it. The menu is obviously influenced by France, going way back to the days when Vietnam was French Indochina. There are also hints of Chinese and Thai influences. This is a room with sophistication and fine food for those weary of the many stripped-down Vietnamese eateries elsewhere in town. Don't forget to end the evening with some homemade coconut or mango ice cream. All said and done, you are looking here at one of a small handful of really good Asian restaurants in the downtown area.

JUMP CAFÉ & BAR *International*
Melinda Street in Commerce Court East • map 10 • 416-363-3400 • jumpcafe.com • lunch Monday – Friday, dinner Monday – Saturday • dinner $150 for two • all major credit cards • reservations recommended, especially late in the week.

Jump is buried in the heart of the country's most influential business and financial district and its patrons ooze everything that's successful. The bar is packed with happy souls when the market rises. The lunch crowd shows its appreciation for one of the most discussed kitchens in town. The room is bright and cheerful, overlooking the inner plaza of Commerce Court. Venison, salmon, rack of Australian lamb and grilled portobello mushrooms adorn plates brought to the table by experienced and friendly servers. For dinner you could also consider air-dried bresaola and aruga, followed by a spinach and lobster ravioli, topped off with some molten chocolate cake and banana ice cream bathed in crème anglaise. As befits the new century, the wine list applauds the New World.

KEG MANSION *Steakhouse*
515 Jarvis Street • map 21 • 416-964-6609 • toronto.com • dinner daily • dinner $90 for two • all major credit cards • reservations advisable.

There might be around 30 places in Toronto claiming to be steakhouses. But no other steak house in town offers its customers the real thing more than the Keg

Mansion. It's housed in the impressive old McMaster mansion, one of the last great houses south of the Rosedale ravine. One customer describes it this way: "It's the only restaurant I've been in where there's a fireplace in the women's washroom." The Keg Mansion is also noted for its very good steaks and friendly service at a reasonable price. For many years, the customers just keep coming back. And the wine list, though not nearly as thorough as many of its expensive competitors, is well within reason. You won't find too many food critics wandering around, but it is quite possible you might bump into a ghost or two.

KOREA HOUSE *Korean*
666 Bloor Street West • map 23 • 416-536-8666 • lunch and dinner daily • dinner $80 for two • Mastercard and Visa • reservations are not necessary.

Korea House has been honing its reputation in this neighbourhood for a long time. If you're a neophyte when it comes to Korean food, the complete dinner for about $25 relieves you from making a whole lot of uninformed decisions. The meal includes rice, loads of barley-flavoured green tea and fresh dessert fruits. The waitresses are aware that too much spice could upset your comfort level, so let them know whether the chef should "turn it down a notch." If you want to wander further afield, try hakmool changol, which is a seafood and vegetable hotpot. If you take the kids, it's a polite tradition for them to pour the tea for adults.

LA MAQUETTE *International*
111 King Street East • map 11 • 416-366-8191 • lamaquette.com • lunch Monday – Friday, dinner Monday – Saturday • dinner $150 for two • all major credit cards • reservations recommended. If you reserve online you are eligible for a 10% discount on the food portion of your check.

This establishment, housed on the edge of the historic Town of York neighbourhood, has a fine reputation for elegant surroundings, memorable food, artistic presentation and a varied menu. There's a relaxing and intimate atmosphere with muted jazz usually permeating the place at dinner. Service is good natured and attentive. It's little wonder the place has a reputation for romantic dining. Choose seating on the patio, in a solarium, or next to a cozy winter fire. Although a popular early *prix fixe* meal for theatre patrons costs around $20 per person, you will find it rewarding to linger in this room to fully enjoy your evening. Your reward could be a wild mushroom strudel, followed by wild game ravioli and topped off with a generous portion of cedar plank salmon. Convinced?

LAI WAH HEEN *Chinese - Cantonese*
Metropolitan Hotel, 108 Chestnut Street • map 15 • 416-977-9899 • metropolitan.com • lunch and dinner daily • dinner $175 for two. There's a prix fixe executive lunch for two for $52 and a deluxe dinner for six for $328 • all major credit cards • reservations recommended for lunch and dinner.

Toronto is favoured with a couple of excellent hotel restaurants. When the first class Metropolitan Hotel decided to open its Cantonese restaurant on the outskirts of Chinatown, it went all out to please and impress. When *New York Times* says that the best dim sum in North America likely resides here, you get the impression that this is no ordinary Cantonese restaurant. *En Route* magazine noted that the restaurant boasts "edible masterpieces rarely savoured outside Hong Kong." *Gourmet Magazine* elevated Lai Wah Heen to its Top Table list. This is, quite simply, the finest Chinese restaurant in the city – perhaps even in the whole country. The décor in beige and black is dramatically modern and betrays the influence of high Hong Kong style. The baked shark's fin soup comes to the table covered in puff pastry. Service is impeccable. If you judge a good Chinese restaurant by the number of Chinese businesspeople seen with out-of-town guests, go no further than here.

LATITUDE WINE BAR & GRILL *International Fusion*
89 Harbord Street • map 19 • 416-928-0926 • travel.yahoo.com • lunch and dinner daily • dinner $110 for two • Mastercard and Visa • reservations a good idea for dinner.

Nestled close to the University of Toronto, Latitude has gradually built a solid reputation for fine food and expert service. Scented candles set a tone for what has become one of the city's favourite places to dine. The menu offers an array of flavours ranging from Latin to Asian with unexpected hints of other national origins. An oyster and mango combination contrasts with lemongrass salmon and chicken with roasted pumpkin seeds. This is quite a cozy establishment with limited seating, so make sure of your reservation.

LE PAPILLON *French Canadian*
16 Church Street • map 11 • 416-363-3773 • lepapillon.ca • lunch and dinner Tuesday – Sunday • dinner $80 for two • all major credit cards • reservations suggested for dinner.

Toronto has surprisingly few French restaurants specializing in dishes from Québec. Le Papillon bases its menu on *la belle province* in airy and pleasant surroundings that lend themselves to quiet conversation among friends. Situated close to both the St Lawrence and Hummingbird centres, the room has become a favourite place to go for the theatre crowd. There's an abundance of choices among *hors d'oeuvres*, salads and soups, but keep an appetite for the over-sized Breton-styled crêpes. The wine list is adequate, but diners often opt instead for the hard Granny Smith apple cider. It would be a good idea to spend some of the evening here, without concern for an approaching show time just around the corner.

LEE GARDEN *Chinese - Cantonese*
331 Spadina Avenue • map 14 • 416-593-9524 • torontolife.com • dinner daily • dinner $90 for two • reservations not accepted.

There are places in Chinatown that seem to have been around forever. Yes, the old timers know this one well. The only problem with this extremely popular place is getting in. Lineups seem to be the order of the day, especially at weekends when droves of folk come for the lack of MSG and fat. No one has a problem with recommending this hugely popular place right in the heart of Chinatown. Line up, be patient and reap your reward.

LEMON MERINGUE *International*
2390 Bloor Street West • map Toronto • 416-769-5757 • lemonmeringue.com • lunch Tuesday – Friday, dinner Tuesday – Saturday, brunch Sunday • dinner for two $185 • all major credit cards • reservations recommended, especially at weekends.

Dinner doesn't come much better in this part of town. Not only is the food of exceptional quality, but its presentation borders on an art form. There are always seasonal adjustments on the menu and, if you're lucky the night you're there, you might encounter the now famous Miso-glazed salmon served with wilted greens and ginger and carrot salad. It hasn't taken long for this room to leap close to the top dozen in town. Even though a lemon meringue might not always appear on the desert list – but you could settle for lemon mousse with blueberries – you might also consider for the apricot frangipani. The wines offer a full range of vintages to suit your mood and taste.

LUCKY DRAGON *Chinese*
418 Spadina Avenue • map 14 • 416-598-7823 • torontolife.com • lunch and dinner daily • dinner for two $45 • all major credit cards • reservations aren't necessary.

There are places around any city where you can indulge in good food at a very reasonable price. This is one of those places and it's where you can find something on the menu from just about any province in China. Here's a good place for those oriental tidbits and more than generously proportioned main dishes. Just about everything on the menu comes in at under $10. The room is long and narrow, brightly lit with no nonsense tables and chairs. People have been coming this way for years just for the food and the bill comes as a very pleasant afterthought.

MAMMINA'S *Southern Italian*
6B Wellesley Street West • map 20 • 416-967-7199 • torontolife.com • lunch Tuesday – Friday, dinner Tuesday – Saturday • dinner for two $110 • all major credit cards • reservations recommended, especially at weekends.

When select Hollywood folk come here for the Toronto International Film Festival, they call into Mammina's to get away from the crowd and bathe in an overdose of civility. For one thing, it's a small place and easy to miss. That means you can usually escape the foreign press. Second, word has spread around Tinseltown that Mammina's surrounds itself with a discreet and quiet professionalism. The food, rooted in southern Italy, is always memorable; the service is smooth and low-key; the room is sparsely decorated and the lighting low. What's more, a bottle of Italian wine will cost you less here than anywhere else in town because the mark-up is a comparatively miniscule $5. Everything considered, you can't do much better.

MANDARIN *Chinese Canadian buffet*
2200 Yonge Street • map 34 • 416-486-2222 • mandarinbuffet.com • lunch and dinner daily • dinner for two $55, lower prices for seniors • all major credit cards • reservations strongly advised for the weekend, Mother's Day and Chinese New Year.

There are never any surprises at one of the large Mandarin restaurants. For over 25 years this popular chain of expertly-run family dining rooms has won numerous media awards for the all-you-can-eat buffet, salad bar and Chinese food. The welcome and service are almost embarrassingly warm and polite. The food's quality and presentation never varies. Balancing a wide range of conventional Chinese dishes is a dinner menu of prime rib and fresh crab legs, or lobster in season. Desserts vary from traditional Chinese pastries to flans, cakes and fresh fruit to freshly made waffles and cream. At least six ice cream and yogurt flavours are on hand. The beverage list is limited, with average house wine, liqueur, creative cocktails and beer all usually under $5 each. Washrooms set a standard for cleanliness that could well be copied by more upscale establishments. Dress is as casual as you like. Some other city locations are at 2206 Eglinton Avenue East and 1027 Finch Avenue West.

MATA HARI *Malaysian - Asian*
39 Baldwin Street • map 14 • 416-596-2832 • toronto.com • lunch Tuesday – Friday, dinner Tuesday – Sunday • dinner for two $110 • all major credit cards • reservations advisable at weekends.

There's a tempting historic blend of Chinese and Malay cuisines rippling through a menu that offers about two dozen main dishes. The service could well have been rooted in the legendary Raffles: it's discreet and polite to a fault. There are little touches like a lowered public telephone, barrier-free access for disabled persons and dietary considerations that take into account most needs. The wine list, usually meagre in south Asian restaurants, is even a pleasant surprise. Although competitive neighbours along Baldwin Street surround Mata Hari, they hold their own. (By the way, there are no exotic Dutch dancers around to spy on you!)

MÖVENPICK MARCHÉ *Continental*
161 Bay Street inside Heritage Square • map 10 • 416-366-8986 • movenpickcanada.com • daily 7:30 AM – 2:00 AM • dinner for two $50 • all major credit cards • no reservations.

Mövenpick has a knack for being different. And from the moment Marché opened on the Galleria just inside the Yonge Street entrance to Heritage Square, it became an instant hit. It's worth waiting in line to get in and then wandering around the market atmosphere getting a bevy of chefs to prepare your food just the way you like it. You get a tab when you set out and at each station they jot down all the goodies you select for your meal. If you opt for a seat outside in the Galleria, then you've got the best indoor view in the city. Not bad when you consider that this experience is worth writing home about yet won't break the bank.

NAMI *Japanese*
55 Adelaide Street East • map 11 • 416-362-7373 • torontolife.com • lunch Monday – Friday, dinner Monday – Saturday • dinner for two $130 • all major credit cards • reservations are a good idea for lunch and recommended for dinner.

The starkly modern black on white exterior gives way to a more restful interior orchestrated by kimono-clad attendants. The sushi bar is on the right, traditional seating straight ahead and privately screened rooms immediately on the left. Choose from the familiar greaseless tempura or beef teriyaki, or proceed to an adventure from the main menu. The overall food quality, artistry of presentation and serene service out-score most of the similar places in town. An established place with a solid and well-earned reputation.

NORTH 44° *International*
2537 Yonge Street • map 34 • 416-487-4897 • north44restaurant.com • dinner Monday – Saturday • dinner for two $240 • all major credit cards • reservations recommended.

When lists of favourite restaurants are published, it's unusual if North 44° is not one of the top half-dozen. The establishment is an expensive place to dine, but it's an elegant, modern and stylish place with an enviable reputation for well-executed cuisine, creatively served by a professional and knowledgeable staff. Menu selections challenge a mostly upwardly mobile, well-heeled and well-dressed crowd. Sage braised rabbit and quail in sesame marinade are but a prelude to the indulgent desserts. This is one of those places where you go for a special celebration. North 44°, by the way, is Toronto's latitude.

OLD MILL INN *International - British*
21 Old Mill Road • map Toronto • 416-236-2641 • oldmilltoronto.com • lunch and dinner daily • dinner for two $210 • all major credit cards • a good idea to reserve at weekends.

The Old Mill Inn opened as an English Tudor-styled hotel the day WWI was declared. It's built next to the ruins of the old King's Mill and has expanded into a spa, dining establishment and hotel complex. It seems all overly British at times, complete with a live salon orchestra at dinner – making it a real throw back to the days of Empire, though not quite up there with Victoria's quaintly eccentric Empress Hotel. Expect the food to take on echoes of an elaborate English Sunday dinner, complete with parsnip soup and beef with Yorkshire pudding. If you want to unshackle yourself from the bonds of tradition, you might venture into bok choy alongside a roasted quail. And, to make it a truly authentic British eating out experience, there's a customary $4.95 cover charge at weekends.

PAESE *Southern Italian*
3827 Bathurst Street • map Toronto• 416-631-6585 • torontolife.com • lunch Monday – Friday, dinner daily • dinner for two $125 • Visa and Mastercard • reservations suggested for weekends.

Paese seems to hold the mortgage on fine southern Italian cuisine north of the 401, much to the chagrin of those who think everything that's good is south of the expressway. The room has an upscale environment without formality and attracts regular patrons from the affluent north Bathurst area. Appetizers range from bruschetta to smoked salmon and there are about a dozen pasta dishes. Mains concentrate on traditional chicken and veal. However, it is possible to opt for something more local, such as rack of venison with a cranberry and ginger glaze. A varied wine list with 500 labels is on hand with prices ranging from quite affordable to something nearing your next car payment.

PANGAEA *International*
1221 Bay Street • map 25 • 416-920-2323 • torontolife.com • lunch and dinner Monday – Saturday • dinner for two $190 • all major credit cards • reservations recommended.

Over recent years this spot on the eastside of Bay Street, just north of Bloor Street West, has seen several optimistic restaurants open to fanfare and close in silence. Inside, the present occupant espouses the term 'cuisine vitale'. That appears to be a high-priced name for fusion. And most everything here comes at a price, including the afternoon tea at $15 a head. Pangaea attracts the Bloor West shopping crowd, tired from browsing around Hermès and Chanel. The décor has a feeling of Zen about it. As one critic noted: "There are few wall pieces to distract from the $200 haircuts." Despite the seeming pretension of the place, the kitchen is one of the best in Yorkville and the menu changes monthly. There are even 19 wines by the glass, which is a blessed event in this part of town.

PAPPAS GRILL *Greek*
440 Danforth Avenue • map Toronto • 416-469-9595 • lunch and dinner daily • dinner for two $80 • Visa and Mastercard • reservations a good idea on Friday and Saturday nights particularly.

The Danforth is the centre of North America's largest Greek neighbourhood. So it's no surprise that the street is filled with good restaurants and a Mediterranean atmosphere. Pappas is a big, noisy, friendly place and the outdoor patio is a magnet during the summer, bringing in folks from all over town. Lots of vegetarian stuff and pizzas fresh from clay ovens are on the luncheon menu. When the sun sets, out come all the traditional Greek dishes served by a large, friendly staff. If you are thinking of bringing along up to 100 close friends, Pappas can accommodate you with no problem whatsoever. Just let them know ahead of time that you're coming. You might even get your own floor. Opa!

PHO HU'NG *Vietnamese*
350 Spadina Avenue • map 14 • 416-593-4274 • lunch and dinner daily • dinner for two $50 • credit cards not accepted • reservations not taken.

In Chinatown, where mediocre Vietnamese restaurants seem to be opening on every corner, it's good to know where to find Pho Hu'ng. As its name suggests, this is a great place for soups. But this is only a start to the 200 menu items that promise a truly wide excursion into Vietnamese cuisine with all its seductive Asian aromas. Strengths are directed towards beef and chicken dishes that come topped off with crunchy bean sprouts, lime and basil. This is not a place where alcohol dominates the drinks list, so go local and enjoy the tangy tropical juices. This is a cash only establishment, but the bill for even a whole group of people is a pleasant surprise.

PLANET HOLLYWOOD *American*
277 Front Street West • map 9 • 416-596-7827 • planethollywood.com • lunch and dinner daily • dinner for two $90 • all major credit cards • if a whole bunch of you are going, and you want to sit together, better reserve a ring side seat.

It doesn't get any more American than this. If you want to munch next to Sharon Stone's ice pick, or slurp your soup near the motorcycle Richard Gere rode in *An Officer and a Gentleman*, then this is your place. The cuisine is called 'California new classic' (a.k.a burgers 'n fries), including an apple pie supposedly invented by Arnold Schwarzenegger's mother. You can try it out for dessert close by the sled featured in *Home Alone*. Absolutely nothing promotes Hollywood better than Hollywood. So grab yourself a plateful of the American dream before or after a game at the Rogers Centre. Oh, and please don't forget to use your spare change to load up on souvenirs.

PREGO DELLA PIAZZA *Italian*
150 Bloor Street West • map 25 • 416-920-9900 • pregodellapiazza.ca • lunch and dinner daily • dinner for two $170 • all major credit cards •reservations recommended.

In a city awash with good Italian restaurants, this one seems to rise above most others. Not surprisingly, it caters to a high-end Yorkville clientele including a constant smattering of recognizable personalities. The room has a lushly modern look, while the summertime patio is definitely a place on which to be seen. There's a prevailing air of professionalism and perfection. And there's praise for superb food that defines itself as a 'new Italian wave'. For example, you might enjoy roast quail in agre dolce for lunch. At dinnertime, be tempted by fusili with smoked chicken and wild mushrooms in a sweet plum tomato sauce followed by monkfish picatta with Tuscany black olives and roasted tomato coulis.

PROVENCE *French contemporary*
12 Amelia Street • map 22 • 416-924-9901 • reataurantprovence.com • lunch and dinner Tuesday – Sunday, brunch Saturday – Sunday • dinner for two: prix fixe $60, gastronomic $140, brunch $35 • all major credit cards • reservations a wise move.

In the cosmopolitan area around Parliament and Carlton streets, several little restaurants have opened to cater to the diverse cultural mix of neighbourhood people. Provence has been the mainstay of diners here and has earned its stripes over the last 25 very successful years. Its reputation has spread far beyond Old Cabbagetown. The bright room spreads out on to the sidewalk during summer and lures folk into the pleasures of its highly regarded kitchen. Southern France is evident in the décor, service and selection of fine foods. You can choose from an extensive *à la carte* menu, an accommodating *prix fixe,* or a special gastronomic presentation. The wine cellar represents several countries and has won the *Wine Spectator* Award of Excellence for the last five years. Check out their extensive Web site for complete menu information.

PURE SPIRITS OYSTER BAR AND GRILL *Seafood*
55 Mill Street, building 62A • map 12 • 416-361-5859 • torontolife.com • lunch and dinner daily • dinner for two $110 • all major credit cards • reservations recommended.

The Distillery District has become one of the most impressive places in the city. Cobblestone lanes, going back over 175 years, reveal restaurants, stores and galleries magnificently restored inside with jaw-dropping effect. It's in this old treasure trove of warehouse buildings that Pure Spirits set up its seafood room within a space dominated by distressed brick walls, rough hewn beams and wooden booths – all lit with theatrical understatement. During the summer, you can spill out to a large patio and join folk doing the same thing in other nearby restaurants. If you order clams, they come in a curry-coconut broth. Oysters can be ordered almost any way you want. The chopped calamari salad with bacon lardons and olives is a pleasant surprise. This is a place you go not only for the memorable ambience of the setting, but for the food. It's a perfect combination indeed and cannot easily be ignored.

QUARTIER *French*
2112 Yonge Street • map 33 • 416-545-0505 • torontolife.com • lunch and dinner daily • dinner for two $140 • all major credit cards • reservations assure your comfort level at weekends.

The Davisville crowd has some good restaurants along Yonge Street that have captured a lot of attention. Quartier is among the best with a traditional French bistro menu that includes duck confit with pomme salardaise, five spice pickerel with organic risotto, and a hearty filet mignon. The smoked trout with asparagus salad is also worth considering. Modestly priced wines are selected from France, Ontario and California with most available by the glass. Dessert tempts you with offerings like wild blueberries (in season) with lemon curd. The service here is pleasantly professional and everything is done to make sure you'll consider a return visit. During summer months there's a small sidewalk plot where you can sit amid flower pots and take in the street scene. This part of Yonge Street is not exactly glamorous, mind you, and there's an adult establishment close by. But, hey! Doesn't that remind you of Paris?

RAIN *Asian*
19 Mercer Street • map 9 • 416-599-7246 • torontolife.com • dinner Tuesday – Saturday • dinner for two $180 • all major credit cards • reservations still required.

When this place opened it had all the mystique of New York's old Studio 54, complete with a bouncer who forbade entrance to those not considered sufficiently chic. You simply had to be anointed to enter. Legend has it that a Hollywood star was turned away, even when trying to attend her own party. A prominent food critic was once given the wave. Things have now become more accommodating. Inside, the walls feature waterfalls and the relaxed atmosphere is a testament to one of the finest restaurant designs in town. Rain has played to its generic Asian strength in a city nicely seasoned with Chinese, Japanese, Thai, Vietnamese and Malaysian restaurants. But, even then, it can stray into dishes not readily associated with this part of the world. If you want to experience how the chic folk graze, especially on five spice Peking duck, Rain is worth a visit – as long as they will still let you in!

ROSEWATER SUPPER CLUB *International*
19 Toronto Street • map 11 • 416-214-5888 • worldsbestbars.com • lunch Monday - Friday, dinner Monday – Saturday • dinner for two $230 • all major credit cards • reservations should get you in for dinner.

In an area where serious competition is only a few steps away, the Rosewater Supper Club has opted for expensive pleasure bordering on decadence. Persian carpets and a marble dance floor start to give you some idea. So will the 20 foot ceilings and velvet chairs that look more like thrones than seats for mere mortals. But before you settle in, drop into the lounge for a drink and some nostalgia from a throaty singer who might evoke memories of Garland, or Dietrich. The complex is populated with the well-heeled Bay Street crowd who can afford to strut their stuff in syncopation with live dinnertime music. Some menu items embrace the trendy fusion style while others stick to more traditional offerings. The wine list is noteworthy.

RUBY *Chinese - Cantonese*
1571 Sandhurst Circle • map Toronto • 416-298-1638 • lunch and dinner daily • dinner for two $105 • all major credit cards • get reservations for end of week dinners.

This is a large room capable of seating well over 500 happy diners. Situated within easy reach of Scarborough's booming Chinese community, Ruby is a beehive of activity at lunchtime as a seemingly unending cavalcade of dim sum carts skirt around tables to deliver scrumptious goodies. Dinner patrons have been craving the Peking duck here for years. And the shark's fin soup and choice abalone creations have never failed to please since the establishment opened. If you want to get a real bargain, check out the $83 Peking duck and lobster combination for four or six people. If you are fussy about ingesting MSG, just ask them to put it on hold. Ruby is one of the restaurants in suburbia that gives good reason for jaded downtowners to venture north for the evening.

RUTH'S CHRIS *Steakhouse*
Toronto Hilton Hotel, 145 Richmond Street West • map 10 • 416-955-1455 • ruthschris-toronto.com • closed for lunch, except during December, dinner daily • dinner for two $240 • all major credit cards • reservations an inspired idea at weekends

It's possible for 200 carnivores to pack into the five rooms here and sample expensive US prime steaks brought to the table sizzling in butter. There are ten choices of potato, each with an additional price tag of course. You can partake of a popular bread pudding with whiskey sauce, or opt instead for a cigarette in a special lounge – a rarity now that the city disapproves of almost anyone smoking virtually anywhere. It all comes at a price with this establishment topping most other expensive purveyors of steak in town.

SAUVIGNON *French*
1862 Queen Street East • map Toronto • 416-686-1998 • torontolife.com • lunch and dinner Tuesday – Saturday • dinner for two $130 • all major credit cards • reservations needed at weekends.

This is an atmospheric room trying to replicate a nice breeze off the Mediterranean. Needless to say, this is the kind of atmosphere that goes down well in the suburban Beach neighbourhood where interesting little restaurants keep opening to make nightlife interesting. The varied menu here tends to sail outside France on occasion to embrace other European shores. One of the neat things is the in-store bakery that assures you of fresh breads and way above average cakes and pastries. Duck takes its place alongside monkfish and steak to give you a nice selection of mains. Service is neither extraordinary nor inefficient, but rather reminds you of the celebrated *l'attitude* that seems to abound in the south of France.

SCARAMOUCHE *French*
1 Benvenuto Place • map 29 • 416-961-8011 • scaramoucherestaurant.com • dinner Monday – Saturday • dinner for two $210 • all major credit cards • reservations are respectfully advised.

Scaramouche, housed in a tastefully decorated and muted room, has the distinction of being up there among some of the most expensive and respected restaurants in the city. And, quite frankly, it caters to a conservative and very well off clientele. That said, Scaramouche also has one of the most extensive wine lists in Toronto and includes several *grands crus*. Desserts have won acclaim from serious diners. Arguably, it has one of the city's best kitchens and most professional table staff. An appetizer of pickled cherries with vanilla and hazelnuts on a toasted brioche complemented with Riesling jelly is a perfect prelude to venison loin roasted with smoked bacon. For an elegant evening away from the downtown buzz, this would be a fine choice indeed.

SEGOVIA *Spanish*
5 St Nicholas Street • map 20 • 416-960-1010 • segovia.ca • lunch Monday – Friday, dinner Monday – Saturday • dinner for two $100 • all major credit cards • reservations advised.

When you look north along St Nicholas Street from the Wellesley Street corner you can't help noticing a splash of colour on Segovia's exterior walls. That kind of attention extends inside, where you're greeted by old-world service from people well versed with the day's offerings. There's a nice range of tapas on hand before a traditional Gazpacho Anduluz and on to something like seafood Zarzuela, with its heady mix of saffron and brandy. This is a traditional Spanish room with dark woods and muted strains of a classical guitar. Many regulars opt for what the chef is preparing that evening and never seem to be disappointed. Segovia has earned a reputation for around 20 years for fine Spanish food and wines at reasonable prices.

SOUTHERN ACCENT *American - Cajun Creole*
595 Markham Street • map 23 • 416-536-3211 • southernaccent.com • dinner Tuesday – Sunday • dinner for two $120 • all major credit cards • reservations suggested for weekends.

Situated on one of the most distinctive, if not a little quirky, streets in town, Southern Accent manages to revive the steamy New Orleans feeling of the Forties. Jambalaya, of course, is on the menu, together with a to-die-for pecan pie. A plate of jumbo shrimp, swimming in a bread-dunking sauce, shouldn't be passed by, and neither should the slow-cooked beef ribs in tomato sauce. Speaking of bread, the wholesome and varied basket that comes to the table costs $5 (an exceedingly rare event in Toronto) but it's worth every penny. The service here is a pleasant relief from the attitude of so many restaurants these days. The smiles are actually genuine. Lots of cozy nooks and crannies abound in the two-storey Victorian house, so you can do a bit of hand holding without too many people noticing.

SPOON *International*
391 King Street West • map 9 • 416-599-7000 • spoonrestaurant.com • dinner daily • dinner for two $165 • all major credit cards • reservations recommended.

Spoon is a good example of the folly of trying to categorize a restaurant. While it bills itself as American contemporary, critics label it as either eclectic or pan Asian. With a menu that often includes quail along side Persian barbary bread, lamb shank and jicama and sour apple slaw, you can see the conundrum. That said, here is a slickly minimalist room, subtly bathed by warming skylights, specializing in fine service and a consistently regarded for its high standard of cuisine. Although the wine list is not outstanding when compared with other establishments, it does provide a reassuring and complimentary balance to your dish of choice. In the summer months, try a table on the patio where you have the added enjoyment of people watching.

SPRING ROLLS *Thai - Asian*
40 Dundas Street West • map 15 • 416-585-2929 • springrollsonline.com • lunch and dinner daily • dinner for two $40 • Visa and Mastercard • reservations not accepted.

The minimalist and stylishly inviting décor of a large Spring Rolls' room seems to deny the possibility that this is a chain of restaurants. But a chain it is. There are three of them downtown, and growing in number, with their popularity based on an impressive array of delectable Asian creations and topped off with a very manageable price. Make your selections from equally enticing Thai curries, Vietnamese pho, Singapore noodles, Szechuan stir fry and, as the name suggests, nine different kinds of spring rolls. This enterprise has taken Asian dining rooms in a totally different direction, well away from their predictable cultural clichés, and right into a smart and very trendy dining environment. To make things more appealing, you can take advantage of their take-out service.

STARFISH *Seafood*
100 Adelaide Street East • map 11 • 416-366-7827 • torontolife.com • lunch and dinner daily • dinner for two $150 • all major credit cards • better phone ahead for a seat at weekends.

Toronto is not over-blessed with a plethora of good seafood restaurants. However, this is one of the city's best non-Asian establishments. For starters, it has a world champion oyster shucker on hand and 18 different kinds of oysters to keep him busy. Grilled shrimp, nicely seared scallops, or even oxtail meat stuffed into tender squid can raise your taste buds to exciting new heights. And when was the last time you had the opportunity to order fresh grilled sardines? Now's your chance to bring back those memories of that beachfront café in Spain or Portugal. Desserts are not forgotten here, including the possibility that their lemon tart, topped with a crisp meringue and served with minted grapefruit sections, might be on the menu the night you arrive. And what would a renowned oyster place be without beer? Choose from any of ten on tap. Wine lovers aren't forgotten and can usually find selections by the glass from an interesting selection of locales.

STORK ON THE ROOF *Continental*
2009 Yonge Street • map 33 • 416-483-3747 • storkontheroof.com • lunch Tuesday – Friday, dinner Tuesday – Saturday • dinner for two $125 • all major credit cards • a reservation might be a good idea for dinner.

This is what you call an upscale Dutch treat. Among the fine restaurants in midtown is this gem with culinary roots planted in the Netherlands. You'll find hints of Indonesian influences and exotic Asian herbs mixed with lemon and sesame flavours. An almost boneless roasted quail with sweet grilled figs is a nice starter. Escargots in red wine and garlic are served in a phyllo cup. Try the sautéed shrimp and scallops and finish the meal with some Dutch apple pie or perhaps a Stilton and port. There are more than a half-dozen wines by the glass and an interesting and varied choice of bottles. The décor here is a bit off the beaten path, but it's a place where you can relax and enjoy your night in the company of pleasant, friendly and personal staff.

SUSHI KAJI *Japanese*
860 The Queensway • map Toronto • 416-252-2166 • torontolife.com • dinner Tuesday – Sunday • dinner for two $270 • all major credit cards • reservations seriously recommended.

Experienced habitués of some of Japan's finest restaurants rate this room highly. One exuberant customer went so far as to put it among the world's top ten Japanese restaurants. All this praise comes at a price. Sushi Kaji might well be the city's most expensive place for a meal. The chef is a stickler for only the freshest fish, carefully selected according to the season, and presents his prize to you with meticulous respect for presentation. The menu is extensive, the service is gracious and the list of sakes is impressive. If you have money and a true appreciation of the finest Japanese cuisine, you have found a perfect marriage of the two.

SUSUR *International Fusion*
601 King Street West • map 8 • 416-603-2205 • susur.com • dinner Monday – Saturday • dinner for two $230 • all major credit cards • reservations required.

Dining at Susur is an experience you will not easily forget. Within a room displaying almost stark minimalism and bathed in ever-changing soft light, you'll discover what is arguably one of the city's two or three best restaurants. Why such a low-key décor? So it won't distract from the presentation of the food. This is no ordinary place. The main course is served first, for example. Soup comes just before dessert. Highly professional table staff discuss your preferences well ahead of serving gastronomic experiences that change daily and embrace the finest dictates of worldly kitchens. The wine list flirts with vintages from Austria, Portugal and Canada to complement French, Italian and Californian labels. If this is your first time at Susur, be encouraged by one of the five tasting menus, two of which are vegetarian. No one knows until about an hour before mealtime what these menus will contain. It depends on what's available in the markets that day. Your are strongly advised to visit **susur.com** before going. You'll see why. Expect to be intrigued. Expect to be seduced.

TAKESUSHI *Japanese*
22 Front Street West • map 10 • 416-862-1891 • torontolife.com • lunch Monday – Friday, dinner Monday – Saturday • dinner for two $120 • all major credit cards • reservations accepted.

There was a change in Takesushi a little while ago after another praised Japanese restaurant, Nami, took it over. The décor is different and a bit more modern, but the standard of excellence never missed a beat. If you want to dine in traditional omasake fashion, there are three dinners to consider: one for $50 and the others for either $70 or $90. It's not usual for people to go into raptures over dessert at a Japanese restaurant, but here you will tell your friends about the chocolate mousse in ice wine jelly. Hardly traditional Japanese, but definitely out of the ordinary. The room's new design is an abstraction of restful rocks and bamboo rods, ensuring the calmness of Japanese traditions. There's a wide range of beers, but less than half-dozen sakes available. The sushi bar gives you a glimpse of folk scurrying past along the Front Street sidewalk.

TOM JONES *Steakhouse*
17 Leader Lane • map 11 • 416-366-6583 • tomjonessteakhouse.com • lunch Monday – Friday, dinner daily • dinner for two $210 • all major credit cards • reservations necessary for dinner.

Upscale steakhouses have come and gone, but this restaurant has been around for a long time and so has the building erected over 200 years ago. Rich woods and discreet period pictures combine with white tablecloths to give the three rooms a traditional steakhouse appearance. The menu is also traditional with a smattering of choice seafood like lobster, Alaska king crab and Dover sole. Red meats, from prime rib to an assortment of steaks, cover the full spectrum of beef while adding veal and lamb. After 10:00 PM you can order a cheese or beef fondue. The wine list is well regarded and you shouldn't have a problem selecting just the right bottle for your dinner. Service is attentive and the staff is well versed in the ways of the kitchen. For now, management has set aside a special smoking room in case the soothing piano music doesn't do its job of calming your nerves. A final note: gentlemen are encouraged to wear a jacket and tie.

TOWN GRILL *International*
243 Carlton Street • map 17 • 416-963-9433 • torontolife.com • lunch and dinner Tuesday – Friday • dinner for two $125 • Mastercard and Visa • reservations advisable by week's end.

Old Cabbagetown is one of those eclectic neighbourhoods, brimming with history and harking to the beat of a very diverse social and cultural mix of people. Residents here are fiercely loyal to their special piece of Toronto. Little wonder they don't stray far from the neighbourhood to patronize some of the city's more interesting places to eat. The Town Grill positions itself towards the upper end of the nearby eateries and has won a faithful following from people much further afield than Parliament and Carlton. There's a distinct freshness about the menu, thanks to some subtle and creative spicing. This is mostly familiar fare. Wonderful beef tenderloin with Dijon mustard crust, for example, but executed with encouraging zeal. A well-balanced assortment of about 40 wines is available for your pleasure, many of which can be ordered for under $20.

TRUFFLES *International*
21 Avenue Road (Four Seasons Hotel) • map 25 • 416-928-7331 • fourseasons.com/toronto • dinner Monday – Saturday • dinner for two $230 • all major credit cards • reservations recommended.

Hotel restaurants, once the great gastronomic temples of the Thirties, are starting to regain their historical glory in selected places around the globe. This is one of them, situated on the mezzanine floor of Four Seasons' hometown hotel. If international salutes by *Gourmet* and *Hotel* magazines, and over a decade's worth of consecutive Five Diamond awards from AAA/CAA, are anything to go by, Truffles is considered up there with the world's best top ten hotel restaurants. There is a timeless air about this room, with tables arranged to afford privacy on the one hand, or tasteful display on the other. Seasonal changes to the menu reveal constant culinary surprises and flawless execution amid superbly professional service. Rabbit rolled in nutmeg spinach and served with chestnuts gives you some idea of the creativity you should expect. The same originality is applied to the tarragon ice cream accompanying a galette of warm apple and quince. This restaurant is an excellent choice indeed for that very special occasion. Smart casual attire is requested, though it's preferable that gentlemen wear a jacket and tie.

VIA ALLEGRO *Italian*
1750 The Queensway • map Toronto • 416-622-6677 • torontolife.com • lunch and dinner daily • dinner for two $180 • all major credit cards • reservations a wise move at weekends.

Here is one of the best reasons to get away from downtown and Little Italy to experience wonderful Italian food in an atmosphere that oozes the charms of the Mediterranean. The strip mall environment should be utterly ignored because, inside, a whole new gastronomic world unfolds within a room that can hold hundreds of people from families to lonely food nerds. You wouldn't expect to find one of the continent's biggest wine cellars here (45,000 bottles), nor will you automatically assume that the menu will contain such a tantalizing variety of selections, or that the kitchen will turn out some of the best Italian food you've ever eaten. All this and a friendly table staff who always seem to have the knack of making you comfortable among 'family'. By the way, there are no less than six sommeliers on hand for wine service. So, unshackle yourself from the constant lure of downtown's predictable culinary chic and venture westward for a meal to remember.

WAH SING *Seafood*
47 Baldwin Street • map 14 • 416-599-8822 • torontolife.com • lunch and dinner daily • dinner for two $110 • Visa and Mastercard on purchases over $20, otherwise cash • reservations recommended for lunch and dinner as the week progresses.

Although Chinese restaurants all feature seafood in one form or another, this one specializes in the art of its preparation. Wah Sing is regarded as being near the top of the crustacean heap. The room is modest, with pink table-cloths, comfortable sitting surfaces and small white lights. Seafood lovers can agonize over about 100 combinations before zeroing-in on their favourite section of the menu. See if the two-for-one lobster special is available the time you visit. Or try the sizzling grouper with ginger and scallions. Competition among good restaurants along this stretch of Baldwin Street is fierce. Wah Sing won't make you wish you went some place else.

WAYNE GRETZKY'S *Canadian Sports Bar*
99 Blue Jays Way • map 9 • 416-979-PUCK • gretzkys.com • lunch and dinner daily • dinner for two $120 • reservations essential for game nights.

Anyone who enters this world of Gretzky will be submerged in hockey stuff. The address – #99 – was Wayne's jersey number. The telephone number is PUCK. Wayne, of course, is Canadian, but the food is American. As with Gretzky himself, this haunt is a bit larger than life. There's a 280 sq m patio on the roof and almost as much hockey history stashed around the room as you'll find in the Hockey Hall of Fame. The menu boasts Wayne's favourite meals, such as steak tenderloin. If you can't bear tearing yourself away from the Great One, at least you can take away a memory from the souvenir shop. And, if you don't know who Wayne Gretzky is, then you'd better go back home and take up croquet.

XAM YU *Seafood - Chinese*
339 Spadina Avenue • map 14 • 416-340-8603 • torontolife.com • lunch and dinner daily • dinner for two $50 • Visa • reservations not necessary.

One of the authentic things about Chinatown's restaurants is the seeming endless list of dishes chalked up on the walls. Couple this with the formal

Xam Yu menu and the decision-making process can exhaust the most decisive person on the planet. Xam Yu prizes its expertise in the preparation of seafood, but that shouldn't stop you from ordering mushroom soup, eggplant or tofu. Any way you choose, the bill is a welcome surprise. The kitchen is inventive, the presentation is a cut above most of its neighbours and the staff is helpful and polite.

YOUNG THAILAND *Thai*
165 John Street • map 9 • 416-593-9291 • youngthailand.com • lunch Monday – Friday, dinner daily • dinner for two $100 • Visa and Mastercard • best bet is to reserve for weekend dinner.

Many folk say that this is one of the top two Thai places in town. The bright and airy room with nicely spaced tables goes a bit overboard with plants, but it's what turns up on the plate that counts. Fish cakes with lime, or chili with green onions provides a good start, followed by a beef coconut curry packing the right amount of seasoning. If you are one of those people who crave Thai food once in awhile, you certainly won't be disappointed with this long-standing room where everything appears to be just right. The atmosphere is casual and the staff practices the art of politeness. There are two other central locations: 81 Church Street and 2038 Yonge Street.

Local information

Finally, here's some local information you should know. Toronto, like other cities, has its particular way of doing things and many of them might be different from what you're used to at home. Here's where we show you the differences.

Alcohol & bars, 213
Clothing, 213
Crime, 214
Cycling, 214
Directions, 214
Distress centres, 215
Driving, 215
Drugstores, 216
Electrical current, 216
Gay community, 216
Holidays, 217
Hospitals, 217
Media, 217
Medical & dental, 218

Metric system, 219
Multiculturalism, 219
People with disabilities, 219
Politeness, 220
Postal services, 220
Prostitution, 221
Security, 221
Smoking, 221
Taxes, 222
Telephones, 222
Walking, 222
Washrooms/toilets, 223
Weather, 223
Toronto trivia, 225

Emergency Police, fire & ambulance **phone 911**

ALCOHOL & BARS

Toronto is still a bit Victorian when it comes to its drinking laws. The legal drinking age is 19. Regular bar hours are 11:00 AM – 2:00 AM daily. Wine, spirits and some imported beers are available from government operated Liquor Stores. Look under *Liquor Control Board of Ontario* in the phone book for a list of outlets, or visit their Web site at **lcbo.com**. Regular beer is sold at government operated Beer Stores. You'll find them in the telephone book under *Beer Store*, or on the Internet: **thebeerstore.ca** If a restaurant is 'licensed under the LLBO' (Liquor Licensing Board of Ontario), it means that alcohol is served. Some restaurants will let you bring your own wine, so phone ahead to find out. There's a move afoot by the provincial government to bring Ontario more into line with Québec and have alcohol available in corner stores. Driving with a blood alcohol level of 0.08 or higher is punishable under the *Criminal Code of Canada.*

CLOTHING

People here dress casually all year round. However, you're never out of place wearing business attire at formal meetings and in high-class restaurants. Wear 'smart casual' for other occasions, restaurants, or when off to the theatre. At other times, wear anything that feels comfortable. Remember that

213

summer can be hot and humid in Toronto; winter can be bitterly cold; spring wet and variable; and fall nice and cool in the evening. So dress accordingly. If you're not used to cold weather, it's best to 'layer' your clothing when you go outside. Don't wear good shoes outside in the winter. Get some boots or overshoes because they will protect you from all the salt used to melt sidewalk ice.

CRIME

Toronto is one of the safest major cities on the continent, and the safest major Canadian city. This doesn't mean we don't have our share of trouble around town. It just means we have less per capita crime than most other big cities. Most murders happen among people who know each other. Total crime in the city has been falling over the last decade. To put it into some perspective, Washington, DC, has 40 times Toronto's murder rate. St Louis, MO, beats us 35-1 in that category. In overall crime, Montreal has over three times as much, Vancouver almost five times more, and Birmingham, AL, clobbers us by seven to one. Just the same, our good fortune is nothing to brag about. When you're in town, be sensible and don't take unnecessary chances. Incidentally, you can get a breakdown of the crime statistics from **statcan.ca**

CYCLING

With 2,000 parks and ravines covering 8,000 ha of green space, you're never far from a great place to cycle. Toronto is one of North America's most bike-conscious cities and you might be surprised to see so many people out cycling on summer weekends. There are even special bicycle lanes along some major downtown streets. The first thing to know is the law stating that everyone under the age of 18 has to wear a helmet when they're riding a bike. The vast majority of adults wear one voluntarily. Cycles are permitted on TTC subway and RT trains, streetcars and buses during non-peak hours, from 9:30 AM to 3:30 PM, and 6:30 PM to 6:30 AM. Despite this, vehicle operators and ticket collectors have the right to refuse access to bicycles, in the event of crowding or emergencies. Finally, don't leave your bike lying around unattended. About 12,000 bicycles are stolen each year and police find only about five per cent of them. So, make sure your bike is immobilized when you leave it some place. There's a whole lot of cycling information, including maps of city bicycle paths, on the city's Web site: **city.toronto.on.ca/cycling** For information about taking your bike on the TTC, log on to **ttc.ca** or phone 416-393-INFO.

DIRECTIONS

A lot of people get confused trying to find their way around Toronto. It's mainly because the locals never seem to use the words 'right' and 'left' when giving you directions. By and large, Toronto is laid out on a grid pattern: most main streets run at right angles to each other. Yonge Street is the north-south spine that divides the city between east and west. It's second nature for Torontonians to think in terms of the compass when they're getting around town. If you ask someone for directions, instead of them saying: "Go up Yonge and turn right at Carlton…" they'll tell you to "Go north on Yonge and east on Carlton…" You'll also come across this on the subway, with notices telling you whether trains are eastbound, northbound, etc. North is at the top of all maps in this book.

DISTRESS CENTRES

The phone numbers below will put you in touch with someone ready to help you. Even if you have had only the slightest reason to talk with someone about a problem you might have, now is the time to do it:

Drug/Alcohol Addiction
416-397-4636

Kid's Help Line
1-800-668-6868

Children's Aid Society
416-924-4646

Sexual Assault
416-597-8808

Community Services
416-397-4636

Suicide
416-598-1121

DRIVING

Toronto, like other large cities, has its share of traffic congestion and frustrating delays caused by weather, road repairs and accidents. Here are some general rules and tips to help you get around town more easily:

- You can turn right on red lights providing there's no notice to the contrary. Come to a full stop first, make sure the way is clear, then proceed with caution.

- When a school bus has its lights flashing, all vehicles in *both* directions must come to a complete stop.

- All traffic must come to a complete stop to allow people to cross the street at clearly marked pedestrian crossings. It's customary for pedestrians to raise their arm to signal that they're about to step off the curb.

- Traffic must come to a full stop behind streetcars that are loading or unloading passengers. Do not overtake the streetcar until all its doors have fully closed.

- Always remember to use your turn signals when changing lanes, or making turns.

- Although it's not illegal to use a phone while you're driving, common sense dictates this is not a safe thing to do behind the wheel. If you have an urgent call to make, pull off the road.

- Be sensible about safety. Lock your vehicle and don't leave stuff in obvious view inside. You might feel more secure by using a steering lock. Radar detecting devices are illegal and will be seized if discovered.

- Daytime running lights are mandatory on all vehicles sold in Canada. Telling another driver he's got his headlights on in the middle of the day only lets him know you're a tourist.

- There's an old saying in Toronto: "Drivers experience two seasons: winter and road repairs." It's another reason to leave your vehicle in the garage and take the TTC.

Parking

This falls into two general categories: on the street, or in a parking lot. If you park on the street, make sure your vehicle is not in violation of any parking signs. In most downtown locations you have to buy a ticket from the nearby Municipal Parking solar-powered ticket dispenser. When you take it out of the machine, put it *face up on your dashboard*. Private companies run some parking lots while others, showing the big green letter 'P', are operated by the city. There's not much difference in their prices. Try **greenp.com** to find the nearest municipal lot. Parking lots in the central downtown core are expensive during the day, and even more expensive if they're close to major events. Try to get a space before 9:00 AM when all-day rates are much cheaper. If your car is missing, phone the police at 416-808-2222. It might have been stolen or towed to the pound. The best advice, once again, is not to use your vehicle downtown. Use the TTC instead.

Gasoline

Gas prices are always going up and down, often in both directions on the same day. This craziness prompted the Web site **torontogasprices.com** to come into being. Its main function is to let you know where to find cheap gas. You can search by location, brand, or where motorists have come across a sudden price drop. It also lists the most expensive gas stations. Most major-brand stations don't have full-service outlets, whereas all the small company stations have someone to fill your tank. These smaller stations generally charge less than their larger competitors. All stations serve regular and premium gas, but diesel isn't universally available. Leaded gasoline is not sold in Canada.

DRUGSTORES

All drugstores and pharmacies in the city have a pharmacist on duty. Most Shopper's Drug Mart stores are open till midnight daily. Phone 1-800-363-1020 for their locations and 24 hr services, or go online at **shoppersdrugmart.ca** If you are downtown, there's a 24 hr store on the corner of Gerrard Street West and Bay Street (see map 15).

ELECTRICAL CURRENT

Toronto operates on the standard North American 110-volt system. Overseas visitors should bring adapters for their electrical equipment.

GAY COMMUNITY

This is a very gay-positive city. Gay and lesbian marriages are legal and you can walk into city hall to tie the knot. There are some churches performing marriages as well. Whereas Gay Pride festivities in other cities around the world seem to be losing their cachet in recent years, the one here remains a big summer hit and attracts huge turnouts. Fashion Cares, a blockbuster artistic fundraiser for the HIV-AIDS community, continues to be the hottest ticket in town. The centre of things is still the Church-Wellesley Village (map 21) which has undergone a major sprucing-up that some believe has made it more metrosexual. Other gay areas have sprung up, taking over the once seedy area around Parkdale and the trendy areas of Bloor West Village, The

Annex, Davenport and Trinity-Bellwoods. They don't have the focused commercial gay business base of Church-Wellesley Village, but they seem to attract those who have given up the overt lifestyle and just want to settle down. Get a copy of the bi-weekly newspaper *xtra!* to find out what's going on. You can also get it online at **xtra.ca**

HOLIDAYS

All banks and government offices are closed on each of the following holidays. Stores are usually closed on New Year's Day, Good Friday, Easter Sunday, Canada Day, Simcoe Day, Thanksgiving and Christmas Day. The TTC operates a reduced service on these days as well.

PUBLIC HOLIDAYS

Date	Occasion	National/Local
January 1	New Year's Day	National
March/April, date varies	Good Friday	National
March/April, date varies	Easter Monday	National
May, third Monday	Victoria Day	National
July 1	Canada Day	National
August, first Monday	Simcoe Day	Local
September, first Monday	Labour Day	National
October, second Monday	Thanksgiving	National
November 11	Remembrance Day	National
December 25	Christmas Day	National
December 26	Boxing Day	National

HOSPITALS

This sounds obvious, but hospitals are for really sick people. So don't go to a hospital's emergency department if you think you might be coming down with a cold. Go to a walk-in clinic instead (see the next page). The largest concentration of major hospitals is centred in the Discovery District (map 15) downtown. Other big downtown teaching hospitals are St Michael's (map 11) and Toronto Western (map 13). Suburban hospitals are shown on the *Toronto* map. Expect to be seen fairly quickly when you go to emergency, but then get ready for a wait that could last for several hours. The most urgent cases get first priority. When you enter a hospital in Toronto, you're likely to come across handwashing dispensers. Take a moment to use these devices both when you first enter the hospital and again when you leave. If you want to be doubly cautious about not getting, or spreading, infections go into a washroom and give your hands a good scrub with soap and water.

MEDIA

Toronto is the centre of Canada's communications industry. The percentage of homes here that are wired for cable and satellite delivery systems is one of the highest in the world. We are also the only country to carry the full television service of the United States on its domestic system. There are over 70 channels on the basic television service, including those from both countries. Additional tiers of service can increase available channels to nearly 200. The cable connection also carries dozens of radio stations. The country's three national English television networks each have their headquarters here. Toronto has four major daily English newspapers (the same as New York City) and four major local foreign language papers which are detailed on the following page.

TORONTO DAILY NEWSPAPERS				
Newspaper	Language	Publication	Telephone Area 416	Website
Corriere Canadese	Italian	Mon - Sat	785-4300	corriere.com
El Popular	Spanish	Mon - Sat	531-2495	diarioelpopular.com
Globe & Mail	English	Mon - Sat	585-5000	theglobeandmail.com
Korea Times	Korean	Mon - Fri	787-1111	koreatimes.net
National Post	English	Mon - Sat	383-2500	nationalpost.com
Sing Tao	Chinese	Daily	861-8168	singtaotor.com
Toronto Star	English	Daily	367-2000	thestar.com
Toronto Sun	English	Daily	947-2222	canoe.ca

In addition to the major newspapers listed above, there are three free English tabloids: *24 Hours* (**24hrs.ca**), *Metro* (**metronews.ca**) and *Dose* (**dose.ca**), available from boxes Monday through Friday.

MEDICAL & DENTAL

Canada's Medicare system is available without cost only to Canadian residents with a valid Health Card. If you are visiting from outside the country it is strongly advised that you get health insurance coverage before you leave home because uninsured treatment can become very expensive, especially if your condition is serious and you need hospitalization.

Medical emergencies

Go straight to the nearest hospital, or phone 911 if you need ambulance assistance. If your condition is not of an urgent nature, go to a walk-in clinic. Choose one listed under 'Physicians' in the *Yellow Pages* phone book. If you believe that you or your child has been poisoned by something that was swallowed, contact the Poison Control Centre at the Hospital for Sick Children immediately. It's open 24 hr. (See map 15 for its downtown location on University Avenue at Gerrard Street West.) **sickkids.on.ca**, or phone 416-813-6621.

Dental emergencies

If you have a dental emergency, and can't get an immediate appointment with a local dentist, go to the emergency walk-in dental clinic at 1650 Yonge Street (map 32). The clinic is staffed by a revolving roster of local dentists and is open daily from 8:00 AM till midnight. Payment is by cash, Visa, or Mastercard. If you subscribe to a dental insurance plan, the folks there will give you the forms to fill out for a reimbursement. Phone 416-485-7121.

Sexually transmitted diseases (STD)

Phone the Toronto Health Department at 416-392-2437 for the nearest treatment centre, or visit their Web site at **city.toronto.on.ca/health**. For additional contact information regarding HIV-AIDS look in the phone book under *AIDS and HIV Services*. Gays and lesbians might prefer to go to the Hassle-Free Clinic, 66 Gerrard Street East, 2nd Floor, at the corner of Church Street (map 16) for anonymous testing for all STDs. However, AIDS testing requires an appointment that you can organize when you get there. For clinic hours, phone the following numbers for recorded information: men 416-922-0603 and women 416-922-0566. Their Web site is **hasslefreeclinic.org**

METRIC SYSTEM

Canada has used the metric system of measurement for decades. Despite this, clothing measurements remain in inches and no one seems to think that's strange. People state their height in feet and inches, rather than metres and centimetres, and that seems normal too. So, you can talk to us in metric, Imperial, or American measurements and we'll nod our heads knowingly and understand you completely. **sciencemadesimple.net/conversions** is a good place to go on the Web if you find all this metric conversion stuff confusing. But, please don't think Toronto is a cold place when you see the temperature here is only 30. That's 30 degrees Celsius, which converts to 86 Fahrenheit.

MULTICULTURALISM

Toronto is one of the world's most culturally diverse cities. When you walk down the street, you can't help noticing people from all over the world, often speaking their native language. Even so, English is the social and business language. We all seem to respect each other's differences and customs and get along surprising well when you consider the racial tensions in other places. When you come to Toronto, look upon it as a global experience. It's where you can eat superbly prepared exotic food and take part in lots of 'foreign' cultural activities. *Vive la différence.*

PEOPLE WITH DISABILITIES

Toronto has demonstrated that it's a very manageable city for wheelchair users and people with disabilities. For example, there's 24 hr access to the Centre for Independent Living which can help solve any problems you might encounter.

- If you arrive at Pearson International Airport, you'll find the terminals are designed to assist you. So are Union Station and the Toronto Coach Terminal. To get downtown from Pearson, use an accessible limousine like Air Cab, or Airline Limousine, or take the airport bus. Each bus has room for two wheelchairs. If you prefer to drive, vehicles with hand controls are available from most of the rental car companies at the airport.

- The major downtown hotels served by the airport bus have rooms specially adapted for people with disabilities. When you get into the city, you'll find all sidewalks slope to the street at intersections and public buildings are wheelchair accessible. However, the public transit system (TTC) is not universally accessible to wheelchair users. To compensate for this, the TTC operates a special 'Wheel-Trans' service of adapted buses. Wheel-Trans vehicles give you door-to-door service and you pay only the regular TTC fare. However, you need to book this service four days in advance.

- If you usually have difficulty communicating with people, Wheel-Trans can supply you with a special *Accessible Service Flashcard*. Just show this card to the driver when you want special assistance. Visitors can get a temporary pass to use Wheel-Trans, or an *Accessible Service Flashcard*, by calling the TTC's administration office weekdays between 8:00 AM – 4:00 PM.

- Celebrity Taxi and Royal Taxi each have vehicles equipped to handle wheelchairs. Call Royal in the morning for afternoon service on weekdays and 24 hr in advance for weekends. Celebrity asks you to book 24 hr in advance.

PEOPLE WITH DISABILITIES
Transportation and help information

Service Provider	Telephone	Web site
Air Cab	416-225-1555	
Airline Limousine	905-676-3210	
Celebrity Taxi	416-398-2222	
Centre for Independent Living	416-599-2458 24 hr 416-599-5057 TTD	cilt.ca
Royal Taxi	416-785-3322	
TTC Disability Information	416-393-4636	city.toronto.on.ca/ttc
TTC Wheel-Trans	416-393-4111	city.toronto.on.ca/ttc

POLITENESS

Many American visitors have made a point of saying how polite people are in Toronto. That's certainly true when you compare the locals with those in places like New York or London. It's also true that you seem to hear the words 'thank you', 'I'm sorry' and 'you're welcome' a lot more here than in other cities. Torontonians often hold doors open for each other, which is considered quaintly Medieval by less enlightened folk. However, it's interesting to observe that the more affluent the Toronto neighbourhood, the less polite and courteous people seem to be. Just the same, a smile and kind gesture go a long way to making your stay in town more enjoyable.

POSTAL SERVICES

Despite the prevalence of email and digital camera cell phones, lots of folk still like to send postcards home when they're on vacation. Post offices are open Monday through Friday, 8:00 AM – 5:00 PM, with some open Saturday till 1:00 PM. These days, however, the regular big post office is becoming a thing of the past. Most of their business has been taken over by small postal outlets throughout the city – mainly in drugstores – that can handle all your postal needs. These outlets often operate daily during the store's regular hours. When you buy stamps, you'll be charged an extra 7% (GST) tax. You can also buy American and British stamps at the historical First Post Office, 260 Adelaide Street East. It's the only post office in Canada where you can do this. This post office is open daily. See map 11, or visit the Web site: **townofyork.com** For general postal information visit **canadapost.ca**

PROSTITUTION

Adult prostitution – straight or gay – is technically legal in Canada, but soliciting for the purposes of prostitution is illegal. Only in Canada could we come up with such a social compromise! That said, there's a flood of escort advertisements in the daily *Toronto Sun* newspaper, as well as the weekly *NOW* and *eye* newspapers. The Web site **sexworktoronto.com** puts it in some sort of practical perspective: "Even if police did want to pursue unusual charges that technically fit Criminal Code requirements, they aren't likely to stick. Where charges against off-street, consensual prostitution do result in convictions, punishments are typically just light fines." People generally think the police have better things to do than to bust consensual adult sex acts in private. After all, it was the late Pierre Elliott Trudeau, as federal justice minister, who said "the state has no place in the bedrooms of the nation." Just the same, don't do it in a vehicle. It has been ruled in court that doing it there is not "in private". For safety's sake, always use a condom.

SECURITY

Toronto isn't as uptight about security as cities in the United States, or many throughout Europe. The thought of a terrorist attack here doesn't seem to be on peoples' radar screen. However, you will have to go through security check points at the airport, in courthouses and in the provincial legislature. Apart from that, there are surveillance video cameras in most stores, malls, buildings, underground garages, gas stations and other places where people congregate. These are installed for private and corporate security reasons and not as a result of government anti-terrorism measures. You won't find any barricades around town stopping you from driving to where you want to go, nor will you see police or military personnel standing around with their guns at the ready. Don't expect any *Big Brother* video street surveillance either, like you'll find all over the place in London. The people of Toronto are a pragmatic lot and are very secure in their freedom to go where they want, when they want.

SMOKING

For all practical purposes, you can't smoke in bars, restaurants, public buildings, on public transit, in taxis, the workplace, hotel lobbies, or in virtually any enclosed space outside your own home or vehicle. There are complicated exceptions, but bylaws are already in place to squash these exceptions as time goes by. Make life easy for yourself – butt out and go with the flow. Business owners, and lots of non-smokers, have given up labelling city council as being Draconian, so your complaints won't change anything. There's always the sidewalk if you can't control the urge. It is illegal to sell tobacco products to people under the age of 19. You can't even give a cigarette to a kid without risking the wrath of authority and a heavy fine. It's getting almost impossible these days to buy a pack of 25 for under $10. There are no cigarette vending machines in the city and drugstores are prohibited from selling tobacco products.

TAXES

Canadians are the most heavily-taxed people in North America. That's why we can afford a national health scheme and all sorts of guaranteed pensions. Two of those taxes are consumption taxes. Combined, they add 15% to the cost of virtually everything you buy, with some weird and illogical exceptions. The Provincial Sales Tax (PST) is 8% and the federal Goods and Services Tax (GST) is 7%. The PST on hotel bills is reduced to 5% to encourage tourism. There are rumours that the city might soon be able to invent additional taxes, so be prepared to feel yet another hand in your pocket some time soon. The receipt you get will itemize all the taxes you have paid. If you're a visitor from outside Canada, you can take heart. Under certain conditions the government will reimburse you for some of the money you've spent on GST and PST. See page 12 for information regarding a Custom's rebate for visitors. If you want to immerse yourself in tax information, log on to **canada.gc.ca** and **gov.on.ca**

TELEPHONES

Local public telephone calls cost 25 cents. Long distance calls can be paid by American Express, Mastercard and Visa credit cards, telephone company cards, or telephone cash cards available at most convenience and drugstores. Follow the instructions on the phone's digital electronic display screen. Toronto has two local area codes: 416 and 647. You must dial the area code as part of all local calls made within the city – a total of 10 digits. Do not dial 1 first. The *White Pages* phone book lists residential numbers in the front and government numbers at the back. The separate *Yellow Pages* phone book lists commercial and professional entries. Toronto is extensively equipped to handle all your voice and data needs, and was one of the first cities in the world to immerse itself in cellular and wireless technology. For more information, check out **bell.ca**

WALKING

Summer and fall are the best times to join the locals out for a stroll. Late September and early October are particularly rewarding if you enjoy a dazzling display of fall colours. You'll find that city streets are safe any time of the day or night and the tremendous variety of neighbourhoods will give you a sense of discovery. Here are some tips to increase your enjoyment of exploring Toronto at street level:

- Look through the *Inner-city Neighbourhoods* maps to find places that interest you most. Think of combining your walk with visits to attractions. Plan ahead by checking out the restaurants you will pass along the way.

- If you enjoy nature more than concrete, take a look through the *Parks, beaches, squares and zoos* section of the *Places* chapter. You might also want to check out **city.toronto.on.ca/parks** that has information about the city's Discovery Walks program, including maps you can download. This is a great way to meet like-minded people, enjoy the fresh air, get some exercise and discover some cool stuff.

- Don't forget the PATH underground walkway system shown on page 21. It's a 10 km (6 miles) labyrinth of climate-controlled pedestrian passages under the city core that are filled with over 1,000 shops, restaurants and services. It's a fascinating place to spend a day walking around, regardless of the weather.

- Two places that offer quiet pleasures for the walker are the University of Toronto campus (map 19) and Rosedale (maps 30, 31). Weekends are best for the university so you can avoid crowds of students. Rosedale is wonderful if you enjoy looking at lovely old homes set along mature, tree-lined streets. Strangely, neither area is well-known to people living in other parts of the city, let alone visitors.

- When walking around town, cross the street at pedestrian crossings and obey the pedestrian walk signals. Jaywalking is not the local thing to do, but there's no law making it illegal. However, there is a law saying that if a vehicle or bicycle has to avoid you while you're crossing the street, then you can be charged with interfering with traffic. Also remember that vehicles can turn right on a red light, providing they stop first. Just because they seem to be waiting for you, don't bank on it!

- While on the subject of bicycles, always keep an eye open for bicycle couriers. In the downtown core, especially during the summer, they can be a menace because they often have a dangerous habit of wanting to share the sidewalk with you when you least expect them.

WASHROOMS/TOILETS

Toronto doesn't go out of its way to provide public toilets. It just seems natural that we take advantage of the facilities in restaurants, bars, hotel lobbies, coffee shops, public buildings, shopping malls, gas stations and department stores. Some have changing facilities for babies in both the male and female sections. Others, but not many, like to reserve their facilities for patrons. If you're visiting us from the UK, just a reminder that the terms 'loo' and 'WC' are not readily understood here, so it's best to stick with "Where's your washroom?" One of the rare stand-alone public toilets in the city is on King Street West opposite the Royal Alexandra Theatre.

WEATHER

Nothing pre-occupies the minds of Torontonians more than the weather. Precipitation is spread fairly evenly throughout the year with August being the driest month and January having the most precipitation. Spring can be fairly wet with temperatures ranging all over the place. Summer is generally warm early on and hot as you get into July and August. It can also become quite humid with thunderstorms. Fall is usually clear and cool and considered by many to be the nicest time of the year. Winter is another matter. It's not unknown to see temperatures fall around 20 degrees overnight in January and February. Our record minimum temperature has hit minus 32C. That compares with our record summer high of 41C. In short, our annual temperature range has had a spread of 73C. Winter can be very cold, but usually there aren't too many major snowstorms. Just dress warmly and remember your sense of humour. If you're already in town, tune in to *CablePulse24* (**pulse24.com**) on cable channel 24. This hip local television station has the weather and live highway cameras on screen 24/7/365. Radio AM680 (**680news.com**) gives weather and road conditions every 10 minutes. All English-language newspapers have a weather section inside. For out-of-towners, log on to **theweathernetwork.com** for present, short, and long-term forecasts. The Weather Network also gives you updates on how the weather is affecting road conditions throughout Ontario. It's worth checking them out if you're driving here, especially in the winter.

The following tables show the city's average weather statistics:

AVERAGE ANNUAL WEATHER STATISTICS
Temperatures in Celsius, precipitation in mm, relative humidity

Month	Temperature		Humidity		Precipitation	Wet Days
	Min	Max	AM	PM		
January	-9	-1	78	70	69	16
February	-9	-1	78	67	61	12
March	-5	3	76	62	66	13
April	1	2	74	56	64	12
May	7	17	73	55	74	13
June	12	23	78	58	69	11
July	15	26	79	56	74	10
August	14	25	83	58	69	9
September	11	21	87	60	74	12
October	4	13	87	62	61	11
November	-1	6	82	68	71	13
December	-6	1	80	71	66	13

The chart below shows the one above converted into American standard measurements:

AVERAGE ANNUAL WEATHER STATISTICS
Temperatures in Fahrenheit, precipitation in inches, relative humidity

Month	Temperature		Humidity		Precipitation	Wet Days
	Min	Max	AM	PM		
January	16	30	78	70	2.72	16
February	16	30	78	67	2.40	12
March	23	37	76	62	2.60	13
April	34	50	74	56	2.52	12
May	45	63	73	55	2.91	13
June	54	73	78	58	2.72	11
July	59	79	79	56	2.91	10
August	57	77	83	58	2.72	9
September	52	70	87	60	2.91	12
October	39	55	87	62	2.40	11
November	30	43	82	68	2.80	13
December	21	34	80	71	2.60	13

Wet Days on the charts means that at least 0.25 mm (0.01 inches) of precipitation (rain or snow) is likely to fall on that number of days. This is the equivalent of a passing light shower.

Local information Toronto trivia

! Here's an odd collection of facts and observations concerning life in our fair city.

How much does it cost to change a light bulb?

No, this isn't the beginning of a joke. But read on anyway. How much does it cost? Well, if it's a light bulb in one of Toronto's oldest social housing complexes, then the answer is about $500, plus parts. First, a qualified union electrician, who is paid $60 an hour, must change the bulb. Because the bulb is way up there, a cherry picker and union drivers have to be used. That costs money too. (Apparently it's really profitable being a unionized civic worker in Toronto.) Recently, it cost the city close to $10,000 to change the bulbs on 20 posts outside a complex where 1,000 people live.

Towering ambitions

Two adventurous Greenpeace activists were the first people to scale the CN Tower in its 25-year history. The assault began at 4:00 AM on July 16, 2001, when Steven Guilbeault from Montréal, and Chris Holden from the UK, climbed as far as the observation deck – an impressive 181 storeys. There, they unfurled a banner protesting global warming. "It's high. It's a great view of Toronto," Guilbeault said. Following their four-hour descent, they were arrested and charged with mischief. They appeared in court 13 months later and were given conditional discharges and told not to go within 50 metres of the tower ever again.

Pittsburgh North

One of the highest-rated programs on America's *Showtime* cable network is *Queer as Folk*. Although it would have us believe that the earthy lifestyle of its gay and lesbian characters is set in Pittsburgh, the program is shot in Toronto. 'Liberty Street' is really Church Street in Toronto's gay Church-Wellesley Village. Woody's is a real bar at 467 Church Street and, a block further north at 553 Church, you'll find Babylon. The interior scenes for both bars are shot in a studio. When Michael goes shopping for comic books, he drops by 1,000,000 Comix at 530 Yonge Street. And, when the guys pump iron, they do so at a gym on the corner of Yonge and Charles streets. Some folk in Toronto's gay community have wryly speculated that the American producers couldn't find any signs of gay life in Pittsburgh, so they came here.

Party favours

When 'Honest' Ed Mirvish, Toronto's entrepreneurial czar, has a birthday it's the guests who receive the presents. His late-July bash around Mirvish Village usually attracts about 30,000 partygoers who get through 18,000 hot dogs, 20,000 bags of chips, 20,000 pastries, 8,000 Popsicles and 225 kilos of chocolate. If Ed feels you've been waiting in line too long for the free good-ies, you'll likely get a box of dried pasta, or a stick deodorant for your trou-ble. Ed was born in 1912.

Hurricane Hazel

This was the most severe storm to hit Toronto in living memory. After caus-ing considerable damage throughout the Caribbean, the force 4 hurricane slammed into the Carolinas and went on an erratic path north along the east-ern US seaboard, claiming hundreds of lives. On October 15, 1954, it crossed Lake Ontario and devastated parts of Toronto. Environment Canada estimat-ed that 300-million tonnes of rain fell on the city that day. Some streets com-pletely disappeared and 83 people died. Some of their bodies came ashore on the New York side of Lake Ontario.

Windy city

That wind turbine (windmill) you can see down by the lake, just a few kilometres east of the city limits, is the biggest in North America. Rising 117 metres, it's the same height as a 30-storey building. The blades are 39 metres, or longer than the wings on a 747 jet. It generates 1.8 megawatts of power - enough to serve 600 homes – and the blades rotate at a maximum of 15.7 rev-olutions per minute.

Worldly possessions Part 1

The 10,776 sq m Prayer Palace, built in 2001, is the largest church in town. It sits on 6.5 ha of land near Highway 400 and Finch Avenue West, and cost $23,357,000 to build. There's a television studio inside and parking for 814 vehicles outside. According to the *Toronto Star*, the evangelical church has a congregation of 3,000. If you want to make comparisons, Washington's Na-tional Cathedral is a mere 7,110 sq m, and Toronto's two largest cathedrals combined would seat fewer people than the Prayer Palace.

Worldly possessions Part 2

While on the subject of record sizes, the city's largest house was built – by a Russian businessman according to the local media – in the ultra-upscale Bridle Path neighbourhood. The living area covers 4,180 sq m. There's no word on how much it cost.

The Mouse

It seems the roller ball mouse that's connected to countless computers throughout the world could have originated in Toronto. In 1952, a top-secret Canadian Navy project used a five-pin bowling ball in a porcelain cradle to operate a rudimentary, computerized radar-tracking device on board ships carrying out covert missions on the Great Lakes. The clumsy apparatus was called a 'Digital Automated Tracking and Resolving System.' One of its inventors, Tom Cranston, said, "the whole idea was pretty wacky for the 1950s. Then, it was totally laughable."

Longevity

People living in Toronto have an average life expectancy of 79.3 years – one year more than the national Canadian average. A Canada-wide survey also revealed that 17% of Torontonians are daily smokers (the national average is 22%), and 11% of adults are obese, below the national average of 15%. In Vancouver, people smoke less and aren't as fat, but they live, on average, a year less. Go figure!

There's no business like show business

Although Toronto is regarded as being the world's third-largest centre for English theatre, it has been some time since our stages became the envy of the world. That will change in 2006 when local theatrical entrepreneur, David Mirvish, brings the world premiere of *Lord of the Rings* to Toronto's Princess of Wales theatre. It's the most expensive stage production in history, costing a whopping $27,000,000. The original cast is mostly Canadian.

Index

For references to streets, see the Neighbourhood Street index, *pages 94–97.*

A

A W Hockridge, 62
Absolutely, 80
ACC, 32, 33, 175
Acqua, 42, 187–88
Acrobat, 90
Acton, 40
Adega, 52, 188
Adriatico, 80
African restaurants, 183
Agincourt, 22
AGO, 50, 51, 122, 126
AIDS Memorial, 64, 65, 126
Air Canada Centre, 32, 33, 175
Airport Lounge, 58
airports, 6–8, 13
Albany, 68
Albert Campbell Square, 136
alcohol and bars, 213
Alexandra Park, 38, 48, 49, 50
Algonquin Island, 24, 25
Alice Fazooli's, 40
Alize, 90
All the Best, 82
Allan Gardens, 54, 55, 136
Allen Gallery, 46
Alliance Atlantis, 161–62
Alumnae Theatre, 46
Amadeu's, 50
Amalfi, 54
ambulance, 211
AMC, 162
American restaurants, 183
Amore, 90
Amsterdam Bridge, 32
Amsterdam Guest House, 56, 101
Angelini's, 64, 188
Angus & Co, 76
Annapurna, 76, 188
Annex Books, 76
Annex Grill, 78
Annex, The, 21, 70–71, 72, 73, 78, 80, 102
Annex Theatre, 58
annual events, 148–59

Anshei Minsk Synagogue, 50
Antiques Canada Show, 149
Antiques Collectibles, 56
Arabesque, 46
Archer, The, 130, 142
Arctic Bear, 72
Arena Gardens, 54, 55
Argonauts, 169–70
Arlequin, 72, 188
Armadillo, 42
Armour Heights, 22
art, 126–35
Art Gallery of Ontario, 50, 51, 122, 126
Art Nouveau, 46
Art Shoppe, 88, 89
Art Zone, 68
Artful Dodger, 64
Artists' Gardens, 32
Asahi, 56
Asean, 50
Ashai Sushi, 74
Asian Legend, 92
Asian restaurants, 183
Atrium on Bay, 52
Au Lit, 88
Auberge du Pommier, 17, 189
Audience, The, 30, 134
Austin, James, 79, 114, 133
Auto Pound, 32
Automotive Building, 26, 106
Avalon, 40, 189
Avant Goût, 80
Azul, 38

B

Bahá'í Centre, 70
Baldwin Steps, 78, 79
Ballenford Books, 68
ballet, 160–61
Balloon King, 48
Balzac's, 46
Ban Vanipha, 50, 189
Bangkok, 50
Bangkok Garden, 52, 189–90

Bank of Nova Scotia, 58
Bank of Upper Canada , 44, 45, 113, 115
Banknote, 38
Banting Institute, 62
Banting, Frederick, 63, 142
Bar 501, 64
Bar Italia, 58
Barberian's, 52
Barn-Stables, 54
Baroli, 54
bars, 163–64
Bata Shoe Museum, 70, 71, 126–27
Bathurst Street Theatre, 58
Bay, The, 74
Bayview Village, 17
BCE Place, 43, 106
beaches, 136–38
Beaches International Jazz Festival, 149
Beaches, The, 22
bed and breakfasts, 103
Bedford, 22
Bedford Academy, 70
Belle Epoque, 80
Bellini's, 72
Belt Line Trail, 84, 86, 88, 89
Ben Wicks, 56
Benfica Aguia, 48
Berczy Park, 44, 116, 128
Berkeley Street Theatre, 46
Berkeleys, 46
Betty Oliphant Theatre, 64
Between the Eyes, 32
Biagio, 44, 190
Biff's, 44
Bin-Scarth Road (#61), 84, 85
Birk's, 72
Bistro du Parc, 72
Bistro 990, 62
Bistro Tournesol, 76, 190
bistros, 184
Black Bull, 40
Black Creek Pioneer Village, 17, 113–14, 164–65
Black Eagle, 64

Black Sheep, 92
Bloor Cinema, 68
Bloor East, 74–75, 103
Bloor Street Church, 70
Bloor Street Diner, 90
Bloor-Yorkville, 21
Bloorcourt Village, 22
Blue Jays, 169, 179
Blue Jays' Bullpen, 30
Bluffer's Park, 17, 137, 138–39
Bluma Appel Theatre, 44, 180
Boathouse, 32
Boba, 72, 190
Bobbie Rosenfeld Park, 30, 32, 33
Bocconi, 86
Boddington's, 74
Boiler House, 46
Bombay Host, 90
Bombay Palace, 44, 190–91
Bond Place Hotel, 54, 101
Book City, 68, 86
Bordello, 68
Boss, 72
Bouchon, 44
Boujadi, 17, 191
Boulevard Café, 58, 191
Bow & Arrow, 88
Braem & Minnetti, 80
Branksome Hall, 74
Brass Taps, 56
Brassai, 40
Brasserie Aix, 58
Bravi, 44
Brockton, 22
Brown Stone, 64
Browne's Corners, 22
Brunswick House, 70, 71
Budd Sugarman, 72
Buddhist Temple, 38
Buddies in Bad Times Theatre, 64, 172
buffets, 184
buildings, 104–113
Bull & Firkin, 88
Bulldog, 54
Bullet, 38
Bumpkin's, 64
buses, 11, 19
Butler's, 68
Butt'a, 58
Buttonville Airport, 8
Bvlgari, 72

By the Way, 68
Bymark, 42, 191–92
Byzantium, 64

C

Caban, 34, 40
Cabbagetown, 56, 66–67
Cabbagetown Cultural Festival, 150
Cadogan & Co, 80
Cafe California, 64
Café Diplomatico, 58, 59
cafés, 184
Caffe Brasiliano, 48
Caffe Doria, 80, 81
Caffe Volo, 64
Calvin Presbyterian, 86, 87
Cambridge Suites Hotel, 44, 100
Campbell House, 42, 127
Canada Blooms, 150
Canada Day, 150
Canada Quay, 32, 33
Canadian Airmen's Memorial, 127
Canadian Children's Dance Theatre, 66, 160
Canadian Children's Opera Chorus, 166
Canadian International Air Show, 150–51
Canadian International Auto Show, 111, 151
Canadian International Marathon, 151
Canadian National Exhibition, 27, 151–52, 165
Canadian Open Tennis, 170
Canadian Opera Company, 166
Canadian restaurants, 184
Canadian Stage Company, 46, 172, 180
Canadian Tire, 74, 75
Canadiana Backpackers Inn, 40, 100
Canary, 46
Candy Machine, 76
Canoe, 42, 192
Canon Theatre, 54, 175
Capitol, 58
Captain John's, 34, 35
Caravan, 158
Caribana Parade, 152

Carlu, 52
Carman's, 64
Caro, 86
Carrington's, 62
Cartier, 72
Casa Barcelona, 17, 192
Casa di Giorgio, 34
Casa Loma (building), 78, 79, 104, 133
Casa Loma (district), 76, 77, 78–79
Casa Mexico, 64
Castle Frank Road (#8), 84, 85
CBC, 40, 41, 106
Cedarvale, 22
Celebrate Toronto Street Festival, 152
Celia Franca Centre, 106
Cenotaph, 42, 119, 127
Centenary Hospital, 17
Centennial Park, 17, 139
Central Fire Hall, 44
Central Technical School, 58, 59
Centre Island, 8, 24, 25, 145
Centreville, 25, 165
Centro, 90, 91, 192
Champion House, 50
Chanel, 72
Chaplin Estates, 88, 89, 90
Charlies, 34
Cheers, 90
Cheese Dairy, 68
Chelsea Inn Hotel, 52
Cherry Beach, 137
Chiado, 17, 193
Children's Aid Society, 215
Children's Conservatory, 136
CHIN Picnic, 150, 152–53
China Gourmet, 56
Chinatown, 21
Chinese Baptist Church, 50
Chinese Consulate General, 70
Chinese New Year, 153
Chinese Railroad Memorial, 30, 31
Chinese restaurants, 184
Ching Kwok Buddhist Temple, 48, 49
Chocolate, 44
Choo Choo, 76
Chorley Park, 84

229

Christ Church, 86, 87
Christie Pits Park, 68, 69
Church of St George the
    Martyr, 50
Church of St Stephen-in-
    the-Fields, 60, 61, 114
Church of the Assumption
    of the Virgin Mary, 48
Church of the Holy Trinity,
    52, 114, 146
Church of the Messiah, 80
Churchmouse, 64
Church-Wellesley Village,
    54, 64–65, 102, 154
Churrasqueira Vila Verde,
    48
CIBC Stage, 32
Cilantro, 90
cinema, 161–63
Cinema Shoppe, 68
Cineplex Odeon, 162
Cinespace studios, 34
Cinesphere, 26
Circle, 86
Cities, 38
City Centre Airport, 20
City Hall, 52, 53, 104
City of Toronto Archives,
    78
City People, 43, 127
CityPlace, 28, 30
CITY-TV, 40, 41
Civello, 74
Civic Garden Centre, 140
Clairlea, 22
Clarion Hotel & Suites
    Selby, 64, 65, 102
Clark's Corners, 22
Clarke Beach, 137
classical music, 166–69
Clay, 60
Cliffside, 22
Cloak and Dagger, 58
clothing, 213–14
Cloud Gardens, 42
Club Toronto, 54
clubs, 163–64
CN Tower, 30, 31, 33, 105,
    225
CNE, 27, 151–52, 165
Coco Lezzone, 58
Coco Rice, 38
Cocoberry Café, 32
Colborne Lodge, 17, 128,
    140
Cole Haan, 72

College Park, 52
College Street Bar, 58
Comfort Hotel
    Downtown, 64, 102
Comfort Suites City
    Centre, 54, 101
Commensal, 52
Commerce Court, 42, 105
Community, 74
Community Services, 215
concert halls, 175–80
Condom Shack, 74
Constantine, 80
continental restaurants,
    184
Convention Centre, 32, 33,
    42, 110–11
Convocation Hall, 60
Conway & Gower, 80
Coppi, 17, 193
Corktown, 44, 46, 47
Corner House, 78, 79, 193
Coroners Courts, 62
Corso Italia, 58
Corso Italia Toronto Fiesta,
    153
Cosmo, 56
Court House, 52
Courthouse Restaurant, 44
Courthouse Square, 44, 45
Courtyard, 72
Courtyard Marriott Hotel,
    64
Cpused, 76
Craigleigh Gardens, 84,
    85
Cranberries, 66
credit cards, 183
Crews, 64
crime, 214
Crockery Barn, 86
Crocodile Rock, 42
Croissant Tree, 64
Crowne Plaza Hotel, 17, 99
Crystal Palace, 27
Cube, 64
Cugini, 52
Cuisine of India, 92,
    193–94
Cultures, 74
currency, 13
Curry's, 62
customs and immigration,
    11–12
customs tax rebate, 12
cycling, 214

D

Daio, 54
dance, 160–61
Dance Cave, 68
Dancemakers, 160
Danforth, The, 22, 156
Daniel Brooke Building,
    114–15
Daniel et Daniel, 56
Danny Grossman Dance
    Company, 160–61
Davenport, 76–77
Davenport Art Gallery, 78
David A Balfour Park, 82,
    86
David Crombie Park, 34,
    44, 46
David Mirvish Art Books,
    68, 69
Davisville, 88–89
Days Hotel, 54, 101
De Boer's, 52
De La Salle College, 80, 81
De La Salle Institute, 44,
    45, 115
Deer Park, 86
delicatessens, 184
Delisle Court, 86
Dell'Ernia, 88
Delta Chelsea Hotel, 101
Delta Toronto East, 17, 99
Demarco Perpich, 80
Dempsey Store, 92, 93
dental emergencies, 218
Design Exchange, 42
Designer's Walk, 78, 80
Direct Energy Centre,
    106–107
directions, 214–15
disabilities, 219–20
Discovery District, 21, 50,
    52–53, 60, 101
Discovery Walks, 139
Dish, 78
Distillery District, 36, 37,
    46, 47, 116–17
distress centres, 215
Doc's Leather, 38
Dock Shoppe, 34
Docks, The, 36, 37
Dominion Hotel, 46
Dominion Public Building,
    42
Dominion Square, 46, 47
Don Mills, 22
Don Valley, 17

Donatello, 52
Dooneys, 68
Dorset Park, 22
Dos Amigos, 76
Double Take, 56
Downsview, 22
Dragon Boat Race Festival, 157
Dragon Dynasty, 17, 194
Draped Reclining Woman, 129, 130
dress, 213–14
driving, 11, 215
drugstores, 216
Drumsnab Road (#5), 84, 85
Dufflet, 38
Duke of Kent, 90
Duke of York, 70
Duncan Street Grill, 42
Dundas Square, 54–55, 101, 139, 147, 155
Dynasty, 72, 194

E

East General Hospital, 17
East Side Marios, 42
Eastern Orthodox Church, 56
Eaton Centre, 52, 53, 105, 114, 128, 134, 146
Eaton, Timothy, 105, 155
Edo, 17, 194
Edoya Sushi, 86
Edwards Gardens, 140, 145
Egerton Ryerson statue, 54
Eggstacy, 54
Ein-stein, 50
El Bodegon, 58, 195
El Rancho, 58
El Trompo, 50
electrical current, 216
Elgin & Winter Garden Theatres, 44, 175
Èlise, 60
Elixir, 68
Ellesmere, 22
Elm Avenue (historic houses), 84, 85
Elmer Iseler Singers, 166–67
Embros, 80
emergencies. *Call 911*

Enoch Turner School, 46, 47, 115
entertainment, 148–81
Entertainment District, 21, 40, 41, 42
Epicure Café, 38
Epicure Shop, 56
EQ3, 38
Esco-Pazzo, 88
Eskimo Art, 32
Esplanade, The, 34, 35
Ethan Allen, 88, 89
Ethiopian House, 62
Eurolite, 34
Europa Grill, 62
Everybody, 66
Ex, The, 27, 151–52, 165
Excess, 54
Exhibition Place, 26–27, 28, 120, 165

F

Factory Theatre, 38, 39
Fairmont Royal York Hotel, 8, 42, 100, 109
Fairview Mall, 17
family entertainment, 164–66
Famous People Players, 172–73
Famous Players, 90, 162
Far Niente, 42
Farmer's Market, 44, 124
Fashion Cares, 153–54
Fashion District, 30, 38, 40–41, 100
Fat Cat, 17, 195
Ferrari, 72
Ferret & Firkin, 70
Fez Batik, 40
Fieramosca, 70
55 Degreez, 76
Fig Leaf, 44
Filet of Sole, 42
Film Festival, 158
Financial District, 21, 42–43, 100, 106
Fionn MacCool's, 40, 86
fire, 213
Fire Hall #7, 56
Fire Station #8, 58
Fire Station #23, 76
First Canadian Place, 42, 43, 105–106
First Church of Christ Scientist, 70

First Narayever Synagogue, 60
First Post Office, 44, 45, 123, 135
First Public School site, 44
509 Dance, 66
Flamingo House, 56
Flatiron Building, 44, 115–16, 128
Flatiron Mural, 128
Flemingdon Park, 17
Flight Stop, 128, 134
Floor Works, 76
Flow, 72
Flower and Garden Show, 150
Fluid, 42
Fluid Living, 46
Foggy Dew, 38
Forest Hill, 22
Forestview, 50
Fort York, 28, 29, 116
Four Seasons Centre, 42, 161, 176
Four Seasons Hotel, 72, 102
Fox & Fiddle, 70
Foxes Den, 62
Frascatti, 52
Free Times, 60
French Country, 80
French restaurants, 184
Friendly Thai, 38, 62
Fringe Festival, 157, 174–75
Frisco's, 40
Fujiyama, 50
Funhaus, 38
Furama, 50
fusion restaurants, 184
Future, 68

G

Gabby's, 90
galleries, 126–35
Gallery Boutique, 62
Gallery Gabor, 68
Gallery Hi Art, 62
Gallery of Inuit Art, 42, 128
Gamelle, 58
Gardens, The, 54, 55
Gardiner Museum of Ceramic Art, 131
Garlic Pepper, 62
Garrison Commons, 26, 28, 29

231

Garrison Creek, 38, 39
gasoline, 216
gay places and events, 54, 64, 154, 216–17
Gehry, Frank, 51, 126, 131
George Brown College, 78
George Brown Theatre, 46
George Weston Recital Hall, 92, 93, 176, 180
German Consulate, 70
Gerrard Glass, 56
Gerrard Street Methodist Church, 56
Gibson House, 92, 93, 128–29
Ginger 2, 54
Giovanna, 38
Glen Road (historic houses), 84, 85
Glenn Gould Studio, 40
Global, 70
Global Guest House, 102
Global Village Backpackers, 40, 100
Globe and Mail, 41, 61
GO Transit, 13, 112
Gold Stone, 50
Golden Mile, The, 22
Golden Thai, 44
Goldfish, 70
Goldsmith, Phil, 106
Gooderham and Worts, 36, 37, 116–17
Goodwill, 56
Government Bookstore, 62
Gowans, 86
Graffiti's, 50
Grand Hotel, 54, 101
Grange Park, 40, 50
Grange, The, 50, 51, 121–22
Grano, 88
Grazie, 90
Great Fire of 1849, 117, 119, 120, 121, 125
Great Salmon Hunt, 154
Greek Islands, 62
Greek Orthodox Church, 46
Greek restaurants, 184
Green Papaya, 90
Green's, 66
grill restaurants, 184
Groundhog, 74
Group of Seven, 129, 130

Gucci, 72
Guerlain, 72
Guildwood, 22
Guvernment, 34

H

Habitat, 38
Hair of the Dog, 64
Hanlan's Point, 24, 25, 137
Hanna's Kitchen, 88
Happy House, 68
Happy Seven, 50, 195
Harbord Bakery, 60
Harbord Collegiate, 58, 59
Harbour Sixty, 32
Harbour Sports Grill, 32
Harbour Square, 32
Harbourfront Centre, 32–33, 99, 129, 165
Harbourfront Centre Theatre, 32, 176
Harbourfront Park, 30–31, 99, 140
Hard Rock Café, 30, 54
Hare Krishna Temple, 80
Harry Rosen, 72
Hart House, 60, 130
Harvest Wagon, 82
Hassle Free Clinic, 54
Havergall Ladies' College, 106
Hawthorn Gardens (#2), 84, 85
Hazelton Hotel, 72, 102
Hazelton Lanes, 72, 73
Healey's, 38
Hemispheres, 52
Henry Farm, 22
Henry Moore sculptures, 129–30
Henry Scadding House, 117
Herbs, 17, 195–96
Heritage houses, 66, 70, 74
Heritage Square, 42, 43, 106
Hermès, 72
Hey Good Cooking, 78
High Park, 17, 22, 128, 140, 141
Highland Creek, 22
highways, 8–10
Hillcrest, 76, 77
Hillcrest Village, 22
Hilton Toronto, 42, 100
Hiro Sushi, 44, 196

history of Toronto, 14–15
HMCS York, 28
HMV, 54
Hockey Hall of Fame, 42, 170
Hogtown, 69
Holiday Inn on King, 40, 100
holidays, 217
Hollace Cluny, 80
Holt Renfrew, 72
Holy Smokes, 34
Holy Trinity Church (Anglican), 52, 114, 146
Holy Trinity Church (Greek Orthodox), 58,
Holy Trinity Church (Russian Orthodox), 50
Homeproud, 40
Homero, 62
Honest Ed's, 68, 69
Hong Shin, 52
Hoops, 62
Hooters, 40, 90
Horse Feathers, 80
horse racing, 171
Horseshoe Tavern, 40
Hospital for Sick Children, 52, 53, 122–23
hospitals, 217. See also names of individual hospitals
Host, 72, 196
Hot House, 44
Hotel Isabella, 64
Hotel Le Germain, 100
Hotel Victoria, 42, 100
hotels, 99–103. See also names of individual hotels
House of Tea, 82
House on Parliament, 56
Howard Johnson's Hotel, 72, 102
Howard, James Scott, 123, 135
Howard, John George, 113, 125, 140, 144
Hudson Bay Centre, 74
Hudson's Bay Company, 43, 74
Hughie's, 52
Hugo Quattrocchi, 80
Humber Arboretum, 141
Humber Bay Park, 17, 141
Humber Summit, 22

Humberlea, 22
Hummingbird Centre for the Performing Arts, 44, 177
Hunan Palace, 58
Hungarian Reformed Church, 60
Hungary Thai, 50

I

Ichiban Fish House, 92
Ichiriki, 74
Il Bun Ji, 68, 196
Il Fornello, 86
Il Posto Nuovo, 72, 196–97
Imagine, 40
IMAX, 26, 27, 107, 162
Imperial Opera Theatre, 46
Imperial Pub, 54
index of streets, 94–97
Indian Flavour, 52, 197
Indian Hut, 74
Indian restaurants, 184–85
Indian Rice Factory, 76
Indochine, 52, 74, 197
Indoors Out, 88
Indyfest, 155
inner-city neighbourhoods, 23
Innocenti, 38
Inside Out Lesbian and Gay Film and Video Festival, 163
Insomnia, 68
Intercontinental Hotel, 42, 72, 100, 102
International CHIN Picnic, 150, 152–53
International Boat Show, 158
International Festival Caravan, 158
International Film Festival, 158, 163
International Marketplace, 32
international restaurants, 185
Intheory, 38
Irene's, 48
Irie, 38
Isabella Hotel & Suites, 102
Island Airport, 8, 24
Island Thyme, 68
Islands, 20, 24–25, 145

Islington, 22
Italian Consulate, 50
Italian Cultural Institute, 70
Italian restaurants, 185
Ithica, 74
Izu, 88

J

J J Muggs, 52
J M Barnicke Art Gallery, 130
J S Bonbons, 78
Jaipur Grille, 88
Jalan, 38
Jalapeño, 38
James Joyce, 70
Jamie Kennedy, 44
Jane Mallett Theatre, 44
Japan Sushi, 68
Japanese restaurants, 185–86
Japango, 52
Jardin, 68
Jarvis Street Baptist Church, 54
Jarvis, William, 65, 75, 85
Java Jive, 64
Javaville, 56
Jean Sibelius Square, 70
Jet Fuel, 66
Jing Peking, 58
Jodhpore, 50
Joe Badali's, 42
Joe Inc, 42
John Bassett Theatre, 40, 111
John Mulvey House, 38
John Quay, 30
Johnny G's, 56
John's, 50
Joker, 40
Joons, 68
Jump Café & Bar, 42, 197
Jun Jun Sushi, 58
Junction, The, 22
Just Desserts, 64

K

Kabuki, 44
Kalendar, 58
Kama, 42
Kamimura Gallery, 80
Kaolin, 76
Kathmandu, 64

Keg Mansion, 64, 65, 197–98
Keg (St Lawrence), 44
Kensington Kitchen, 60
Kensington Market, 48, 49, 50, 51, 114, 123–24
Ketchum Park, 72
Kew Beach, 137
Kid's Help Line, 215
Kilgour's, 68
Kim Bo, 48
Kim Sang, 52
King Edward Hotel, 44, 100
King's, 50
King's Garden, 42
King's Park, 46
Kingsway, The, 22
Kipling Heights, 22
Kitchen Stuff, 74
Kiyomizu, 92
Klaus, 46
Knox Church, 60, 61
Kober Wrentree, 46
Koolhaus, 34
Korea House, 68, 198
Korea Town, 68–69
Korean Presbyterian Church, 76
Korean restaurants, 186
Korean Village, 68
Kos Café, 76
Kromer Radio, 48

L

L'Atelier, 80
La Bodega, 50
La Hacienda, 38
La Maquette, 44, 133, 198
La Palette, 50
La Parette, 76
La Vecchia, 90
Lai Wah Heen, 53, 198–99
Laila, 68
Lakes, 80
Lane, Henry Bowyer, 117, 119, 125
Lansing, 92
Large Two Forms, 129
Lastman, Mel, 93, 142, 180
Latitude Wine Bar & Grill, 60, 199
Latvian House, 58
Laughlen Lodge, 52, 53
Lawren Harris Park, 74, 85
Lawrence Park, 22

233

LCBO, 34, 35, 83
Le Bifthéque, 42
Le Germain Hotel, 40
Le Gourmand, 40
Le Papillon, 44, 199
Le Paradis, 78
Le Royal Meridien King
    Edward Hotel, 44, 100
Le Select, 40
Le Trou Normand, 72
Leafs, The, 33, 171
Leao D'Ouro, 60
Leaside, 22
Lee Garden, 50, 199
Lee's Palace, 68
Left Bank, 38
Lemon Meringue, 17,
    199–200
Lennox, E J, 75, 79, 85, 110,
    118, 125
Lenwil, 78, 79
Leoni's, 40
Lester B Pearson Airport,
    6–8, 112, 219
Lettieri, 40
Liban, 64
Liberal, 48
Libeskind, David, 73, 132
Librairie Champlain, 46
Lileo, 46
Limelight, 88
Lionel Conacher Park, 81
Little Anthony's, 42
Little George Hotel, 45
Little Italy, 48, 49, 58–59
Little Norway Park, 28, 29
Little Poland, 39
Little Tibet, 38
Little Trinity Church, 46,
    47, 115, 117–18
Living Well, 62
Lobby, 72
Loblaws, 34, 76
Local 4, 64
local information, 213–27
Loft, 38
Long Branch, 22
Loretto College, 70
Lorraine Kisma Theatre for
    Young People, 174
Los Iguanas, 68
Lotto Prize Office, 74
Lotus Garden, 50
Louis Vuitton, 72
Lüb, 64
Luciano's, 66

Lucid, 40
Lucky Dragon, 50, 200

M

Macdonald, Sir John A, 63
MacGregor, 40
Mackenzie House, 54, 130
Mackenzie, William Lyon,
    91, 130, 142
Madigan's, 70
Madison Manor Boutique
    Hotel, 70, 102
Maggie's, 58
Malaysian restaurants, 186
Malta Village, 22
Malvern, 22
Mammina's, 62, 200
Mandarin, 90, 91, 200–201
Manor Arms, 88
Manufacturers Life
    Building, 74, 75
Map Room, 80
Maple Leaf Gardens, 54,
    55
Maple Leaf Quays, 30
Maple Leafs, 33, 55, 171
Margarita's, 50, 56
Mariachi's, 88
markets, 123–25
Marlene's, 76
Marlowe, 58
marriage, 216
Marriott hotels, 52, 74, 102
Mars Centre, 52
Martin Goodman Trail, 34,
    36, 37, 138
Maryvale, 22
Massey Hall, 54, 177
Mata Hari, 50, 201
Matignon, 62
Matthew Berger, 80
Mayday Malone's, 76
Mazzoni's, 92
McMaster Hall, 118
McMaster House, 65
media, 217–18
Media Tower, 52
medical emergencies, 218
Medicare, 218
Medieval Times, 26, 27
Megacity, 15
Mel Lastman Square, 92,
    93, 141–42, 150, 155
Mel's, 68
Melina's, 90
Menagerie, 66

Mendelssohn Choir, 168
Mercurio, 70
Messis, 60
Meteorological Office, 70
metric system, 10, 219
Metro Cigar, 62
Metro Square, 42
Metronome, 28, 31
Metropolis, 54, 55
Metropolitan Hotel, 52,
    101
Metropolitan United
    Church, 44, 118
Mexican restaurants, 186
Mick E Fynn's, 54
Middle Eastern restau-
    rants, 186
Milano, 40
Miles Nadal Jewish
    Centre, 70
Milestones, 40, 92
Milk Children's Festival of
    the Arts, 154
Mill Street Brewery, 46
Mimico, 22
Mink, 42
Mint Corner, 43
Mirvish, David, 69, 173,
    178
Mirvish, Ed, 69, 132, 173,
    178, 180, 225–26
Mirvish Village, 68, 69
Mo Mo's, 60
MOCCA, 131
Molson Amphitheatre, 26,
    27, 177
Molson Indy, 154–55, 170
Monarch Tavern, 48
Money, 42
Moneysworth & Best, 34
Mont Blanc, 72
Montana, 40
Montgomery Tavern, 91
Montgomery's Inn
    Museum, 17, 130–31
Monument to
    Multiculturalism, The, 43
Moore Park, 22
Moore, Henry, 129, 130
Mooring Basin, 24, 28, 29
Morba, 38
Moriyama, Raymond, 108,
    110, 111, 127, 136
Morningstar, 62
Morton's, 72
Moss Park, 44, 46, 54

motels, 99–103
Mount Pinatubo, 76
Mount Pleasant Cemetery, 86, 142
Mount Sinai Hospital, 52
Mountain Equipment, 40
Mövenpick, 42, 201
movies, 161–63
Moxie's, 92
Moya, 68
Mr Greek, 92
Mugg's Island, 24, 25
Mul Rae Bang-A, 68
Mullins, 62
multiculturalism, 219
Musa, 48
Musashi, 80
Museum of Ceramic Art, 72, 131
Museum of Contemporary Canadian Art, 131
museums, 126–35
music, classical, 166–69
Music Garden, 30, 31, 146

N

Nami, 44, 201
Nataraj, 70
Nathan Phillips Square, 42, 52, 93, 130, 141, 142, 155
National Ballet of Canada, 30, 161
National Ballet School, 64, 106
National Trade Centre, 26, 106–107, 179
Native Canadian Centre, 70
Nature Trail, 84
Navaro, 38
Necropolis, 66
Neill-Wycik Hotel, 54, 101
New Sky, 50
New Toronto, 22, 91
New Year celebrations, 155
News Café, 78
newspapers, 218
Newtonbrook, 22
93 Harbord, 60
Nonna's, 38
Noodle Bowl, 70
Normal School, 54, 144, 145

North 44°, 90, 91, 201–202
North Rosedale, 84–85
North Toronto Railway Station, 82, 83, 107
North York Centre, 92–93, 103
North York Hospital, 17
Northbound Leather, 62
Northfield House, 106
Northwood, 22
Novotel hotels, 34, 92, 99, 103

O

O'Grady's, 64
O'Keefe House, 54
Oakham House, 54
Oasis, 60
Okonomi House, 62
Old Cabbagetown, 56, 66–67
Old City Hall, 42, 118–19
Old Garrison Burying Ground, 119
Old Mill, 17, 202
Old Rectory, 52, 117, 146
Olive and Lemon, 60
Olivet Congregational Church, 73
Olliffe, 82
Olympia, 76, 64
Olympic Island, 24, 25
Olympic Spirit, 54, 171
One King West, 107
One, The, 52
One-of-a-Kind Craft Show, 155
Ontario College of Art and Design (OCAD), 50, 131, 145
Ontario Decorative Hardware, 46
Ontario Gallery of Chinese Arts, 50
Ontario Medical College for Women, 56, 57
Ontario Place, 26, 27, 165–66
Ontario Science Centre, 17, 107–108
opera, 166–69
Opera Atelier, 167
Opus, 70
Orange Room, 34
Oro, 52
Orthodox Church, 68

Osgoode Hall, 42, 53, 119
Oxygen, 40
Oyshi, 32

P

P J Mellon's, 64
Paddy Murphy's, 38
Paese, 17, 202
Paisley Garden, 72, 73
Palavrion, 40
Palm House, 54, 136
Palmerston, 58, 68
Panasonic Theatre, 64, 178
Pangaea, 72, 202–203
Pantages Hotel, 54, 101
Pantages Theatre, 54, 175
Papamios, 76
Paper Moon, 88
Pappas Grill, 17, 203
Paramount Cinemas, 40
Park Drive Reservation, 82, 84
Park Hyatt Hotel, 72, 102
Park Road (historic houses), 85
Parkdale, 22
parking, 216
parks, 136, 138–47. *See also names of individual parks*
Parks Department, 139
Parliament Street (#600), 66, 67
Passione Italiana, 86
Pastis, 80
Patachou, 82
PATH walkway, 21, 43, 105, 106, 108, 111, 223
Patty's, 66
Paul Bishop Houses, 119–20
Paul Hahn, 80
Paul Kane House, 64
Paupers, 68
Pavilion, 38
Peach, 54
Pearson Airport, 6–8, 112, 219
Peartree, 56
Pegasus, 52
Pelican, 66
Penelope, 44
people with disabilities, 219–20
People's Foods, 78
Peruvian restaurants, 186

Peter Pan, 40
Philosopher's Walk, 62, 72
Pho Hu'ng, 50, 203
Pi Tom's, 64
Piazza Manna, 32
Pickford, Mary, 53, 161
Pier 6, 32
Pietà, 121
Pine Point, 22
Pink Palace, The, 63
Pink Pearl, 72
Pioneer Festival, 114
Pisces, 82
Planet Hollywood, 40, 203
Plantation, 68
Play, 64
Plaza Flamingo, 58
Plum Tomato, 68
police, 213
politeness, 220
Pomegranate, 58
Pony, 58
Poor Alex Theatre, 70
Port Area, 34, 36–37
Portobello, 38
Portugal Village, 48–49
Portuguese Café, 48
Portuguese Market, 48
Portuguese restaurants, 186
Portuguese Seventh-Day Adventist Church, 58
postal services, 220–21
Posterity, 66
Posticino, 88
Pour House, 78
Power Plant, 32, 33, 132
Prada, 72
Praha, 78
Prego Della Piazza, 72, 203–204
Premier Dance Theatre, 32
Priape, 64
Primrose Best Western Hotel, 54, 101
Prince Hotel, 17
Princess Margaret Hospital, 52
Princess of Wales Theatre, 40, 69, 132, 178
Prinziples, 86
Privilege, 40
prostitution, 221
Provence, 66, 204
Provincial Legislature, 62, 63, 108

public art, 126–35
public holidays, 217
pubs, 186
Pure Spirits Oyster Bar and Grill, 46, 204

Q

Quail and Firkin, 82
Quakers Meeting House, 70
Quality Hotel, 44, 70, 100, 102
Quartier, 88, 204–205
Queen Street West, 38–39
Queen's Park, 62–63, 101, 142–43
Queen's Quay East, 34–35, 99
Queen's Quay Market, 34, 35
Queen's Quay Terminal, 32, 33
Queen's Quay West, 28–29, 35, 100
Queen's Wharf Lighthouse, 28
Queensshead, 38
Queensway Hospital, 17
Question Period, 63, 108
quotes about Toronto, 16

R

R G Perkins, 80
Radisson Plaza Admiral Hotel, 30, 99
Rain, 40, 205
Rainbow, 50
Ramada Hotel, 54, 101
Ramsden Park, 80, 81
Rancho Relaxo, 60
Raptors, 33, 170–71
Rashnaa, 66
Rasoee, 40
Rathnelly, 78, 80
RCYC, 24, 25, 37
RD's, 42
Real Thailand, 70
rebate, tax, 12
Rebel House, 80
Reclining Crows, 43
Red Book, 50
Red Indian, 38
Red Lion, 64
Red Planet, 64

Redpath Sugar Museum, 34, 35, 132
Redwood Grille, 90
Reference Library, 74, 111
Regal Beagle, 70
Regent Park, 56–57, 101
Rehabilitation Institute of Toronto, 76
Reisman, 86
Remington's, 54
Remy's, 72
Renaissance Toronto Downtown, 30, 99
Residential Lighting, 76
restaurants, 182–212. See also names of individual restaurants
 - listing by cuisine, 183–87
Reverb, 38
Rexall Centre, 17, 178
Rexdale, 22
Rhodes, 86
Richview, 22
Ricoh Coliseum, 26, 107, 179
Riverdale, 22
Riverdale Farm, 56, 57, 66, 67, 143
Riviera, 58
Rivoli, 40
Robert Deveau, 46
Roberto's, 90
Rock 'n Roll, 54
Rogers Centre, 30, 31, 33, 179
Rol San, 50
Rolls-Royce, 72
ROM, 72, 73, 132–33, 145
Romagna Mia, 44
Romaris, 74
Ron's, 78
Roots, 80, 86
Rose & Crown, 90
Rose Windows, 132
Rosedale, 74, 82–83
Rosedale Diner, 80
Rosedale Presbyterian Church, 74
Rosedale Ravine, 66, 74, 75, 84, 85
Rosedale Road (#30), 85
Rosedale United Church, 84
Rosehill Reservoir, 86, 87

Rosetta McClain Gardens, 143
Rosewater Supper Club, 44, 205
Rouge Hill, 22
Rouge Park, 17, 143–44
Roundhouse Park, 30, 31, 32
Rowers, 60
Roy Thomson Hall, 42, 179–80
Royal (cinema), 58
Royal Agricultural Winter Fair, 107, 155
Royal Alexandra Theatre, 42, 69, 112, 180
Royal Bank Plaza, 42, 43, 108–109
Royal Canadian Military Institute, 52
Royal Canadian Yacht Club, 24, 25, 70
Royal Conservatory of Music, 72, 85, 118
Royal Ontario Museum, 72, 73, 132–33, 145
Royal St George College Chapel, 68
Royal Thai, 68
Royal York Hotel, 8, 42, 100, 109
Roycroft Park, 78
Ruby, 17, 205–206
Ruchiro, 62
Rug & Design, 78
Runnymede, 22
Ruth's Chris, 42, 206
Ryerson University, 54

S

Sable-Castelli Gallery, 72, 73
Saddle Bag, 86
Saffron Tree, 52
Sage, 62
Sai Wah Heen, 52
Saigon, 50
St Alban the Martyr Church, 68
St Alban's Square, 68
St Andrew's Lutheran Church, 54
St Andrew's Playground, 40
St Anne's church, 129

St Basil's, 62
St Batholemew's Church, 56
St Clair Centre, 86
St Enoch's Gerrard Street Church, 66
St Francis of Assisi Church, 48
St Francis of Assisi School, 48
St George Campus, University of Toronto, 122
St George's Hall, 52, 53
St James Cathedral, 44, 45, 110, 117, 120
St James Cemetery, 66, 67, 144
St James Square, 54, 55, 144–45
St James-the-Less Chapel, 66
St James Town, 66, 67
St Lawrence Centre, 44, 180
St Lawrence (district), 34, 44–45, 46, 100
St Lawrence Hall, 44, 45, 120–21
St Lawrence Market, 44, 45, 124–25
St Louis, 88
St Marc, 64
St Mary Magdalene Church, 58, 59
St Mary's Church, 38
St Matthias Church, 48
St Michael's Catholic Cathedral, 54, 121
St Michael's Cemetery, 86
St Michael's Hospital, 44, 45
St Patrick's, 52
St Paul's Anglican Church, 74, 75, 110, 132
St Paul's Catholic Basilica, 46, 121
St Peter's Church, 56, 68
St Simon the Apostle, 66
St Stanislaus Kostka, 38, 39
St Stephen-in-the-Fields Church, 60, 61, 114
St Thomas Church, 70
St Vladimir Cathedral, 48, 49
Sakura, 44

Salmon Run, 30, 31, 133, 135
Sam the Record Man, 54
Samraat, 70
Sandra Ainsley, 46
Sangam, 52
Santa Claus Parade, 155–56
Sapphire Tower, 42, 107, 109, 112
Sassafraz, 72, 73
Sauvignon, 17, 206
Scadding Cabin, 26, 27, 113, 120
Scadding House, 52, 146
Scallywags, 86
Scaramouche, 80, 206
Scarborough Bluffs, 137, 138
Scarborough Civic Centre, 110, 136
Scarborough Philharmonic Orchestra, 167
Scarborough Town Centre, 17
Scarlett Woods, 17
Schmooze, 40
School of Toronto Dance Theatre, 66
Science Centre, 17, 107–108
Scotia Plaza, 42
Sculpture Garden, 44, 133
Se Jong, 68
seafood restaurants, 186
Search Light, Star Light, Spot Light, 32, 33
Seashell, 92
Seaton Village, 68, 69, 76, 77
Second City, 40
security, 221
Segovia, 62, 207
Sen Ming, 50
Senator Diner, 54
Sen5es, 40
Serendip, 82
Serra, 70
7 West, 62
Severn Creek Park, 74, 75, 85
sexual assault, 215
sexually transmitted diseases, 218–19
Shakespeare's, 70

Shanghai Lily, 50
Sheraton Hotel, 7, 42, 100
Sherway Gardens, 17
Shrine of Our Lady of
    Lourdes Church, 64
Sick Kids' Hospital, 52, 53,
    122–23
Sightlines, 30
Silver City, 90
Silver Hills, 22
Simcoe Day, 116
Simcoe Place, 42, 43, 135
Simcoe, Elizabeth, 25, 138
Simcoe, John Graves, 37,
    47, 98, 116, 134
Simply Thai, 86
Sistemlux, 40
Six In One, 38
Six Points, 22
SkyDome. See Rogers
    Centre
Skywalk, 32
Slack Alice, 64
Sleep Country, 82
Smokey Joe's, 92
smoking, 221–22
Sneaky Dee's, 58
Snow, Michael, 128, 134
Snowbirds, 151
Snug Island, 24, 25
Soho Metropolitan Hotel,
    40, 100
Solo, 40, 64
Som, 90
Sotto Sotto, 72
Sotto Voce, 58
Soulpepper Theatre, 46,
    173
South Annex, 59
South Hill, 80
South Rosedale, 84–85
Southern Accent, 68, 207
Southside Louie's, 58
Spacco, 90
Spadina Circle, 60, 61
Spadina House, 78, 79,
    114, 133
Spanish restaurants, 186
Speakers' Corner, 41
Spice Thai, 30
Spiga, 86
Spinello, 44
Spirits, 74
Splendido, 60
Spoon, 40, 207

sports, 169–71
sports bars, 186
Sports Centre, 86
Sportsmen's Show, 107,
    159
Spotted Dick, 74
Spring Rolls, 52, 207–208
squares, 136, 139, 141–42,
    144–47. See also names
    of individual squares
stadiums, 175–80
stage companies, 172–75
Stanley Park, 38, 39
Starfish, 44, 208
steakhouses, 186
Steamworks, 64
Stewart Building, 52
Stollery's, 72
Stork on the Roof, 88, 208
Strathcona Hotel, 42, 100
street index, 94–97
street names, origins of, 98
streetcars, 19
Stubbe, 72
Studio Gallery, 46
suburban Toronto hotels,
    99
suburbs and neighbour-
    hoods map, 22
subway, 18, 19. See also
    TTC
Sugar, 42
Sullivan, 22
Sultan's Tent, 44
Summerhill, 78, 80–81, 82,
    86
Summit Grill, 90
Sunnybrook Park, 17, 145
Sunnybrook Women's
    College Hospital, 17, 62
Sunnyside Beach, 138
Sunrise, 52
Sunset Grill, 90
Superior, 54
Sushi Kaji, 17, 208–209
Sushi Rock, 90
Sushi Supreme, 88
Sussex-Ulster, 58, 60, 68
Susur, 38, 209
Sutton Place Hotel, 62,
    101
Swansea, 22
Swarkovski, 72
Sweet Rosie's, 86

T

Taddle Creek Park, 70
Tafelmusik, 167
Takara, 86
Takesushi, 42, 209
Tam O'Shanter, 17, 22
Tanenbaum Opera
    Centre, 46
Taro, 38
Tarragon Theatre, 76, 77,
    174
Taste of Spain, 92
Taste of the Danforth, 156
Tasty, 68
tax rebate, 12
taxes, 222
TD Centre, 42, 43, 111
Teatro, 58
telephones, 222
Tempo, 58
1055, 82
Tengye, 70
Tequila Bookworm, 38
Terroni, 86
Textile Museum of
    Canada, 52, 53, 133–34
Thai Magic, 80
Thai Mango, 92
Thai Princess, 40
Thai restaurants, 186–87
Thai Thai, 88
Theatre for Young People,
    44, 174
Théâtre Français, 46
Theatre Passe Muraille, 38,
    174
theatres, 175–80
Thistletown, 22
Thomas, William, 45, 120,
    121
Thorncliffe Park, 22
thoroughbred horse rac-
    ing, 171
350 Fahrenheit, 70
360 Restaurant, 30, 187
Tiffany & Co, 72
Timothy's, 66
tipping, 182
Toba, 44
Todmorden Mills Harvest
    Festival, 156
Todmorden Mills
    Museum, 17, 134
toilets, 223